# The Future of Adventism

# The Future of Adventism
*Theology, Society, Experience*

*edited by*

Gary Chartier
*La Sierra University*

Griffin & Lash, Publishers
*Ann Arbor, Michigan*

The cover image is *Alegora nadzei* (1807),
by Kazimierz Wojniakowski.

Published by
Griffin & Lash, Publishers
Ann Arbor, Michigan

ISBN 978-0-692-52021-5

This corrected printing is the fourth printing of this book.

This book was printed in the United States of America
on acid-free paper.

*The Future of Adventism: Theology, Society,
Experience* / edited by Gary Chartier
Includes index.
1. Theology, Doctrinal 2. Seventh-day Adventists—Doctrines
I. Chartier, Gary, 1966-

*In honor of*
*Fritz Guy*
*and in memory of*
*Paul J. Landa*

# Contents

# Acknowledgments

This book grew from the "Great Disappointment, Greater Hope" lecture series that took place on the La Sierra University and Loma Linda University campuses in 1994. I am grateful to the many people who helped to make the series a success, including:

- the lecturers—Alden Thompson, Antonius D. Brandon, Charles Scriven, Charles Teel, Jr., Dalton Baldwin, Frederick G. Hoyt, Fritz Guy, Jacques Doukhan, John Brunt, Niels-Erik A. Andreasen, Paul J. Landa, Ronald D. Graybill, Roy Adams, Roy Branson, Sakae Kubo, Richard Rice, and Wayne Judd—for their thoughtful and stimulating insights;
- the respondents—Adeny Schmidt, Bernard Taylor, David R. Larson, Gayle Saxby, Gerald R. Winslow, Harvey Elder, Ivan Blazen, James Walters, John R. Jones, Jonathan Butler, Karl Kime, Lee Johnson, Lorenzo Grant, Lynn Mallery, Madelynn J. Haldemann, Monte Andress, Rennie Schoepflin, Sheryll Prinz-McMillan, and Steven G. Daily—for their openness to thinking critically and provoking conversation;
- the members of the faculty of what is now La Sierra University's H. M. S. Richards Divinity School, for their endorsement of my proposal for the series;
- the members of the La Sierra University and Loma Linda University media services teams, for ensuring the successful delivery of the initial lectures as well as their recording and preservation;
- Jeffrey Cassidy, for stepping in when needed;
- John R. Jones and Marvella Beyer, for the administrative assistance they provided at more than one point; *and*
- the members of the La Sierra University and Loma Linda University administrative teams—notably Fritz Guy and Lawrence T. Geraty—for their support for the series.

*The Future of Adventism* has benefited as well from the valuable contributions of others, including:

- Arthur Patrick, who, though not a participant in the original lecture series, permitted me to include his essay in this collection, recognizing its natural fit with the focus and tenor of the book;

- Linn Tonstad, Hanz Gutierrez, Edward Vick, Rennie Schoepflin, Trisha Famisaran, Chris Oberg, and Michael Pearson for their willingness to pen endorsements;
- the members of the faculties and staffs of the La Sierra University and Loma Linda University libraries—notably Barbara Lear, Chelsi Cannon, Chris Cao, Chris Cicchetti, Christina Viramontes, Daryl Swarm, David Ramos, Denise Bell, Elton Jornada, Gilbert Abella, H. Maynard Lowry, Hilda Smith, James Walker, Jeff de Vries, Jenni Subriar, Jill Start, Jon Hardt, Kitty Simmons, Marilyn Crane, Petr Cimpoereu, Sam Cho, Sandra Hartson, Vera Mae Schwartz, Victor Hernandez, and others— for research assistance and general human decency;
- Donna L. Carlson, for useful comments and suggestions;
- Gary Ross and Edward Vick, for catching multiple errors;
- A. Ligia Radoias, who facilitated the completion of the book in more than one way, as, for instance, by helping to improve the cover; *and*
- Lalé Welsh, for welcome opportunities for dialogue and exchange.

This book honors the memory of Paul J. Landa and the continuing scholarship and teaching of Fritz Guy.

- When I initially proposed the "Great Disappointment, Greater Hope" lecture series, Paul immediately saw its potential and invested enthusiastically and tirelessly in turning vision into reality. Paul's involvement in the series was one of many ways in which he contributed to scholarship, education, and the life of the Seventh-day Adventist Church. His incisive mind, clarity of thought and expression, high expectations of students and colleagues, and breadth of intellectual and pastoral concern made him a crucial member of the La Sierra University community for decades.
- From its conception in 1992, the book slated to emerge from the lecture series was intended to recognize Fritz's gifts and his distinctive value to La Sierra University and the Seventh-day Adventist community. The premier North American Adventist systematic theologian of his generation, Fritz is both brilliant and widely learned and, at the same time, gracious and generous. He has given unstintingly for over six decades to the church family he loves—prompting reflection and debate, offering challenging insights, and nurturing not only the Adventist community as a whole but also multiple generations of individual students and congregants. His analytical rigor and creative vision continue to bear fruit in the lives of those who read his work and in the diverse ministries of those who continue his own ministry of scholarship and teaching.

Paul was not, unfortunately, the only contributor to *The Future of Adventism* to die before its publication. I regret—and the blame lies on my shoulders—that Arthur Patrick, Dalton Baldwin, and Roy Branson were not able to see the book completed. Each of them made my life better in different ways, and I am sorry to have been unable to share with them this testament to their work.

- It was a pleasure to work with Arthur during his tenure as editor of *Adventist Heritage* when I served as the journal's managing editor, as also to talk with him about a range of topics and to read his carefully crafted and graceful prose.
- Dalton offered a uniquely Adventist perspective on a range of issues in philosophical and systematic theology during his decades of teaching at Loma Linda University, enabling colleagues and students to see familiar issues in new ways and maintaining a friendly attitude that made it possible for him to engage constructively across ideological divides.
- Roy touched many lives in memorable ways as a key founder of the Association of Adventist Forums, during his tenure as editor of *Spectrum* and as a teacher at Andrews and Loma Linda Universities and at what is now Washington Adventist University, and in virtue of his work as a Sabbath School teacher on both the East and West Coasts. I appreciate both the vote of confidence reflected in his selection of me as *Spectrum*'s news editor and book review editor and the chance these roles afforded for hours of conversation. (He was also too modest to mention the fact he himself led out in the formation of the Interreligious Coalition on Smoking OR Health, involved in the public health activism discussed in his chapter.)

And of course I happily acknowledge the usual suspects—Lalé Welsh, A. Ligia Radoias, Aena Prakash, Alexander Lian, Andrew Howe, Annette Bryson, Carole Pateman, Charles W. Teel, Jr., David B. Hoppe, David Gordon, David R. Larson, Deborah K. Dunn, Donna Carlson, Elenor Webb, Eva Pascal, Fritz Guy, Jeffrey Cassidy, Jesse Leamon, John Thomas, Maria Zlateva, Nabil Abu-Assal, Patricia M. Cabrera, Roger E. Rustad, Jr., Ronel Harvey, Ruth E. E. Burke, Sarvi Chan, Sel J. Hwahng, Sheldon Richman, W. Kent Rogers, Wonil Kim, and Xavier Alasdhair Kenneth Doran—for the usual reasons.

# Foreword

Randal R. Wisbey

The book captures a remarkable moment in the life of the Seventh-day Adventist Church when many of our denomination's leading theologians came together to think about its future. It is clear, in reading these stimulating and deeply encouraging essays, that they have much to say to the moment we today inhabit.

It is also evident that many in the Adventist Church are today caught up in thinking about the very issues these essays address. What does it mean to be part of a global family? How does theology shape practice? And, perhaps most importantly, will we embrace the future in a spirit of hopefulness? To this last question, the writers of these essays would encourage us, unequivocally, to say "Yes!" While there is a firm anchor in the reality of the church and the world—its joys and its deepest challenges—these writers consistently point us forward.

I am in no way surprised that the campus I am blessed to today call home was the place in which this conversation occurred. La Sierra and Loma Linda have long been at the forefront of thinking about the future in ways that are intrinsically helpful to the church as it confronts an ever-changing and challenging world. I am incredibly grateful and mindful of the gift of dedicated theologians and biblical scholars who continue to shape our understanding of God and of Scripture by being a constructive and inquisitive voice for the continuing development of the Seventh-day Adventist Church, asking appropriate questions and working diligently to find the best, and most powerful, responses.

Reading these essays has been a deeply satisfying experience for me personally. I have known many of these individuals as teachers, as mentors, and, in later years, as valued colleagues. As I read their words, I hear their distinctive voices—hopeful, passionate, committed. I also am reminded of how significant their contributions have been in linking my own understanding of the connection between theology, society, and experience.

I also note my gratitude for Gary Chartier who has edited this work and authored one of its chapters. Gary's remarkable scholarly contribution has been very important to La Sierra. This volume bears the stamp of his intelligence and overt optimism in the power of words and the ability they embody to help us shape the future we most long for.

In 1994, a remarkable group of individuals came together and shared a vision of how Adventist theology and identity could best shape the church and the world it served. How grateful I am that now, twenty-one years later, their essays are available to a much larger audience. As you make your way through this book, I am certain that you will be challenged, encouraged, and invigorated.

# Introduction

## Gary Chartier

The Seventh-day Adventist community of faith has been committed since its inception to a continuing, dialectical conversation between heritage and hope in a quest for "present truth." Adventists have sought to reclaim the best of the Christian heritage even while asking, in different ways, what new insights, new discoveries, might be worth affirming and celebrating in the contemporary world.

This quest for present truth is the responsibility of the entire church. For, while pastors and scholars have engaged repeatedly with the task of rethinking Adventism's nature and mission, it is among Adventism's strengths that members with diverse backgrounds and professional roles have welcomed the opportunity to join in the conversation about the optimal shape of Adventist life and thought.

Central to many different conceptions of Adventist identity has been a future-oriented sense of mission, an ineradicable hope, an openness to the future. Adventists have disagreed vigorously about the church's future and the world's, but they have consistently shared an awareness that the future matters and deserves our careful, prayerful, thoughtful, active attention. That awareness underlies this book.

The programmatic essays that make up this book—concerned with a range of issues in Adventist belief and practice—embrace a variety of theological and ecclesial perspectives. They are united by a passionate desire to foster the growth and flourishing of the Adventist family of faith by encouraging deliberate reflection on the trajectory of the development of Adventism as a community and as an intellectual tradition thoroughly open to the future even as it builds appreciatively on the insights of faithful people accumulated over millennia past. They focus on familiar theological topics, but also on central features of Adventist life.

In 1861, Adventist pioneer J. N. Loughborough famously declared:

> The first step of apostasy is to get up a creed, telling us what we shall believe. The second is, to make that creed a test of fellowship. The third is to try members by that creed. The fourth to denounce as heretics those who do not believe that creed. And fifth, to commence persecution against such.[1]

While the contributors to this volume defend particular viewpoints, sometimes quite vigorously, none of these essays is intended to serve as the basis for a creed. None is designed to foreclose discussion. None is offered as the definitive, conversation-stopping last word on its subject. Rather, each is intended to provoke rumination, stimulate conversation, and encourage reflective disagreement.

The contributors were not asked directly to react to each other's work, but I am confident that, if they had been, dissent would have been respectful, but also, certainly, both evident and vigorous. I am similarly confident that I do not speak only for myself when I suggest that I do not assert here anything of which I am certain or anything I have proven or discerned infallibly. Rather, what I write expresses that for which I *hope*. And I take positions I believe I can defend while very much aware that there are countervailing considerations, that I could be thoroughly mistaken; I invite all those who read this book to challenge and disagree. I hope this volume's readers will welcome what they find helpful while appreciatively proposing alternatives to what strikes them as unconvincing. We honor the Adventist heritage of commitment to present truth most appropriately when we continue our conversation, when we keep listening to each other and so, through each other, for a word from the God we hope will spur insight and discovery in and through the words of finite, fallible, sinful people. As we do so, we can help constructively to understand and shape the future of Adventism.

---

[1] Qtd. "Doings of the Battle Creek Conference, Oct. 5 & 6, 1861," *Review and Herald*, Oct. 8, 1861: 148.

# God

## Richard Rice

To many people, religion means certainty about many things. But they are most religious who are certain of but one thing, the world-embracing love of God.[1]

## OUR UNDERSTANDING, DOCTRINE, AND EXPERIENCE OF GOD

The doctrine of God has never been a defining aspect of Seventh-day Adventism. Unlike certain religious groups, we are not known for our distinctive perspective on the divine reality. In fact, in the many decades that Seventh-day Adventists have been around, the topic of God has seldom been the central focus of theological concern. For the most part, the descriptions of God that appear in our doctrinal books do not break new ground, but merely restate standard theological formulas. For example, in its two-column article on "God,"[2] the *Seventh-day Adventist Encyclopedia* of 1966 offers nothing more than brief comments on the statements that God is spirit, love, self-existent, immutable, omniscient, omnipresent, omnipotent, faithful and holy.

This is not to say that God is relatively unimportant to Adventists, only that we have not given the topic extensive formal attention. A community's understanding of God involves much more than formal doctrinal statements; it involves concrete religious intuitions as well. This is why I like the phrasing of the original lecture title I was assigned—"the Adventist Understanding of God." This expression seems to strike a nice balance between "Doctrine of God," on the one hand, and "Experience of God," on the other. To describe the Seventh-day Adventist understanding of God, we

---

[1]Charles Hartshorne, *Beyond Humanism: Essays in the New Philosophy of Nature* (Lincoln, NE: U of Nebraska P 1968 [1937]) 44.

[2]Five columns are devoted to the "Sanctuary" article, and thirty-six to the "Sabbath" article.

need to appreciate the importance of both elements. We must be sensitive to doctrines *and* to experience.

Of the two, experience is more fundamental to our understanding of God than is doctrine. Philosopher Richard Rorty says, "It is pictures rather than propositions, metaphors rather than statements, which determine most of our philosophical convictions."[1] The same is true in religion. Here, too, our most fundamental convictions are framed in symbols rather than in clear-cut concepts and propositions. Story, picture, and metaphor—things that speak directly to our imaginations—have a greater influence on the way we apprehend God than homiletical discourse or theological essay.

My own understanding of God certainly reflects this fact. Looking back to the earliest stages of my own spiritual odyssey—which has never taken me outside the Seventh-day Adventist community—I have become aware of the profound influence of stories, pictures, art, and music on my religious development. The very first book I remember was volume 1 of *The Children's Hour*, by Arthur S. Maxwell. At the age of three, I was sitting on the couch of our family's apartment in Los Angeles, looking at a picture of two native Americans in full headdress gazing over the prairie, when I somehow tore the page from top to bottom. I was dismayed, but Mother got some scotch tape and repaired the damage. I pulled the book off the shelf the other day and found the Indians, still staring into the distance, the tape, now yellowed with age, still holding the page together.

Paging through that book and the four that followed it, I recalled the stories that so entertained me as a child—stories that guided my life, fostered my values, molded my attitudes, and, most importantly, shaped my view of God. As its many readers know, children are the central characters in most of Uncle Arthur's stories. His favorite plots seem to involve three things: the dire consequences of a child's disobedience or bad judgment; the rewards of obedience—which weren't nearly as exciting; and miraculous deliverances from peril, often in direct answer to prayer.

It is interesting to reflect on the view of God that such plots communicate to young minds. God is firmly in control of the world and takes a keen interest in boys and girls, particularly in their behavior. God rewards those who are obedient to the divine will—or to their parents or teachers, who act in God's stead. And those who disobey meet with dire consequences. God answers prayer in remarkable ways, protecting us from harm or meeting a desperate need just in the nick of time. We may not think of mor-

---

[1] Richard Rorty, *Philosophy and the Mirror of Nature* (Princeton: Princeton UP 1979) 12.

alistic anecdotes as primary sources of doctrine, but the widespread exposure to such stories by several generations of Adventists has had a significant influence on our collective view of God. My guess is that over the years, and especially years ago, Uncle Arthur has contributed more to the way Adventists feel about God than all the books our theologians have written.

As we explore the Seventh-day Adventist understanding of God here, we will focus on doctrinal formulas. But we should bear in mind that they are only part of the picture. Religious experience has a powerful effect on the life of a religious community, too. On the one hand, we give our collective apprehension of God conceptual formulation in response to emerging challenges to communicate and defend our faith.[1] On the other hand, our concepts of God also shape our apprehensions and expectations of God. So, our experience of God gives rise to doctrines about God, and our doctrines, in turn, affect the way we experience God.

## Analysis: Enduring Tensions within the Seventh-day Adventist Understanding of God

If we look closely at the Seventh-day Adventist understanding of God with this dialectic of doctrine and experience in mind, we find a number of profound tensions.

On the formal level, our statements about God often lack coherence and consistency. Some of these conflicts lie *within* our doctrine of God. Some of the things we say about God are inconsistent with other things we say about God. We say, "God is creator, supreme in power and intelligence. All that lives owes its existence to God, who sustains the universe on a moment by moment basis." We also assert that God's government is at risk. Divine sovereignty is threatened by a massive rebellion on the part of creatures. Now, how can God be everything our doctrine of creation affirms, and yet God's sovereignty be jeopardized by creaturely revolt?

There are also conflicts that arise *between* the doctrine of God and other doctrines. We say that God offers us love and unconditional acceptance, but there are elements in Seventh-day Adventist theology that cloud the assurance this affirmation should bring.

One is our intense concern with personal behavior. "Salvation is a gift," we say, "but . . . there are certain strings attached. You haven't accepted the gift unless you are eating, drinking, dressing, and worshipping a certain way. After all, we are God's commandment-keeping people. Unlike those who pick and choose among

---

[1] It is sometimes said that heresy is the mother of orthodoxy.

God's requirements, modifying the eternal law for personal convenience, we take all God's commandments seriously."

Another is our view of judgment. We say that God is love, but we believe that God keeps an exhaustive record of our lives. In the vaults of heaven, every misdeed and every idle word is meticulously recorded. Unless they are all taken care of, we will never enter everlasting life.

A third factor that saps our assurance is our dramatic eschatology. We say that God is love, but Seventh day Adventist views of the future are filled with ominous events and tremendous tests of character. We look forward to terrible persecution, fantastic deceptions, the withdrawal of divine mercy from the wicked earth, indescribable devastation, the most intense anguish that God's people have ever been called to endure. Expressions like *remnant, last warning message, close of probation, seven last plagues,* and *time of Jacob's trouble* seem to conflict with the notion of a loving and forgiving God.

In addition to these doctrinal tensions in Adventism, we also encounter tensions on the experiential level. What we feel about God sometimes conflicts with what we say about God. Our experience of God contradicts the list of attributes we formally ascribe to God.

Sometimes our doctrines are preferable to our apprehensions. On a theoretical level, we assert that God accepts us unconditionally, loves us beyond calculation, and freely forgives our sins. We can believe that on one level, while on another level we still have the feeling that God's approval depends on our behavior. Many Seventh day Adventists have the nagging fear that they will never survive the judgment unless their characters are perfect, unless they remember and confess every sin they have ever committed. *In such cases, we need to let our doctrine inform our religious intuitions, and strive to bring our feelings into harmony with our beliefs.*

There are also times when our personal apprehensions of God seem to be "ahead of" our doctrines. People with a strong devotional life often sense God's love and care for them on a day by day, even moment by moment, basis. They feel that the events of our lives make a difference to God as they actually happen. But our standard doctrinal statements assert that God is immutable, or changeless, that nothing about God could be different in the slightest. We typically enthrone God in the remoteness of eternity, far above the tumult of earthly affairs. *In this case, we need to bring our doctrines into harmony with our religious intuitions. It is nearly impossible to read the biblical descriptions of God without sensing God's profound involvement in human affairs, God's deep sensitivity to human decisions and actions. We may find it necessary to revise the traditional formulations in light of these biblical themes and personal insights.*

## RETROSPECT: SOME IMPORTANT DEVELOPMENTS IN THE SEVENTH-DAY ADVENTIST UNDERSTANDING OF GOD

I will not attempt here a comprehensive review of all that Adventists have said about God. Since the doctrine has never dominated Seventh-day Adventist theology and only occasionally occupied the center of attention, this would be difficult to do, and the results may not be all that interesting. Nevertheless there have been some notable developments in the Seventh-day Adventist understanding of God, and I would like to touch on three of them: (1) the defense of God's personness, which involved two episodes about fifty years apart; (2) the gradual emergence of Trinitarian orthodoxy, which is arguably still underway; and (3) the interpretation of the great controversy concept, which suggests interesting possibilities and raises significant problems.

1. The question of God's personness became a contested issue among Adventists twice during Ellen White's ministry—during the 1850s and around the turn of the twentieth century. On both occasions Ellen White staunchly defended the definite personality, or personness, of God.

The "spiritualizers" of the 1840s and '50s responded to the Great Disappointment by asserting that Christ had in fact returned as the Advent Movement had predicted. But they construed the Second Coming as a spiritual event, not a physical, visible return to earth. They also spiritualized other aspects of Christian faith, including the nature of God, whom they viewed as a pervasive influence in the world rather than a specific center of consciousness. Important Adventists such as James White and Uriah Smith countered by denying the Trinity and asserting that Christ is both clearly distinct from and subordinate to the Father.[1]

In response to charges that she taught spiritualist views, Ellen White did not explicitly deny the Trinity, but she did assert that she had seen the Father and the Son in vision as distinct physical realities. "I have often seen the lovely Jesus, that He is a *person*," she wrote in 1851. "I asked Him if His Father was a person and had a form like Himself. Said Jesus, 'I am in the express *image* of my Father's Person.'"[2] Although on this view the Father and the Son apparently have identical physical forms, only that of the Son is visible, even in vision. Three years later, Ellen White described God as revealed to her in vision—as a physical presence, but not one that

---

[1]Malcolm Bull and Keith, Lockhart, *Seeking a Sanctuary: Seventh-day Adventism and the American Dream*, 2d ed. (Bloomington: Indiana UP 2007) 74-5.

[2]Ellen G. White, *Early Writings of E. G. White* (Washington, DC: Review 1945) 77.

human eyes could directly behold "The Father was enshrouded with a body of light and glory, so that His person could not be seen; yet I knew that it was the Father and that from His person emanated this light and glory. When I saw this body of light and glory rise from the throne, I knew it was because the Father moved . . . ."[1] So, God could not be a mere spirit, because God is a person, that is, God has a concrete physical form (even though it is invisible).

In the early Ellen White, divine individuality and possession of a physical form were closely connected. But this is not true of her more mature statements on God. Fifty years later, she returned to the question of God's individuality, and this time she defended it on entirely different grounds.

In response to what is often called the "pantheism" crisis, Ellen White produced her most sustained discussion of the nature of God and God's relation to the world. It was published as Section 5 of *Testimonies for the Church*, Volume 8. In this passage, she repeatedly affirms the personal nature of God, but not once does she refer to a physical divine form to defend this point. She rejects "the theory that God is an essence pervading all nature,"[2] more because the idea is inadequate than inaccurate. "God is the mighty power that works through all nature and sustains all things," she asserts, but this does not say enough. This power is "not merely an all-pervading principle, an actuating energy. God is a spirit; yet He is a personal being, for man was made in his image."[3] This opens the door for her to posit a physical correspondence between human beings and God, but this is not the avenue she takes. We must understand God as personal in nature, she argues, that is, as a distinct conscious being, because we see intelligent agency at work in human origins, in the ongoing course of nature, and most significantly, in the life and ministry of Jesus. Note that she does not deny that God is "all-pervading principle." Her point is that God is more than this expression conveys. God is a personal being, a center of consciousness, capable of decision and action.

On both of these occasions, the question of God's personness had to be answered decisively in order to prevent widespread misunderstanding as to what Seventh-day Adventists believed. In each instance, the response seems to have been pointed and effective, but there was a significant difference between the two. To distinguish themselves from the spiritualizers, Adventists attributed to God a physical form and sharply distinguished between God and Christ. In

---

[1]White, *Writings* 92.
[2]Ellen G. White, *Testimonies for the Church*, 9 vols. (Mountain View, CA: Pacific 1948) 8: 291.
[3]White, *Testimonies* 8: 263.

response to pantheism, however, they did neither. Their descriptions of the divine reality are metaphysical rather than physical. They focus on God's relation to the created world rather than God's physical movements in heaven.

2. Whereas Seventh-day Adventists developed their concept of God's personness in a succession of rather distinct episodes, the view of God as Trinity emerged within Adventism through a process of gradual evolution. Even though it never crystallized as an "issue" that stimulated extensive discussion or precipitated official action, we find striking differences between the views of early Adventists and the church's current thinking. As George R. Knight observes, so removed is the church's position now from what it was at the beginning that "[m]ost of the founders of Seventh-day Adventism would not be able to join the church today if they had to subscribe to the denomination's Fundamental Beliefs."[1] Important early Adventists directly opposed the idea of the Trinity. For Joseph Bates it was unscriptural, for James White it was an "absurdity," and for M. E. Cornell it was a fruit of the great apostasy that also included Sunday keeping and the immortality of the soul.[2] In fact, C. Mervyn Maxwell concludes that early Adventists were "about as uniform in opposing Trinitarianism as they were in advocating belief in the Second Coming."[3]

In contrast, Seventh-day Adventist thinkers today are as uniformly supportive of the idea. They use explicitly Trinitarian language to talk about God and they interpret the concept of Trinity with care and subtlety. For example: in an *Adventist Review* article entitled "The Mystery of the Trinity: God as Father, Son, and Holy Spirit," Raoul Dederen, professor *emeritus* of theology at the Seventh-day Adventist Theological Seminary, Andrews University, defends the doctrine of the Trinity as biblically based, even though, as he notes, the word itself is not found in Scripture. He also rejects all tritheistic or modalistic conceptions of God and urges us to respect

---

[1] George R. Knight, "Adventists and Change," *Ministry*, Oct. 1993: 11.

[2] Knight 11. Knight cites Joseph Bates, *The Autobiography of Elder Joseph Bates* (Battle Creek, MI: Adventist 1868) 20-5; James White, "The Faith of Jesus," *Review and Herald*, Aug. 5, 1852: 52; M. E. Cornell, *Facts for the Times* (Battle Creek, MI: Cornell 1858) 76. Knight also mentions two examinations of early Adventist anti-trinitarianism by SDA scholars: Erwin R. Gane, "The Arian or Anti-Trinitarian Views Presented in Seventh-day Adventist Literature and the Ellen G. White Answer (MA thesis, Andrews U 1963), and Russell Holt, "The Doctrine of the Trinity in the Seventh-day Adventist Denomination: Its Rejection and Acceptance" (term paper, Andrews University. 1969).

[3] "Sanctuary and Atonement in SDA Theology: An Historical Survey," *The Sanctuary and the Atonement: Biblical, Historical and Theological Studies*, ed. Arnold V. Wallenkampf and W. Richard Lesher (Washington, DC: General Conference of Seventh-day Adventists 1981) 530, qtd. Bull and Lockhart 69.

the essential mystery of God's triune reality.[1] The widely circulated commentary on the church's 1980 Statement of Fundamental Beliefs is equally explicit in affirming the Trinity and it, too, explores the meaning of the idea, albeit briefly. The Godhead comprises a relationship of love that comes to expression in the work of salvation, and most clearly at the cross of Christ. The Trinitarian differentiations within God correspond to the various saving activities of God.[2]

When and how did these transformation take place? I'm not sure we can tell. The earliest version of the Fundamental Beliefs of Seventh-day Adventists (1932) describes "the Godhead, or Trinity," as consisting of "the Eternal Father," "the Lord Jesus Christ," and "the Holy Spirit." The 1980 revision of the Statement curiously omits the word *Trinity*, but clearly affirms and further develops the idea. Belief 2 asserts, "There is one God: Father, Son, and Holy Spirit a unity of three co-eternal Persons," and Beliefs 3, 4, and 5 deal, respectively, with "God the Eternal Father," "God the Eternal Son," and "God the eternal Spirit."

In spite of the solid and growing support the understanding of God as Trinity has received from the church's official doctrinal statements and publications over the years, there have been rumblings of opposition along the way. In a 1968 paper discussing hermeneutical principles in the E. G. White writings, Arthur L. White, then Secretary of the Ellen G. White Estate, notes that Ellen White never employs the term *Trinity* and asserts that our denominational forefathers were consistently averse to the doctrine as defined in the church creeds. (They saw it as spiritualizing away both Jesus Christ and God.) He argues that Ellen White's early descriptions of God the Father and Son in heaven as having physical forms—the ones we cited above—should be taken literally and provide a lasting safeguard against the threat of spiritualizing the divine reality.[3] So, the emerging Trinitarian consensus among Adventists has not been unanimous.

One of the church's most significant liturgical sources also points to a doctrinal transition over time. Looking at the *Seventh-day Adventist Hymnal* of 1985 alongside the 1949 *Church Hymnal* it replaced, we surmise that there were reservations among Adventists about the concept of the Trinity in the late '40s but that these res-

[1]Raoul Dederen, "The Mystery of the Trinity: God as Father, Son, and Holy Spirit," *Adventist Review*, Aug. 26, 1993, 8-11.

[2][P. Gerard Damsteegt et al.,] *Seventh-day Adventists Believe: A Biblical Exposition of 27 Fundamental Doctrines* (Washington, DC: Ministerial Association, General Conference of Seventh-day Adventists 1988) 17-25.

[3]Arthur L. White, *The Ellen G. White Writings* (Washington, DC: Review 1973) 156-61.

ervations were largely overcome within the next three decades. The 1949 publication altered a number of familiar Christian hymns in order to remove their Trinitarian references. The 1985 publication restored the Trinitarian references to these hymns. Thus, the closing line of "Holy, Holy, Holy" in the 1949 hymnal—"God over all who rules eternity"—becomes in the 1985 hymnal "God in three persons, blessed Trinity!" The 1949 version of "Come Thou, Almighty King" deletes a stanza that begins with the words "To Thee, great One in Three, Eternal praises be." The 1985 version restores that stanza. The 1985 publication also adds no fewer than ten new hymns containing straightforward Trinitarian language. Consequently, we can now sing the following lines: "Praise the Father, praise the Son, and praise the Spirit, three in One" (in hymn 2); "Holy Father, Holy Son, Holy Spirit, three we name You" (in hymn 30); "The Trinity whom we adore, forever and forever more" (in hymn 148).

If a community's worship provides an important indication of its religious understanding, it is clear that significant developments have taken place in the past few decades in the Seventh-day Adventist understanding of God. In contrast to the decisive affirmations of God's personness we noted above, our move toward Trinitarian orthodoxy has been subtle rather than dramatic, gradual rather than abrupt. But it is a genuine change and a profoundly important change, nonetheless. It has brought our understanding of God into harmony with the profound insights of some of the earliest Christian thinkers, who recognized this affirmation of God's complex unity as the only adequate way to safeguard the central claim of Christian faith, "God was in Christ." And it places us squarely within the circumference of orthodox Christianity. Our doctrine of God distinguishes us from other religious movements that originated about the same time Seventh-day Adventism arose and to which we are often compared. Unlike Jehovah's Witnesses, Mormons and Christian Scientists, Seventh-day Adventists accept the view of God adhered to by the dominant stream of Christian tradition. However other doctrinal concerns may distinguish us from Christians generally, our doctrine of God shows that we are distinctive within rather than apart from Christianity at large.

3. The concept of the great controversy plays an important role in Ellen White's writings. The great controversy vision of 1858 provided the basis for a series of volumes entitled *Spiritual Gifts*. This was later enlarged to form a second four-volume series, *The Spirit of Prophecy*, and ultimately expanded into the five-volume Conflict of the Ages Series, which Adventists widely regard as her *magnum opus* and the definitive expression of Adventist thought. "The Great Controversy" is the title of the fifth and most influen-

tial book in this series. In his book-length study of this concept in
Ellen White's thought, Joe Battistone correctly identifies it as her
central theological idea, the comprehensive framework within
which she deals with all her important concerns.[1]

The idea of the great controversy is that of a conflict between
superhuman powers of good and evil that engulfs the entire universe. God's loyal followers are engaged in a struggle with the followers of Satan, the instigator of this massive rebellion against divine sovereignty. Satan was once the archangel Lucifer, the highest
of created beings, who stood in the presence of God and served as
leader of the heavenly host. However, after becoming resistant to
divine authority and particularly resentful of the Son's superiority,
Lucifer left his honored place, rejected God's appeals to repent, and
persuaded a significant number of his fellow angels—the estimate is
one-third—to join him in rejecting God's rule and engaging in an
open revolt. God expelled them from heaven and ever since they
have been working to foment suspicion, dissatisfaction and ultimately rebellion throughout the universe.

The great controversy is central to Ellen White's theology. She
invokes the idea of a massive, superhuman rebellion against God to
illuminate critical moments in the arc of human history, beginning
with creation and concluding with the final destruction of the
wicked and the establishment of God's eternal kingdom on earth.
The mighty fallen angel was the power that tempted the first humans in the Garden of Eden. Speaking through the serpent in the
Garden of Eden, the devil persuaded Eve to eat from the forbidden
tree and gained control over humankind when Adam followed
suite. Variously identified as the devil, Satan, the enemy of souls,
this great antagonist has been active throughout human history to
foment sin and suffering. He is the ultimate cause of all the misery
on this planet. So, the course of human history is one of sustained
warfare between God and the devil, as God pursues divine objectives in creating, populating this planet with loyal beings happy in
God's service, and the devil strives to undermine all that God seeks
to accomplish.

The decisive battles in this protracted conflict occurred during
the ministry of Jesus. Satan worked on two fronts to thwart Christ's
mission. He tried to persuade Jesus to distrust and rebel against
God, and he stirred up opposition to Jesus' ministry. In the face of
powerful temptations, Jesus remained loyal to the Father, and faith-

---

[1]Joseph Battistone, *The Great Controversy Theme in E. G. White Writings* (Berrien Springs, MI: Andrews UP 1978). To my knowledge this is the only book-
length treatment of the great controversy idea. However, it is by and large a
summary of Ellen White's narrative from the origin of evil to restoration of the
earth. It is not a critical assessment of the concept.

fully followed the path of suffering servanthood to the cross. The Son's condescension to the level of humanity and submission to a humiliating death on the cross played a key role in resolving the great controversy. By demonstrating beyond all doubt that God is generous, caring, and self-denying they provided a decisive refutation of the devil's charges against God. They belie the devil's charge that God is tyrannical, overbearing, and unfair. The concept of the great controversy is crucial to Ellen White's understanding of the atonement. As she describes it, Lucifer's rebellion presented the government of God with a profound crisis. It not only led to open revolt on the part of a significant number of the God's intelligent creatures, it generated even wider suspicion that God's self-characterization as loving might be false. In other words, there was widespread confusion resulting from what the devil said, if not considerable sympathy for his charges. There were lingering questions about God's true attitude toward creatures and particularly about the fairness of the divine requirements. Was it possible that in spite of God's claim to goodness, God is ultimately a tyrant, that divine commands are unreasonable, and that the divine government ultimately requires the groveling acquiescence of creatures to superior power?

There was only one way for God to respond to this problem: it was necessary to provide a manifestation of divine love so powerful that no rational creature could possibly deny it. This is precisely what the cross represented. It showed beyond all doubt that God is unrelentingly committed to the welfare of the creatures—and is willing to suffer and sacrifice in order to win their confidence. This display of divine love laid to rest any lingering suspicions regarding God's benevolence. In so doing, it exposed Satan's charges for exactly what they were—pure fabrications spun from a mind filled with self-promotion. In view of the slander against God and its deadly consequences, God was fully justified in bringing the rebellion to an end.

The concept of the great controversy, a crisis of cosmic proportions threatening God's government, a collapse of confidence which God overcomes by giving Jesus for the salvation of the human race, also provides a basis for interpreting the concluding events in human history. God can bring the reign of sin to an end without appearing vindictive once everyone understands that sinners are entirely responsible for their own destruction. God does not arbitrarily terminate their existence, but reluctantly allows them to experience the consequences of their own choices. In separating themselves from God, they have, in effect, chosen death. So, the final judgment is not a display of divine vengeance, but the natural destination of those who remove themselves from the source of all life.

The notion of the great controversy has important implications for the Seventh-day Adventist understanding of God. It also raises questions that deserve further exploration.

The most important implications of the great controversy concerns the fundamental nature of God. It places love clearly at the center of the divine reality. Love is not merely an attribute of God—not even the most important of divine attributes; rather, it describes the very essence of the divine being. Love is not something God happens to do, it is something that expresses God's inner reality. It is God's nature to love. In loving us, God is most fully God.

In recent years a number of Seventh-day Adventist writers have underscored the importance of love for an understanding of God. Alden Thompson appeals to the freedom-loving nature of God to establish a continuity between the God of the Gospel and the God of the Old Testament.[1] In the opening essay of a symposium volume expounding Arminian theology, Fritz Guy observes that love is the one word that Christians apply to God without qualification. Accordingly, he maintains, love is more basic to God's character than qualities such as power and justice. It leads God to take enormous risks and provide extravagant displays of affection. It also makes God dynamically responsive to creatures and vulnerable to disappointment. Moreover, there is no limit to its scope and its endurance.[2]

No Seventh-day Adventist thinker has concentrated more exclusively on God's love than A. Graham Maxwell. In his book, *Servants or Friends? Another Look at God*,[3] Maxwell reiterates the themes that his large following has appreciated for many years. Taking as his key text Jesus' statement to his disciples, "I do not call you servants any longer, but friends,"[4] Maxwell insists that the notion of friendship is central to an adequate understanding of God and emphasizes the central role that trust plays in a mature relation to God. God is eminently friendly toward us. God respects our freedom and individuality and invites us into intimate, personal friendship. In contrast to the servant obedience of those who erro-

---

[1]Alden Thompson, *Who's Afraid of the Old Testament God?* (Grand Rapids: Zondervan 1989).

[2]Fritz Guy, "The University of God's Love," *The Grace of God, The Will of Man: A Case for Arminianism*, ed. Clark H. Pinnock (Grand Rapids: Zondervan 1989) 31-49.

[3]A. Graham Maxwell, *Servants or Friends? Another Look at God* (Redlands, CA: Pine Knoll 1992).

[4]Jn. 15:15.

neously think of God as an exacting master, the response of those who understand the truth about God is love and trust. Based on their friendship with God, they are able to tell the truth about God.

The idea of the great controversy has important implications for God's relation to the world. It points to a genuine interaction between God and creatures. God does not achieve God's purposes simply by willing them to be so. This is most obvious in connection with human salvation. Adventists have traditionally believed that God offers salvation to all, but that not all receive it. While faith does not contribute to the gift, the gift has no effect unless we accept it. This means that our understanding of salvation is clearly Arminian. It places great emphasis on human freedom. In attributing genuine freedom to God's creatures, Arminianism sharply diverges from the theological tradition that dominates western Christianity and received its definitive expression in Calvinism. According to this perspective, God's most important qualities are supreme power and knowledge, God's relation to the world is one of sovereignty and control, and the ultimate purpose of God's activity is divine glory. In contrast, Arminianism emphasizes God's love and sensitivity to the creatures, God's dynamic interaction with their decisions and experiences, and God's willingness to take risks and make sacrifices on their behalf.

As is the case with most Arminians, Adventists generally retain a number of traditional theistic concepts that conflict with their more basic theological convictions. They insist that not only God's essential reality, but also God's experience of the world, is utterly changeless. This requires that God's knowledge of the world be changeless as well, which means that divine knowledge of the future must be as complete and invariant as divine knowledge of the past. Thus, one finds "foreknowledge" defined in the *Seventh-day Adventist Bible Dictionary* as "that aspect of God's omniscience by which future events are known to Him before, and apart from, any objective indication that they are to take place."[1] The attempt to explain how a changeless God can know a changing world has generated ingenious theological inventions, from explorations of retrocausation to a recovery of the idea of "middle knowledge." But for clarity and probative power, I still believe, none of them matches the simple solution that God's knowledge accurately reflects the contents of the world. Since the world is temporal, God's knowledge is temporal. As the former develops, so does the latter.[2]

But whether or not Seventh-day Adventist theology ever embraces my solution to the problem of divine foreknowledge, in one

[1] *Seventh-day Adventist Bible Dictionary* (Washington, DC: Review 1960) 360.
[2] See my discussion in *God's Foreknowledge and Man's Free Will* (Minneapolis: Bethany 1985; rptd. Eugene OR: Wipf 2004).

way or another it must apply its Arminian insights more extensively
to the doctrine of God. When we affirm creaturely freedom in the
area of personal salvation, we invoke an image of God that stands in
striking contrast to traditional views of divine majesty. We envision
God as fellow sufferer rather than supreme sovereign, as friend and
companion rather than monarch and master.

At the same time, the concept of the great controversy presents
us with some perplexing problems to which Adventists have not
devoted much attention. In some ways, it seems to stand in tension
with the sovereignty of God.

For one thing, it presents us with a view of reality that seems to
be dualistic. The entire universe is engulfed in a conflict between
good and evil which will have eternal consequences. This seems to
give the devil immense power, and this seems to compromise
God's status. Adventists stand squarely with orthodox Christianity
in affirming God's ontological superiority to the creaturely world.
The world and its inhabitants all owe their existence to God, while
God owes existence to no one else. In the language of classical theology, God and God alone is self-existent. Moreover, God not only
brought creatures into being to start with, but sustains them in existence moment by moment. To quote Paul's quotation of a pagan
poet, "In him we live and move and have our being."[1] Ellen White
expresses essentially the same idea in what is probably her most
straightforward metaphysical assertion: "All created beings live by
the will and power of God. They are dependent recipients of the
life of God. From the highest seraph to the humblest animate being, all are replenished from the Source of life."[2]

In view of the fact that everything owes its existence to God,
what are we to make of the enormous stature the devil enjoys in
the great controversy scheme? Here we encounter a personality so
powerful it can evidently present itself as a plausible rival to God for
the allegiance of intelligent creatures. How is this possible when the
devil is just as dependent on God for existence as everything else in
the universe, and when presumably perceptive beings like angels
would have no difficulty recognizing this fact? What could an intelligent being hope to gain from contesting God's supremacy, knowing all the while that God could instantly annihilate him?

Suppose we reply that the devil's challenge to God is moral rather than ontological in nature. That is to say, it is not God's supreme power that he threatens, but God's standing in the eyes of
creatures. The devil does not hope to dethrone God, but to foment
the widespread suspicion that God is a tyrant who rules only by

[1]Acts 17:28.
[2]Ellen G. White, *The Desire of Ages: The Conflict of the Ages Illustrated in the
Life of Christ* (Mountain View, CA: Pacific 1947) 785.

force and pursues nothing beyond self-gratification. Construed this way, the issue of the great controversy is not God's power, but God's reputation.[1] If creatures are persuaded that God is nothing but a tyrant, they will respond with groveling acquiescence, not heartfelt praise, and the relationship God desires with them, based on love and joyful appreciation of the divine character, will be destroyed. What is at stake, then, is not God's supremacy, but the kind of supremacy God seeks. If God's government were based on sheer power, then there could be no controversy, because nothing could threaten it. God would simply overwhelm detractors or annihilate them, and that would be that. But if God's government is based on the loving response of God's creatures, then a serious misconception of who and what God is can pose a threat.

This interpretation of the great controversy dissolves the metaphysical dualism that the concept initially seems to imply, but it raises a difficult question of its own. How is it possible to distrust God? In the great controversy scenario the devil accuses God of tyrannical behavior. Evidence for God's true motives accumulates over the long course of human history, reaching its climax in the sacrifice of Christ. God's creatures weigh the evidence and conclude that God is who God claims to be—a benevolent, loving parent who really cares for them. With this conclusion the devil loses his argument and the conflict is over—case closed.

However, the notion of "God on trial" seems problematic. The idea of creatures evaluating Satan's charges in light of the evidence and concluding that God is truly benevolent after all presents us with difficulties. First, it holds God accountable to some moral standard, and this calls into question God's supremacy. If, as many theologians hold, God is by definition good, the divine character itself the supreme standard of goodness, then there is no independent standard by which to evaluate God. There is nothing beyond God to which God is accountable, against which we can evaluate God's character. If God is by definition good, then the notion of God on trial makes no sense. How could the ultimate standard of goodness fail to be good? So, either God is less than ultimate goodness or the notion of God on trial makes no sense.

God's ontological supremacy also calls into the question the possibility of a creaturely investigation of the divine character. An objective evaluation of something presupposes two things: reliable evidence and unbiased investigators. To conduct such an inquiry, we must be confident that the evidence before us has not been

---

[1]For a scholarly examination of God's reputation in the context of the biblical book of Revelation, see Sigve K. Tonstad, *Saving God's Reputation: The Theological Function of* Pistis Iesou *in the Cosmic Narratives of Revelation* (Edinburgh: Clark 2007).

tampered with and that our minds have the capacity to weigh the evidence and reach their own conclusions. In other words, we must have confidence in the structure of reality and in our own cognitive processes.

The fact that God's power sustains all that is, however, means that God is involved in every aspect of reality. There is evidence at all only because divine power sustains it. Our minds work the way they do because God has designed them that way. To trust evidence for anything is ultimately to trust God, and to trust our minds is ultimately to trust the one who designed them and guides their operation. Every cognitive process thus presupposes that God is trustworthy. But this is precisely what is at stake in the great controversy. It seems, then, that we cannot determine *if* God is trustworthy unless we assume *that* God is trustworthy. Once again, we find ourselves begging the question. The trustworthiness of God is therefore a necessary presupposition of all cognitive activity. Every claim to knowledge implicitly expresses confidence in God.

There are some less theoretical questions that the great controversy concept raises as well. One wonders, for example, about the practical consequences of the idea that our world is populated with angels and demons fiercely struggling with one another over the souls of human beings. In a book published several years ago,[1] Steve Daily criticized Adventists for failing to take the great controversy seriously, just when other Christians have developed a deeper appreciation for demonic power. He called for a balanced approach to the demonic, but he also encouraged Adventists to consider the possibility of confronting the forces of darkness more directly. Personally, I find the prospect of engaging the forces of darkness on a face-to-face, first-name basis rather troubling. I fear that attempting to do so has the potential to cause great harm, and I find no strong precedent for it in Seventh-day Adventist history. So, I wonder, is the great controversy theme a powerful metaphor designed to heighten our sense of the importance of spiritual issues? Or does it literally describe the unseen forces waging war all around us?

At the same time, there are cultures and there are situations where the notion of such conflict has a powerful influence. It underscores the seriousness of the decisions we make. And it can provide reassurance to those cowed by forces over which they have no control. The prospect of divine victory over all God's enemies and all our enemies—over everything that harms and troubles us—can provide enormous reassurance.

---

[1] Steven G. Daily, *Adventism for a New Generation* (Portland, OR: Better Living 1993).

There may be some who also wonder about connecting the language of love and the language of violence. For example, one edition of *"The Great Controversy" uses the title,* "The Triumph of God's Love." The word "triumph," like the words "conquest" and "victory," connotes a war zone. It presents us with God the warrior, going into battle, defeating enemies, taking captives, wreaking havoc and destruction. This could lead to the supremacy of superior power, but how could love ever "triumph" in this way? Love and force are alien operations. Love does not take, it gives. It does not subjugate, it liberates. It does not rise to triumph, it stoops to serve. The terminology of conquest seems ill-suited to express the central feature of God's character.[1]

## SOME RECENT DISCUSSIONS

Since I delivered the lecture from which this chapter emerged, Adventists have done a lot more thinking about God, and some of these developments deserve attention here.

One important aspect of the doctrine that has received further attention is the concept that God is best thought of in terms of the trinity. Thanks to the work of Gilbert Valentine, some of the factors that led Adventists to embrace a Trinitarian view of God have become much more clear.[2] As Valentine describes it, the emphasis on righteousness by faith for which the General Conference of 1888 is remembered generated a deeper appreciation for the importance of Christ's work as our savior. This, in turn, led to an affirmation of Jesus' divinity, since a human being, let alone a fallen human being, could hardly be the source of our salvation. And this led to the realization that God the Son was coeternal with God the Father. The close relation between them of which Jesus speaks in John 17, for example, refers not just to his earthly ministry, but to his life with God before the Incarnation. *Desire of Ages,* one of Ellen White's more influential books, is noteworthy for emphasizing Je-

---

[1]One wonders if the idea of the Great Controversy results from the confluence of two great revivals—the Methodism of the eighteenth century and the Millerite movement of the nineteenth—and thus brings together two somewhat diverse elements—Methodist piety and apocalyptic eschatology. Love was a central theme in Methodism. John Wesley defined Christian perfection as the loving of God with all one's powers. One of Charles Wesley's hymns portrays Jesus as "pure, unbounded love." Apocalyptic eschatology, with its focus on the return of Christ and the imminent end of the world, was the theme of the Millerite movement. Although Ellen White's Conflict of the Ages series begins and ends with the words, "God is love," the entire course of history in between is portrayed as a protracted military campaign between superhuman forces of good and evil, battling for the loyalty of the moral universe.

[2]Gilbert M. Valentine, "Clearer Views of Jesus and the Doctrine of the Trinity in the Seventh-day Adventist Church," *Spectrum* 42.1 (Win. 2014): 66-74.

sus' divinity in a number of memorable passages. Ellen White's own growing understanding and the wide influence of *Desire of Ages* and other works slowly led to a broad consensus regarding the Trinity.

According to Valentine, two prominent Adventists contributed substantially to this important development, W. W. Prescott and A. G. Daniells, both of whom were working in Australia in the 1890s. Prescott was preparing a series of Sabbath School lessons on the Gospel of John, and his careful study of the book, particularly the "I am" sayings of Jesus, led him to the conclusion that Christ was the Yahweh of the Old Testament and therefore fully God and co-eternal with the Father. The key for him was the link between Jesus' "I Am" statement in John 8:58 with the "I Am" declaration of Yahweh in Exodus 3:14.

Following a series of evangelistic meetings that Prescott conducted in in Melbourne, A. G. Daniells and other ministers studied Andrew Murray's devotional book *The Spirit of Christ,* a copy of which Daniells had acquired in a secondhand book store.[1] This book on the person and work of the Holy Spirit proved to be spiritually and theologically helpful to Daniells and his colleagues. The concept that that the Spirit was the "third person of the Godhead" was first publicly expressed in writing by Ellen White in 1897, in letters written to ministers.[2] It was also reflected in the *Desire of Ages* published in 1898.[3] The topic of the trinity was a sensitive issue among Adventists for a number of years afterward, but the seeds were sown, and there were forthright descriptions of the Trinity in the statement of Adventist beliefs that appeared in the 1931 *SDA Year Book.*

My own reflections on the church have brought me to the conclusion that Christian community is best understood as having a basis in the triune nature of God. As described in the biblical book of Acts, the saving ministry that Jesus began continued in the work of his apostles through the power of the Holy Spirit. And the presence of the Spirit in the lives of Jesus' followers makes it possible for them enjoy an experience of profound care and concern for one another. Furthermore, as the Johannine writings in particular indicate, Christians in their life together both reflect and participate in the love that defines God's own life as an intimate community of Father, Son, and Spirit.[4]

---

[1] Andrew Murray, *The Spirit of Christ* (New York: Randolph 1888).

[2] Ellen G. White, *Special Testimonies for Ministers and Workers,* [Series 1] no 10 (Battle Creek, MI: General Conference 1897) 25, 37.

[3] White, *Desire* 538.

[4] For a fuller discussion development of these ideas, see "The Trinitarian Basis of Christian Community," *Ministry,* Feb. 2009: 13+.

This view of God has profound implications for the entire range of Christian beliefs, including, for example, the doctrine of the church. It indicates, for one thing, that the church is the primary manifestation of God's presence in the world, and, for another, it places the church at the center of the Christian life. If salvation involves participating in the fellowship that defines God's own life, then one's relation to God involves participating in the community that God's love established. The experience of salvation is therefore social as well as individual. It has a public as well as a private dimension. It changes our relations to others as well as to God.

The doctrine of God has also received careful consideration in the writings of two professors of theology at Andrews University Theological Seminary. In "Doctrine of God," his contribution to the *Handbook of Seventh-day Adventist Theology*,[1] Fernando L. Canale approaches the topic along the lines of classical theological reflection. He discusses various divine attributes, such as "eternity" and "immutability," as well as divine love, certainly God's preeminent biblical attribute. And though he strongly affirms the divine Trinity, he also appeals to divine mystery as a way of accounting for the challenge of conceiving God as both three and one.[2] Canale also maintains that God genuinely interacts with the world, although he insists that this is compatible with the traditional view that God's knowledge encompasses the entire future, as well as the present and the past. Basic to Canale's approach to the doctrine of God is his insistence that "our understanding of God must stand free from human speculations," and human philosophy must be "subject to the Bible, since divine philosophy is already available in the Scriptures."[3]

In a recent book, John C. Peckham provides a detailed discussion of God's love. *The Love of God: A Canonical Model* is the most extensive exploration to date of this central divine attribute by a Seventh-day Adventist thinker.[4] He proposes an alternative to two objectionable views of God--the "transcendent-voluntarist model," which insists on a radical separation between God and the world, and the "immanent-experientialist model," which holds that God

---

[1]Fernando L. Canale, "The Doctrine of God," *Handbook of Seventh-day Adventist Theology*, ed. Raoul Dederen, Commentary Reference Series 12 (Hagerstown, MD: Review 2000).

[2]Canale seems to come rather close to tritheism when he describes the persons of the Trinity as "three individual centers of intelligence and action," or "centers of consciousness and action," but he insists that the idea that God is "one single reality" "transcends the limits of our human reason" and must be accepted by faith (150).

[3]Canale 105.

[4]John C. Peckham, *The Love of God: A Canonical Model* (Downers Grove, IL: IVP 2015).

could not exist without a world. Peckham prefers "the forecondi-
tional-reciprocal model." On this model, God is essentially independent from the world--God created because God chose to—yet
God is genuinely affected by the world. To unpack this, Peckham
describes God's love as having five important aspects—volitional,
evaluative, emotional, "foreconditional" (his novel expression), and
reciprocal—and he devotes a chapter to each of them. As he describes it, God's love is subjectively unconditional, meaning that
God's love for the creatures never varies, but objectively conditional, in the sense that those who reject it do not experience it.

The book's subtitle, "a canonical model," expresses a conviction that Peckham shares with Canale, namely, that our view of
God should be based exclusively on the biblical writings. Though
there are important aspects of the doctrine of God that the book
does not take up, such as the Trinity, its careful exploration of
God's love has a good deal to offer.

Although Adventist views of God have developed significantly
over time, and there may be noteworthy variations among them
today, there is little question that for Adventists across the board
love is the preeminent divine attribute. We all embrace the words
with which Ellen White's Conflict of the Ages Series begins and
ends, "God is love." No theological challenge for the church is
more important than to explore the full meaning of this affirmation.[1]

## PROSPECT: TOWARD A SEVENTH-DAY ADVENTIST
## VIEW OF GOD—WHAT NEEDS TO BE DONE

Let me draw these reflections to a close by suggesting several
ways in which our thinking about God could develop in the future.

One would be to give the doctrine of God explicit theological
attention. It has developed among us more or less spontaneously
over the years. In some ways that is good, because it has prevented
us from formally committing ourselves to erroneous views. But the
time has come to give the doctrine of God the attention it deserves.
We cannot let our understanding of the central theme of Christian
faith grow like Topsy. Developing theologically in this way leads to
doctrinal disintegration. This means that we must elevate our doctrine of God to a position of paramount theological importance. As
many Christian theologians now acknowledge, God is the central
and all-encompassing article of Christian faith. Everything else the
church has to say is commentary on this one, fundamental doctrine.

Second, as we develop our doctrine of God, we need to draw
on all the resources that bear on our understanding. This means at-

[1]For a succinct account of the themes that this would involve, see Guy.

tending to neglected Biblical themes, particularly those dealing with the inner life of God. We give far too little attention to such phenomena as divine repentance and divine sensitivity, in spite of the fact that they are central to the biblical portrait of God. We also need to attend to the insights of our own religious experiences. Our personal apprehensions of God often provide a helpful corrective to traditional theoretical formulations.

Third, we need to determine what is central and what is peripheral to our understanding of God. If love is really the most important divine attribute, then everything Adventists have to say is a commentary on divine love. We need to demonstrate how the definition of God as love transforms our understanding of God and we need to explore the consequences of this transformation for everything else we believe. This will lead us to expand our understanding of God as Trinity. One of the reasons our Trinitarian thought has been arrested is our failure to link the love of God with the essence of God. To correct this, we should draw on some of the powerful resources of Christian tradition, as they explore what it means to proclaim that God is love. This is what the concept of the Trinity is all about. It is not a Hellenistic corruption of the Gospel, nor a philosophical departure from primitive Christianity. Rather, it is a profound meditation on the meaning of God's self-giving in the mission of Christ to redeem the fallen world.

Fourth, we need to bring the doctrine of God into direct conversation with the challenges that Christian faith faces today. One is the challenge of unbelief in modern culture. We need to develop a rationale for believing in God that addresses contemporary challenges to its credibility. In the past two centuries, atheism has become a viable possibility for vast numbers of people for the first time in human history. There have always been individuals here and there who questioned the existence of God, but never before have so many rejected the idea, never before has doing so been the mark of an age. And in the past two decades, so-call "new atheists" have been particularly vocal in objecting to the idea of God. If Seventh-day Adventism is to be a vibrant force in the developed countries of the world, it must address the serious doubts people have about God. This calls for something like a philosophical or foundational theology.

Another challenge to Christian faith is the religious pluralism of the world today. Unbelief is not by any means the only alternative to Christian faith in God. We are surrounded by divergent religious perspectives. In fact, if we could identify all the religions that exist in southern California, within a hundred mile radius of where this paper was first delivered, we would find more of the world's religious traditions represented in a single locale than at any other time in history, with the possible exception of ancient Alexandria. All the world's great religious traditions are manifested here— Christianity in many different branches, eastern as well as western, along with Judaism, Islam, Hinduism, Buddhism. Along with them we would find some of lesser known religions, such as Sikhism and Taoism. And we would also find various new age movements, whose concepts of self-discovery, reincarnation, and channeling seem to confirm the oft-repeated observation that, when people cease to believe in God, they come to believe, not in nothing, but in anything.

A contemporary doctrine of God must also explore the relation between traditional perspectives on God and social structures that have perpetrated racial and sexual oppression. Eurocentrism and patriarchy are examples. The picture of God as a large white male (as in Michelangelo's famous portrayal in the Sistine Chapel) not only fails to speak to millions of God's children, it makes it difficult, if not impossible, for them to believe in God. For some, it is reminiscent of horrendous atrocities that have been committed in the name of Christianity; it symbolizes humankind at its worst.

Finally, we need to give fuller expression to our most distinctive theological perspective and frankly face the perplexing questions it raises. The great controversy theme provides us a dramatic interpretation of history, a unique and highly suggestive response to the problem of evil, and a dynamic, interactive view of God's relation to creation. It deserves further exploration along all these avenues.[1]

All this serves to show that we have a lot of work to do in developing our understanding of God. We have rich resources; we face significant challenges. We need to mine our resources more fully and take our challenges more seriously. The first great commandment is a call to worship God. So, too, is the first angel's message. A doctrine of God, therefore, is more than part of the Advent message; properly understood, it *is* the Advent message. We will never fulfill our mission unless we expand our vision of God. To complete the Adventist mission we must develop an adequate understanding and a convincing portrait of the God we call the world to worship.

---

[1]For a discussion of the great controversy in relation to the problem of suffering, see my book *Suffering and the Search for Meaning: Contemporary Responses to the Problem of Pain* (Downers Grove, IL: IVP 2014).

# 2

# Revelation and Inspiration

## Sakae Kubo

Revelation and inspiration are very closely connected. The first has to do with disclosure and the second with the bestowing of wisdom or skill, the guiding of the minds of prophets, and the stimulating of the people of God to perform their various functions and offices.[1] Inspiration is more generally understood as God's superintendence through the Holy Spirit of the communication of revelation to ensure its authenticity. Regarding revelation—or, more specifically, special revelation—among Christian theologians the issue has revolved around the nature of what is disclosed—propositions, or God in person.

With the neo-orthodox emphasis on God personally as the content of revelation, not propositions, Seventh-day Adventists now have specifically included God but have maintained the emphasis upon propositions.[2] Because there is a general agreement regarding this aspect of special revelation, this has not been an area of discussion. The area in which the question of inspiration and revelation has surfaced in Adventist discussion is the extent to which special revelation is required in such books as Acts, Chronicles and Kings, and the Wisdom books, such as Proverbs and Ecclesiastes. Discussion has centered more specifically in the area of the use of particular methods in the study of Scripture as it relates to inspiration. The future of the Adventist understanding of revelation and inspiration will revolve around this issue.

[1]See C. F. D. Moule's discussions in *The Interpreter's Dictionary of the Bible*, 4 vols. (New York: Abingdon 1962) 2:713-24 and 4:54-8.

[2]Raoul Dederen, "The Revelation-Inspiration Phenomenon according to the Bible Writers," *Issues in Revelation and Inspiration*, Adventist Theological Society Occasional Papers 1, ed. Frank Holbrook and Leo Van Dolson (Berrien Springs, MI: Adventist Theological Society 1992) 13.

## 1844-1900: THOUGHT INSPIRATION ESPOUSED

A General Conference action of November 16, 1883, gives us the first indication of the church's understanding of inspiration.[1] It was voted to

devote critical thought to the grammatical perfection of the writings, . . .

*Whereas*, We believe the light given by God to His servants is by the enlightenment of the mind, thus imparting the thoughts, and not (except in rare cases) the very words in which the ideas should be expressed; therefore

*Resolved*, That in the republication of these volumes, such verbal changes be made as to remove the above-named imperfections, as far as possible, without in any measure changing the thought; . . . .[2]

Two things should be noted. It is clearly acknowledged that a prophet is not preserved from "grammatical imperfections" and, therefore, that revisions of a prophet's work are not out of order. The other more significant point is the fact that thoughts and not words are imparted by God. Obviously these two points clearly show that for the early Adventists who supported this resolution, inspiration did not take place by dictation.

Although not a primary source for the period, W. C. White's letter to L. E. Froom of January 8, 1928, confirms this picture.

This statement made by the General Conference of 1883 was in perfect harmony with the beliefs and positions of the pioneers in this cause, and it was, I think, the only position taken by any of our ministers and teachers until Prof. [W. W.] Prescott, president of Battle Creek College, presented in a very forceful way another view—the view held and presented by Professor Gausen [sic]. The acceptance of that view by the students in the Battle Creek College and many others, including Elder Haskell, has resulted in bringing into our work questions and perplexities without end, and always increasing.

Sister White never accepted the Gausen [sic] theory regarding verbal inspiration, either as applied to her own work or as applied to the Bible.[3]

W. C. White confirms the position of the General Conference thinking about inspiration and the thinking of the pioneers at that

---

[1]Previous to this, criticism of William Miller's interpretation of Scripture appeared. Liberal views of Scripture were first appearing in the United States at Miller's time. Naturally, the Millerites felt that churches which opposed Miller by interpreting the little horn as Antiochus Epiphanes were affected by these modern views. They referred to this new approach as neology (see Kai Arasola, *The End of Historicism: Millerite Hermeneutic of Time Prophecies in the Old Testament* [Uppsala: Arasola 1990] 58-9; P. Gerard Damsteegt, *Foundations of the Seventh-day Adventist Message and Mission* [Grand Rapids: Eerdmans 1977] 63-77). Notice that this is an instance in which the discussion is not focused directly on inspiration but on interpretation.

[2]Ellen G. White, *Selected Messages*, 3 vols. (Washington, DC: Review 1958-80) 3: 96.

[3]W. C. White, letter to L. E. Froom, Jan. 8, 1928, White, *Messages* 3: 454-5.

time but adds another point of interest—that a deviation from that view was promoted by W. W. Prescott at Battle Creek College. Prescott was president from 1885 until 1894. Therefore, it was probably after the General Conference of 1883 that he promulgated his Gaussen-influenced views.[1]

Clearly, Prescott was advocating a novel position which has never been the official position of the church.[2] Yet he must have been influential, since this view seems to have prevailed in the church generally in his time and after. No doubt this was the reason for his reluctance to correct data in the *Great Controversy* when he was asked to assist with its revision.

[1]François Samuel Robert Louis Gaussen (1790-1863) was a Swiss clergymen who published his book *Theopneustie* in Geneva in 1840. The English translation, *Theopneustia; The Plenary Inspiration of Scriptures*, was published in London in 1841. Gaussen believed that the Bible came by dictation. Philosopher William Abraham writes: "For my part, I must emphasize that Gaussen really did believe in dictation. The original shows this clearly:

> . . . elle (L'écriture) est entièrement dictée par le Saint-Esprit, elle nous donne les propres paroles de Dieu, elle est entièrement donnée par le souffle de Dieu.
>     . . . toute la partie des Ecritures apelée Prophetie, quelle qu'elle soit, a été complétement dictée de Dieu; en sorte que les mots memes, aussi bien que les pensées, y ont été donnés de lui.

The analogies that Gaussen uses bear this out. The writers are said to be 'the pens, hands and secretaries, of the Holy Ghost'; and he compares the relation of God to the writers of Scriptures to that between Racine and a village schoolmaster who writes out a drama at his dictation" (William J. Abraham, *The Divine Inspiration of Holy Scripture* [Oxford: OUP 1981] 28-9).

[2]Such a view demands inerrancy. Though today proponents of this view reject the dictation method, inerrancy was based originally on dictation and logically flows from it. While dictation is denied, the current form of explanation ends up essentially affirming dictation. While *Review and Herald* editor, Kenneth Wood wrote: "But though we stand foursquare for the Bible as God's inspired Word, we do not contend for 'inerrancy' in the autographs as the hallmark of inspiration" ("The Divine-Human Word," *Review and Herald*, June 24, 1976: 2). Don Neufeld, then associate editor of the *Review*, stated: "If Seventh-day Adventists had not had demonstrated in their midst how inspiration operates, then they would probably stand with Dr. Lindsell in his position with regard to inerrancy. His position is a philosophical deduction based on how he assumes God operates" (Donald Neufeld, "The Battle for the Bible," *Review and Herald*, July 26, 1979: 15). George Reid, director of the Biblical Research Institute, declared: "Adventists also find themselves uncomfortable with Evangelical inerrancy. The idea of defending the error-free status of lost autographs rings hollow. It seems to be a form of shadowboxing" ("Is the Bible Our Final Authority?" *Ministry*, Nov. 1991: 8).

Arthur White wrote: the Adventist concept "partakes neither of the modernistic, liberal views that destroy the authority of God's Word nor the ultraconservative views that make the prophet a mere automaton—a machine, as it were-speaking or writing words he is impelled to utter or to record" ("Toward an Adventist Concept of Inspiration," *Review and Herald*, Jan. 12, 1978: 4.

Another matter of interest was the publication, beginning January 15, 1884, of a series of articles on inspiration by George I. Butler when he was president of the General Conference. He proposed in this set of articles the view that there are different degrees of inspiration in the Bible. Moses and Christ—with the latter, of course, much superior to the former—stand at the pinnacle of inspiration because "the subject matter they present is more important, the light revealed is clearer, and their words more impressive and profound."[1] He was careful to state that he respected all Scripture though with varying degrees and that he did not question any statement anywhere. He accepted all of the books of the Bible as inspired.

What is interesting in Butler's presentation is that he clearly recognizes the difference between the revelation given to Moses and that given to Solomon, between what we have in Genesis and what we have in, say, the Song of Solomon. He also recognizes the different modes of revelation and inspiration.

In 1886, Ellen White stated that the authors, not the words, of the biblical books were inspired. They were imbued with thoughts but not words or expressions.[2]

In 1889, she wrote what was apparently a response to the series of articles by Butler.[3] She opposed those who had taught that "some things in the Scriptures were inspired and some were not" at the Battle Creek Tabernacle and Battle Creek College. In fact, however, Butler had not taught that some parts of Scripture were inspired while others were not, but that some parts, such as the Pentateuch and the Gospels, were more inspired than Proverbs and Song of Solomon. It would be interesting to know whether Ellen White was concerned specifically with what Butler wrote or if she was opposed to the notion of degrees of inspiration as such.

---

[1]George I. Butler, "Inspiration: Differences in Degrees and Manner of Bestowment," *Review and Herald*, Jan. 14, 1884: 44. He shows the varied ways in which God gave light to human beings. 1. God spoke audibly in giving the law and announcing Christ. 2. God instructed Moses and Christ after taking them into the special divine presence. 3. God gave visions and dreams. 4. God influenced people through the Spirit. God "illuminated the memory of those who had been acquainted with important events, so that they could correctly place them on record." Butler is, no doubt, referring here to historical works such as 1 and 2 Samuel, 1 and 2 Kings, 1 and 2 Chronicles, Luke-Acts. 5. The Spirit was with Solomon and others, "and especially illuminated their natural faculties," so that they set forth good thoughts which we have in such books as the Proverbs, Job, etc. "These books seem to have been given in a different manner from most of the other books of the Bible" (44.)

[2]White, *Messages* 1: 21. This passage comes from Manuscript 24, 1886.

[3]White, *Messages* 1: 23. The letter included in the above work was written in 1889.

## 1900–1954: Inerrantists Gain Ground

As we survey this next period, it appears as though Prescott's influence while at Battle Creek College affected very strongly the view of inspiration held by many church leaders and members. While there were those who still maintained the position held by the church's mainline in the nineteenth century, it is evident that the majority of the church members and probably most of the leaders outside of Washington had adopted a Gaussen-like view of inspiration.

Because of the analogy one could make between the Bible and Ellen White (since Adventists consider both inspired), it is of interest to us to consider instances where the inspiration of Ellen White was considered. Bert Haloviak points out three different attitudes towards Ellen White's writings in the early twentieth century.[1] The first group, including A. T. Jones, E. J. Waggoner, and J. H. Kellogg, can be classed as inerrantist. They were literalists who could not allow for apparent contradictions or inconsistencies. A prophet could not contradict herself. Thus, they concluded that what appeared like contradictions were not from the prophet but came from some external source. By 1910 most of the first group had rejected Ellen White and left the church.[2]

Haloviak mentions two other approaches to Ellen White that existed at that time. Stephen Haskell, George Butler, and J. S. Washburn also maintained a literal interpretation of Ellen White's writings but downplayed the apparent inconsistencies and contradictions. They could thus consider them as inspired. The third group including Daniells, Prescott, and W. C. White "emphasized the need for a non-literal, contextual approach. . . . ." They did allow for errors but did not believe that the presence of errors in Ellen White's writings meant that they were not inspired.

It was also during this period that a number of articles in the *Review and Herald* dealing with higher criticism appeared.[3] This was

[1]Bert Haloviak with Gary Land, "Ellen White and Doctrinal Conflict: Context of the 1919 Bible Conference," *Spectrum* 12.4 (June 1982): 23.

[2]Haloviak with Land 32.

[3]They allude to the Michigan *Christian Herald's* reference to great revivals coming but indicate that such is not possible with churches influenced by higher criticism (Leon A. Smith, "The True Basis for a Genuine Revival," *Review and Herald*, Jan. 5, 1905: 5), to the *Hibbert Journal's* article on "Shortcomings of the Decalogue" (Leon A. Smith, "Modern Criticism of the Decalogue," *Review and Herald*, Jan. 26, 1905: 6), the Baptist Congress at Baltimore, Maryland, on November 12, 1905, discussing the question of Jesus's virginal conception (C. M. Snow, "The Higher Critics and God's Word," *Review and Herald*, Nov. 28, 1907: 4), the desire of higher critics in the Episcopal Church to change the Ten Commandments (C. H. Edwards, "Facing the Crisis," *Review and Herald*, May 18, 1911: 3-4), liberal theology's failure to offer anything in place of what it had tak-

no doubt due to the fundamentalism-liberalism debate that was go-ing on in the Protestant world at that time. (The Niagara Confer-ence, which spelled out the five fundamentals, met in 1895 and the publication of the *Fundamentals* took place in 1909.) There is noth-ing in these articles to indicate that they were directed to persons within the church.

According to Haloviak, the first decade of the twentieth centu-ry was characterized predominantly by support for a more literalistic view of Scripture, probably under the influence of Prescott. What Daniells said at the 1919 Bible Conference confirms this. "We have made a wonderful change in nineteen years, Brother Prescott. Fif-teen years ago we could not have talked what we are talking here today."[1] Yet the Conference reports show that there was fear that what was being discussed would be leaked out, belying the claim that great changes had taken place. While some held more liberal views, it seems that there was a strong undercurrent of support for an ultraconservative view through the first four decades of the twentieth century. The aftermath of the 1919 Bible Conference on-ly strengthened this position. Nevertheless, the fact that the 1919 Bible Conference took place and an open discussion was permitted on touchy issues regarding the Spirit of Prophecy is indicative of the fact that some changes had taken place.

The 1919 Bible Conference took place because of the conver-gence of two factors: the development of this ultraconservative view of inspiration and the fact that people who were acquainted with Ellen White and how her writings were put together, and had been involved in changes made in her writings, were still alive, were leaders of the church, and had a different view of inspiration. The latter factor and the fact that those acquainted with her spoke out openly, frankly, and yet with sensitivity and respect regarding her writings made this conference unique. What should be kept in mind throughout is the analogy of Ellen White's modus operandi with that of the Bible. What was said about her writings could be said about the Bible. In fact, the participants at the conference indi-cate that one could be more critical of the Bible than of Ellen White.[2]

---

en away (F. M. Wilcox, "Nothing to Offer," *Review and Herald*, Oct. 5, 1911: 10-1); and William Newton Clarke of Colgate University, who referred to the Millerite movement as "the great calamity of 1843" which could have been pre-vented by higher criticism (Earle Albert Rowell, "Higher Criticism the Enemy of Seventh-day Adventists," *Review and Herald*, Nov. 9, 1911: 7.

[1]Molleurus Couperus, "The Bible Conference of 1919," *Spectrum* 10.1 (May 1979): 57.

[2]Prescott (Couperus 39) and Daniells (Couperus 43) both felt that disagree-ments over whether the Bible was verbally inspired or not would not cause as much disturbance as the same disagreement focused on the work of Ellen White.

What are the significant conclusions regarding inspiration that emerged from this conference?

1. Daniells's statement that Ellen White "never claimed to be an authority on history, and never claimed to be a dogmatic teacher on theology"[1] is an important one. The implications of this, as Daniells further explained, was that there could be historical errors in her writings. At one point Daniells put forth "one illustration of a mistake in the Bible: In Samuel it says a man lifted up his hand against 800 men whom he slew; then in Chronicles this same thing is spoken of, and it says that he lifted up his hand against 300 men, whom he slew."

2. There was a unanimous consensus supporting the view that Ellen White's writings were not "verbally inspired." Those in attendance at the conference knew how her books had been put together. James White corrected her works, while secretaries assisted in making grammatical changes and added historical material that were not included by her.[2]

3. A major problem which was not addressed was how to deal with the "slippery slope" problem which surfaced several times. C. L. Benson articulated this problem best when he asked:

> If there are such uncertainties with reference to our historical position, and if the Testimonies are not to be relied on to throw a great deal of light upon our historical positions, and if the same is true with reference to our theological interpretation of texts, then how can we consistently place implicit confidence in the direction that is given with reference to our educational problems, and our medical school, and even our denominational organization? If there is a definite spiritual leadership in these things, then how can we consistently lay aside the Testimonies or partially lay them aside when it comes to the prophetic and historic side of the message? and place these things on the basis of research work?[3]

It seems to me that we need simply to accept this kind of problem as a fact of life. On the one hand, we never will have an inerrant canonical document and on the other hand, we will never be faced with a document that is totally and absolutely unreliable. The human condition is such that truth is not served to us on a silver platter. Rather, we must ever search and investigate; and because of our backgrounds, educations, and experiences, will not always come out in the same place, though we will share our views with our communities.

The fact of the matter is that the position taken by Daniells and others regarding grammatical correction and historical errors was so convincing that, no matter what kind of slippery slope they found themselves on as a result of adopting it, they could not disavow

[1] Couperus 34.
[2] Couperus 50, 54.
[3] Couperus 46.

their position. Whatever else they might be wrong about, they knew they were right about this because of their own personal acquaintance with the methods used in preparing Ellen White's books. Prescott himself could never forget the corrections made in *The Great Controversy*. Whatever solutions suggested must begin with these basic facts.

While there seems to be some progress indicated by the openness and frankness of the discussion that took place at the 1919 Bible Conference, the reaction to it once it was publicized led to dismissal of faculty members at Washington Missionary College and later to Daniells' removal from office as General Conference president.[1] Obviously a conservative backlash resulted and has affected the church even to the present. In 1932, F. M. Wilcox noted the consequences of this conflict: the churches were stirred up and students went witch hunting for "modernist" professors.[2]

## 1954-1966: The Figuhr Era—A New Openness

Reuben Figuhr became president of the General Conference in 1954. His support of education—evinced in the establishment of two universities and the Geoscience Research Institute (GRI)—and his encouragement of some important publications indicated a shift from the ultraconservative past.[3]

It was also during Figuhr's administration that the Theological Seminary was moved from the shadows of the General Conference in Takoma Park, Maryland, and its isolation from other academic influences, to the campus of Andrews University in Berrien Springs (1959). Coincidentally with this move, another important change was taking place in the faculties of the Seminary and the religion departments of our colleges. Where we lacked trained biblical scholars and theologians, now scholars trained at non-Adventist universities began to teach in these fields. Formerly, Adventist

[1] Haloviak with Land 30-32.
[2] Haloviak with Land 32.
[3] Richard Hammill, "Fifty Years of Creationism: the Story of an Insider," *Spectrum* 15.2 (Aug. 1984): 34-6. Hammill attributes to him the following: the establishment of two universities, Andrews University in 1957, and Loma Linda University in 1961; the publication of the *Seventh-day Adventist Bible Commentary*, ed. Francis D. Nichol *et al.*, 7 vols. (Washington: Review 1957); the publication of [R. A. Anderson, LeRoy E. Froom, and W. E. Read,] *Seventh-day Adventists Answer Questions on Doctrine* (Washington, DC: Review 1957) and General Conference of Seventh-Day Adventists, Committee on Problems in Bible Translation, *Problems in Bible Translation* (Washington, DC: Review 1954); the establishment of a committee to study "sensitive problems" in Daniel; the recommendation to financially support trained geologists to do basic research and the establishment of the present Geoscience Research Institute (1958).

teachers had received their doctorates in "safe" areas outside of theology or biblical studies. With this development came a disturbing but refreshing change, stimulating the study of the Bible in ways not possible before, as Adventist scholars wrestled with ideas discussed by scholars everywhere, bending and shaping them within an Adventist framework. These new ideas, however, challenged some old ideas and conflicts developed regarding inspiration, Ellen White and exegesis, the proof-text method, and some Adventist interpretation of Scripture. There was also a more open attitude toward the search after truth. One's thinking was not enclosed and limited by narrow boundaries. Different ways of thinking were not *verboten*.

The Geoscience Research Institute pursued research and field studies instead of merely apologetic approaches designed to uncover evidence to support positions already accepted. These studies led to the awareness that it was not possible, in light of all the relevant data, to maintain that the earth was only 6,000 years old—and this in turn led to the problem of how to understand the inspiration of Ellen White, who had supported this view.

This period is important for our purposes because a more honest look at Scripture and Ellen White was possible and questions began to be raised about the nature of inspiration. Responsible examination of geological phenomena led to questions regarding the traditional view of the age of the earth, which was thought to be biblical and which had clearly been endorsed by Ellen White.

## 1966-2003: ATTEMPTS MADE TO CLOSE PANDORA'S BOX

This heady period of openness did not, however, last very long. With the election of Robert Pierson as General Conference President, things began to change.[1] The Seminary felt the pressure. Soon all the members of the New Testament department as well as the one person trained in systematic theology had found new positions. The personnel in the Geoscience Research Institute were replaced as a result of Pierson's attendance at the 1968 Field Conference and the resultant fear of what GRI scientists were thinking, saying, and doing.[2] Their work threatened a short chronology for earth history, and with it—some thought—the inspiration and authority of Ellen White.

Other changes followed. Gordon Hyde, an ardent conservative not trained in theology, became director of the Biblical Research

---

[1] Hammill 39.
[2] See Edward Lugenbeal's account in "The Conservative Restoration at Geoscience," *Spectrum* 15.2 (Aug. 1984): 23-31.

Institute in 1969. The Bible Conferences of 1974, ostensibly intended to counteract "higher critical methodologies," was promoted by the Biblical Research Institute. Later, similar conferences were held in other parts of the world field.

In 1976, Pierson asked Richard Hammill to prepare a statement on inspiration and revelation which Hammill says was

> drastically revised at the Nosoca Pines Conference in February of 1978. Two sections of the document were excised: one of these dealt with the human element in revelation and the resulting problems of contradictions or differences where there are multiple accounts in the Bible of certain events; the other excised section dealt with the role of reason in seeking to understand inspired writings. I was not included as a member of the subcommittee which excised these sections and further revised the document, no doubt because I had just made known my views about that in a paper on inspiration which I had presented earlier in the conference.[1]

Willis J. Hackett initiated the development of a statement on the subject of creation and the early history of the earth in 1976. This statement was published in the *Adventist Review* of June 17, 1980. The statement occasioned contention because it only affirmed "a short history for life and the human race," whereas some wanted more specificity, *i.e.*, an explicit endorsement of a 6,000-year history for the earth. Later, another "Statement of Affirmation" was published by the *Adventist Review* and *Ministry*;[2] it stated that "the biblical record requires a short chronology of approximately 6000 years in contrast to tens of thousands or millions of years." The West Coast Bible Teachers went on record in May of 1977 opposing the development of statements on inspiration, revelation, and creation.[3]

A very important development in the history of inspiration in the Adventist Church took place in the seventies. Several scholars published articles and a book, *Prophetess of Health*, documenting the use of historical sources, including their errors, by Ellen White.[4] After reviewing the developments in this area, Don McAdams concludes:

> Three points have been clearly established. One is that Ellen White took much material from other authors. And she did not use secular literary sources just to provide clear descriptions of historical events, health

[1]Hammill 45n3.

[2]"Statement of Affirmation," *Adventist Review*, Dec. 8, 1983: 15; "Statement of Affirmation," *Ministry*, Dec. 1983.

[3]See the report in *Spectrum* 8.4 (Aug. 1977): 44-7. Apparently no official use was made of these statements, though the idea of "loyalty oaths" has been taken up by the Adventist Theological Society (see below) as a means of screening prospective members.

[4]See Donald R. McAdams, "Shifting Views of Inspiration: Ellen G. White Studies in the 1970s," *Spectrum* 10.4 (Mar. 1980): 27-41.

principles or other information revealed to her in vision; she also used these sources to provide information not seen in vision.

Second, Ellen White was a part of late nineteenth-century American culture and was influenced by contemporary health reformers, authors and fellow Adventist church leaders. . . . Without diminishing one whit from the special revelation of the Holy Spirit to Ellen White, we must acknowledge that she was shaped by her environment just as all of us have been shaped by ours.

The third point which recent Ellen White scholarship has established is that Ellen White was not inerrant. Inevitably, as she incorporated into her own articles and books contemporary ideas and the words of contemporary historians, health reformers and devotional writers, she passed along errors of fact and some of the misconceptions of her generation.[1]

These conclusions, if they are as "clearly established" as McAdams believes, have very significant implications regarding the present debate on inspiration and hermeneutics.

These studies led to the admission by W. P. Bradley[2] and Arthur White[3] that Ellen White did use materials from other sources and that inaccuracies in her historical writings are possible and, in fact, present.

The decade of the eighties began with the conference at Glacier View regarding Desmond Ford's view of the sanctuary. An interesting blip in the history of interpretation was Consultation II (1981), at which the historical-critical method, shorn of objectionable presuppositions, was deemed acceptable for the study of the Bible.[4] This is interesting because it followed the 1974 Bible Conference and Glacier View and took place during the period Gordon Hyde was director of the Biblical Research Institute.

About this time (1981), Gerhard Hasel was appointed dean of the SDA Theological Seminary. He was very influential with the church administrators already through his association with the Biblical Research Institute, but in his new position he became even more influential in shaping the thinking of church administrators who, fearful of "liberal" influences, were more than ready to follow his very conservative leadership.

[1]McAdams.

[2]"Ellen G. White and Her Writings," *Spectrum* 3.2 (Spring 1971): 58.

[3]Arthur L. White, "Historical Sources and the Conflict Series. The E.G. White Historical Writings," *Adventist Review*, July 26, 1979: 9-10.

[4]Alden Thompson, who participated in this consultation (the results of which have not been published), affirms that the consensus reached by the working groups at Consultation II was that "the descriptive aspects of the so-called historical-critical method could indeed be separated from naturalistic presuppositions and thus could be used by Adventist scholars" (*Inspiration: Hard Questions, Honest Answers* [Hagerstown, MD: Review 1991] 272).

One immediate result was the turnabout reflected in the statement on Methods of Bible Study[1] regarding the assessment of the historical critical method. Hasel's contention[2] that it is not possible to use a modified version of this method without swallowing the presuppositions that its original formulators accepted[3] appears in this document. Reviewing this argument, Jerry Gladson shows that it is possible to use this method without the naturalistic presuppositions, that it has been a "long-standing Adventist practice," that it was used in the *Seventh-day Adventist Bible Commentary*, that Hasel himself has used the historical critical method, and that it helps *"the church come to terms with the genesis of Ellen G. White writings."*[4]

Other significant and ominous events in recent times have been the reactionary tendencies exhibited by the Religion Department at Southern Adventist University (which requires that its chair foreswear even a modified form of the historical critical method and that its faculty sign statements indicating their positions regarding the church's fundamental doctrines),[5] and the establishment of an organization and publications devoted to the promotion of ultraconservative theology. Because of the dissatisfaction with the dominance of progressives within the leadership and membership of what is now the Adventist Society for Religious Studies, conservatives began their own organization. Membership in the Adventist Theological Society, which was initiated in 1988 by the Southern College Religion Department, is obtained by recommendation of two members and "receipt of a signed application indicating acceptance of the society's constitution and bylaws, and unqualified commitment to the society's criteria of membership as presented in the preamble, . . . ."[6] The Southern College Religion Department began its publication, *Adventist Perspectives*, in 1987, and in the same year a conservative group began publishing *Adventists Affirm*; the *Journal of the Adventist Theological Society* was first issued in 1990.

---

[1]"Methods of Bible Study Committee (GCC-A)—Report," *Adventist Review*, January 22, 1987, 18-20.

[2]See Jerry Gladson, "Taming Historical Criticism: Adventist Biblical Scholarship in the Land of the Giants," *Spectrum* 18.4 (April 1988): 19-34.

[3]*Understanding the Living Word of God* (Mountain View, CA: Pacific 1980) 24-26, 28.

[4]See Gladson. Surprisingly Gladson thinks that the report approves "a cautious use of historical criticism . . ." (30), even though it states that "[e]ven a modified use of this method that retains the principles of criticism which subordinates the Bible to human reason is unacceptable to Adventists" ("Methods" 18) He can argue that the term "a modified use" is not what is significant but rather the clause "that retains . . . reason." Almost every scholar has argued otherwise.

[5]See Gladson 28, 29, 32; *Adventist Perspectives* 1:1 (1987: 50.

[6]J. R. Spangler, "Adventist Theological Society," *Ministry*, December 1989, P. 24-25.

A most significant event in Adventist history of interpretation was the publication of Alden Thompson's *Inspiration: Hard Questions, Honest Answers* in 1991.[1] It is significant because it is the first time a position using a reasoned, historically sensitive approach to deal with the problem of errors and differences in the Bible was openly offered for discussion by the church. The response to Thompson's book by the Adventist Theological Society was swift and strongly apologetic and polemical in tone.[2] Much discussion has been initiated by *Inspiration* and the ATS volume designed to reply to it, and the dust has not yet fully settled.

## ANALYSIS OF ADVENTIST HISTORY

The inspiration debate today does not focus on the question of dictation. All sides today agree that God did not dictate the Bible, although this view has been held in the past. Rather, the debate is concerned with verbal inspiration and inerrancy.[3] Verbal inspiration is distinguished from dictation. In dictation God actually dictates the Scripture word by word. A commitment to verbal inspiration presupposes that God prepares prophets from birth and so shapes them that one can say that not only their thoughts but also their words, although their own, are also God's. There is obviously a very fine line between dictation and verbal inspiration. In fact, as Old Testament scholar Dewey Beegle says:

> Notwithstanding repeated denials of the charge, the doctrine of inerrancy leads eventually into the mechanical or dictation theory of inspiration. God could not have given a verbally inerrant Scripture through human charnels without dictating the correct information directly to the biblical writers where they or their sources were in error.[4]

Non-Adventist Christians looking at the question of inspiration in the Adventist church would be immediately struck by the fact that the real debate does not focus on whether the Scriptures are verbally inspired and inerrant. The real debate focuses on whether one uses the historical-critical method, however modified, which

[1]Thompson.

[2]Holbrook and Van Dolson.

[3]Abraham maintains that, while inerrantists do not believe in the dictation method, their view of inerrancy is based on the dictation method of Gaussen.

[4]Dewey M. Beegle. *Scripture, Tradition, and Infallibility* (Grand Rapids: Eerdmans 1973) 239.

Kern Robert Trembath, himself an evangelical, calls verbal inspiration theories "dictation theories in all but name." His reason is that "Once it is assumed that human moral fallibility is unable to be utilized by God as a vehicle of divine inspiration, and it is instead assumed that the doctrines of biblical certainty and perspicuity require the overriding of fallible contributions to Scripture, then some form of dictation is present" (*Evangelical Theories of Biblical Inspiration: A Review and Proposal* [New York: OUP 1987] 91).

implies for the conservatives that one considers human reason superior to Scripture, and thus sits in judgment over Scripture. The real issue, then, is whether one considers human reason superior to Scripture, whether we subordinate Scripture or whether we subordinate ourselves to Scripture.

The reason the debate takes the form it does is the fact that a contemporary prophet, Ellen White, has lived and worked among us and also has written about the process of inspiration. Enough is known about how her writings came about that it is not possible to believe in dictation or verbal inspiration. She is also very clear in regard to this:

> It is not the words of the Bible that are inspired, but the men that were inspired. Inspiration acts not on the man's words or his expressions but on the man himself, who under the influence of the Holy Ghost, is imbued with thoughts. But the words receive the impress of the individual mind.[1]

Regarding inerrancy, when asked "Don't you think there might have been some mistake in the copyist or in the translators?" Ellen White responded in the affirmative. Although that was not the question, some have assumed from this that she would have answered in the affirmative also concerning mistakes in Scripture not due to copyists.[2] One could argue that this answer does not refer to the autographs themselves but the fact is that she admits to the probability of mistakes in manuscripts and translations which we consider the word of God. Adventists have never stood behind the autographs regarding inerrancy because we have never defended inerrancy directly. However, one Adventist scholar, Samuel Koranteng-Pipim, makes this bold statement: ". . . all claims that the Bible makes on any subject—theology, history, science, chronology,

---

[1] White, *Messages* 1: 21. George Reid has pointed out an apparent contradiction in Ellen White's view of inspiration in *Testimonies for the Church*, 9 vols. (Mountain View, CA: Pacific 1948) 4: 9, where, referring to biographical accounts in Scripture, she wrote, "The scribes of God wrote as they were dictated by the Holy Spirit, having no control of the work themselves." The statement is so explicit that it is difficult to explain it otherwise than written. She believed at least for these accounts (probably one can extend it for much of Scripture) that God literally dictated the Scripture. Reid's explanation for the contradiction is that in this passage what she meant was that the "writers were impelled to tell the whole truth about Bible characters rather than yield to the normal temptation to lionize, omitting unpleasant facts" (9). Surely this is not the obvious meaning and this explanation is not the only one possible. Another explanation could be that her statements on inspiration found in *Great Controversy* were based on an external source (Calvin E. Stowe, *Origin and History of the Bible* [Hartford, CT: Hartford 1867]), while her writing here—not dependent on such a source—indicates how she really thought inspiration operated. However, it is difficult to square this with what her own experience would have taught her unless she differentiated between her mode of inspiration and those of the biblical writers.

[2] White, *Messages* 1: 16.

numbers, etc.—are absolutely trustworthy and dependable (2 Pet. 1:15-21)."[1] Similar claims are made by those evangelical writers who believe in inerrancy.[2]

While Koranteng-Pipim has been straightforward regarding where he stands, others seem to be working on this basis but are not willing to state it as boldly and candidly as he. Thus, after reviewing the White Estate's response to *Prophetess of Health*, Gary Land comments:

> The foregoing have been examples of how the White Estate's adoption in practice, although not in theory, of the inerrancy approach to inspiration has led it to make arguments that do not fit the facts.[3]

Edward Lugenbeal makes the same point in regard to the approach of conservatives to geological problems at the Geoscience Research Institute:

> Conservatives agreed in theory that Ellen White was fallible, but their actions indicated otherwise. They consistently defended every one of Ellen White's published scientific comments—no matter how incidental to the message of the passage. When asked, for example, about her statements attributing vulcanism to the burning of coal or her assertion that giant men had been found in the fossil record, not once did the Geoscience Research Institute conservatives suggest these statements might illustrate the fallibility of a prophet. Without fail they defended each statement's validity in terms of contemporary scientific knowledge. In short, they treated the entire corpus of Ellen White's writings as inerrant.[4]

One gets the feeling as one reads the responses to Thompson's book that members of the Adventist Theological Society believe in an inerrant Bible without—except for Koranteng-Pipim—admitting it.[5]

---

[1] Samuel Koranteng-Pipim, "An Analysis and Evaluation of Alden Thompson's Casebook/Codebook Approach to the Bible," Holbrook and Van Dolson 63n3.

[2] Lindsell (*Battle* 30-1) affirms: "However limited may have been their knowledge, and however much they may have erred when they were not writing sacred Scripture, the authors of Scripture, under the guidance of the Holy Spirit, were preserved from making factual, historical, scientific, or other errors. The Bible does not purport to be a textbook of history, science, or mathematics; yet when the writers of Scripture spoke of matters embraced in these disciplines, they did not indite error; they wrote what was true."

[3] "Faith, History, and Ellen White," *Spectrum* 9.2 (March 1978): 54.

[4] Lugenbeal 25.

[5] Gulley ineluctably accepts an inerrant view of inspiration when he literally accepts the analogy between inspiration with the incarnation. "In other words, this unity of the divine and human makes both Christ and the Bible unique, different from any other person or book" ("An Evaluation of Alden Thompson's 'Incarnational' Method in the Light of His View of Scripture and Use of Ellen White," Holbrook and Van Dolson 75). Obviously if the human part of the Bible is like the human part of Christ, the Bible would be inerrant as Christ was sinless. How literally would one want to carry this analogy? This means that the

Obviously because of Ellen White's clear statements on inspiration, conservatives have sought to bring the debate onto a different field—higher criticism and human reason, since it is through these that inerrancy comes to be questioned. Ellen White does speak against these. But as we have seen there is higher criticism and there is higher criticism and the distinction is great. George Eldon Ladd, a noted conservative New Testament scholar, shies away from the term "historical criticism" because of the baggage it carries. He says:

> "Criticism," as we would define the term, does not mean sitting in judgment on the Bible as the Word of God. Criticism means making intelligent judgments about historical, literary, textual, and philological questions which one must face in dealing with the Bible, in the light of all of the available evidence, when one recognizes that the Word of God has come to men through the words of men in given historical situations.[1]

Rejecting naturalistic suppositions, progressive Adventist scholars, like Ladd, recognize the need to use criticism not to judge the Bible but to understand it better. Because of the historical nature of the Bible, questions regarding the text, the chronology, the literature demand criticism and the making of intelligent judgments.

At the time of Ellen White such distinctions could not be drawn. However, because she speaks against it, it is easier to criticize those who use it—regardless of their care in not using its naturalistic presuppositions—than to defend belief in biblical inerrancy.

This tack also permits those who accept it to claim "literal" biblical support for the positions they espouse and wish to maintain and to label all other positions as unbiblical and liable to undermine Scripture. Thus, the first issue of *Adventists Affirm*, which deals with the ordination of women, states:

> What is at stake is the authority of the Bible for defining SDA beliefs and practices. . . . If such a Biblical teaching [1 Cor. 14:34, 37] is regarded as limited to the culture of Paul's time, the same could be said of Biblical teachings regarding creation, Sabbathkeeping, clean and unclean meats, footwashing, tithing, etc. The authority of Scripture as a whole would thus be undermined and discredited."[2]

James Smart says in regard to this kind of approach:

---

inspired persons became indefectible as Christ when they wrote their books which means a kind of verbal inspiration.

Davidson is more specific than Gulley when he says, "Ellen White is not talking about the fallibility of Scripture, any more than she is implying sinfulness in the 'imperfect' humanity of Jesus" ("Revelation/Inspiration in the Old Testament: A Critique of Alden Thompson's 'Incarnational' Model," Holbrook and Van Dolson 112). The Bible must be inerrant because Christ was sinless in his humanity.

[1] George Eldon Ladd, *The New Testament and Criticism* (Grand Rapids, MI: Eerdmans 1967) 37.

[2] See the discussion in *Adventists Affirm* 1.1 (Spring 1987): 1.

It is important to note that the immediate effect of a theory of literal inspiration was not to reinforce the authority of God's word in Scripture as a word in which man must ever afresh seek guidance in the affairs of life but rather to make the Scriptures useful as the divine validation of a system of doctrine and practice. The infallibility attributed to the Scriptures was transferred directly to the doctrines and practices that were considered to be founded in Scripture, with the consequence that a static religious order came into being.[1]

Smart sets forth the ultimate case against inerrancy:

The theory of literal infallibility, far from being an expression of genuine respect for Scripture, is open to the accusation of being a means whereby, subtly, under a semblance of extreme respect, an established order of religion makes use of Scripture for its own purposes and subordinates it to itself, thereby removing from God's word in Scripture its power to revolutionize the existing order.[2]

Despite protestations to the contrary, what is happening here is that, by means of this view of inspiration, human reason in fact controls, subordinates, and imprisons God and Scripture to itself.

Another reason for the shift in focus from inerrancy to higher criticism and human reason is that this argument is one that administrators can readily agree to. It produces strong negative reactions. Even progressive administrators have a difficult time keeping their balance, since they feel the pressure from the majority of laypersons who have a strong conservative leaning. A. G. Daniells's experience in this regard can lead them to waffle. The Adventist Theological Society has been readily and publicly supported by administrators. How can they not put their arms around an organization that is so strongly "supportive" of the Bible, the ministry of Ellen White, and traditional Adventist beliefs even though it may be exclusive and divisive.

Hasel's approach to hermeneutics, which also attacks the higher critical method indiscriminately, is an attempt to safeguard the kind of conservative conclusions he espouses. However, the assumption that those who have a high view of Scripture will use the correct

---

[1] James D. Smart, *The Interpretation of Scripture* (Philadelphia: Westminster 1961) 182-3. Smart shows how this approach destroys Scripture of its freedom to judge us. "In short it was a method of interpretation that robbed the revelation of Scripture of its freedom. God was no longer free to contradict the established religious order. The doctrine of the infallible inspiration of Scripture had the same effect later in Roman Catholicism, making the Scripture the bastion of an infallible church and denying any possibility that the word of Scripture might seriously sit in question on the order of the church. So also in scholastic Protestantism it was used to validate the established Protestant doctrine and order and claim for it an infallibility similar to that claimed by the Roman church. Doctrines and practices soundly based on an infallible Scripture could not be subject to any essential change. There could be no error in them. Thus has man in different ages used Scripture to establish his own or his own human church's authority over men" (183).

[2] Smart 183.

hermeneutics and, therefore, arrive at common biblical doctrines founders on the harsh rock of reality. In fact, the most heated debates on doctrines take place among conservatives who have a high view of Scripture. Fundamentalist Harold Lindsell maintains that some things in the Old Testament are not binding on Christians. He says, "I have in mind dietary laws."[1] Obviously Hasel does not agree with Lindsell here, nor with regard to the Sabbath, the state of the dead, the sanctuary, and other matters. A high view of inspiration does not lead to an orthodox uniform set of beliefs. Even a conservative hermeneutical method without "higher criticism" does not guarantee this.

The precise refinements of a doctrine of inspiration lose their significance in the interpretive process. The best proof of this lies in the fact that the adherents of inerrancy vary considerably in their interpretation of key biblical issues. It would seem that if God were really so concerned about giving communication inerrantly in and through the autographs, God would be equally concerned to help biblical interpreters determine that inerrant meaning.[2]

In his presidential message to the Evangelical Theological Society, which is officially committed to inerrancy, Robert Gundry said: "Unresolved differences of hermeneutical approach becloud the unity of our subscription to inerrancy."[3] He went on to examine the hermeneutical principles that conservatives use that conflict with their concept of inspiration.

> On the really tough problems we usually resort to one of two approaches. We can propose a solution that theoretically or technically is possible, but that is something less than a natural or obvious meaning we would assign the passage were it not for the existence of an apparently discrepant parallel. The other approach is to suspend judgment speak of it as an apparent discrepancy incapable of natural resolution at this time. . . . However, proponents of both alternatives have to be ready to defend themselves against the charge that neither takes the words of Scripture as seriously as the word "inerrancy" suggests. Why? Because, it is charged, neither will accept the obvious conclusion based on the most neutral meaning of the passages: An actual discrepancy exists. It can be argued that both contorted harmonization and suspension of judgment deny the clarity of Scripture, which is to deny the view of inspiration they are intended to uphold.[4]

[1] Harold Lindsell, *The Bible in the Balance* (Grand Rapids: Zondervan 1976) 295.

[2] Beegle 96.

[3] See Stanley N. Gundry, "Evangelical Theology: Where *Should* We Be Going?" *Evangelicals and Inerrancy*, ed. Ronald F. Youngblood (Nashville: Nelson 1984) 242.

[4] Gundry 243.

If the ultimate goal of God's word is communication and God has not guaranteed inerrant interpretation, God is obviously not as concerned about inerrant Scripture, either.

The third observation is that apparently all participants in the debate agree on the legitimacy of lower or textual criticism,[1] although here human reason and historical-critical methods are used. One of the basic principles of textual criticism is that when there are two readings for a particular verse, the more difficult reading is probably the original.[2] For example, where there are two variants, one which gives the correct Old Testament author of a passage quoted in the New Testament and one an incorrect author, the latter would be considered the original because of the tendency to correct errors in the manuscript. In other words, this principle goes against the desire to have a Bible without errors since it favors errors or differences. The basic procedure in establishing original readings is not different from that employed in higher criticism. The only difference, it seems to me, is that the scope of its operation is generally outside the sensitive areas of sources, authorship, and interpretation.

Indeed, a conservative scholar can deal freely with questions of sources, authorship, and interpretation with higher critical tools and reasoning in the context of, say, the liberal Society of Biblical Literature. In fact, this is done all the time. One cannot present papers to a group whose basic presuppositions are so different from one's own that communication is impossible. Communication and discussion are possible because there is a common understanding of the ground rules for research. Conservative scholars simply have to choose their topics so that they will not be affected by their basic presuppositional differences from their liberal colleagues, by, *e.g.*, her or his view of the miraculous.[3] I am contending that whenever conservative writers present papers at meetings of general theological society, publish articles in scholarly journals, or write theses or dissertations, they are obliged to use the historical-critical method even though they may not show their hands in the areas in which their presuppositions come into conflict with those of the scholars who will be evaluating their research. The unwritten rule is that, if they want to communicate with the scholarly community or have their papers or books accepted for publication, they must follow the rules of the game accepted by editors and readers.

---

[1]Gerhard Hasel accepts human reason in textual criticism. See *Understanding the Living Word of God* (Mountain View, C A: Pacific 1980) 93.

[2]See Hasel 93; Hasel subscribes to this principle.

[3]One can present a paper dealing with the miraculous from the standpoint of a descriptive analysis, not from the standpoint of historical reality.

Because of the stigma attached to the term "higher criticism," there is studied avoidance of this nomenclature in favor of some others such as *historical-grammatical* or *grammatical-historical* or *historical-theological* or *theological-historical* method—anything but *higher critical*, even though, as Gladson has shown, the refusal to use this expression is a semantic game. At any rate, the focus has been upon the word "criticism," though the word itself is not determinative since its meaning has to do with careful investigation rather than negative judgment. Therefore, those who use the new terms prefer to use the words "approach" or "method," although the basic meaning would not be altered if the word "criticism" were used.

However, what is being reacted to is not so much the word "criticism" as used in the expression but the historical-critical method with its presuppositions that things happened always the way they happen now. Basically, this method excludes divine interventions or miracles from history. And yet in all the new terms used the word *historical* is still used. This is strange, perhaps, but it reflects the fact that the critics of the historical-critical method all want their findings to have validity. To say one's method is grammatical or theological only seems to imply that one's concern is focused in the wrong place, since the Bible is predominantly history. To speak of a *modified historical method* is as good as the use of any alternative—better, certainly, than references to a *conservative* or *evangelical historical method*.

Any argument against the use of human reason in religious reflection is an argument that cuts both ways. Not to use human reason is to put oneself at the mercy of emotions or feelings. Reason, like speech, is a divine gift to humanity. Obviously, either can be abused but, like it or not, it has to be used. The question is not whether we should use it or not but how we should use it. We have to use reason—what else *could* we use?—to help us determine whether the Bible is the Word of God to us. It doesn't come as part of our being. On the basis of reason, some may reject it. Others will accept it. How does this take place except through reason acted on by the Holy Spirit?

The judgment of the mind which accepts the legitimacy of the Bible as the only valid source of religious data and norms logically antedates the Bible as that source and thus is shown as the source of whatever certainty the person experiences with the Bible. "Certainty" is a category of the mind, not of external reality. When the mind accepts a particular book as being of ultimate religious certainty and authority, it is the mind that judges it to be certain and not the book which somehow presses certainty onto the mind from without.[1]

This does not mean that reason is superior to Scripture, since reason by accepting Scripture deliberately subordinates itself to it. But, having accepted Scripture, reason is not left on the shelf. Our reason comes into play in many ways—particularly when it encounters something that is unusual or atypical.[2] The gospels of Matthew and Luke relate the same story of the temptation of Jesus; but Matthew's second temptation is Luke's third. Confronted with an anomaly like this, the mind begins to reason why and seeks a reason for it. One cannot believe that both accounts of Matthew and Luke are chronologically accurate, so one must use reason to explain the difference. Using reason to address this kind of problem is not subordinating the Bible to reason but investigating the Scripture to understand it more accurately. The use of reason or biblical criticism is not to criticize the Word of God but to try "to understand the Word of God and how it has been given to man."[3] It is a "reverent criticism" and it is demanded by the historical nature of Scripture. Take, for example, the Gospels. They, especially the three Synoptics, portray the life, death, and resurrection of Jesus. Why are they so similar? Why are they also different? Why is John so different from the others? As Ladd says, *"anyone who tries to answer these questions is a critic."*[4]

Inerrancy itself is an inference of the mind. The Bible does not state anywhere that it is inerrant. Neither does the Bible say anywhere that the grammatical-historical approach is the correct method to use in the study of the Bible. Reason determines this. Indeed, reason can use a view of inspiration to imprison and subordinate Scripture or to free Scripture to judge us. Reason is used by both conservatives and progressives; it is unavoidable. The only question is how we will use it.

---

[1]Trembath 34.

[2]Richard Davidson, "Revelation/Inspiration" 107, gives as one of the basic presuppositions of his method that "biblical data are accepted at face value and not subjected to an external norm to determine truthfulness, adequacy, intelligibility, etc." However, Randall W. Younker, "A Few Thoughts on Alden Thompson's Chapter: Numbers, Genealogies, Dates," in the same volume (183-4), dealing with the problem of Amram's prolific brothers, does not accept the data at face value (Amram and Jochebed were not Moses' biological parents) and uses external norm to support his position (arguing that it was an acceptable practice in antiquity to abbreviate genealogical lists). Furthermore all through his discussion the use of reason is very evident. The only difference between his approach and that of Thompson is that he is using every reasonable means to support his position over against Thompson's. Furthermore, his whole approach is a modified form of higher criticism.

[3]Ladd 217.

[4]Ladd 38.

## THE FUTURE OF THE DOCTRINE

The progressive view of inspiration is in basic agreement with the conservative view in affirming that:

- the Bible is inspired;
- reason must submit to the authority of God;
- naturalistic presuppositions must be set aside in the study of Scripture; methods appropriate for the study of God's word must be employed;
- there is a basic unity in Scripture;
- the guidance of the Holy Spirit should be sought to enable a thorough understanding of Scripture; and
- the context of a verse, a paragraph, a book, and the whole Bible is important for the understanding of a passage.

The basic difference is simply that the progressives believe in the infallibility of the Bible in matters relating to faith and practice but do not require inerrancy regarding matters that are peripheral and incidental to the message of the passage. The conservatives want to maintain a "high" view of Scripture so that infallibility extends to everything including "theology, history, science, chronology, numbers, etc."[1] Notice the etc. However, by adopting this understanding of inspiration they would effectively eliminate Ellen White as an inspired writer. Progressives recognize and acknowledge that Ellen White's writings in this respect are not different from the Bible; therefore, their view can acknowledge both the Bible and Ellen White as inspired.

At present, the conservatives have gained a foothold by establishing their own society and publications which have gained the support of church administrators. By their membership policies, which exclude those who differ from them, and their publications, which criticize and undermine the credibility of those who disagree with their approach to Scripture, they have made an effective, strategic bid for future dominance. Coincidentally, the title of their society and their publication have allowed them implicitly to claim to represent Adventists in general. If membership in the society is used, overtly and covertly, as a means of appointing faculty or of selecting administrators, the future looks bleak.

If recent history instructs us in any way, the progressives in the church with their understanding of inspiration are in for a difficult period. If what happened in the Missouri Synod and the Southern Baptist Convention are pointers to what can happen in the Adventist Church, progressives may be in for some tough times.

However, there is one major difference between Adventists and these other denominations. Adventists have had a modern prophet

---

[1]Koranteng-Pipim 63.

in their midst. Because of this, they are very familiar with how a prophet works and how inspiration operates. Beginning in the '70s, studies have investigated the process of inspiration. Their conclusion: the fact that a text is affected by its cultural environment and its sources and that it includes errors does not mean that it is uninspired. In other words, while administrators, conservatives, and the majority of laypeople may wish for and promote a "high" view of inspiration, the inspiration of Ellen White belies this artificial, theoretical, and human-made model of inspiration.

Thus, Adventist conservatives who hold to a high view of inspiration face a dilemma: they can maintain their view and accept Scripture but reject Ellen White as a prophet who does not meet these criteria or reject their high view of inspiration, which would leave them free to accept both Ellen White and the Bible. While there seem to be no other options, what could very well happen is that the conservatives could mount a Herculean *tour de force* to show that the purported errors found in Ellen White's writings were not errors at all. The progressives should not allow this to happen. The conservatives must face this issue. They must either maintain their view of inspiration while rejecting Ellen White or reject their view of inspiration while accepting Ellen White. There really are no alternatives. An adequate understanding of the ministry of Ellen White will save the church from an inadequate view of inspiration.

# 3

# Creation

## Jacques Doukhan

Writing about the "future understanding of creation" is both ironical and challenging. It is ironical because creation is primarily an event of the past. Indeed the present existence of the world, our own personal existence, constitute the very signs of the absolute precedence of creation. I exist, therefore creation took place. Creation is, then, the past event *par excellence*. This consideration in regard to the past implies recollection of and faithfulness to something which we have received from then. On the other hand, it is also challenging, because it projects us into the future, bringing along with it the risk of something new in our understanding of creation. It forces us to the discipline of imagination and creativity to renew our thinking. Thinking about creation implies both the duty to remember and the drive to elaborate. To illustrate my point from the language of creation, I would venture to say that roots as well as flowers are part of the tree. Without roots, the tree cannot produce flowers. Without roots, flowers are either artificial or fading flowers. On the other hand, without flowers, the tree becomes irrelevant and sick; it is just a piece of wood which will ultimately disappear in the anonymous forest or in the hell of the fireplace.

I have thereby indicated my methodology and my approach as well as my goals for this paper. My observations will start with a presentation of what I perceive has been the traditional Seventh-day Adventist understanding of creation. My purpose will be to offer not merely a synthesis of the various trends in Seventh-day Adventist thinking about creation, but also a critical evaluation of the present stage; I will ultimately propose new directions for the future Adventist understanding of creation. This recollection of the past and this opening to the future will work together to, hopefully, make flowers blossom on deeply rooted trees.

## The Seventh-day Adventist Debate
### about Creation

The traditional Adventist approach to the doctrine of creation has been apologetic. Creation theology has been discussed within the framework of a defense against other Christian or secular positions. Seventh-day Adventist research on creation has struggled with the issue of the contradictions between the findings of science and the biblical data, with the question whether the biblical text is a myth or a historical record, and with the question of its implications for science if it is, in fact, history.

The question of the connection between science and religion is certainly the most important issue in the contemporary Seventh-day Adventist discussion of creation. Most writings, debates, and religion courses that address the topic of creation in the Seventh-day Adventist church are concerned with its scientific implications. It is also significant that a research center, the Geoscience Research Institute, has been specifically commissioned to conduct research in this area; the Institute's journal, *Origins*, reflects this preoccupation with the relation between creation and science. On this platform, the discussion evolves essentially around the issue of creation and evolution, and three positions have been advocated.

1. *Evolution is fully rejected.* All the earth—its substance (the matter) as well as its content (the organic matter: plants, animals, and human beings)—was created during the first week of creation, just a few thousand years ago. This approach has the merit of respecting the biblical text as it is; but it brings science and religion into sharp and irreconcilable conflict.

2. *Evolution is fully adopted.* The biblical creation stories are viewed as mythological tales which have more to say about theological meanings than about the real event of creation as history. This approach offers the advantage of agreeing with contemporary currents, whether they pertain to science or to modern hermeneutical methods with their critical presupposition; but it ignores the plain intention of the biblical text.

3. *Evolution is accommodated.* This position has often been defended by traditional teaching on Seventh-day Adventist campuses and therefore deserves more extended treatment. This approach consists, here, in trying to harmonize the biblical chronology with the scientific system of geological ages. Two approaches have been represented. One position reads the fist verse of the Creation story (Gen. 1:1) as a separate unit in the literary course of the biblical text. Thus the phrase "In the beginning God created the heavens and the earth" is read to apply to a precreation of elements, an event which would have taken place several billion years before the actual creation week. Between Gen. 1:1 and Gen. 1:2 a temporal

gap is assumed during which our planet would have existed in a chaotic state. This hypothesis is sometimes called the "gap theory." Another position, the existential or spiritual approach, consists in considering the Genesis creation story as a poetic text or a theological text designed to convey a theological message (redemption, worship etc.), and not to report about a historical event.

These two positions stumble on the biblical text and on the intention of Scriptures.

The so-called "gap theory" stumbles on the stylistic observation of the connection between Gen. 1:1 and Gen. 1:2. On one hand the first line seems to be independent, referring to the absolute beginning, on the other hand the phrase of Gen. 1:1 could be read in a single breath, linked with Gen. 1:2. "In the beginning of the creation by God of the heavens and earth, as the earth was . . . then God said."[1] This reading, which is adopted by a good number of Bible translations, is justified on the basis of syntax, structure, and canonical interpretation. The Hebrew phrase *bere'shit* (in the beginning) is not only pointing to the universal and absolute creation, as suggested by its Masoretic accentuation and the fact that the phrase refers only to that event of creation; this phrase could also be analyzed as a construct state meaning "in the beginning of."

Anxious to deny the mythological interpretation of the text of the Genesis creation story, some Seventh-day Adventist scholars sometimes overlook the fact that the text does allude to mythology. Thus, they miss an important aspect of the interpretation of the Bible. The first allusion to the mythological world occurs right at the beginning of the text. The biblical creation story is introduced in the same stylistic manner as ancient Near Eastern cosmogonies. Both the *Enuma elish* and the Atrahasis Epic begin with a similar dependent temporal clause.

This observation does not mean, however, that our text is also of a mythological nature. Similar stylistic constructions show, rather, that the biblical author, aware of the surrounding culture, wants to react to mythology. The biblical author starts the same way as ancient cosmogonies in order to situate the Genesis narrative in response, in reaction to them—engaging in a classic rhetorical approach that is attested elsewhere in the Bible.[2] This deliberately anti-mythological writing betrays at least the intention of the biblical author that the text should be received as a serious historical formation. This intention is further supported by the fact that the literary genre of the biblical creation account is a genealogy. Not

[1] Gen. 1:1-3.
[2] See Job 18-19.

only does the text exhibit the characteristic features of the genealogy, but it is explicitly designated as a genealogy.[1]

This observation has important bearing on how the biblical text should be understood and interpreted. Literary and historical contexts are important. The text should not be analyzed *in vitro*. It belongs to a particular setting in life. Before trying to look for what it means, the reader of the text should first try to look for what it meant. The interpretation of the biblical text should start from the text as it stands, rather than from today's data or categories of thought.

The existential reading of the text stumbles on the historical intention of the text. Now, if the text presents itself as essentially historical, it would be an exegetical mistake to interpret it as a myth whose only purpose would be to convey a spiritual or a theological message. For in Hebrew, "it is the thought that follows the event and not the reverse. . . . Here the thought is not initiated and controlled by the thought, but is generated and governed by the adventures of history."[2] This important principle of Hebrew thought should keep us from falling into the trap of some biblical interpreters who see creation as an expression of the theology of Redemption. To be sure, the Bible relates creation to redemption. But the theology of Redemption is not the starting point from which the biblical author will infer the event of creation. Rather, the theology of redemption has its *Sitz im Leben* in the event of creation. It is the miracle of creation as a historical event which inspires hope and faith and facilitates the intellectual elaboration of the theology of redemption and not the reverse.

If the biblical author's intention is to be received as someone who reports history and testifies that the event indeed happened, does that mean that the text has a scientific intention? Is the text supposed to provide scientific data? The biblical text contains no formulæ of physics or chemistry. Does this absence mean that the text has nothing to say about scientific phenomena? The nature of the connection between science and history is complex and has too often been oversimplified. Two mistakes have been committed in this respect: either 1) history and science have been confused, or 2) history and science have been separated. The reality is much more nuanced. 1) The first position is generally held by concordists, who overlook the fact that history and science do not use the same language and do not deal with the same conceptual material. The historical report must be understood in light of the frame of reference of the reporter.

[1] Gen. 2:4a.

[2] Jacques Doukhan, *Hebrew for Theologians: A Textbook for the Study of Biblical Hebrew in Relation to Hebrew Thinking* (Lanham, MD: UP of America 1993) 192.

2) On the other hand, it is also a mistake to ignore the connection between this history reported by religious revelation and science. Most scientists, but also many theological scholars today, have become convinced that the two domains, the two ontologies, are absolutely separated: only experimental disciplines qualify as sciences. Metaphysical analysis is impossible. Metaphysical questions cannot be treated by rational analysis. From this philosophical presupposition has germinated the idea that absolute truth does not exist in the religious-theological area. Knowledge is only the province of science. Religion is just a matter of subjective preference. But what matters is not whether we *prefer* science or religion, Athens or Jerusalem. The only real serious question in religious matters just as in scientific matters is to know the Truth. It is a question of honesty. Now, if it is true that the biblical text conveys the history of the world, it follows that it concerns nature and is therefore pertinent to scientific investigation. Both history and science are concerned with Truth. Therefore, they belong together. Inasmuch as the biblical text has been accepted as God's revelation by Seventh-day Adventists and theological scholars, they should then try to work under its direction and control. The plain meaning of the text is that the whole creative origination of the human universe took place then, at the same time, during the same week.

But the biblical scholars have stumbled on a serious scientific problem: the time element. Several solutions have attracted biblical scholars concerned with the scientific truth. 1) The text is not in agreement with science because it is mythological, hence ahistorical. The biblical data are, therefore, irrelevant in the scientific quest for truth about origins. I have already discussed this approach above. 2) The text should be in agreement with science, it was therefore forced into the evolutionist mold or into the "gap theory." Traditional Seventh-day Adventist scholars have generally opted for the latter.

I would like to suggest a third option which I find implied in the text itself. I have already indicated that the analysis of the literary structure of the text reveals a regular parallelism between the two biblical creation accounts. This literary device invites a synchronic reading of the two texts and witnesses to the author's intention to provide the reader with a hermeneutical key. The first key text should be read in the light of the second and vice versa.

Now, the second creation account shows creation as a short process. Human being is created adult, the trees are created with their leaves and fruit and the rivers are created flowing. It is as if time had been contracted or simply swallowed. What normally takes hundreds of years took only a minute. God has this power. The same kind of power over time is suggested in the miracle of

the sun which stops its course at Gibeon,[1] or which moves back-
ward ten degrees on the sundial of Achaz,[2] or even in the miracle of
the water which is turned into old wine at the Cana wedding.[3]
Now, if we accept this miracle of time as it is implied in the second
creation account, we should, then, be able to assume the same phenomenon in the first creation account. The fact that in Gen. 2,
human beings, trees, and rivers are described as if they were created
grown up, mature, suggests that, likewise, in Gen. 1, rocks, lights,
and seas came into being in the same extraordinary way. The question of the age of the earth becomes then a futile one. If we believe
in the miracle of creation of a mature (even very old) world, then
science and the Bible can be brought in agreement with each other
on this difficult question of time.

The scholar's task should not, however, be limited to the necessity of bringing Bible and science into agreement. As noble as this
effort may be, it is not enough. And to work only with that concern in mind may create biases and eventually produce suspect results; it will also, I am afraid, bring a generation of inquisitors. The
scholarly enterprise should, therefore, aim beyond the "holy" duty
of serving the church, and aim simply at Truth whatever this may
be. Although we must believe that the God who revealed the biblical story is the same as the God of science, since the Revealer is also
the Creator, the question still remains whether the biblical text will
ever be in total harmony with the findings of science—not because
the two revelations are in conflict, but because the human understanding and interpretation of those two revelations will always remain incomplete.

There will always be gaps and mistakes in both science and biblical exegesis. The idealistic dream of an agreement between science
and Bible should not lead us astray. Presently, our work as well as
our results remain limited, and they are suspect if they are conducted within the context of apologetics and the presupposition of con-
cordism. After all, the concordist approach has led to an evolution-
istic understanding of the biblical creation story (Teilhard de Chardin, the day-age theory). Certainly, the relationship between Seventh-day Adventist scientists and biblical scholars is crucial, but it
should be a very complex relationship. It should be a relationship of
communication but not of dependence. The biblical scholar should
not dictate his theological understanding of the truth to the scientist. And inversely, the scientist should not impose her or his scientific interpretation on the biblical scholar. The ideal should be that
the two would reach the same conclusion independently. This does

[1]Josh. 10:12.
[2]Isa. 38:8.
[3]Jn. 2:9-10.

not mean that they could not learn from each other or even gather from each other clues which would be helpful for their own research. But the truth they may have received from each other should not replace their research, but rather stimulate it while opening their minds to new questions and avenues. This tension is not easy to bear. But every scholar knows that truth is achieved only when tension is assumed.

Another reason why Seventh-day Adventist research should work beyond the requirements of apologetics is that this approach has limited the understanding of truth. The fact that Seventh-day Adventist research on creation has confined itself to the fields of apologetics has led our scholars to be concerned only with defending the claim that creation did take place. Very little has been achieved beyond these limits. We may have today more arguments showing that belief in special creation is a reasonable option. These arguments may have strengthened our faith and our confidence in this church, but they have not enriched our understanding of creation. Ironically Seventh-day Adventist theology includes no theology of creation.

The future of Seventh-day Adventist reflection on creation would thus gain if it were pursued in this direction.

## Seventh-day Adventist Theology of Creation

Creation is supposed to be very important in Seventh-day Adventist theology. The doctrine of creation has been qualified by the Seventh-day Adventist commentary as "the indispensable foundation for Christian and biblical theology." Indeed, faith in creation is implied in the name *Seventh-day* Adventist and is emphasized in the Three Angels' Messages. The doctrine of creation is therefore an essential part of Seventh-day Adventist identity and deserves a central place in Seventh-day Adventist theology. Unfortunately, although faith in creation is strongly asserted, very little creation theology has been developed. Thinking stopped with this faith, while it should have started there.

Because creation has come to us as a revelation—after all, we were not there to witness it—any theological reflection on creation should start on the track of the biblical account of creation. Because Seventh-day Adventists believe in the authority and the inspiration of the Bible, the biblical testimony to creation, especially the Genesis creation account,[1] should be of primary importance and should be studied for its own truth. To be valuable and effective this study should be conducted independently from scientific, philosophical,

[1] Gen. 1:1-2:4.

or doctrinal presuppositions. This is the difficult task of exegesis: to pursue the biblical truth "inductively," from the text to the theological conclusion, and not *vice versa*. Now, the Bible, and the creation account in particular, do not provide the reader with a systematic theology. Only the raw event is affirmed. It is, then, the duty of the reader to decipher the biblical material, to understand it and eventually to draw from this data relevant theological implications. Thus, the way the biblical text tells about creation leads to a specific theology.

1. The miracle of creation *ex nihilo* has, for instance, an important bearing on our understanding of God, the human person, and of human history and its final destiny. The fact that God has created from nothing constitutes a revelation of divine independence and power. God is self-sufficient. Creation is also a revelation of God's grace. The gift of creation was free and could not be a response to something or someone, since nothing and no-one was except God. On the other hand, the fact that the world, "the heavens and the earth" and all that was in it, "the host of them"[1] was created out of nothing means that these realities are not divine in nature. They did not exist by themselves before God's creative act. They had a beginning and were brought into being by God. They are therefore limited, dependent on God and subject to divine control. Also, the fact that creation *ex nihilo* was possible conveys a lesson of faith and hope for the believer. We know then that death is not the last word and that new beginnings and restoration are conceivable. The doctrine of creation *ex nihilo* offers definite lessons which are not only crucial in the context of contemporary Christian existence—as they alert us of the miracle of new life and of conversion—but also with reference to ultimate questions of human destiny—as it testifies to the power that makes resurrection possible.

2. The wise and harmonious organizations of the work of creation teaches lessons of law but also of love. The principle of law pervades the text. God divides light from darkness, delimits the waters. Divine power appoints the stars for signs and for fixed times and specific functions. The living creation is required to be fruitful and to multiply. Human being is ordered to subdue the earth and to enjoy its fruit. The technical word for law (*sawa*) is used in this instance,[2] and the seventh day is set apart. God sets hedges for the natural order which every species has to respect.

Also, with the discipline of the law and the restraints of justice, the attention given to the beauty of creation brings along the breath

[1]Gen. 2:1.
[2]Gen. 2:16.

of grace and love. The artistic, literary arrangement of the creation narrative, the harmonious repetition of the ten words of God, the rhetorical rhythm of seven and the refrain "it was good" and the concluding statement "it was really good" (the Hebrew word for good, *tob,* means both good and beautiful), express the æsthetic perfection of creation. Nature is presented here as a positive gift from God.

3. The place of human being in the Genesis creation accounts suggests that humanity stands as the climax of the created order. The whole narrative moves toward the creation of Adam and Eve and everything is made for their benefit. They enjoy a special and privileged relationship with the Creator. While they share with nature the same destiny, they alone are made in the divine image. They are the only beings whose formation involves God personally. Their nature and destiny are thus described in relationship with God. Humans cannot exist or survive outside of this relationship. They exist biologically and spiritually (the word *ruah,* "spirit," means both "air," the principle of life, and spirit). Humans are also social beings, and are described in relation to nature, animals, and ultimately, to their life partners. Thus, God's image implies physical, spiritual, and social-conjugal dimensions as well. As the last creation, human being is viewed as a total being. Another meaning of the divine image is that humans were created as unique as God is unique. The human individually signifies God's image, and indeed is a sign of God's existence.

4. Finally, a theology of worship is implied in and by the holiness of the Sabbath announced in the creation story. At the end of God's work, the whole creation is contemplated. For the first time humans are present. The mention of the human rhythm, "evening and morning," is therefore no more needed. Now, in time, within the historical flesh of the twenty-four-hour day, all the theological lessons discovered throughout creation are now captured together. And the Sabbath adds a new lesson to them: the duty for humans to respond to and praise God.

Subsequent biblical reflection on creation can be organized around three main theological themes.

*a. Creation and history.* The miracle of creation has inspired a theology of history and salvation, a *Heilsgeschichte.* This connection abounds especially in the historical and prophetic books of the Bible. Thus, this event of the Exodus which encapsulates the history of the national salvation of Israel is told in the language of creation.[1] Israel, saved from Egypt and the waters of the sea, is said to be

---

[1]Ex. 15:8.

"created" (*bara*) by God.[1] Likewise, Israel's return from Babylonian exile is predicted in terms of a new creation.[2] God's eschatological salvation is conceived of as a real creation of "new heavens and earth."[3] This reference to creation in the heart of the theological reflection on salvation shines through the liturgical life of the religious community, especially in the ritual of the Day of Atonement and the Christian baptism.

*b. Creation and Existence.* Creation is meaningful in the daily and secular life of the believer. Existential reflection on the significance of creation is particularly vivid in Wisdom literature and has been characterized as "a theological anthropology." In this context, creation is the basis for an ethical life.[4] The purpose of this wisdom reflection on creation, however, is not so much "wisdom" *per se* as the encounter with the Creator[5] and the acute awareness of divine omnipresence.[6]

*c. Creation and Praise. Creation* lies at the heart of the worship experience. Significantly, in the Psalter, creation is most associated with worship.[7] The Psalms are not so much concerned with the creation or nature as they are with the Creator. All creatures are called to praise God.[8] Creation and praise are persistently linked in the Old Testament. And this tradition continues through the book of Revelation.[9]

Ironically, not only has the study of the biblical text been neglected in Seventh-day Adventist thinking about creation, but very little attempt has been made to integrate creation into Seventh-day Adventist theology in general. We have not yet explored the connections between creation and other key Adventist theological themes, such as the sanctuary, eschatology, health reform, baptism, tithe, the law and the Sabbath.

*1. The Sanctuary.* The biblical connection between sanctuary theology and creation theology appears immediately in the story of the building of the wilderness sanctuary in the book of Exodus.[10] This story parallels the literary structure of the Genesis creation story.[11] Like the creation story, the sanctuary text moves in seven steps and closes at the seventh step with the same stylistic phrase and the

---

[1]Isa. 43:1, 2; 15-7.
[2]Isa. 44-5; Ezek. 37.
[3]Isa. 65:17; 66:22-23; Heb. 12:26, 27; 2 Pet. 3:13; Rev. 21:1.
[4]Eccl. 12:1, 6; Prov. 6:6-11.
[5]Job 42:5-6.
[6]Prov. 5:21; 15:3.
[7]Ps. 29:2-11.; 66:4; 86:9; 95:6; 96:9-10, etc.
[8]Ps. 148:3.
[9]Rev. 14:7.
[10]Ex. 25-40.
[11]Gen. 1:1-2:4a.

same Hebrew words, "finished His work."[1] Amazingly, the story of the construction of the Jerusalem temple by Solomon unfolds also in seven steps and the last step is also marked by the same language—"finished the work."[2] In the whole Hebrew Bible, significantly, the association of these words is only found in these three passages, suggesting some kind of relation between the sanctuary-temple and creation. This connection is again pointed out in the Psalms.[3] This identification between creation and the sanctuary suggests that for the ancient Israelites, the Day of Atonement may have meant more than the mere cleansing of the tent of the temple. It seems to have carried a cosmic connotation, pointing to the cleansing of the world, hence a re-creation. This is perhaps why Daniel 8 describes the cosmic Day of Atonement in terms taken from the language of the creation story—"evenings and mornings"[4]—since this very rare expression is only found in the context of the creation narrative.[5] This close connection between creation and sanctuary is widely supported in ancient Jewish writings.

As far as Seventh-day Adventist theology is concerned, certainly, this connection may have tremendous implications regarding, for instance, the interpretation of the cleansing of the sanctuary and the theology of the Day of Atonement. Rather than bringing out only the mystical and idiosyncratic dimension of Kippur, this connection also draws attention to the historic dimension, a perspective which fits better the categories of Hebrew thinking. As a result, sanctuary theology becomes more universal, therefore more human and more relevant, shall we say—and less boring.

*2. Eschatology.* Since creation took place, since the world had a beginning, it is therefore not eternal: it will have an end. On God's level, creation means that since the beginning was God's, so, too, is the end. Protology leads to eschatology.

Also, the very nature of the miracle of creation, as an *ex nihilo* creation, points to the miraculous character of the end event. The Bible speaks about the final salvation of the world in terms of recreation and resurrection. The biblical theology of the new realm— "new heavens and earth"—is based on creation. Therefore, belief in the final resurrection implies the same quality of faith as belief in creation. The Epistle to the Hebrews refers to this type of faith when it defines faith precisely by reference to creation and the hope of the realm of God. Faith, it says, is the substance of things hoped for (God's realm), the evidence of things not seen (creation). This

---

[1] Ex. 40:33; cp. Gen. 2:2.
[2] 1 Kgs. 7:40, 51.
[3] Ps. 78:69.
[4] Dan. 8:14.
[5] Gen. 1:5, 8, 13, 19, 23, 31.

definition of faith (the only one in the Bible) is followed by a poem, the hymn of faith, which is itself framed by reference to creation in the beginning[1] and hope for God's new realm at the end.[2]

It is interesting that the same observation has been made regarding the Bible as a whole which is also framed with this double reference to the beginning and the end. Whether one considers the
Hebrew Bible (Gen. 1-2 to Mal. 3 or 2 Chr. 6:21-3), or the two
testaments of the Christian Bible (Gen. 1:1 to Rev. 22:17-21), the
canon starts with a reference to creation and closes with a references to the coming, future, hoped-for Realm of God.

Now, it is noteworthy that the association between these two
events lies in the very heart of Seventh-day Adventist identity. Our
name, *Seventh-day Adventists*, links our faith in creation and our
hope in God's coming realm. It is, therefore, no accident that the
proclamation of the Third Angel's Message in Rev 14:7 plays such
a significant part in Seventh-day Adventist theology. Creation and
judgment, that is, the event of the beginning and the event of the
end, constitute the essence of the message of the eschatological
remnant.

*3. Health Reform.* Seventh-day Adventist understanding of what
has sometimes been called "health reform" has not yet exploited
the mine contained in creation theology. The church's emphasis on
healthful living has essentially been discussed in the context of apologetics and has been expressed in negative terms, rather than articulated within a consistent and positive theology. We have not yet
fully realized that our wholistic view of humankind is indebted to
our doctrine of creation. The fact that human being has been created as a totality has implications not only for human destiny (the totality of death), but also human life here and now. The way we eat,
the way we drink, the way we think, the way we behave, etc., affect our total being.

It is also interesting to note that whenever the Bible points out
dietary laws, it highlights their roots in creation. God's provision of
food for humans as well as for animals is given in the context of
creation.[3] Other ancient extra-biblical texts show indeed that "there
was a widespread belief in Antiquity that man and animals were
once vegetarian."[4] The prophetic hope that one day "the lion shall
eat straw like ox"[5] reflects this idea. The messianic era is, then,
characterized by a return to the original quality of life given at creation. When the prophet Daniel chooses his vegetarian menu he us-

[1]Heb. 11:3.
[2]Heb. 11:39-40.
[3]Gen. 1:29.
[4]Gordon J. Wenham, *Genesis 1-15* (Waco, TX: Word 1987) 33.
[5]Isa. 11:7; 65:25; cp. Hos. 2:20; 2:18.

es a language which alludes to the Genesis creation account (Dan 1:16). His discourse contains an association of three words ("give," *ntn*, "vegetables," *zr'*, and "eat," *'kl*) which is found only in the biblical creation story.[1] This reference to creation is, in fact, intended as a response to the royal usurpation of God's role as Creator.

More specifically, the dietary rules, with their distinction between clean and unclean meat, point to the Genesis creation story. The language of Lev. 11 reports them with the same technical words and expressions as in Gen. 1 ("beasts of the earth," "creeping animals," "according to its kind," etc.). Also, the list of the animals in Lev. 11:1-23 follows the same sequence as in Gen. 1:24-66, during the creation of the sixth day (animals on land, Lev. 11:2-8; cp. Gen. 1:24; animals in water, Lev. 11:9-12; cp. Gen. 1:26a; animals in the air, Lev. 11:13-23; cp. Gen. 1:26b; reptiles, Lev. 11:29-31, 41-3; cp. Gen. 1:26c). Also, in Leviticus 11 just as in Gen. 1:24-26, the relation between humans and animals is associated with the relation between God and humans. In Gen. 1:26, the human duty to have dominion over the animals is associated with the fact that humans have been created in God's image. Likewise, in Leviticus 11, the human duty to distinguish between clean and unclean meat is associated with the principle of the *Imago Dei*—"you will be holy as I am holy" (Lev. 11:44-5). The restriction on eating blood is given in the context of the recreation of the flood, in Gen. 9; there also the dietary restriction is associated with the principle of *Imago Dei* (Gen. 9:3-7; cp. Gen. 1:27).

The choice of this particular diet should, then, go beyond the selfish desire to be healthy; it says, rather, something about our *faith* in the Creator and is, therefore, a choice of a religious nature: because of God.

4. *The Law. Creation* is also pertinent to theological reflection about the law. We have already indicated how the organization of God's work and the order of nature testified in the creation story to the significance of law. On the other hand, the law refers back to the event of creation. The ten commandments move in the same rhythm as the ten words of creation. Significantly, the Sabbath, memorial of creation, occupies the geometric and thematic center of the structure of the Decalogue, that is, the very place where seals were stamped in ancient covenant documents. Obedience to the divine principles is, thus, supposed to derive not from a magic mentality—as a means of obtaining God's approval—but simply from our awareness of our natural condition as creature. The human person as well as the world survive insofar as they respect those rules. So understood, the law is not designed to limit; it is not an unbear-

---

[1]Gen. 1:29.

able burden. Instead, it is the only way to fulfill our destiny, to be ourselves, and therefore to be free and happy, virtues we have not always discerned among promoters of the divine law. (This observation holds, of course, for advocates of the health laws.)

5. *Baptism*. All the ingredients of the event of creation are present in the Seventh-day Adventist ritual of baptism. The water, the invocation of the Holy Spirit, the word, and, ultimately, the gestures involved in the ritual—namely, immersion and the baptized person's departure from the water—recall the miraculous event of creation, thus pointing to a cluster of theological points. First of all, this connection between baptism and creation conveys the memory of the past event of creation, refreshing the quality of faith necessary to believe in the *ex nihilo*, out-of-darkness miracle. Then, it points to our hope in the future recreation of the world and the resurrection of humankind, our resurrection. Finally, it is the sign of our personal decision in the midst of our present existence, our decision to change our ways and live a new life with Christ, our decision to be ready always to question our choices and to be able to repent and change direction throughout our lives. More than a "rite of initiation" into the community of believers, baptism is the concrete and dynamic symbol which comprehends the whole plan of salvation. It has not only a historical or an existential but also a cosmic significance. Therefore, the neophyte who decides to be baptized cannot be a small child. A person who goes into the waters of baptism to obey or please her or his parents, or to imitate her or his peers, hardly knows the experience of baptism. In this condition, baptism remains a meaningless tradition instead of a bearer of new meaning. In our evangelistic zeal to reach out and bring about great numbers of baptisms to fill in reports or generate statistics, we may miss the real meaning of baptism. Loaded with the reference to creation, in essence, baptism speaks against habits and traditions, and militates against what Albert Camus rightly called "the religion of bureaucrats." Baptism does not exalt the laziness of repetition but highlights, on the contrary, the challenge of future.

6. *Tithing*. The practice of tithing is first mentioned in the book of Genesis, in the context of Melchizedek's encounter with Abraham.[1] Significantly, Melchizedek's blessing refers to the God of Abraham as "the possessor of heaven and earth"[2] before Abraham offers him the tithe. The same association recurs at the conclusion of the book of Leviticus. Before entering the promised land the people of Israel were to be reminded that this land was God's.[3] Thus, all the "tithes of the land" should be considered as "holy to

[1]Gen. 14:18-24.
[2]Gen. 14:19.
[3]Lev. 25:23.

the land"[1] and were therefore to be offered as an acknowledgment of God's ownership. Now, this particular recognition of God's ownership of space belongs to the biblical theology of creation. The Psalms in particular develop this theme in relation to creation:

> The earth is the Lord's and all its fullness,
> The world and these who dwell therein.
> For He has founded it upon the seas,
> And established it upon the waters.[2]

The tithe is more than a shrewd invention to help the priestly community to survive and prosper. It is a concrete expression of faith in the God who has everything and, therefore, to the God whom I owe everything. No wonder then that the practice of the tithe is associated with the trust that God will bless and give abundantly.[3] This promise is concerned with the theological meaning of tithing as an expression of faith in the Creator and dependence on divine grace and creative power; it is not intended to promote the view that tithing is a magic device or a good recipe for becoming wealthy. Seventh-day Adventists should understand this principle and shape their thinking and behavior accordingly. We do not pay our tithes in order to acquire more possessions; rather, we give our tithes because we can lay claim to nothing. An interested faithfulness in that matter would be totally out of place. Tithe points to the reality of God's realm. This symbolic gift of our minimum speaks about the gift of divine maximum. Put in the perspective of creation, tithe is not understood as a business transaction with God or the church as an institution. It is the expression of my awareness that I can lay claim to nothing. It is, therefore, absurd to assert a supposed right to prosperity on the basis of tithe. A sign of the divine ownership, tithe becomes sacred not only for those who give it, but also and perhaps more so, for those who spend it.

6. *The Sabbath.* Unfortunately, Seventh-day Adventist Sabbath theology has often been conceived in terms of a defense. Sabbath is "not Sunday." Besides this apologetic concern very little has been achieved in regard to the meaning of the Sabbath itself. Among the various theological dimensions contained in the Sabbath, the dimension of creation is certainly the most important one. The primary function of the Sabbath is to call us "to remember" the event of creation. Sabbath theology contains all the lessons of creation theology. But it brings to our reflection on creation an additional dimension. Creation is understood there in relation to the human person. In the Genesis creation account, both the human person and the Sabbath enjoy God's blessing. In the structure of the text,

---

[1]Lev. 27:30.
[2]Ps. 24:1-2; see also Ps. 89:1-12, Ps. 100:3; Job 41:11, etc.
[3]Mal. 3:10.

humans, like the Sabbath, appear at the end of the work of creation, as its ultimate goal. "The Sabbath was made for humankind."[1]
The Sabbath is creation received by humanity. The function of the
Sabbath is, then, to call us to relate to creation as to a gift. From the
perspective of the Sabbath, the theology of creation is essentially a
theology of grace. Creation theology becomes at this level a theology of praise and thanks to the Creator. It is worship at its best.
The history of humankind begins on this note, with the awareness
that human existence is received from God and implies the reality
of God. Against the Sartrean statement "I exist, therefore God does
not exist," Sabbath theology asserts "I exist, therefore God exists."
The first theological reflection took place on Sabbath. Sabbath theology is the root of all theology.

## CONCLUSIONS AND PERSPECTIVES

A renewed attention to creation in Seventh-day Adventist theology would open up perspectives in two opposite directions, in di-
alectal tension.

On the one hand, creation brings us closer to our biblical
sources and to our mission. Thus it strengthens our Seventh-day
Adventist roots and refreshes our Seventh-Adventist identity. Moving beyond apologetics, Seventh-day Adventist attention to creation should be more creative. The searching of the biblical documents and the intellectual exercise of thinking should proceed *for
the sake* of truth and not just *in defense* of truth. The biblical creation
story should be explored not only to justify the position that we are
right in believing in the event of creation, but also to inspire and
nurture our thinking as we explore new insights, travel new theological paths. The mystery of creation will always remain a challenge, a constant invitation to our questions, our research, and our
meditation.

Also, to rethink Seventh-day Adventist doctrines in relation to
creation will help to draw a coherent picture of Seventh-day Adventist theology. All those theological truths which were scattered
and disconnected before can be tied up together with the bond of
creation. Seventh-day Adventist theology is essentially a theology of
creation. Certainly this discovery can sharpen the awareness of our
specific mission and identity and confirm our confidence in this
church.

On the other hand, this attention to creation propels us beyond
our borders and brings us closer to the world. Instead of proclaiming our doctrines in the jargon of a marginal sect, Seventh-day Adventist theology, because of its anchor in creation, should embrace

[1]Mk. 2:27.

a universal scope and speak a universal language. Because creation is important in Seventh-day Adventist theology, Seventh-day Adventist theologians should address themselves to the theologians of evolution who have been working under the influence of the process philosophy of Whitehead and Hartshorne (Cobb, Ogden, Overmann, etc.), or of the cosmic Christology of the controversial Jesuit Teilhard de Chardin (Rahner, Herlsbosch, Schoonenberg, Pendergast, etc.). But more importantly, Seventh-day Adventist theology should address the contemporary issues which shape and shake the present world in general, all the more so as a revival of interest in the theme of creation has been occasioned by concern with various contemporary problems. Issues such as ecology (Lynn White, Matthew Fox, F. Elder, F. G. Van Dyke, etc.), ethics (Roger L. Shinn, G. Wingren, etc.), economics (D. Lim, A. Christiansen, A. and J. Meyer, etc.), the problem of evil (Jon Levenson), and even the holocaust (Hans Küng, E. Berkovits, M. Ellis) are being discussed from the perspective of creation. Seventh-day Adventist scholars should not ignore these thinkers, not only because Seventh-day Adventist people face the same problems, but also because they share with these thinkers the same basic belief in creation. Seventh-day Adventist theologians should not only try to argue and oppose them but also strive to understand them, to learn from them, to enrich Seventh-day Adventist theology.

This appeal of creation theology to reconcile ourselves with the world should also affect the worldview of Seventh-day Adventist theologians and lay members. The old problems of dualism and the contempt of the physical world, including the human body, originates in Platonism. In Christianity, it was first advocated by Marcion in the second century, who opposed creation to redemption, law to grace, YHWH to Jesus. This view gained increasing acceptance in the wake of the reaction to the Arian heresy; afraid of linking Christ too closely with creation, as the Arians did, early theologians and church leaders, encouraged by Athanasius, argued forcefully for the divinity of Christ at the expense of the truth of creation. For, if Christ is not divine (is only a creation), then no redemption is possible. The dilemma is clear: it is either redemption or creation. I believe this view is still current in most Christian theologies today because of the powerful influence of Bultmann (also called "the modern Marcion"). Many Christian theologians have deliberately chosen to emphasize redemption at the expense of creation; if they do approach creation, it is from the perspective of redemption. Because Seventh-day Adventists have chosen to receive creation in history as God's gift, they should free themselves from the grip of dualism. They should learn to relate to creation, to appreciate life, beauty and enjoyment, even sensual enjoyment.

The tension generated by creation theology is, in fact, a vital tension in Christian life. On the one hand, we are confirmed in our distinctiveness of character and our vocation; on the other hand, we are urged to be sensitive to the world and to open ourselves to the life of this world. Abraham Joshua Heschel called this tension the requirement "to be holy and human."

Seventh-day Adventist scholars should then study and think about creation in tension. This is why, where this crucial doctrinal theme is concerned, all areas of expertise, all sensitivities should be mobilized. The horizon of creation is too vast to be apprehended by one person, or one group of persons. As Pascal said: "The space of this infinite frightens me." Only humility and the awareness of our limitations will enable us to do justice to the nature of any reflection on creation. On this subject, shortcomings and ignorance are unavoidable. Therefore, I would like to think that the scientist, the biblical scholar, the theologian, the philosopher, and also the poet and the artist, the left-brained and the right-brained person, all have something to contribute. Only an interdisciplinary approach is adequate. The ultimate lesson of creation is the obligation of tolerance and cooperation. Seventh-day Adventist scholars have not been very good in that regard. This lesson does not mean, however, that just any idea or any phantasm will be acceptable. In fact, working together brings consensus while it enriches us and opens us up to new perspectives. The future Adventist understanding of creation will survive only on this condition, only if it allows for these riches and this variety: roots, deep and reliable, but also flowers, gracious and delicate. Isn't this—after all—the first and most simple lesson of creation?

# 4

# *Sabbath*

## Niels-Erik A. Andreasen

Nearly fifty years ago, the legendary British Old Testament scholar H. H. Rowley made the following observation regarding the Sabbath in post-exilic Judaism: "In post-exilic days, if there had been no synagogues, it is difficult to see how . . . [the Sabbath] could have survived, and it is significant that in our day impatience with the Sabbath as a day of rest is the accompaniment of the widespread abandonment of the Sabbath as a day of worship."[1]

My thesis in this essay is that the Seventh-day Adventist church is entering something like a "post-exilic" experience, and that the survival of the Sabbath as a day of rest among us depends on the degree to which we maintain it as a day of worship. In short: no Sabbath worship, no Sabbath rest. But that is not how Sabbath keeping among us began one hundred and seventy years ago, and how it has been sustained in recent times.

## HOW ADVENTIST SABBATH KEEPING BEGAN

It is remarkable to realize that worldwide Sabbath observance by millions of Seventh-day Adventists had its beginning in quiet conversations among three or four members of several churches in the mid-nineteenth century. Before that time, immigrant Jews introduced the Sabbath to the new world in both South and North America, and Seventh-day Baptists brought their practice to Newport, Rhode Island in 1664.[2] In 1844, Seventh-Day Baptist Rachel Oakes and her Methodist pastor Frederick Wheeler met, talked and ended up becoming Sabbath observing Adventists. Subsequently,

---

[1] *Worship in Ancient Israel* (Philadelphia: Westminster 1967) 241.
[2] Raymond F. Cottrell, "The Sabbath in the New World," *The Sabbath in Scripture and History*, ed. Kenneth H. Strand (Washington, DC: Review 1982) 245.

Thomas M. Preble, a Millerite, and sea captain Joseph Bates discovered in intense private study and conversations that the Sabbath and the advent belong together.[1]

This association of Sabbath and advent crystalized during a series of conferences four years later (1848), leading to the now familiar and persuasive Seventh-day Adventist Sabbath theology. In his examination of this topic, Cottrell attributes the worldwide success of the Seventh-day Adventist church to the association of Sabbath and advent.[2] In fact, the point is often made by Seventh-day Adventists that those Millerites who survived the Great Disappointment of 1844 did so through a study of the sanctuary, leading them to conclude that Christ entered the sanctuary in heaven, there to begin a ministry of intercession and judgment in preparation for his soon return to earth. In that same sanctuary was kept the law of God, including the fourth (Sabbath) commandment, so long neglected by the majority of Christians, but now brought to light by the Adventists. It connected the sanctuary ministry of intercession and judgment with the soon awaited Second Advent by means of the Sabbath commandment. Loyal Sabbath observance, they explained, implies worship of the Creator, which in turn becomes an identifying "seal of God" on the saints, in distinction from the mark of the beast (loyalty to Satan), associated with Sunday worship.

Early Adventist theology made Sabbath observance into one of Adventism's most central teaching. As a result, Adventists became careful Sabbath keepers, who developed long, unofficial but nevertheless widely recognized lists of approved Sabbath activities, often to the frustration of young church members. At the same time, they defended members' legal right to take the seventh day off from work and opposed Sunday laws vigorously. The greatest Adventist heroes of faith were individuals who kept the Sabbath in the face of economic ruin, lost educational opportunities, and imprisonment. In short, Seventh-day Adventists believed that without the Sabbath God would not be worshipped truly as creator and redeemer.

This approach did not necessarily rob Sabbath observers of the rest, joy, and blessings which this special day also brings. It did, however, obscure these benefits from the sight of some believers, because it focused so strongly on the believer's legal obligation before God.

## BROADENING THE BASE

This understanding of the Sabbath continued into the mid-twentieth century and received a fresh statement by M.L. Andre-

[1]Cottrell 246.
[2]Cottrell 256-9.

asen in *The Sabbath: Which Day and Why?*[1] Fifteen years later, when questions were raised about the role of the Sabbath in Seventh-day Adventist theology, this interpretation was reaffirmed with only slight modification in the book known as *Questions on Doctrine.*[2] The authors explained that the seventh-day Sabbath belongs within the moral law, and that a special moral accountability is attached to Sabbath observance in "these last days" when all Bible truth is being made known throughout the world. The mark of the beast refers to "the attempted change of the Sabbath of the fourth commandment of the Decalogue by the Papacy, its endeavor to impose this change on Christendom, and the acceptance of the Papacy's substitute by individuals."[3] However, there are indications that this interpretation of the Sabbath was leading some to a legalistic understanding of salvation, for the authors take pains to explain that "Seventh-day Adventists do not rely upon their Sabbath keeping as a means of salvation or of winning merit before God. We are saved by grace alone. Hence our Sabbath observance, as also our loyalty to every other command of God, is an expression of our love for our Creator and Redeemer."[4]

This more grace-oriented approach to the Sabbath came to clear expression during the 1952 Adventist Bible Conference. In the presentation by Edward Heppenstall, "The Covenant and the Law," the Sabbath is interpreted primarily within the context of the new covenant, not the law. "As we examine the law of God in the light of the everlasting covenant, we find that it is the Sabbath commandment that sets God's seal upon it, and at the same time becomes the symbol and test of the new Covenant."[5] That covenant was sealed by Christ on the Cross. "The text (Heb 4:3-4) declares that the significance of the Sabbath is related to the completed works of God at creation."[6] "This rest of God signified by the seventh-day Sabbath is very definitely indicated at the cross, when Christ completed the work of re-creation."[7] "The rest of God signified by the Sabbath means continual communion. . . . The seventh-day Sabbath stands for eternal communion."[8]

---

[1]M. L. Andreasen, *The Sabbath: Which Day and Why?* (Washington, DC: Review 1942).

[2][R.A. Anderson, LeRoy E. Froom, and W.E. Read,] *Seventh-day Adventists Answer Questions on Doctrine* (Washington, DC: Review 1957) 149-85.

[3]Anderson, Froom, and Read 181.

[4]Anderson, Froom, and Read 153.

[5]Edward Heppenstall, "The Covenant and the Law," *Our Firm Foundation*, 2 vols. (Washington, DC: Review 1953) 1: 488.

[6]Heppenstall 490.

[7]Heppenstall 491.

[8]Heppenstall 492.

The direct association of the Sabbath primarily with the new covenant rather than primarily with the law, eventually and inevitably invited new approaches to Seventh-day Adventist Sabbath theology. The most celebrated such study is Samuele Bacchiocchi's *Divine Rest for Human Restlessness.*[1] This energetic defense of the seventh-day Sabbath as a central part of biblically based Christian doctrine distinguishes itself from most earlier Seventh-day Adventist treatments of the subject by not once listing the word "law" in the table of contents or chapter headings. But it devotes a whole chapter to the Sabbath covenant. Even the title is significant, for it underscores that the Sabbath is a "divine rest," thereby focusing upon God's gift of rest, rather than God's requirement of rest. The subtitle identifies the subject of the book as "the good news," indicating that the author wants to emphasize the Sabbath as an expression of the gospel, rather than of the law. Two years earlier, Sakae Kubo had articulated a similar approach to the Sabbath in his book, *God Meets Man: A Theology of the Sabbath and the Second Advent.*[2] The same year I published *The Christian Use of Time.*[3] Other works followed in the same vein.

While none of these set out to contradict earlier interpretations of the Sabbath, they certainly fostered something of a paradigm shift away from a narrow focus on what God requires to what God provides, namely a new covenant relationship of which the Sabbath is a sign. To the earlier emphasis on the Sabbath as command was added a new emphasis on the function of the Sabbath in the life of the believer. In reality, this new approach did not intend to set aside earlier emphases, nor did it seek to chart an entirely different course for Seventh-day Adventist theology, though some may have seen it that way. Rather, it simply attempted to rescue Sabbath observance from visible neglect among many Seventh-day Adventists who refused to be frightened into Sabbath keeping by the authority of the law and local denominational practices, but who in keeping with a contemporary mindset were searching for redemptive religious practices along with the truth about them. Thus, these new Sabbath studies offered additional reasons why all believers should embrace the Sabbath with its promise of rest, blessings, and divine presence. In one of his most picturesque but less felicitous illustrations, Bacchiocchi compares the Sabbath at the end of the week to the tasty tomato sauce on top of a dish of spaghetti—why would anyone

---

[1] Samuele Bacchiocchi *Divine Rest for Human Restlessness* (Berrien Springs, MI: Biblical Perspectives 1980).
[2] Sakae Kubo, *God Meets Man: A Theology of the Sabbath and the Second Advent* (Nashville: Southern 1978).
[3] Niels-Erik Andreasen, *The Christian Use of Time* (Nashville: Abingdon 1978).

want to do without either, he asks matter-of-factly. In short, these new studies of the Sabbath were evangelistic, aimed at a new generation of Adventists who, like Sunday keepers before them, were about to lose the Sabbath to the long weekend. To them the message went out that the Sabbath conveys the gospel, that it represents the good news of God's redemptive grace, that it brings untold blessings to the lives of individuals and families, and that it is a foretaste of eternity, symbolically illustrating the rest that awaits the people of God,[1] as Edward Heppenstall put it so forcefully in his ground breaking study of 1952. Thus the earlier approach to Sabbath observance through the law (God requires us to rest) was joined by a new approach to the Sabbath through the covenant relationship of grace (God offers us rest). That grace orientation has begun to take hold, but not without problems.

## Looking to the Future

Well over half a century after the conference at which Heppenstall articulated his broadened view of the Sabbath, more than 170 years after the Great Disappointment, well into the twenty-first century, the Sabbath question once again challenges the Seventh-day Adventist community in the same way it challenged the Jewish community in the post-exilic period.

Common to the experiences of both communities is their gradual movement into the bright light of the larger world surrounding them. Consider what happened to the Jewish community. Prior to the exile, the people of Israel had lived in their own land, surrounded by clearly marked borders, with their own king, army, monetary system, language, and religion. Of course, the external world repeatedly threatened them during pre-exilic times, and sometimes nearly succeeded in entering and overwhelming their realm, as in the time of King Hezekiah. Then followed the captivity in 586 BC, the return to Jerusalem in 536 BC, and the emergence of Judaism in the post-exilic period. Now, the Jews lived in a province belonging to another kingdom, used a new international language (Aramaic), and faced new political and economic realities. Additional places of worship (mostly synagogues, but also temples) were erected, sharply differentiated religious parties (Pharisees, Sadducees, Essenes) emerged, and the Jews were confronted by other religions, both in Judea and in the Diaspora. As a result, post-exilic Judaism, unlike pre-exilic Israelite faith, became a religion in the world, not of the land. At first that new world was Persian, a world of toleration, with a reasonable measure of freedom, previously un-

[1] Heb. 4:4-5.

known in ancient times, and thus a favorable context for Judaism to establish itself as a religion of the larger world.

In such an environment, Judaism had to define itself from the inside out, as it were. Whereas formerly king, priest, and prophet had defined Israelite religion, it now became the Jewish heart and mind, informed by the emerging canon of Scripture, preserved and articulated by priest, rabbi, and scribe that spoke for religion. That puts all religious practices in a new light. Sabbath observance was also affected by this change, as is evidenced in the post-exilic literature. No longer does it focus upon Sabbath laws proscribing work on the seventh day (as in Exodus, Leviticus and Deuteronomy) nor upon the universal Sabbath obligation placed upon the people of the new covenant (as in the prophets Isaiah and Jeremiah). Rather, beginning with the post-exilic period, the Sabbath became associated with holiness, with the temple and its services, when the Levites defended it in their capacity as leaders of worship and sacred services.[1]

In the Diaspora with no temple nearby, this kind of sacred Sabbath keeping as Sabbath worship continued in every home, synagogue, and community, thanks to the Talmudic scholars who transformed the now lost holiness of the temple into a new holiness of every household, synagogue, and community, by means of Talmudic interpretation followed by new application of the Biblical and Mishnaic laws. While historians of early Christianity have sometimes deplored this development as both legalistic and devoid of spirit, the history of Judaism has shown just how effective the emphasis upon this type of religious observance— the transfer of temple holiness into every household and synagogue—has been. Neither 2,500 years, nor dispersions around the world, nor lack of organization, nor holocausts and wars, nor ideological differences within the community have succeeded in erasing Jewish identity and the Sabbath which has helped to guarantee it. As Rowley concluded, following the exile, Sabbath *worship* preserved Sabbath *rest*.

The Seventh-day Adventist church has entered for some time and continues with accelerating speed to enter just such a "post-exilic" environment. No longer do most Seventh-day Adventists live, worship, and work within denominational boundaries. Instead, church membership is growing rapidly, especially in developing countries, propelling the church and its members into the public arena. At the same time, church institutions must comply with local and federal regulations and thus will continue to move outside the narrow fold of church organization and administration. Increasing

[1] I Chr. 9:32, 23:30-31; 2 Chr. 2:4. 8:13; 31:3; 36:21; Neh. 9:14; 10:31, 33;13:15-22.

numbers of church members, no longer self-employed in rural areas, find work in the public and private sectors of our economy, and participate in the economic, political and social lives of their communities. As a result, new pressures and stresses fall on our religious life, including our Sabbath observance.

Especially, like the post-exilic Jewish community, our church no longer seems able to maintain Sabbath observance among its members simply by appealing to the law and its requirements. A comparison of Ezra, the post-exilic religious leader, and Nehemiah, the political leader, is instructive here. Ezra, a teacher of the law, attempted, apparently not very successfully, to institute Sabbath keeping by appealing to the law.[1] Nehemiah did it, evidently with greater success, by posting Levites, who had purified themselves, as guards by the city gates at the onset of the Sabbath to keep foreign merchants from entering and trading with Jews.[2] Thus, when the line separating the church arena from the world arena is blurred, a strong appeal to holiness is needed to preserve religious life, including Sabbath observance.

In our time, keeping the seventh day separate from working days is relatively easy for most people in the west, thanks to liberalized labor laws and the long weekend. Shift work still creates problems for some, but relatively few church members are threatened with economic ruin if they observe the Sabbath. However, keeping the Sabbath distinct from the long weekend of recreation remains a pressing problem for many. As a result, the Sabbath laws in the Bible, originally designed to proscribe work on the seventh day, are often used to identify appropriate Sabbath activities. Instead of serving as a defense of Sabbath keeping, by protecting the seventh day from intrusive work activities, the Sabbath laws have become the arbiters deciding what kinds of work and recreational activities may be engaged in on that day. Consequently, as in the time of Ezra, the Sabbath laws have become trivialized in the minds of some struggling Sabbath observers.

In the same way, the church cannot maintain Sabbath observance simply by inviting a grace orientation to this religious practice. Jeremiah's promises of divine blessings on Sabbath keepers were evidently addressed to those who ignored the sanctity of the Sabbath by carrying merchandise through the gates of Jerusalem on that day.[3] Isaiah's promise of grand benefits to Sabbath keepers[4] concludes a chapter dealing with an external, formal, and very dis-

---

[1]Ezra 9-10; Neh. 10:30-1.
[2]Neh. 13:15-22.
[3]Jer. 17:19-27.
[4]Isa. 58:13-4.

appointing religious life.[1] The association of Sabbath observance and membership in the covenant community[2] was directed to eunuchs and foreigners who were yet to be accepted as fully-fledged members of the congregation. Evidently, the vivid prophetic invitations to accept the Sabbath as a vehicle of God's grace fell on the largely deaf ears of people who had lost both the passion for and the memory of Sabbath observance as an expression of joy in God's salvation. In short, a grace orientation to religious teachings does not insure their observance either.

In our congregations, such a grace orientation has become the watchword for all our church teachings, inadvertently reducing them essentially to variations on a single theme in the minds of many, and frequently without any accompanying strong commitment to the basic tenets of a religious life. For example, the grace orientation to the Sabbath does not necessarily encourage Sabbath observance among believers for whom this day arrives regularly and painlessly as a free insert in the long weekend, provided by society, without any special effort or planning required of the Sabbath keeper. Thus, the readily available long weekend has tended to "cheapen" the grace orientation to the Sabbath.

If neither appeal to Sabbath law nor invitation to Sabbath grace by themselves have the ability adequately to restore Sabbath observance in a "post-exilic" experience, how can this restoration occur? How may the future Seventh-day Adventist Sabbath be secured? As in that first "post-exilic" period, so today we must return to Sabbath worship in its full sense to secure a place for the Sabbath in our future.

Sabbath worship is the neglected aspect of Sabbath observance for a growing number of Adventists in our time. Thanks to the lasting and powerful influence of the Sabbath laws on social legislation, we now have the right to take time off from work once a week, and thanks to the prevalence of Sabbath grace we now enjoy such time each week without fear, but with all the benefits it brings to individuals and families. The Sabbath law has done its work, and Sabbath grace is extended to us all in rich measure. But Sabbath worship is being neglected, and as a result we stand to lose both our rest from work as well as the blessings and grace of a Sabbath rest all within the long, amorphous weekend. How then can Sabbath worship be restored?

*Place of Sabbath Worship*

While Sabbath worship is primarily associated with time, places also have a role to play in it—particularly two places, home and

[1] Isa. 58:1-5.
[2] Isa. 56:4.

church. In fact, in our time Sabbath worship brings together home and church, just as it brought together home and synagogue in post-exilic Judaism. Sabbath worship begins at home with the arrival of the seventh day, when we exit the world of work and enter the world of rest. It continues next morning in the house of God, and it concludes somewhere in God's world as we re-enter the world of work. Sabbath worship gives special meaning to these places, transforming the home into a sanctuary of rest, of grace and of God's presence, and making of the church sanctuary a home for community life and learning. As we cross the borders between these places during the Sabbath, life itself is transformed by our worship. Thus, the cares of the world are laid aside as we enter home and church for Sabbath worship, while in turn God's presence flows out from there into the world and permeates it during the week of work. In post-exilic Judaism, a Judaism without a holy land, without secure borders, without a special language and (for many and eventually for all) without its sacred temple, Sabbath worship gave new meaning to two new places, home and synagogue, where life could be lived and faith nurtured. In our time, Sabbath worship helps us rediscover the sanctity of home and church, places where our life and faith receive nurture by God's very presence.

*Time of Sabbath Worship*

The time for beginning Sabbath worship, at sunset on the sixth day, is quite practical in most parts of the world, but not entirely convenient in the view of many. A little later would perhaps be better, some have thought, and others quietly implemented one alternative or another. That way, we could drive home from work as usual, pick up a few items from the store as usual, arrive as usual for supper, and watch the evening news as usual. That would be more convenient, some have thought—but it would not enhance our Sabbath worship, because worship is our response to God's presence in our lives and it is an ordered response, ordered primarily by time. Therefore, Sabbath evening worship requires us to break the "as usual" evening activities and establish a different, "unusual" time around which Sabbath worship is ordered. The Sabbath evening sunset, according to Scripture, is that point in time, deliberately chosen, from which to order our Sabbath worship. There must be nothing "usual" about it, for it is not our "usual" work pattern, but the "unusual" Sabbath pattern that determines it.

Worship protects Sabbath time from slipping into the "usual." If we neglect worship at these times, we may still enjoy free time from work for a while, thanks to social legislation, but we will lose the Sabbath. We may still find rest, joy, and fellowship in our back yards, thanks to the long weekend—but no Sabbath remains. Only Sabbath worship protects Sabbath time from becoming "usual" time, because it marks the borders around the Sabbath, borders that separate between two worlds, God's and ours. Consequently, Sabbath worship in all its variety must be regular, a custom from which we do not deviate.[1] In short, Sabbath worship protects our Sabbath rest and blessings from being nibbled at first second by second, then minute by minute, and finally hour by hour until it is all swallowed up by the weekend.

*Manner of Sabbath Worship*

How does Sabbath worship work? Notice how Scripture uses action verbs referring to mind and heart when describing Sabbath observance: remember, observe, delight in, rest from, be finished with, do good to. If these verbs are to characterize our Sabbath worship we need to allow variety and breadth in our approach to it. The many *do not's* with which we have grown up must be turned into even more *do's*. Consider the many possibilities these action verbs will allow during Sabbath worship at home, in church, and in community. Jesus sums them up when he affirms that it is right to do good things on the Sabbath.[2]

Because the lines separating church from society are becoming increasingly blurred in this "post-exilic" time, new challenges to Sabbath worship will emerge regularly. Sometimes, we must help society around us function on the Sabbath. For example, many of our health care institutions participate in the daily lives of their larger communities to such a degree that these communities rely on them for life-preserving services; our full attention to duty may thus be necessary even on the Sabbath. Only a strong commitment to Sabbath worship in its full sense can prevent us from losing this day to the many work duties required of Sabbath observers in such settings. That is to say, when all necessary, needed, and proper Sabbath activities are structured and conceptualized as worship activities, broadly understood, through which Sabbath sanctity permeates our homes, our institutions, and our communities, the Sabbath will be protected and preserved. Understood this way, the preparation and serving of a meal on the Sabbath, the cleaning and making of a bed, a response to an emergency, or the provision of any service for the good of others on this day will be an occasion for Sabbath worship, rest, and celebration, and not an opportunity for profit-making or a grudging submission to duty—thanks to a restoration of Sabbath worship. Thus an attitude of genuine Sabbath worship

[1] Cp. Luke 4:16.
[2] Matt. 12:12.

will help keep proper and needed activities on the Sabbath true to the meaning of genuine Sabbath observance.

## Conclusion.

Well over a century and a half after the Seventh-day Adventist church began, the Sabbath remains one of our distinguishing marks and we are the only major Christian church to uphold it. We have been successful in proclaiming Sabbath keeping. As a result, over 18 million Christians observe the Sabbath throughout the world, most of them doing so without oppression and persecution, and millions more take time off from work on that day inadvertently, thanks to the long weekend. Similarly, the many benefits and blessings that have always accrued to Sabbath keepers are now awaiting millions of people throughout the world, thanks to this long weekend, along with the rest, recreation, and joy it offers individuals and families. These are magnificent gains for a church whose members were frequently ridiculed and even imprisoned just a few years ago simply for honoring the Sabbath instead of Sunday. In the face of these gains, what is left for Seventh-day Adventists to do at this time when we remember our beginnings? We must protect the Sabbath as a day of worship, because in the words of H.H. Rowley, "it is significant that in our day impatience with the Sabbath as a day of rest is the accompaniment of the widespread abandonment of the Sabbath as a day of worship." Thus, the future Adventist understanding of the Sabbath includes a vigorous restoration of the Sabbath as a day of worship in its full Scriptural meaning, because without Sabbath worship we will find no genuine Sabbath rest.

# 5

# *Humanness*

## Dalton D. Baldwin

The Seventh-day Adventist understanding of humanness is rooted in that of the Millerite movement. In his preaching and
writing, William Miller did not give a prominent place to his view
of humanness. Primarily, of course, he emphasized the time of the
second coming of Christ. In a certificate dated September 5, 1822,
he explained that he had prepared for his brethren, friends, and children a brief statement of his faith. We can find some clues to his understanding of humanness in the second, third, and fourth articles:

> ART. II. I believe in one living and true God, and that there are
> three persons in the Godhead,—as is in man, the body, soul and spirit.
> And if any one will tell me how these exist, I will tell him how the
> three persons of the Triune God are connected.
> ART. III. I believe that God, by his Son, created man in the image
> of the Triune God, with a body, soul and spirit; and that he was created
> a moral agent, capable of living, of obeying, or transgressing the laws of
> his Maker.
> ART. IV. I believe that man, being tempted by the enemy of all
> good, did transgress and became polluted; from which act, sin entered
> into the world, and all mankind became naturally sinners, thrust out
> from the presence of God, and exposed to his just wrath forever.[1]

Placing the body, soul and spirit parallel with the three persons
of the Godhead seems to give a degree of independent existence to
the body, soul and spirit in a human being. The tripartite character
of humanity, body, soul and spirit, is the image of God in which
humans were created. Miller definitely believed that humans were
created with free will. They could obey or disobey without their
actions being predestined one way or the other by factors in their
causal pasts. He believed in original sin in the sense that after the fall
everyone is born responsibly guilty and deserves to be lost. Articles
V and VI indicate that after the fall original sin does not exclude
free will, with which a person accepts or rejects salvation.

---

[1]Sylvester Bliss, *Memoirs of William Miller* (Boston: Himes 1853) 77-8.

Although there is some ambiguity, Miller seemed to believe in the immortality of the soul and the eternal punishment of the wicked, which were beliefs of the Calvinist Baptist church with which he was affiliated. He did not mention immortal souls in his statement of faith. Article X said that those who have faith "can never perish." In Article XIII he said that "final impenitents will be destroyed from the earth, and sent away into a place prepared for the Devil and his angels." He probably meant that their souls still exist after being destroyed from the earth and are therefore immortal.

His statement on the resurrection could be interpreted to support conditional immortality. In Article XVII he said that the "just, or believers," are resurrected at the second coming of Christ before the millennium and "will receive everlasting life." The "unjust" are resurrected after the millennium and receive "eternal condemnation." We could regard this as saying that everlasting life is only given on condition of free choice of faith. The use of the term "condemnation" could mean that the wicked are totally destroyed after eternal condemnation in the final judgment. However, the rejection of the conditionalist position of George Storrs twenty-two years later indicates that Miller believed that at the first resurrection the immortal souls of the faithful receive everlastingly living bodies and the immortal souls of the wicked are placed in eternal punishment.[1]

## CONDITIONALISM IN AMERICA

Enlightenment thinking was beginning to have an impact in nineteenth century America when the Millerite movement was in its heyday. Serious questions arose about the justice of punishing a wicked person infinitely for a finite quantity of sin. One response was universalism. Adventist historian LeRoy Froom lists twenty-nine publications between 1781 and 1829 which advocated belief in the universal salvation of all the wicked in the afterlife.[2] Another response was conditionalism. Conditionalists believe that only God has inherent immortality.[3] Humans are naturally mortal and receive immortality only on condition of choosing to receive the gift of faith. The wicked who reject faith do not suffer eternal punishment but are annihilated after the last judgment.

One of the earliest known conditionalists in America was Elias Smith. A book he had bought in Boston reported the beliefs of certain English Christians. They denied that the wicked suffer eternal

[1]Bliss 79.
[2]LeRoy Edwin Froom, *The Conditionalist Faith of Our Fathers: Conflict of the Ages over the Nature and Destiny of Man*, 2 vols. (Washington, DC: Review 1965) 2: 279.
[3]1 Tim. 6:16.

punishment in hell but instead insisted that the wicked will be totally destroyed. These English Christians were called "destructionists." In an autobiographical account, Smith recalled how he decided to show from the Bible that the destructionists were wrong.

> In April, 1805, I concluded one day to take my Bible and Concordance,
> and find eternal misery, and not have my mind any longer troubled about
> 'destruction.' I examined the words, misery, miserable, miserably; and
> found that there was no one place in the Bible where the word was used
> to describe the state of men beyond death. Next I looked for the word
> *torment* and found that was limited, and that there was no torment men-
> tioned beyond the day of judgment. I then looked at the words destroy,
> destruction, death, second death, perish, consumed, perdition, burnt up,
> etc. I examined the similitudes used to describe the end of the wicked,
> such as chaff and stubble burnt up; dry trees cast into the fire, and tares
> burnt; the fat of lambs consumed, whirlwinds, a dream and a noise. All
> these things proved to me that at the last judgment, the wicked would be
> punished with everlasting destruction, which would be their end.[1]

Smith later published a pamphlet with five sermons advocating
conditionalism.[2] He became one of the founders of the Christian
Connection, in which conditionalism was widely endorsed.[3] Both
James White and Joseph Bates were active in ministry in the Christian Connection.[4]

In 1837, a conditionalist tract by Henry Grew entitled *The In-
termediate State* fell into the hands of George Storrs, a Methodist
minister. After pondering the issue for several years, he took a firm
stand against inherent immortality. His new convictions were not
well received by the guardians of Methodist orthodoxy and he also
experienced opposition to his abolitionist activism on the part of
the local Methodist bishop. After fifteen years as a pastor, Storrs
voluntarily resigned from the Methodist ministry.

He wrote three letters carefully explaining his new convictions
to one of his close Methodist preacher friends who in turn encouraged their anonymous publication. In 1841 Storrs published *An Enquiry: Are the Souls of the Wicked Immortal? In Three Letters.*

He found a congregation in Albany whose members did not
object to his conditionalist teachings and became its pastor. When
he preached a series of sermons on conditionalism, many of his lis-
teners urged their publication. In 1842 he published with his name

[1]Elias Smith, *The Life, Conversion, Preaching, Travels, and Sufferings of Elias
Smith* (Portsmouth, NH: Smith/Shores 1816) 1: 347-8 (despite the volume number, there appears to have been only one volume of this work), qtd. Moses
Corliss Crouse, "A Study of the Doctrine of Conditional Immorality in Nineteenth Century America: with Special Reference to the Contributions of Charles
F. Hudson and John H. Pettingell" (PhD diss., Northwestern U 1953) 79.
[2]Crouse 80.
[3]Froom 2: 291. Crouse (80) says that the Christian group of Smith should be
differentiated from the Christian Connection centered in Dayton, Ohio.
[4]Froom 2: 672, 675.

attached, *An Enquiry: Are the Souls of the Wicked Immortal? In Six Sermons.* The work was well received, reaching its twenty-first edition within ten years. By 1880 Storrs had circulated 200,000 copies.[1]

Shortly after publishing the first edition of the *Six Sermons* he resigned as a pastor and began itinerant preaching of the Millerite Adventist message. He did not openly advocate his conditionalist views in his Adventist preaching.[2] In 1843, *The Midnight Cry* published an article by Storrs on the "sanctuary" which was to be cleansed at the end of the 2,300 days. There was no discussion of conditional immortality or the annihilation of the wicked, but he did quote without elaboration the passage in Malachi 4:1 concerning the day of the Lord which will "leave them neither root nor branch." He invited discussion of his proposal regarding the sanctuary by saying, "I have thrown out this whole subject as a matter for examination rather than a settled opinion."[3]

A month later, William Miller responded to the invitation for discussion of this sanctuary proposal with a sweeping rejection of the understanding of humanness contained in the *Six Sermons.*

> I cannot be silent without dissenting from this any longer, it would be a crime against God and man. Therefore I disclaim any connection, fellowship, or sympathy with Br. Storrs' views of the intermediate state, and end of the wicked, or his late hints on the cleansing of the sanctuary, and limitation of the inheritance and kingdom of Judea.

He went on to explain, "One rule I have followed, is, never to adopt anything as a religious sentiment, however, plausible it might appear, if I could bring one plain text against it from the Bible."[4] Miller's declaration leads us to consider the nature of biblical inspiration and its implications for interpretation.

## BIBLICAL INSPIRATION

No doubt Miller had in mind such passages as the story of Saul, who asked the medium of Endor to "bring up" Samuel. Harold Lindsell pointed out that it was "the spirit of Samuel" who spoke in the incident.[5] The account says, "Then Samuel said to Saul."[6]

Since Lindsell believes that the Bible is inerrant in all its parts, it would be easier for him to formulate doctrine using this text in isola-

---

[1] Froom 2: 305-7.
[2] "Storrs, George," *Seventh-day Adventist Encyclopedia*, rev. ed. (Washington, DC: Review 1976) 1264.
[3] George Storrs [article on the sanctuary], *The Midnight Cry*, April 25, 1844: 322.
[4] William Miller, "Letter from Mr. Miller," *The Midnight Cry*, May 23, 1844: 355.
[5] Harold Lindsell, marginal note on 1 Sam. 28:7, *Harper Study Bible, Revised Standard Version* (Grand Rapids: Zondervan 1965) 434.
[6] 1 Sam. 28:15

tion from those like Eccl. 9:5, 6. If this passage says that Samuel after dying could be "brought up" to give counsel to Saul, for him this indicates that after death humans continue in conscious existence.

A more mature view of the inspiration of the Bible realizes that errors from the culture were on occasion incorporated into the text of Scripture. Ellen White, for example, reports the following:

> I saw that God had especially guarded the Bible; yet when copies of it were few, learned men had in some instances changed the words, thinking that they were making it more plain, when in reality they were mystifying that which was plain, by causing it to lean to their established views, which were governed by tradition. But I saw that the Word of God, as a whole, is a perfect chain, one portion linking into and explaining another.[1]

We should not expect that every concept in the Bible is infallible. A change which incorporated an idea from human tradition would include error. We should notice that Ellen White quickly suggests a way to overcome such errors.

The ideas which connect with each other in a self-consistent chain in the Bible as a whole form a stable standard for truth. "And as several writers present a subject under varied aspects and relations, there may appear, to the superficial careless, or prejudiced reader, to be discrepancy or contradiction, where the thoughtful, reverent student, with clearer insight, discerns the underlying harmony."[2] It is not every concept in the Bible that is infallible. It is the underlying harmony of the Bible as a whole that is infallible.

An example of contradiction on the surface of the Bible is the conflict in the two accounts of David's census. The early account says, "Again the anger of the LORD was kindled against Israel, and he incited David against them, saying, 'Go, count the people of Israel and Judah.'"[3] The same story retold many years later, quoting most of the earlier account word for word, includes a striking difference. "Satan stood up against Israel, and incited David to count the people of Israel."[4]

The second account is much more consistent with the teaching of the Bible as a whole about the justice of God than the first. Even though the first account is clearly wrong in saying that God actively incited David to number Israel, we should not question the authority of the Scriptures *as a whole*. From a study of the Bible as a whole we learn that the early Old Testament frequently says that God actively does what in fact God only permits. The infallibility

---

[1]Ellen G. White, *Early Writings of E. G. White* (Washington, DC: Review 1945) 220-1.

[2]Ellen G. White, *The Great Controversy between Christ and Satan: The Conflict of the Ages in the Christian Dispensation* (Mountain View, CA: Pacific 1911) vi.

[3]2 Sam. 24:1.

[4]1 Chron. 21:1.

and authority of the Bible does not reside in each and every concept in the Bible. It is the Bible as a whole that is authoritative and infallible.

This infallible chain derived from the Bible as a whole is not always easy to locate. Sometimes considerable time and effort are required to identify the self-consistent chain of truth.

> The truths of the Bible are as pearls hidden. They must be searched, dug out by painstaking effort. Those who take only a surface view of the Scriptures will, with their superficial knowledge, which they think is very deep, talk of the contradictions of the Bible, and question the authority of the Scriptures. But those whose hearts are in harmony with truth and duty will search the Scriptures with a heart prepared to receive divine impressions. The illuminated soul sees a spiritual unity, one grand golden thread running through the whole, but it requires patience, thought, and prayer to trace out the precious golden thread. Sharp contentions over the Bible have led to investigation and revealed the precious jewels of truth.[1]

The resolution of some surface contradictions requires prolonged, intense dialogue in order to develop consensus on the real teaching of the Bible as a whole. When in such a dialogue participants use the authority of the Bible as a base for each statement, the authority of the Bible is reinforced. This strengthening of biblical authority occurs even when the underlying harmony of the Bible as a whole is used to correct an error in a particular passage.

When we understand the event, which is described with the statement that "the LORD . . . incited David [to] count the people of Israel," as indicating that God *permitted* David to count Israel, the authority for reversing the meaning of the grammar, syntax and contextual meaning of the original biblical passage does not come from human reason alone. The correct understanding of God's action in relation to the census comes from the underlying harmony of the Bible as a whole. A person should not adopt a position contradicting the meaning of the grammatical and linguistic intention of a passage in the Bible using reason alone. It is only safe to deviate from a passage in the Bible on the authority of the underlying harmony of the Bible as a whole.

When dealing with the story of Saul and the medium of Endor, we should not be misled by the King James translation, which has Saul asking for "a woman that hath a familiar spirit."[2] Saul was not asking for a woman who could summon demonic spirits who would impersonate Samuel. He wanted to profit from the valuable knowledge and counsel of Samuel as spirit. On this phrase the *Seventh-day Adventist Bible Commentary* says:

[1]Ellen G. White, *Selected Messages*, 3 vols. (Washington, DC: Review 1958-80) 1: 20.
    [2]1 Sam. 28:7.

Heb. *ba'alath-'ob. Ba'alath* means "mistress." '*Ob* should be rendered "necromancer," or, in modern language, "a medium" (see RSV; see also on Lev. 19:31). The word is also used of necromancy, as in v. 8, where Saul literally says, "Inquire, I pray, for me by necromancy." Our English word necromancy comes from two Greek words, *nekros,* dead, and *manteia,* divination, and describes the art of ascertaining the future by alleged communications with the spirits of the dead.[1]

The *New Revised Standard Version* translates the phrase, "Seek out for me a woman who is a medium." The laws against enquiring from the spirits of the dead show that the common people believed that the spirit of a person continues to exist after bodily death and can provide valuable knowledge and counsel. The people of Israel were prohibited from imitating "the abhorrent practices" of the surrounding nations by seeking "oracles from the dead."[2] Even though Saul had made laws against consulting the dead, he relapsed into the error of the surrounding culture. From the way the story is told, it is clear that the author believed that Saul actually encountered Samuel as spirit. This is an error from the surrounding culture which is not consistent with the underlying harmony of the Bible as a whole, which teaches that the "dead know nothing."[3]

Miller did not realize that a variety of erroneous understandings of humanness from the surrounding culture were reflected in the pages of the Bible. He did not apply his single text veto when he reconsidered the immortality of the soul in the light of 1 Timothy 6:16, which says that it is God "alone who has immortality." Probably he felt secure in his conviction that the Bible is inerrant in all its parts and therefore felt that it was unnecessary to take other passages into account. He should have realized that the teaching of the Bible on a given topic is that position which is consistent with the Bible as a whole even though there may be particular passages which are in conflict with it.

We now turn from this theological parenthesis back to the story of the development of the understanding of humanness in the Seventh-day Adventist Church.

## Adventist Founders and the Love and Justice of God

The conditionalism which permeated the Christian Connection through the influence of George Storrs shaped the context out of which two of the primary founders of the Seventh-day Adventist Church emerged.

---

[1] *Seventh-day Adventist Bible Commentary,* ed. Francis D. Nichol *et al.,* 7 vols. (Washington: Review 1957) 2: 586.

[2] Deut. 18:9-11; cp. Lev. 19:31, 20:6, 27.

[3] Ec. 9:5; cp. Ps. 6:5, Isa. 38:18.

Before one of her husband's voyages as a sea captain, the wife of Joseph Bates slipped a Bible and some religious books into his gear, and later, after responding to a revival, he joined her church, the Christian Church.[1] He became a leader and minister in the Christian Connection and was an activist in support of temperance, abolition, and the Millerite movement. After the 1844 disappointment, he wrote the first tract issued by Sabbatarian Adventists. Although conditionalism was not emphasized in this early writing, his reference to future events which would come "after immortality" shows that he held the conditionalist position.[2]

James White was baptized into the Christian Connection. After teaching a short time, he resigned to join with the Millerites in preaching the approaching Advent. The Christian Connection ordained him as a minister following a winter of itinerant evangelism with a report of 1,000 decisions for Christ.[3]

Ellen Harmon grew up in a devout Methodist home where she records that she "had been taught to believe in an eternally burning hell." She remembered how "the perspiration would start" when the preacher would describe this inferno "where, after the tortures of thousands upon thousands of years, the fiery billows would roll to the surface the writhing victims, who would shriek, 'How long, O Lord, how long?' Then the answer would thunder down the abyss, 'Through all eternity!'"[4] She recalled, "I despaired that so cruel and tyrannical a being would ever condescend to save me from the doom of sin."[5]

In spite of Miller's rejection of conditionalism, he may have been an instrument in relieving Ellen of her picture of a tyrannical God and the understanding of humanness required to support this devastating view of divine mercy. In 1840 and again in 1842, the Harmon family attended Miller's meetings in the Casco Street Christian Church in Portland, Main. Many of those who came to hear Miller continued to attend revival meetings conducted by the pastor of this Christian Connection congregation.[6] He may have been the source of the sermon which Ellen's mother heard that rejected belief in the inherent immortality of the soul and the ever-

[1]Arthur Whitefield Spalding, *Captains of the Host* (Washington, DC: Review 1949) 38-9.

[2]Froom 2: 675-6.

[3]"White, James," *Seventh-day Adventist Encyclopedia*, rev. ed. (Washington, DC: Review 1976) 1420.

[4]Ellen G. White, *Life Sketches of Ellen G. White* (Mountain View, CA: Pacific 1915) 29, 30.

[5]White, *Sketches* 31.

[6]Arthur White, *Ellen G. White: The Early Years* (Washington, DC : Review 1985) 35-6.

lasting punishment of the wicked. Ellen remembered being shocked when her mother seemed convinced of the new teaching.

"Why, mother!" cried I, in astonishment, "this is strange talk for you! If you believe this strange theory, do not let any one know of it; for I fear that sinners would gather security from this belief, and never desire to seek the Lord."

"If this is sound Bible truth," she replied, "instead of preventing the salvation of sinners, it will be the means of winning them to Christ."[1]

After mulling over the issue in her mind for several months, Ellen adopted conditionalism when she herself heard preaching on the subject. Two features of the new understanding of humanness were prominent in her thinking. Replacing eternal punishment with annihilation of the wicked demolished her picture of God as a tyrant and revealed instead a God of justice and love. In the old view, resurrection took the soul from heavenly bliss back to confinement in the "poor mouldering body," but the new view gave the resurrection "new and sublime importance."[2] By the time of the Great Disappointment, her convictions regarding the conditional immortality of the soul and the annihilation of the wicked were similar to those of Joseph Bates and James White.

After the 1844 disappointment, James and Ellen White (now married) and Joseph Bates did not emphasize conditionalism when they sought to rally the "little flock" to confidence in the nearness of the Advent. In an 1848 letter, James White listed only two fundamental doctrines. "The principle points on which we dwell as present truth are the seventh day Sabbath and Shut Door. In this we wish to honor God's most holy institution and also acknowledge the work of God in our Second Advent experience."[3] However, James White revealed his conditionalist position in *A Word to the Little Flock*, published in 1847, by referring to the saints just before the advent as still "in their mortal state."[4]

## CONDITIONALISM BECAME A FUNDAMENTAL DOCTRINE

By 1852, one of the two original fundamental doctrines of the little flock had been dropped. The original shut door doctrine, which denied the possibility of any new conversions because Christ had left the mediatorial throne in the Holy Place, was recognized as

[1]White, *Sketches* 49.

[2]White, *Sketches* 49-50.

[3]James White, letter to "Brother and Sister Hastings," Oct. 2, 1848, qtd. Robert W. Olson, comp., *The "Shut Door" Documents* (Washington, DC: White Estate 1982) 21.

[4]James White, *A Word to the Little Flock* (facsimile reproduction; Washington, DC: Review nd) 3.

an error when new converts began to join the Sabbath keeping Adventists. During these early years, conditionalism was more and more frequently mentioned in the *Second Advent Review and Sabbath Herald*, published by James White. In 1854, he began listing the basic teachings of the Sabbath keeping Adventist community in the masthead as follows:

> Leading Doctrines Taught by the Review.
> The Bible, and the Bible alone, the rule of faith and duty.
> The Law of God, as taught in the Old and New Testaments, unchangeable.
> The Personal Advent of Christ and the Resurrection of the Just, before the Millennium.
> The Earth restored to its Eden perfection and glory, the final inheritance of the Saints.
> Immortality alone through Christ, to be given to the Saints at the Resurrection.[1]

In an editorial, he expressed his hope of publishing articles on the "all important subjects" such as "Atonement, the Advent, Immortality alone through Christ, the Law of God and Bible holiness."[2] The two fundamental doctrines had expanded to five. Conditionalism had become a leading doctrine. This list of leading doctrines was designed to restore Christianity to apostolic purity. In a later editorial James White listed a group of errors that needed correction by the remnant. "As fundamental errors, we might class with this counterfeit Sabbath other errors which Protestants have brought away from the Catholic church, such as sprinkling for baptism, the Trinity, the consciousness of the dead and eternal life in misery."[3]

James White fulfilled his hope of publishing articles on immortality through a series by D. P. Hall. The first article was entitled, "The Mortality of Man: The Only Shield against the Seductions of Modern Spiritualism."[4] Hall was one of the four Sabbath keeping Adventist preachers in Wisconsin. The series used the surge of interest in spiritualism in popular culture to present the biblical teaching that the dead are unconscious and that human immortality is a gift conferred at the resurrection on condition of faith. The six arti-

---

[1] *The Advent Review, and Sabbath Herald,* Aug. 15, 1854: 1; original italicized.

[2] James White, "The Review," *The Advent Review, and Sabbath Herald* Aug. 15, 1854: 4.

[3] James White, "The Position of the Remnant, Their Duties and Trials Considered," *The Advent Review, and Sabbath Herald,* Sept. 12, 1854: 36. In the sixth number the words "Taught by the *Review*" were dropped and the heading merely read "Leading Doctrines" until the eighteenth number, Dec. 26, 1854, after which this feature of the masthead was discontinued.

[4] D. P. Hall, "The Mortality of Man: The Only Shield against the Seductions of Modern Spiritualism," *The Advent Review, and Sabbath Herald* 6 (Aug. 29, Sept. 5, 12, 19, Dec. 12, 19, 26, 1854)17-19, 25-28, 33-36, 41-42, 129-132, 137-139, 145-147.

cles in the series were then combined into a book of 148 pages entitled *Man Not Immortal: The Only Shield against the Seductions of Modern Spiritualism,* which sold for twelve and one half cents.

After these five leading doctrines had flown on the masthead for eighteen issues, they suddenly disappeared without explanation. In the last issue containing them James White placed a notice saying, "In consequence of ill health we shall leave the Office for a few weeks and design visiting the brethren as the way may open."[1] Pressures from economic problems and a severe conflict with Stephenson and Hall over the "Age to Come" seemed to be closing in on James White. When later that year he refused to publish Hall's views advocating an earthly millennium during which many sinners would be converted, Hall joined the Messenger party, the first significant off-shoot from the Sabbath keeping Adventists.[2] He used the rival publication, *The Messenger of Truth,* to attack James White.

The next year, James White published another series on conditionalism by J. N. Loughborough. Perhaps he felt the need to publish teaching on the subject from a more respected author. There were nine articles in the series entitled, "Is the Soul Immortal."[3] Although the new series was not as clear and convincing, it also was published as a book. The 196-page volume was entitled *An Examination of the Scripture Testimony Concerning Man's Present Condition and His Future Reward or Punishment*—and sold for eighteen cents.

About the time that D. P. Hall accepted the Sabbath message in Wisconsin,[4] Uriah Smith attended a series of meetings in Washington, New Hampshire, and began keeping the Sabbath. The next year, at the age of twenty-one, he started using his literary talents by working on the *Review* staff. In 1855, the year of Loughborough's series on conditionalism, the twenty-three-year-old Smith became the editor of the *Review.*[5]

In 1860, Smith published a 128-page book entitled, *Which? Mortal or Immortal? or an Inquiry into the Present Constitution and Future Condition of Man.*[6] He began the book with five statements which summarize his presentation. Man has no inherent immortal

[1]See James White's discussion in *The Advent Review, and Sabbath Herald,* Dec. 9, 1854: 140.

[2]Richard W. Schwarz, *Light Bearers to the Remnant* (Mountain View, CA: Pacific 1979) 445-6.

[3]See J. N. Loughborough's multi-part discussion of the question, "Is the Soul Immortal," in the Sep., Oct., and Dec. 1855 numbers of *The Advent Review, and Sabbath Herald.*

[4]Arthur W. Spalding, *Origin and History of Seventh-day Adventists,* 4 vols. (Washington, DC: Review 1961) 1: 257-8.

[5]"Smith, Uriah," *Seventh-day Adventist Encyclopedia* 1200.

[6]Uriah Smith, *Which? Mortal or Immortal? or an Inquiry into the Present Constitution and Future Condition of Man* (Battle Creek, MI: Review 1860).

principle in his nature; there is no consciousness in death; immortality is given conditionally by Christ; the wicked will not exist forever in misery; and the wicked will be punished in a future state and then cease to exist. The book systematically organized biblical teaching and was a scholarly and literary improvement over prior Adventist works on conditionalism.

In 1873 Smith published *The State of the Dead and the Destiny of the Wicked.*[1] The argument and the basic order of subjects was the same as in the earlier work, but there is clarification and expansion. He added many quotations from respected authors, and there are some seventy names listed in the author index. Further refinement was included in the 1884 edition entitled *Here and Hereafter, or Man's Nature and Destiny, The State of the Dead, the Reward of the Righteous, and the Punishment of the Wicked.*[2] There are more than 180 names listed in the authors index. For many years after the death of Uriah Smith this book remained the standard Adventist work on the subject of humanness.

Perhaps the most effective Adventist public communicator to take up the topic of humanness was Dudley M. Canright. He was described as "a forceful preacher and polemic writer of considerable ability."[3] The first edition of *A History of the Doctrine of the Immortality of the Soul*[4] was a 184-page historical survey which contrasted the pagan doctrine of inherent immortality with the biblical unconscious state of the dead and conditional immortality given to the faithful at the resurrection. Twice in the decade following the appearance of this publication Canright became so depressed with doubts and discouragement that he dropped out of the Adventist ministry. Shortly after returning to the ministry the second time, he published the second edition.[5] The year of publication he dropped out of the ministry the third time for two years of farming near his home town of Otsego, Michigan. A. G. Butler wooed him back for another three years of hyperactive ministry, which included a spirited defense of the authenticity of the spiritual gifts of Ellen G. White which he had denied during his discouragement.

[1]Uriah Smith, *The State of the Dead and the Destiny of the Wicked* (Battle Creek: Seventh-Day Adventist 1873).

[2]Uriah Smith, *Here and Hereafter or Man in Life and Death: The Reward of the Righteous and the Destiny of the Wicked,* Washington, DC: Review 1897).

[3]"Canright, Dudley M.," *Seventh-day Adventist Encyclopedia* 199.

[4]D. M. Canright, *A History of the Doctrine of the Immortality of the Soul* (Battle Creek, MI: Adventist 1871).

[5]D. M. Canright, *A History of the Doctrine of the Soul, Among All Races and Peoples, Ancient and Modern, Including Theologians, Philosophers, Scientists and Untutored Aborigines; Carefully Brought Down to the Present Time,* 2d ed. (Battle Creek, MI: Adventist 1882).

Two years after his fourth and final withdrawal from the Adventist ministry, he published *Seventh-day Adventism Renounced,* a book of 413 pages which by the time of his death had gone through fourteen printings. The book became the weapon most widely used by evangelical Protestants to attack Adventist teachings. Adventist evangelists report that new converts have more difficulty replacing the immortality of the soul with conditionality than replacing Sunday with Saturday as the Sabbath. Remarkably, although Canright attacked most Seventh-day Adventist distinctive teachings, he did not attack the unconscious state of the dead and conditional immortality.[1]

In 1875, four years after Canright's *History of the Doctrine of the Immortality of the Soul,* John Harvey Kellogg graduated from Bellevue Hospital Medical School in New York. He soon became medical director of the Western Health Reform Institute in Battle Creek. He was asked by the General Conference to present a lecture on the "Harmonies of Science and Religion" on October 8, 1878. The next year he expanded this lecture into a book, *The Harmony of Science and the Bible on the Nature of the Soul and the Doctrine of the Resurrection.*[2]

Kellogg held that a human being "has a soul." In support of his position he cited the statement of Jesus that in ordinary death the soul "is not destroyed with the body."[3] "Do not fear those who kill the body but cannot kill the soul; rather fear him who can destroy both soul and body in hell."[4]

For Kellogg, the soul is the identity of the person. He described two kinds of identity, identity of matter and identity of organization. The identity of a rock is constituted by the *matter* of the rock. If other matter, atoms and molecules, are substituted for those in a rock, it has a different identity. The identities of a rainbow, a river and a human are constituted by the *organization* of the matter. The particular atoms and molecules of rainbows, rivers, and people are constantly changing; but there is continuity in the organization. "Organization constitutes human identity during life, and may certainly do so in death if, as we shall see presently, it may be preserved after the death of the body."[5] He held that the soul, or organization, of each individual is preserved in the memory of God after the first death.

[1]Schwarz, *Light-Bearers* 464-70.
[2]John Harvey Kellogg, *The Harmony of Science and the Bible on the Nature of the Soul and the Doctrine of the Resurrection* (Battle Creek, MI: Review 1879).
[3]Kellogg 71.
[4]Matt. 10:28.
[5]Kellogg 93.

This soul is not a person who functions in knowing and loving. The soul is the organization of the person. There is no functioning person without matter. "Force and matter are inseparable. One cannot exist without the other, even for an instant."[1] From the selective damage to thought and feeling produced by selective damage to parts of the brain, he concluded that human functions like consciousness require chemical activity in a body. He quoted Austin Flint, a recognized authority on physiology, in support of his contention that a soul cannot carry on any human function such as knowing or feeling. "At the present day, we are in possession of a sufficient number of positive facts to render it certain that there is and can be no intelligence without brain substance."[2]

Kellogg's emphasis on matter, physiology, and the body in humanness developed into his religion of "biologic living."[3] As the foremost Adventist scientist of his time, he would have been most likely to recognize the significance of science for the theology of humanness. The nineteenth century health reformers had emphasized the religious significance of health. Larkin B. Coles had written that "it is as truly a sin against Heaven, to violate a law of life, as to break one of the ten commandments."[4] Ellen White's first report on her basic health reform vision of June 6, 1863, included, "I saw that it was a sacred duty to attend to our health, and arouse others to their duty."[5] Kellogg's religious zeal for biologic living culminated in his publication of *The Living Temple*.[6] Unfortunately, its contribution to the Seventh-day Adventist understanding of humanness was blunted, even reversed, when he was charged with pantheism and withdrew from the Seventh-day Adventist Church, taking the Battle Creek Sanitarium with him.

The most extensive Adventist treatment of humanness was that of L. E. Froom. His two-volume *Conditionalist Faith of Our Fathers*[7] contains 2,476 pages. In Volume 1, he devoted more than 500 pages to an analysis of the biblical understanding of humanness and then began an historical survey of the pagan source of the idea of the immortality of the soul from 900 BCE onward.

Froom organized the historical development of dominant concepts of humanness with what he called the "theological trilemma."

[1]Kellogg 38.

[2]Austin Flint, *A Text-Book of Human Physiology, Designed for the Use of Practicioners and Students of Medicine* (New York: Appleton 1876) 695, qtd. Kellogg 52.

[3]Richard W. Schwarz, *John Harvey Kellogg, M.D.* (Nashville: Southern 1970) 37-58.

[4]Larkin B. Coles, *Philosophy of Health* (Boston: Ticknor 1848) 216.

[5]White, *Messages* 3: 280 (Ms. 1, 1863).

[6]John Harvey Kellogg, *The Living Temple* (Battle Creek, MI: Good Health 1903).

[7]Froom.

The trilemma consists of three alternative conceptions of human-ness approached eschatologically. The first alternative is condition-alism, with immortality given on condition of faith. The second is innate immortality, with eternal torment of the wicked. The third is universalism, with all the wicked restored to harmony with God in an afterlife.[1] Although the concept of an immortal soul began to penetrate Judaism before the time of Christ, Froom contended that conditional immortality, the unconscious state of the dead, and the annihilation of the wicked was the "preponderant belief of the church" as late as the second century.[2] The influence of Augustine was a major factor making inherent immortality of the soul the pre-dominant faith of the dominant church for the next fifteen centu-ries.[3] In the twentieth century, popular Christianity continued to hold to natural immortality, but Froom cites a number of influential theologians who turned away from this view.

Karl Barth, perhaps the most influential theologian of the twen-tieth century, rejected Platonic, inherent immortality. In a pub-lished radio address he said that according to the Bible human be-ings are not immortal but mortal. Only God is immortal. Human being is a unity in which the soul can be distinguished from the body but never separated.[4]

Rudolf Bultmann, perhaps the most influential New Testament scholar of the twentieth century, noted that Paul rejected the Greek conception of a substantial, immortal soul that can exist apart from the body. Froom quoted the following from Bultmann:

> The investigation of Paul's use of *soma* has already shown that he does not dualistically set body and soul in opposition to each other. Just as Paul does not know the Greek-Hellenistic conception of the immortali-ty of the soul (released from the body), neither does he use *psuche* to designate the seat or the power of the mental life which animates man's matter, as it had become the custom to do among the Greeks.[5]

Though he analyzed a vast array of authors analyzed in the twentieth century, Froom gave special prominence to the writings of Oscar Cullmann. Cullmann's 1955 Ingersoll Lecture on the Im-mortality of Man, given at Harvard, was published as *Immortality of the Soul or Resurrection of the Dead?* He pointed out the "radical dif-ference" between the concept of Socrates and Plato in which at death the body dies and the soul lives on and the concept of the New Testament in which at death both soul and body die. Resur-

---

[1]Froom 1: 523-28, 2: 6-9.

[2]Froom 1: 886-901.

[3]Froom 1: 1070-9.

[4]Froom 2: 1023-6, quoting an English translation of a French translation of the original German.

[5]Rudolf K Bultmann, *Theology of the New Testament*, 2 vols., trans. Kendrick Grobel (New York: Scribner 1951-5) 1: 203-4.

rection involves a new act of creation which "calls back to life not just a part of the man, but the whole man."[1] The "basic distinction" lies in the Christian view that the "body is not the soul's prison, but rather a temple."[2] Cullmann reported that "No other publication of mine has provoked such enthusiasm or such violent hostility."[3] Popular Christianity cherishes the comforting belief that death is merely a beneficial transition in which the soul is ushered into eternal bliss. Cullmann noted that so far none of his critics had "attempted to refute me by exegesis."[4]

We turn now from a primary focus on the past to a focus on the future in the light of the past. Because the subject is so broad, we will select only two features for emphasis.

### AUTHENTIC HUMANITY

The future understanding of humanness has been available longer than we might wish to recognize. From among several important features of this future redemptive understanding we may select two, liberation and relationships.

Perhaps the most celebrated act of God in the Old Testament was the liberation of the people of Israel from slavery in Egypt. Following the last supper during Passion Week, Jesus prays, "I ask . . . that they may all be one. As you, Father, are in me and I am in you, may they also be in us, so that the world may believe that you have sent me."[5] The realization of authentic humanness is only possible through liberation from oppressive human relationships established by sin and through the creation of liberating relationships through divine grace.

"Liberation" and "relationships" are prominent in today's religion book catalogues. In 1993, the Loma Linda University Center for Christian Bioethics published a book by V. Norskov Olsen entitled *The New Relatedness for Man and Woman in Christ: A Mirror of the Divine*.[6] For a number of years the Office of Human Relations in the General Conference has worked on a project which came to fruition in a book written by Sakae Kubo, *The God of Relationships:*

---

[1]Oscar Cullmann, *Immortality of the Soul or Resurrection of the Dead* (New York: Macmillan 1964_ 25-6.

[2]Cullmann 30.

[3]Cullmann 5.

[4]Cullmann 6.

[5]Jn. 17:20-1.

[6]V. Norskov Olsen, *The New Relatedness for Man & Woman in Christ: A Mirror of the Divine* (Loma Linda, CA: Loma Linda U Center for Christian Bioethics 1993).

*How the Gospel Helps Us Reach across Barriers such as Race, Culture, and Gender.*[1]
With the assistance of New Testament scholar William Barclay, join me on a time warp journey to first-century Tarsus in southeastern Asia Minor. The father of little Saul is a Roman, a Gentile. His mother is Jewish. She is proud of her son and hopes he will cherish his heritage and continue to be one of the faithful remnant. She has taught him a customary Jewish morning prayer. She fondly lays her hand on his shoulder as she listens to his words. I thank thee that "thou hast not made me a Gentile, a slave or a woman."[2]

No doubt the prayer was developed because everyone recognized that it was a distinct disadvantage to be a Gentile, a slave, or a woman in Jewish culture. When the prayer seems to attribute the conditions of Gentiles, slaves and women to God it indicates that errors from the culture had been absorbed into a religiously sanctioned value system and world view. Little did Saul then know the trauma that would be involved in the renewal of that value system.

Years later Paul would write, "There is no longer Jew nor Greek, there is no longer slave nor free, there is no longer male nor female; for all of you are one in Christ Jesus."[3] Paul wrote to the Galatian Church, rejecting the requirement that all new converts must be circumcised Jews before joining the worshiping community. This counsel felt like a soul-wrenching attack on the "pillars" of the faith. In the view of many early Jewish Christians, the divinely revealed *Torah* forbade eating and worshiping with uncircumcised Gentiles.

It was easy for the circumcision party of Galatia to find key texts to support its position. Regarding the surrounding nations the Torah says, "Make no covenant with them and show them no mercy."[4] In the promised land the people of a new city in the path of expansion should be offered terms of surrender. If they refused to surrender, "you shall put all its males to the sword." If they surrendered peacefully, "all the people in it shall serve you at forced labor."[5] Foreign slaves could be admitted to the assembly whose members shared the Passover if they became circumcised. Descendants of Ammonites and Moabites should be excluded from "the assembly of the LORD" to the tenth generation, descendants of Edomites and Egyptians to the third generation. "You shall never promote their welfare or their

[1]Sakae Kubo, *The God of Relationships: How the Gospel Helps Us Reach across Barriers such as Race, Culture, and Gender* (Hagerstown, MD: Review 1993).
[2]William Barclay, *Letters to the Galatians and Ephesians* (Philadelphia: Westminster 1976) 32.
[3]Gal. 3:28. Unless otherwise indicated biblical quotations are taken from the *New Revised Standard Version*.
[4]Deut. 7:2; cp. Ex 34:15
[5]Deut. 10:10-3.

prosperity as long as you live."[1] Gentiles did not have the same rights and privileges as the people of Israel.

Circumcision was the symbolic differentiation between the "Chosen People" and the other nations. Circumcision was a "pillar" for the disciples of Jesus and was only dropped after intense conflict. At first Peter ate and worshiped with uncircumcised Gentiles at Antioch. But when the revival and reformation team came from the "General Conference" to Antioch, they no doubt cited the key text which established circumcision as the sign of an "everlasting covenant."[2] The prohibitions against admitting uncircumcised foreigners were likely alluded to. There is no suggestion in the Old Testament that circumcision would be discontinued when the Messiah comes. Peter and then even Barnabas were "carried away"[3] by the charismatic power of what the team claimed was the Holy Spirit. Peter and Barnabas stopped eating and worshiping with uncircumcised Gentiles.

Paul challenged Peter with inconsistency. Several years prior to this incident, after eating and worshiping with the uncircumcised Cornelius, Peter was charged with destructive pluralism at headquarters. He had defended himself by claiming the authority of revelation. God had revealed to him that he should eat and worship with Cornelius. When Peter at first ate and worshiped with uncircumcised Gentiles and then reversed himself, Paul argued that Peter should be consistent with himself. True revelation should be consistent with itself.

Paul seems to be arguing from the underlying harmony of the whole Old Testament. New revelation should be tested for consistency with prior revelation. The noble Bereans "examined the scriptures every day to see whether these things were so."[4] Peter should not have credited his housetop dream with revelation unless it were consistent with prior revelation. Since there is no explicit Old Testament teaching that circumcision should be dropped when the Messiah comes, support for going against the sign of an "everlasting" covenant would need to come from the underlying harmony of the Old Testament as a whole.

Already in the Old Testament, physical circumcision was described as inauthentic when the obedience of faith is lacking. Jeremiah pointed out that those of Egypt and Judah who were physically circumcised were really "uncircumcised in heart."[5] What really

---

[1] Deut. 23:3-8
[2] Gen. 17:7, 13.
[3] Gal. 2:13 RSV.
[4] Acts 17:11.
[5] Jer. 9:25-26.

counts is circumcision of the heart.[1] In harmony with this position, Paul held that "if you break the law, circumcision becomes uncircumcision."[2] He then argued that since "he is not a real Jew who is one outwardly, nor is true circumcision something external and physical," a person "is a Jew who is one inwardly, and real circumcision is a matter of the heart, spiritual and not literal."[3] In his speech at the Jerusalem council Peter seemed to think of circumcision as a "custom of Moses"[4] rather than a divinely initiated law because it would be inappropriate to refer to a God initiated practice as a yoke "which neither our fathers nor we have been able to bear."[5] We do not know all that "human tradition" in Colossians 2:8 includes, but it certainly includes circumcision. Using the authority of the underlying harmony of the Bible as a whole, Paul and the developing Christian church had dropped a central pillar of Jewish faith. The Gentiles had been liberated from an oppressive relationship. They were now welcomed into the nurturing relationships of the worshiping community.

Paul explained that there is "no longer Jew or Greek" because "all of you are one in Christ Jesus." Some hold that the expression "in Christ" limits this passage to soteriological barriers. There is now no distinction between Jew and Gentile with regard to being saved by faith to eternal life in the hereafter, but this fact has no significance for oppressive structures in the here and now. But when, through faith, grace placed Paul "in Christ," this event did not remove a barrier in God to salvation for Gentiles. There never was such a barrier.[6] "The true light, which enlightens everyone"[7] in every time and place is Christ. Everyone in every time and place is empowered by God to be able to choose whether to respond to that light in faith or not, whether to enter into a saving relationship with Christ or not. Being "in Christ" identifies the saving power of grace as the agent of liberation. In this liberation the structures of oppression which gave rise to the prayer, "I thank thee that I am not a Gentile," have been removed. Those who are in Christ no longer refuse to eat and worship with Gentiles. When he said that there is "no longer Jew or Greek," he did not mean that Greeks who are in Christ lose their enriching genetic and sociological diversity.

Many sincere Christians of the American Bible Belt during the nineteenth century believed that slavery was an institution established

---

[1]Deut. 30:6; Jeremiah 4:4.
[2]Rom. 2:25.
[3]Rom. 2:28-29.
[4]Acts 15:1.
[5]Acts 15:10.
[6]Rom 2:14-6.
[7]Jn. 1:9.

by God to regulate the relationships between races. The issue seemed so vital that every major denomination split over the conflict.

The defenders of slavery were so sure that the Bible supported slavery that they attacked abolitionists for destroying the authority of the Bible. Senator William Smith of South Carolina said in 1820 that he would not be "astonished" to find that Northerners were attempting "a new version of the Old and New Testaments," a "new model . . . to suit the policy of the times." They would "throw off such parts as were uncongenial to their interests, and leave the residue to God."[1] An 1820 Richmond *Enquirer* article held that these "most mistaken and misguided people" were replacing the "religion of 1,819 years for the humanity of the moment." The author held that from the time of Diocletian to the present "a blow so heavy has not been inflicted on revealed religion."[2]

If we take the position that the Bible is inerrant in all its parts and that nothing is wrong which is approved by one or more biblical passages, biblically-based opposition to slavery is almost impossible. Slave owners believed that God initiated slavery in the inspired curse of Noah recorded in Genesis 9:20-27. Frederick Dalcho, an Episcopal clergyman, explained that this curse had to be divine in order for Noah to know the "future condition of his idolatrous and wicked posterity."[3] The other main defense of slavery cited the divine approval of slavery in Mosaic legislation. We have already noticed the command to subject conquered peoples to "forced labor."[4] The passage most frequently cited to show divine approval of slavery was Leviticus 25:44-46.

> As for the male and female slaves whom you may have, it is from the nations around you that you may acquire male and female slaves. You may also acquire them from among the aliens residing with you, and from their families that are with you, who have been born in your land; and they may be your property. You may keep them as a possession for you children after you, for them to inherit as property.

John C. Weems, a Maryland Congressman, claimed that this passage shows that God recognized the "right of [slave] property by purchase."[5] Some even found divine approval of slavery in the ten commandments. "You shall not covet your neighbor's house; you shall not covet your neighbor's wife, or male or female slave, or ox, or donkey, or anything that belongs to your neighbor."[6]

---

[1] Larry R. Morrison, "The Religious Defense of American Slavery Before 1830," *Journal of Religious Thought* 37.2 (Fall-Winter 1980-81): 25.
[2] *The Richmond Enquirer*, Jan. 8, 1820, qtd. Morrison 26.
[3] Morrison 17-8.
[4] Deut. 20:11.
[5] Morrison 19.
[6] Ex. 20:17.

The defenders of slavery were suffering from a faulty conception of the nature of biblical revelation. They did not realize that erroneous human tradition has in some cases crept into the Bible. When God reveals that slaves should receive kindly treatment, it is more appropriate to attribute the apparent approval of slavery to a cultural error than to the divine initiative.

Even though every explicit statement about the ownership of foreign slaves in the Bible tacitly approves of slavery, a more careful analysis of the underlying harmony of the Bible as a whole shows that slavery is against God's will. If the people of Israel became so impoverished that they wished to sell themselves, the buyer was told "You shall not make them serve as slaves."[1] Everyone recognized that slavery violated human dignity. They were also told, "You shall have one law for the alien and for the citizen."[2] If they had applied this principle of equal treatment of Israelites and foreigners, they would not have made any foreigners slaves. No one who loves her neighbor as herself and does to others what she would want them to do to her could hold another person as a slave.[3]

Because the defenders of slavery thought that God had initiated and approved of slavery, they thought that Paul's teaching that in Christ "there is no longer slave or free" was a soteriological teaching that should not be applied to social institutions in this life. They believed that pronouncing slavery contrary to God's will in opposition to explicit statements in the Bible which approve of slavery would destroy the authority of the Bible. It was difficult for them to recognize that using the underlying harmony of the Bible as a whole to correct cultural errors which had crept into the Bible would in fact strengthen the true authority of the Bible.

Early Sabbath-keeping Adventists adopted the abolitionist position of the North. Antislavery was so central to their commitment that it became a test of fellowship. A certain church member in Oswego County, NY, advocated taking no stand on the slavery issue. People often say that meddling in social issues like slavery will alienate potential recipients of the gospel. But Ellen White wrote to him, "Unless you undo what you have done, it will be the duty of God's people to publicly withdraw their sympathy and fellowship from you, in order to save the impression which must go out in regard to us as a people."[4]

A simple minded comparison of Ellen White's counsel with the surface approval of slavery in the Bible would lead to rejection of

[1]Lev. 25:39
[2]Lev. 24:22; cp. Ex. 12:49 and Num. 15:16.
[3]Matt. 22:39; 7:12.
[4]Ellen G. White, *Testimonies for the Church*, 9 vols. (Mountain View, CA: Pacific 1948) 1: 360.

her abolitionist view because it seemed contrary to prior revelation. A misguided conscientious appeal to what is explicitly stated on the surface in the Bible will sometimes obstruct constructive pluralism and renewal guided by the underlying harmony of the Bible as a whole. We should not, however, question the sincere biblical commitment of many of these slaveholders. Their willingness to die in battle for their cause indicates that their motive was not merely a love of ease and comfort. Their primary problem was a misunderstanding of the nature of revealed authority.

How could a true prophet like Paul make such an ethical mistake as to send Onesimus back to be the slave of the Christian Philemon? He knew that for those who are baptized into Christ "there is no longer slave or free."[1] Apparently God could not yet reveal to Paul that it was time to abolish slavery since new revelation could only be recognized as valid when it was seen to be consistent with prior revelation. If God is to preserve human freedom, divine revelation cannot correct positions contained in Scripture until the people become aware of the underlying harmony which forms the basis of testing the correction. A premature vision abolishing slavery would have been judged to be erroneous because of its inconsistency with what people thought the Bible taught. Although each sides should have respected the integrity of the other and avoided needless blood shed, the abolition of slavery was part of God's redemptive liberation of authentic humanness.

Why does the word "humanness" in this study sound a little strange to those of us who have for years divided theology into the doctrine of God, the doctrine of Christ, and the doctrine of man? The use of the word, *man* to refer to humanity is one of thousands of conscious and unconscious ways in which the dominance of males over females has permeated our language, thought, and behavior. The morning prayer thanking God for not having been made "a Gentile, a slave or a woman" in a backhanded way protests injustice. It says, I am so grateful that I am not treated unjustly as Gentiles, slaves, and women are.

We look back at the nineteenth-century biblical defenders of slavery with incredulity, wondering how they could be so blind to God's will. We would be more sympathetic if we looked at ourselves struggling over the role of women in Seventh-day Adventist ministry. On the surface the Bible contains powerful prohibitions of the participation of women in human institutions. The biblical principles which constitute the underlying harmony of the Bible as a whole on the role of women lie beneath the surface; and as we

[1] Gal. 3:28.

have noticed, Ellen White says, "It requires patience, thought, and prayer to trace out the precious golden thread."[1]

Those who cherish the Bible are quick to support efforts to defend its authority against erosion from the acids of skepticism in our culture. This wholesome desire to defend the Bible is often vulnerable to the idea that it is inerrant in all its parts. As we have seen, a commitment to verbal inerrancy makes it almost impossible to persuade people to give up such deeply entrenched sins as slavery if there are passages in the Bible which support the behavior.

There certainly are verses in the Bible which support the suppression of women. One of them is found in Paul's instruction to the church at Corinth. "As in all the churches of the saints, women should be silent in the churches. For they are not permitted to speak, but should be subordinate, as the law also says. If there is anything they desire to know, let them ask their husbands at home. For it is shameful for a woman to speak in church."[2]

The attempt to apply this counsel to a local problem generated by the pagan priestesses of Corinth is not persuasive. The verse says that women should be silent in "all the churches of the saints." Speaking in any way by asking a question in Sabbath School, making an announcement in church or offering prayer violates the requirement of this passage for women to be silent in the weekly worship service.

Another passage subordinates women not only in church but in the home and in all human relationships. "Let woman learn in silence with full submission. I permit no woman to teach or to have authority over a man; she is to keep silent. For Adam was formed first, then Eve; and Adam was not deceived, but the woman was deceived and became a transgressor."[3]

When we hire a more qualified woman as the principal of a school with men teachers, as the chair of a department or the president of a university; we act contrary to this passage. Should we reverse this policy? What does the underlying harmony of the Bible say about the role of women?

The first mention of female in contrast to male in the Bible establishes equality. "So God created humankind in his image, in the image of God he created them; male and female he created them."[4] The New Revised Standard Version more adequately than other versions translates the Hebrew word *adam* in this verse as "humankind." At this point in the biblical story *adam* is a generic noun referring to humanity and not yet a proper name. The application of

[1] White, *Messages* 1: 20.
[2] 1 Cor. 14:33-5
[3] 1 Tim. 2:11-4.
[4] Gen. 1:27.

*adam* to both male and female is even more obvious in Genesis 5:2 which says, "Male and female he created them, and he blessed them and named them *'adam'* when they were created." As the crowning act of creation God created woman and man together as equals. They were both equally made in the image of God.

Together they were assigned responsibility for and stewardship over the entire creation. "God blessed them, and God said to them, 'Be fruitful and multiply, and fill the earth and subdue it; and have dominion over the fish of the sea and over the birds of the air and over every living thing that moves upon the earth.'"[1] Their ecological "dominion," like God's, was to be benevolent, cherishing and protecting every part for the benefit of each part and of the whole.

The story of creation in the second chapter of Genesis contributes valuable supplementary understanding of humanness. When there were no plants, God "formed man out of the dust of the ground, and breathed into his nostrils the breath of life; and the man became a living being."[2] But this living male in isolation could not yet realize complete humanity. He needed a living environment for food, fragrance, beauty and the replenishment of oxygen, and so God created plants. But the living male in a vast empty arboretum was yet unable to realize complete humanity. "Then the LORD God said, 'It is not good that the man should be alone; I will make him a helper as his partner.' So out of the ground the LORD God formed every animal of the field and every bird of the air."[3] The animals were helpful but not yet a partner helper. So out of one of Adam's ribs God made a woman. The man said:

> This at last is bone of my bones
>    And flesh of my flesh;
> This one shall be called woman (*ishah*)
>    For out of Man (*ish*) this one was taken.

Perhaps we should not put too much emphasis on the chronological order of these creation events since the two stories differ in the sequence. The order of creation in the two chapters is as follows:

| Genesis 1 | Genesis 2 |
|---|---|
| Light | |
| Firmament | (Dry Land Assumed) |
| Dry Land and Plants | Male Humanity |
| Fish and Birds | Plants |
| Land Animals | Animals and Birds |
| Male and Female Humanity | Female Humanity |

If we combine the helpful insight of the second story with the first, we would say that, when God created humanity, God made Adam a helper appropriate for Eve and Eve a helper appropriate for

[1]Gen. 1:28.
[2]Gen. 2:7.
[3]Gen. 2:18-9.

Adam. It would be a serious mistake to argue that the order in these creation accounts establishes priority because in both stories dirt is created before humans and in the second story monkeys are created before woman. In the first story the highest priority is given to female and male humanity who in one pronouncement are created last.

As male and female they were different. There were anatomical, endocrinological, psychological, and cognitive differences. These differences contributed to their complementary helpfulness. Each needed the differences the other supplied. Equality in the expression of these differences is required in order to realize full humanity.

The Bible records the high value of spiritual gifts received by women. Joel spoke for Jaweh saying, "Then afterward I will pour out my spirit on all flesh; your sons and your daughters shall prophesy."[1] For Paul, "those who prophesy speak to the people for their upbuilding and encouragement and consolation."[2] Since he discussed how a woman wears her hair when prophesying and praying in church, it is clear that women were speaking for the edification of the churches with approval.[3]

When women exercised the gift of prophecy, they were exercising authority over men. In the Pauline list of spiritual gifts[4] prophecy takes precedence over pastors and teachers. A woman prophet, such as one of the daughters of Philip,[5] spoke with authority for men and women of the congregation and with authority for pastors and teachers. The prophet Deborah spoke with authority over Barak, the general of the Israelite army; and when Barak grew faint-hearted, she took over leadership of the army.[6] Recognizing the authority of women over men in this way is contrary to 1 Cor. 14:33-36 and 1 Timothy 2:11-14,[7] but it is consistent with the underlying harmony of the Bible as a whole on the proper role of women

Women prophets like Miriam,[8] Deborah,[1] Huldah,[2] and Anna[3] were encouraged to exercise their authority because no one should

[1] Joel 2:28, repeated in Acts 2:17.
[2] 1 Cor. 14:3.
[3] 1 Cor. 11:5.
[4] 1 Cor. 12:28 and Eph. 4:11.
[5] Acts 21:9.
[6] Judges 4 and 5.
[7] As with regard to slavery, there are many other passages which are not consistent with the underlying harmony of the Bible as a whole. Gen. 3:16; Ex. 20:17 (prohibition of coveting a wife but not a husband because only women are owned as property); Ex. 21:7-10 (contrast Deut. 15:17); Num. 30:3-14; Lev 12:2-5; Deut. 22:28-9; 1 Cor. 11:1-11; Eph. 5:22-4; Col. 3:18.
[8] Ex. 15:20-21.

reject divine spiritual gifts. The spiritual gifts include wisdom, knowledge, healing, forms of assistance, and forms of leadership, which God gives to women equally with men.[4] We thwart the divine purpose for our humanness when we refuse to allow women to exercise these gifts because of passages in the Bible which are clearly inconsistent with the underlying harmony of the Bible as a whole.

The assembled General Conference acted on the teaching of the Bible as a whole in 1990 when it affirmed the equality of men and women and recommended that women should be encouraged to enter into all phases of public ministry for which they have the spiritual gifts. It was a strange self-contradiction, however, when it also recommended that we should not affirm these gifts by officially recognizing them through ordination services and certificates. This action is analogous to asking a person to act as police officer without allowing her or him to wear a uniform and badge and carry police credentials.

The future understanding of humanness will liberate women from the oppression of structures of male dominance which have been produced by sin. We cripple humanity because we prevent the spiritual gifts of women from contributing to the good of the whole. Legislatures, board rooms, faculties and pulpits are languishing for want of women.

Those who vote for legislators and board members, those who sit on faculty search committees, and those who vote in constituency meetings most often do not intend to oppress women. With great sincerity they speak of male-female equality. The structures of oppression which thwart the contribution of women have so permeated society and culture that they feel like the divine design. They have been with us so long that, like slavery, they have crept into the Bible.

For eighteen hundred years we humans were almost blind to the implications of Paul's teaching that because we are all one in Christ Jesus, "there is no longer slave or free." How long will it take us to apply his teaching to the liberation of women? When we cling to oppressive structures, we defeat the divine design for humanness It is time for men and women to yield to God's gracious invitation to become equally helping partners in the eternally expanding enterprise of humanness.

[1] Judges 4:4-5
[2] 2 Kings 22:14.
[3] Luke 2:36.
[4] I Cor. 12:8-11, 27-8.

## 6

# Christ and Salvation

### Gary Chartier

The center of distinctively Christian belief is the twofold conviction that we encounter God in the story of Jesus of Nazareth and that God's self-disclosure in this story is a decisive element in God's response to the human predicament.

I want to suggest here that we consider understanding this twofold conviction in light of, and as an expression of, the belief that God is love. I propose that we begin by thinking about what would be needed to affirm belief in a clearly, recognizably loving God in the face of evil and suffering, noting, in particular, what we would need to say about the kind of divine action we might expect given that God's will is so often not done. I urge us to think about the sorts of models of understanding and discerning God's presence and activity in Jesus that might be compatible with a sensible way of understanding divine action given the need to affirm God's love despite the reality of evil and suffering.

I float the idea that a common Adventist picture of atonement, of "atonement by revelation," fits more naturally with divine love than does the popular alternative of penal substitution. I emphasize the importance of seeing God's love, like God's presence and activity, as inclusive and universal, and of understanding the spiritual status of people outside our community and the meaning of evangelistic mission in light of this recognition. And I suggest that, instead of affirming or rejecting the idea of universal salvation, often thought to be a concomitant of divine love, *in toto*, we recognize that salvation has multiple dimensions, some of which can be guaranteed by God's love but for some of which we may hope in the face of uncertainty.

## SOME POSSIBLE FUTURE DIRECTIONS FOR
## ADVENTIST CHRISTOLOGY

Both because freedom must be on center-stage if we are to confirm God's love in the face of evil and suffering and because love, and so God's love, seeks the willing response of the beloved, a concern with love means a concern with freedom. I want to explore some possible future directions for Adventist Christology by emphasizing this idea. I begin by spelling out reasons for seeing freedom as important before going on to consider what an emphasis on freedom might mean for our response to the problem of evil and suffering and what a credible account of divine action, one that takes freedom seriously, might suggest for our understanding of Jesus's identity and our knowledge of his identity and activity.

*The Importance of Freedom*

Freedom is a persistent Adventist concern. Adventists have stressed that God cherishes creaturely freedom, even though we sometimes use this freedom to make profoundly damaging and destructive mistakes.

We can see creaturely freedom—an essential element of which is robust contra-causal freedom of the will—as real and important for multiple, related reasons.[1] (*i*) It safeguards the authenticity of our relationships with God: real love is given and received freely; were we not free, our love for God would be the love of puppets. (*ii*) It is an essential element of our dignity and worth as genuinely *real* creatures. (Thus, for instance, Adventists have stressed the importance of religious liberty as an expression of this kind of regard for freedom.) (*iii*) It allows us to be created co-creators, exercising our freedom to help shape the world's future even as we freely engage with God. (*iv*) It is an essential element of any credible account believers in God might offer of the problem of evil and suffering in the world.

---

[1]See John Searle, *Rationality in Action* (Cambridge: Bradford-MIT 2001) 269-98; Carl Ginet, *On Action* (Cambridge: CUP 1989); David Ray Griffin, *Unsnarling the World-Knot: Consciousness, Freedom, and the Mind-Body Problem* (Berkeley: U of California P 1998); Thomas Pink, *Free Will: A Very Short Introduction* (Oxford: OUP 2004); Robert Kane, *The Significance of Free Will* (New York: OUP 1998); Austin Farrer, *The Freedom of the Will*, Gifford Lectures 1957 (London: Black 1958); Joseph Boyle, Jr., Germain Grisez, and Olaf Tollefsen, *Free Choice: A Self-Referential Argument* (Notre Dame, IN: U of Notre Dame P 1976); Richard Swinburne, *Mind, Brain, and Free Will* (Oxford: Clarendon-OUP 2013); John Thorp, *Free Will: A Defense against Neurophysiological Determinism* (London: Routledge 1980).

*Freedom and the Problem of Evil*

This problem features several inescapable dimensions. (*i*) Some people unreasonably—purposefully, knowingly, recklessly, or negligently—harm other creatures, sometimes bringing about great loss. Call this *moral evil.* (*ii*) People and other embodied sentients can suffer immensely when physical systems intersect with other physical systems in orderly ways that turn out to have destructive consequences for sentients (cancer or earthquakes or even misplaced banana peels). Call this *physical evil.* (*iii*) Even if good things can and sometimes do emerge from instances of moral or physical evil— heroism or courage may be fostered, for instance—these instances of evil remain genuine losses, genuine occasions for sorrow and regret. That good might or can be brought out of them doesn't make them OK, and so doesn't make intending them OK. Call this *genuine loss.*

Belief in God's love must mean that God does not will or intend the harms resulting from or inherently involved in moral or physical evil: to love a creature is not (whatever else it may or may not be) to will that creature harm. Thus, we can say: God does not will or intend much of what goes on in the world. God's will is very frequently not done in the world. If the assertion that God is in control means that each event that occurs in the world embodies God's will, then to affirm that God is love must be to affirm that God is not in control. Affirming the reality of creaturely freedom— the freedom of creatures to make choices that are inconsistent with God's purposes—and the integrity of natural processes—the fact that such processes function in regular ways even to the detriment of sentient creatures and so contrary to God's will for the good of those creatures—is an essential element of any plausible response to the problem of evil.

Christians (and other theists) can offer and have offered varying proposals regarding the reasons God does not act immediately— coercively, miraculously, in a manner not mediated in and through the free choices of creatures and orderly physical processes—to interfere with the exercise of creaturely freedom and the integrity of natural processes even when doing so might seem to have very good consequences. The proposals worth taking seriously can be classed as moral and metaphysical.

Both sorts of proposals take seriously the reality of evil and suffering and seek to square it with the love of God. Both are subject to serious philosophical and theological challenges, and I am not arguing here that either ought to be accepted. But we need some explanation for the fact that God's will is so persistently not done in the world, or some explanation for the fact that we don't have an explanation, if we are credibly to retain confidence in the reality and love of God in the face of evil and suffering.

(*i*) To say that the explanation of God's respect for the freedom of creatures and the integrity of physical processes is *moral* is to say that God *could* act immediately, unconstrainedly, in the world to stop an act with bad consequences, to stop the consequences, to interrupt a physical process with bad consequences, but that God has good reason not to do so. God's goodness, on this view, depends on God's non-interference. There will be different accounts of what God's good reasons for not acting immediately in the world might be. It might be argued simply that we are warranted in believing that God has such good reasons even if we have no idea what they are.[1] But a standard account might emphasize the inherent worth of creatures' freedom,[2] on the grounds I've already noted, and on the value of a regular, predictable, ordered physical

---

[1]See Daniel Howard-Snyder, ed., *The Evidential Argument from Evil* (Bloomington: Indiana UP 1996).

[2]An approach that emphasized the importance of freedom might well stress the freedom of non-human as well as human creatures. It certainly might emphasize the value of the freedom of at least some non-human animals. And it might also emphasize the freedom of non-human persons. These might include the super-human persons Christians and others have often referred to as angels and demons (on the latter, see, e.g., M. Scott Peck, *People of the Lie: The Hope for Healing Human Evil* [New York: Simon 1982] 182-211; M. Scott Peck, *Glimpses of the Devil: A Psychiatrist's Personal Accounts of Possession, Exorcism, and Redemption* [New York: Free 2005]; and, though it should probably be taken with a grain of salt, Malachi Martin, *Hostage to the Devil: The Possession and Exorcism of Five Contemporary Americans* [New York: Harper 1992]). However, the introduction of non-human persons into the mix doesn't fundamentally change the arguments: it is still necessary to explain God's non-interference with *their* freedom, and there is no reason to think God's reasons for respecting their freedom on a moral account of divine self-restraint in the face of evil would be different from the reasons for God's respecting *human* freedom. Similarly, the problem of suffering caused by physical systems would persist, since it seems as if earthquakes, tidal waves, diseases, and so forth can ordinarily be explained in light of the orderly operation of physical systems, so that reference to the activity of non-human persons in explaining them is superfluous. Still, experiences of encounter with non-human personal evil certainly give us reason to incorporate reference to super-human creatures in our response to the problem of evil and suffering. Adventists have often included God's respect for the freedom of non-human persons in attempts to understand the problem of evil and suffering under the umbrella of "the Great Controversy." But they are not alone in referring to non-human evil in this context: see, *e.g.*, Gregory A. Boyd, *Satan and the Problem of Evil: Constructing a Trinitarian Warfare Theodicy* (Downers Grove, IL: IVP 2001). Richard Rice offers some observations about this approach in his contribution to *The Future of Adventism* and in *Suffering and the Search for Meaning: Contemporary Responses to the Problem of Pain* (Downers Grove, IL: IVP 2014) 75-90.

cosmos as a backdrop to creaturely action, needed both for moral choice and for effective, responsible planning.[1]

Proponents of a moral explanation of the fact that God does not act immediately in the world will differ regarding the kinds of limits on divine action moral reasons constitute. (*a*) Proponents of a moral explanation who are advocates of a *uniformity* view will maintain that moral reasons rule out all immediate, coercive, miraculous divine action while allowing persuasive, providential divine action mediated in and through the free choices of creatures and orderly physical processes.[2] (*b*) Proponents of a moral explanation who are advocates of a *near-uniformity* view will maintain that such reasons are consistent not only with persuasive providence but also with rare instances of miraculous divine action.

Advocates of both views recognize that we persistently experience an orderly world not ordinarily interrupted by miracle. But they differ about whether recognizing the reality of suffering and the integrity of the physical world is congruent with the possibility that there might be *some* instances of immediate, coercive divine action.

(*ii*) To say that the explanation of God's respect for the freedom of creatures and the integrity of physical processes is *metaphysical* is to say that the freedom of creatures, including the non-personal micro-creatures that constitute the world all the way down to the subatomic level, is an inescapable feature of reality.[3] There could not, on this view, be a world distinct from God at all without freedom for creatures and integrity for natural processes.[4] Creation is thus likely to be creation out of chaos rather than creation out of noth-

[1]See, *e.g.,* Austin M. Farrer, *Love Almighty and Ills Unlimited*, Christian Faith Series (Garden City, NY: Doubleday 1961); Richard Swinburne, *Providence and the Problem of Evil* (Oxford: Clarendon-OUP 1998); Brian Hebblethwaite, *Evil, Suffering and Religion* (London: SPCK 2000); Nancey C. Murphy and George F. R. Ellis, *On the Moral Nature of the Universe: Theology, Cosmology, and Ethics* (Minneapolis: Fortress 1996); Keith Ward, *Divine Action* (London: Collins 1990).

[2]See, *e.g.*, Maurice F. Wiles, *God's Action in the World* (London: SCM 1986).Wiles seems to want to rule out not only non-persuasive divine action but, indeed, particular divine action of any sort.

[3]See, *e.g.*, David Ray Griffin, *God, Power, and Evil: A Process Theodicy* (Lanham, MD: UP of America 1991); David Ray Griffin, *Evil Revisited: Responses and Reconsiderations* (Albany: SUNY 1991).

[4]If divine goodness is, as I believe we should take it to be, necessary in a strong sense, then moral constraints on divine action will at the same time be metaphysical constraints. However, accepting *these* sorts of metaphysical constraints is compatible with embracing a mixed view of divine action, while the sorts of constraints on which I focus when talking about metaphysical constraints would seem to be compatible only with a view of divine action as fully persuasive. Thanks to David Larson for prompting me to make this point.

ing.[1] On this view, all divine action is persuasive, mediated in and through the choices of free creatures and the operation of orderly physical processes.

Proponents of a *metaphysical* explanation of the fact that God cannot at least ordinarily be expected to act immediately in the world to prevent, end, or remedy suffering and proponents of the uniformity variant of the moral explanation will take the same view as regards what can be expected in the world, as regards how God can be understood to act in the world, even though their deep explanations for why this is the case will differ. Their underlying philosophical views won't be the same; but their theology of providence, we might suggest, will be identical. We can call the position both views share a commitment to a *fully persuasive* account of divine action. Advocates of the near-uniformity variant of the moral explanation of the (on their view general but not complete) absence of immediate divine action can be said to embrace a *generally persuasive* or *mixed* view of divine action.

Advocates of mixed and fully persuasive accounts of divine action will agree about what to expect as regards God's activity in the world most of the time: both camps will anticipate persuasive rather than coercive divine action in the vast majority of instances.[2] But

---

[1]See, *e.g.*, Charles Hartshorne, *Omnipotence and Other Theological Mistakes* (Albany: SUNY 1984); David Ray Griffin, "Creation out of Nothing, Creation out of Chaos, and the Problem of Evil," *Encountering Evil: Live Options in Theodicy*, 2d ed., ed. Stephen T. Davis (Louisville, KY: Westminster/Knox 2001) 108-24. For a vigorous defense of creation *ex nihilo*, see, *e.g.*, Robert C. Neville, *God the Creator: On the Transcendence and Presence of God* (Chicago: U of Chicago P 1968).

[2]On providence and divine persuasion, in addition to the works already cited, see, *e.g.*, Austin Farrer, *Saving Belief: A Discussion of Essentials* (London: Hodder 1964); Austin Farrer, *Faith and Speculation: An Essay in Philosophical Theology* (London: Black 1967); Timothy Gorringe, *God's Theatre: A Theology of Providence* (London: SCM 1991); Diogenes Allen, *Christian Belief in a Postmodern World* (Louisville: Westminster/Knox 1989) 165-81; Arthur Peacocke, *Theology for a Scientific Age: Being and Becoming, Natural and Divine*, Signposts in Theology (Oxford: Blackwell 1990) 159-63; Arthur Peacocke, "God's Interaction with the World," *All That Is: A Naturalistic Faith for the Twenty-First Century*, ed. Philip Clayton (Minneapolis: Fortress 2007) 45-7; Thomas F. Tracy, ed., *The God who Acts: Philosophical and Theological Explorations* (University Park, PA: Pennsylvania State UP 1994); Langdon Gilkey, *Reaping the Whirlwind: A Christian Interpretation of History* (New York: Crossroad-Seabury 1976) 303-6; Brian Hebblethwaite and Edward Henderson, eds., *Divine Action: Studies Inspired by the Philosophical Theology of Austin Farrer* (Edinburgh: Clark 1990); Ward 119-69; Michael J. Langford, *Providence* (London: SCM 1981); Brian Hebblethwaite, "Providence and Divine Action," *Religious Studies* 14 (1978): 223-36; John Polkinghorne, *Science and Providence* (London: SPCK 1989); Vincent Brümmer, "Farrer, Wiles and the Causal Joint," *Modern Theology* 8.1 (Jan. 1992) 1-14; John R. Lucas, *Freedom and Grace* (London: SPCK 1976); John B. Cobb, Jr. "Natural Causality and Divine Action," *God's Activity in the World: The Contemporary Problem*, ed. Owen C. Thom-

advocates of the mixed view will suggest that some instances of immediate divine action can be expected, and that these instances will be consistent with God's reasons for generally avoiding immediate action. They will be consistent with these reasons, advocates of the mixed account will suggest, because of their especially great revelatory or salvific significance and because the manner of their occurrence need not disrupt the predictability of the physical world or hamper the free development of creatures.

Whether we embrace mixed or fully persuasive accounts of divine action, taking freedom seriously has significant consequences for how we think about Christ and salvation. With regard to how we think about Christ, an emphasis on freedom will affect both our ontology and our epistemology. With regard to how we think about salvation, this emphasis will affect our account of diverse religious experiences and traditions.

## Incarnation and Freedom

Christians speak of Jesus as God incarnate or as incarnating God. The idea of incarnation, of God enfleshed, is powerful and evocative, but it is also open-textured. To speak of incarnation is to say that we encounter God in and through our encounter with Jesus. But of course the meaning of this claim can be worked out in a variety of ways.

An *identity* understanding of incarnation says that the acts of the human being Jesus of Nazareth *just are* numerically identical with, the acts of God.[1] (This will be expressed in slightly different ways on different accounts of Trinitarian theology.) It's not just that they happen to coincide with God's intentions; if that were the case, they would be acts that cooperated with God's, but they wouldn't be God's own acts. On the identity view, Jesus's acts are God's own acts.[2] There could not be an act on the part of Jesus that was not al-

as, AAR Studies in Religion 31 (Chico, CA: Scholars 1983) 101-16 (reprinted from *Idealistic Studies* 3 [1973]: 307-22); Gordon Kaufman, "On the Meaning of 'Act of God'," Thomas 137-61; Gordon Kaufman, *Systematic Theology: A Historicist Perspective* (New York: Scribner 1968) 299-313; Philip Clayton, *God and Contemporary Science* (Edinburgh: Edinburgh UP 1997) 188-269.

[1]I owe this way of putting the matter to Owen C. Thomas. See, *e.g.*, Thomas's *Introduction to Theology*, 3d ed. (Harrisburg, PA: Morehouse 2002).

[2]For some well developed identity Christologies, see, *e.g.*, Lionel S. Thornton, *The Incarnate Lord: An Essay Concerning the Doctrine of the Incarnation in Its Relation to Organic Conceptions* (London: Longmans 1928); Stephen R. L. Clark, *God, Religion, and Reality* (London: SPCK 1998) 108, 116-9; Stephen R. L. Clark, *God's World and the Great Awakening*, Limits and Renewals 3 (Oxford: Clarendon-OUP 1991) 117-44; Brian Hebblethwaite, *The Essence of Christianity: A Fresh Look at the Nicene Creed* (London: SPCK 1996) 84-99; Keith Ward, *Religion and Revelation: A Theology of Revelation in the World's Religions* (Oxford: Clarendon-OUP 1994) 258-82; Wolfhart Pannenberg, *Systematic Theology*, 3 vols.,

so, at the same time, an act of God: that is simply what it means to speak of identity between God and the human being Jesus of Nazareth. And this means, in turn, that Jesus's acts must be understood to have been immediate divine acts. The alternative would be for them to have been mediated divine acts, divine acts occurring in and through free creaturely acts. But mediated divine acts (at minimum, those that involve mediation in and through the choices of creatures) are acts in which creatures who are other than God freely choose to respond to God's providential promptings in ways that to some significant degree realize God's purposes. The creatures who act in response to these promptings are free in relation to God, and so not identical with God. If the acts of Jesus were *mediated* divine acts, then there must have been an independent human subject capable of choosing whether or not at any moment to act in a manner consistent with God's intentions. And this opens up a gap between God and the human subject Jesus of Nazareth: the human mind of Jesus, on this view, would be not a sub-system of the divine mind,[1] but rather an independently existing center of action, and his human acts would have been free responses to God's inspiration, and so not simply God's own acts. In this case, the acts of Jesus in a given case were not necessarily the acts of God, and Jesus was not God incarnate in the sense implied by the identity view.

This means, in turn, that an identity Christology can be worked out only on a mixed view of divine action. For an identity Christology to be successful, at least some divine acts in the world—at minimum, the acts of Jesus—must be immediate divine acts, and only the mixed view allows for such acts.

An *inspiration* model of incarnation stresses the continuity between incarnation, God's presence in Jesus, and immanence, God's presence throughout the created world. Such a model sees incarnation as a particularly focused instance of God's universal presence and activity. On this kind of model, the acts of the human being Jesus of Nazareth are God's acts insofar as they reflect God's inten-

trans. Geoffrey Bromiley (Grand Rapids: Eerdmans 1989-93) 2: 277-396; Thomas V. Morris, *The Logic of God Incarnate* (Ithaca, NY: Cornell UP 1986); Thomas V. Morris, "The Metaphysics of God Incarnate," *Trinity, Incarnation, and Atonement: Philosophical and Theological Essays*, ed. Ronald J. Feenstra and Cornelius Plantinga, Jr., Library of Religious Philosophy 1 (Notre Dame, IN: U of Notre Dame P 1989) 110-27; Ronald J. Feenstra, "Reconsidering Kenotic Christology," Feenstra and Plantinga 128-52; David Brown, *The Divine Trinity* (London: Duckworth 1985) 219-39, 245-71; Richard Sturch, *The Word and the Christ: An Essay in Analytic Christology* (Oxford: Clarendon-OUP 1991); Daniel Helminiak, *The Same Jesus: A Contemporary Christology* (Chicago, IL: Loyola UP 1986); Richard Swinburne, *The Christian God* (Oxford: Clarendon-OUP 1994) 192-215; Adrian Thatcher, *Truly a Person, Truly God* (London: SPCK 1990).

[1] So Morris, *Logic*.

tions in a particularly clear and consistent way, perhaps, in particular, in a way that plays an especially vital role in achieving God's overall purposes in history.[1] God seeks to achieve divine purposes in and through every event in the creaturely world. And no event is completely opaque to God's intentions (even events wildly inconsistent with the divine will still feature existence, order, and so forth). But some events obviously embody God's intentions much more transparently and effectively than others. On an inspiration view of incarnation, Jesus's key choices can be seen as such events. On this sort of view, identity won't be an all-or-nothing matter, but, rather, a matter of degrees, and the consistency with Jesus reveals God's character and enacts God's intentions, the consistency with which Jesus responds to and carries forward God's persuasive providence, can allow us to claim identity between God and the human Jesus of Nazareth, even if less dramatically than the identity view.

So a mixed view of divine action is consistent with, though it does not entail, a view of incarnation as identity. (A Jewish, Muslim, Hindu, or Sikh theist, after all, might embrace a mixed view of divine action while not endorsing the identification of Jesus of Nazareth as God incarnate.) A view of divine action as persuasive could not be combined with a strict identity view. It would, however, be consistent with—though, again, it would not entail—a view of incarnation as inspiration. (Again, theists of various sorts could accept a persuasive view without also judging that the relevant considerations warranted an incarnational understanding of Jesus.) An inspiration Christology could be affirmed by a proponent of either a persuasive or a mixed view of divine activity in the world, while an identity Christology could be affirmed only by a proponent of a mixed view.

[1]See, *e.g.*, John Macquarrie, *Jesus Christ in Modern Thought* (London: SCM 1991); John Macquarrie, *Principles of Christian Theology*, 2d ed. (New York: Scribner 1977) 268-310; John B. Cobb, Jr., *Christ in a Pluralistic Age* (Philadelphia: Westminster 1975); David Ray Griffin, *A Process Christology* (Lanham, MD: UP of America 1990); Karl Rahner, *Foundations of Christian Faith: An Introduction to the Idea of Christianity* (New York: Crossroad 1978) 176-321; Edward Farley, *Divine Empathy: A Theology of God* (Minneapolis: Fortress 1996) 278-85; Arthur Peacocke, "Jesus the Christ—A Naturalistic 'Incarnation'?," *All* 36-41. I think D. M. Baillie, *God Was in Christ: An Essay on Incarnation and Atonement* (London: Faber 1961) 106-32, is reasonably described as articulating the same position as, for instance, Rahner and Macquarrie; see, *e.g.*, John Hick, "The Christology of D. M. Baillie," *Scottish Journal of Theology* 11.1 (1958): 1-12. A complicating factor, however, is that Baillie, as a Calvinist, was not committed in an unequivocal way to belief in human freedom, and this might be thought to reduce the tension between an inspiration and an identity view of incarnation.

*Differing Accounts of Incarnation and Jesus's Human Knowledge*

Human minds are not omniscient, so the human mind of Jesus of Nazareth wouldn't have been omniscient. Both the identity and the inspiration views of incarnation are quite compatible with the recognition that Jesus was immersed in a particular historical setting, that his knowledge, experience, and understanding were those of a first-century Jew. To affirm the reality of divine action in the world, even, as on the mixed view, immediate divine action, is not to suggest that Jesus should be ripped from his historical context. To acknowledge the reality and importance of that context is a crucial aspect of seeing Jesus as truly human.

On a fully persuasive account of divine providence, of course, God's means of shaping Jesus's understanding and action will be, precisely, the same means of persuasive action through which God engages with the world generally. God inspires, on this view. And God does so in and through all of the actions and events of the creaturely world. But even on a mixed view, persuasive action will ordinarily be the way God does everything, and it is likely, therefore, that this will be the way God provides the human Jesus of Nazareth with information. To provide him with information in ways unlike those in which it is provided to other creaturely persons would not be impossible, of course, on a mixed view of divine action. At any rate, though, the philosophical reasons we might have for regarding immediate divine action as rare on a mixed view would be relevant here, as would whatever theological reasons we might have for seeing Jesus's authentic humanity as important, since bypassing ordinary means of knowing would call that humanity into question.

Thus, Austin Farrer, who unequivocally endorses an identity Christology, observes that "[t]he paradigm [of mediated divine action in the world] is Christ's ability to play his part, with a mental furniture acquired from his village rabbi."[1] Or, as Farrer notes elsewhere while expounding Chalcedonian orthodoxy:

> Christ is very God, indeed, but also very man, and an omniscient being who knows all the answers before he thinks and all the future before he acts is not a man at all, he has escaped the human predicament. And . . . how can a person who knows his unique metaphysical status with more than Aristotelian exactitude be a largely self-taught Galilean village boy whose store of ideas derived from the synagogue? How, moreover, can he be tempted at all times like as we are, or fight a lifelong battle of faith, and suffer seeming dereliction on the cross?
> On the other hand, he *knows how* to be Son of God in the several situations of his gradually unfolding destiny, and in the way appropriate to each.

[1]Farrer, *Faith* 103.

> . . . God the Son on earth is a fullness of holy life within the limit of
> mortality . . . .[1]

And we may note, with Karl Rahner, not only that we have
general theological reasons for positing Jesus's authentic humanity
but also that

> the difference between the human self-consciousness and God, which
> forbids us to understand this human self-consciousness as a double of the
> divine consciousness, is shown by the fact that during his public life Je-
> sus first had to learn (here as always we are talking about the objectified
> and verbalized consciousness of Jesus) that because of the hardness of
> heart of his listeners the kingdom of God did not come in the way that
> he had thought it would at the beginning of his preaching.[2]

## Freedom and Differing Accounts of Jesus's Sinlessness

Whether we opt for an identity or an inspiration account of incarnation will affect what we mean when we talk about Jesus's sinlessness.

God could not be other than morally good.[3] It seems likely,
then, that on an identity account, according to which the acts of
the human Jesus of Nazareth are, at the same time, numerically
identical with the acts of God, any act of the human Jesus of Nazareth will also be morally good (otherwise the act wouldn't also be
an act of God). An act under given circumstances can be morally
good, of course, without being the act that an omniscient person
would have chosen under those circumstances. But affirming the
identity of Jesus's acts with the acts of God means that Jesus will not
and could not have yielded to any internal or external temptation.
On the identity view, sinlessness will equal moral flawlessness. Otherwise, it would have been possible at any given moment for some
act of Jesus not to have been good, and so not God's act, and so it
would have been possible at any given moment for Jesus not to
have been God incarnate, despite having been God incarnate all
along up until that point.

This idea seems troubling for at least two reasons: (i) It makes
Jesus's identity as God incarnate a contingent matter from moment

---

[1]Austin Farrer, "Very God and Very Man," *Interpretation and Belief*, ed.
Charles C. Conti (London: SPCK 1976) 135.

[2]Rahner, *Foundations* 249. Rahner is, I think, attempting faithfully to express a
Chalcedonian view here even if (as it seems to me) what he ultimately articulates
is better understood as a kind of Nestorian view—featuring an understanding of
incarnation as inspiration—than as an understanding of incarnation as identity.

[3]See Keith Ward, *Religion and Creation* (Oxford: Clarendon-OUP 1996) 215-
9; Keith Ward, *Rational Theology and the Creativity of God* (Oxford: Blackwell
1982) 135; Richard Swinburne, *The Existence of God*, rev. ed. (Oxford: Clarendon-OUP 1991) 179-83; Robert Merrihew Adams, *Finite and Infinite Goods: A
Framework for Ethics* (New York: OUP 1999) 175-6; David Braine, *The Reality of
Time and the Existence of God: The Project of Proving God's Existence* (Oxford: Clarendon-OUP 1988) 320-32.

to moment, when identity in the relevant sense seems much more robust than that. If I am Gary Chartier at $t_1$, then I will also be Gary Chartier at $t_2$. So it would seem odd (even if not impossible) to suppose that Jesus could be God incarnate at $t_1$ and then cease to be God incarnate at $t_2$. (ii) The notion that Jesus could have made a wrong moral choice at any moment and so ceased to be God incarnate (as this idea is understood on an identity view) seems inconsistent with the idea that it is his being God incarnate that *explains* his moral flawlessness.

This is an idea that those who affirm a view of incarnation as identity should embrace. For it strains credulity to suppose that it is a matter of coincidence that the same person is *both* morally flawless *and* God incarnate, but independently so. And presumably most Christians over time who have affirmed Jesus's sinlessness as moral flawlessness have done so precisely because of their embrace of an identity account of incarnation. Humans sin; and Jesus was human, subject to the internal and external pressures that are endemic to humanity generally.[1] Obviously, none of us has observed all of his public acts, much less his private, inner choices. Clearly, belief in Jesus's sinlessness understood as moral flawlessness could not have persisted if the church's memory of him included moral lapses. But theological argument is needed to fill in the gaps. An identity understanding of incarnation provides good reason to think that Jesus's choices were morally flawless,[2] while, without such an understanding, this view seems to lack support.

On the inspiration view, the factors that dispose the human Jesus of Nazareth to ignore or resist temptation will be, in principle, the same sorts of factors that dispose us to ignore or resist temptation, though of course the inspiration view of incarnation can take on board the recognition that particular persons may be more resistant to temptation to others. Divine identity will provide no safeguards or guarantees in Jesus's case, just as miraculous divine action doesn't provide any safeguards or guarantees in the case of any of us. Jesus must freely choose from moment to moment to do what's right. This sort of view will lend itself to an account of sinlessness as fidelity to vocation: Jesus does not deviate from the big-picture task of revealing God's will for Israel, founding the church, and so forth,

---

[1] Some Adventist proponents of an identity view of incarnation have suggested that Jesus, while genuinely free to sin, was born entirely without the taint of original sin, and so lacked any inclination to sin. But of course the disposition to do wrong reflects a range of internal pressures, some of which aren't moral at all and are features of ordinary humanness, and external factors; and these internal pressures and external factors would have been salient even in the absence of any inner prompting to do evil as such.

[2] Cp. Brown, *Trinity* 114-9.

and this is what we will mean (on the inspiration view) when we talk about him as sinless.[1]

*Freedom and Our Knowledge of Jesus's History*

On a mixed view of divine action in the world, the vast majority of divine acts will be persuasive rather than coercive. On a fully persuasive view, all divine acts will be persuasive rather than coercive. This means that proponents of both sorts of views of divine action will have reason to expect divine action to be persuasive. And this means, in turn, that they will have reason to expect God's self-communication to creatures, in particular, to be persuasive rather than coercive. This means that we should understand God to act in and through the acts of creatures who are free, but also finite and fallible and, when morally responsible, sinful. A satisfactory response to the problem of evil will not exempt divine self-communication from the constraints that make it the case in general that God's will is persistently not done perfectly in the world.[2]

Thus, to affirm that God seeks to ensure that people will know and appreciate the story of Jesus does not mean that God can be expected to miraculously insulate those who first remembered that story, those who wrote about it, and those who transmitted their texts from the effects of human finitude, fallibility, and sin, or otherwise to *guarantee* their infallibility. But God is perfectly capable of conveying important insights through fallible media.[3]

This means, in turn, that there will be no alternative to doing the hard work, the historical and textual work, required to understand the first-century historical figure of Jesus of Nazareth. Such work will include historiography and archæology and anthropology, studying classical literature, examining the relationships between the texts of the various Gospels. There will be no short-cut to care-

---

[1]Macquarrie, *Christ* 397-8, seems to offer a variant of this view. It is not entirely clear how best to read Wolfhart Pannenberg, *Jesus: God and Man*, trans. Duane A. Priebe (Philadelphia: Westminster 1967) 354-64, but Pannenberg might be seen here as defending a kind of vocational account of Jesus's sinlessness, in which what qualifies Jesus as sinless is his ultimate fidelity to his vocation.

[2]See, *e.g.*, David Basinger and Randall Basinger, "Inerrancy, Dictation, and the Free Will Defense," *Evangelical Quarterly* 55.3 (July 1983): 177-80; David Basinger, "Inerrancy and Free Will: Some Further Thoughts," *Evangelical Quarterly* 58.4 (Oct. 1985): 351-4.

[3]See, *e.g.*, Austin Farrer, "Infallibility and Historical Revelation," *Interpretation* 151-64; William J. Abraham, *The Divine Inspiration of Holy Scripture* (Oxford: OUP 1981); John Barton, *People of the Book? The Bible in Christianity* (London: SPCK 1988); David Brown, "God and Symbolic Action," Hebblethwaite and Henderson; L. William Countryman, *Biblical Authority or Biblical Tyranny?* (Cambridge, MA: Cowley 1994); Austin Farrer, *The Glass of Vision*, Bampton Lectures 1948 (London: Dacre 1948); Keith Ward, *The Word of God? The Bible after Modern Scholarship* (London: SPCK 2010).

ful historical investigation. To affirm *incarnation* is to affirm the presence and activity of God in, not outside, history. To affirm the authentic humanness of Jesus is to affirm the appropriateness and inescapability of historical inquiry. We will thus have reason to share Austin Farrer's judgment: "It is my special concern, as a re-formed Christian, to emphasize the necessity of a constant overhaul of dogmatic development by the standard of Christian origins; and 'Christian origins' can only mean in practice the *evidence we have for* Christian origins, and they come down pretty nearly to the New Testament writings, and the primitive sacramental usages."[1] No doubt we have some other sources of historical insight into the first-century world of Jesus; but the point remains that we must continually subject our doctrinal formulations to the test of history, while continuing to be very much aware of the limits of our histor-ical understanding.

To be clear, this need not, should not mean a kind of historical inquiry which begins with the assumption that God is *not* present and active in history—some sort of methodological atheism or methodological deism. But we also cannot begin with the assump-tion that any particular belief about God's activity in history must be correct. Rather, we must seek as carefully and thoughtfully as we can to learn what actually happened in history. We need not ignore the Christian community's collective memory, or the theo-logical appeal of particular interpretations of ambiguous data, or rel-evant *a priori* considerations. But we must be scrupulously faithful to the facts as far as we can ascertain them. And we must be willing to look critically at our own historical assumptions and judgments about the historical figure of Jesus, as at those we make about other matters.

*Discerning God Incarnate in and through Fallible Media*

Recognizing that God can communicate with us through finite, fallible, sinful human beings means that no doctrinal formulation is likely to come to us with a divine stamp of approval. This is true of developed church teaching about Jesus, as it emerged in the Apos-tles', Nicene, and Chalcedonian Creeds. And it is true of the pre-creedal theological understandings of Jesus articulated in the New Testament and in the writings of early post-New Testament Chris-tian intellectuals, as also of the earliest narrative accounts of what Jesus did and underwent. The point is not to dismiss any of these sources, to see God as absent from them. It is simply to recognize that God's communication with us is mediated communication, and that the fact that God seeks to communicate with us through church teachings and through the Bible does not eliminate the need

---

[1] Farrer, "Infallibility" 158.

for us to try to understand what really happened in first-century Palestine and what sorts of doctrinal formulations the relevant history will support. Though theology can figure in our reading of history, we must be willing, to allow historical inquiry to play an integral role in assessing our theological claims, too.

It won't work, then, to appeal to authority when arguing for a particular understanding of Jesus. But there are multiple, sometimes complementary, approaches, we *can* use, including ones that appeal in multiple ways to Jesus's history.[1] I won't try to spell any of these approaches out in detail, or to evaluate them, but I want at least to outline them and note their availability.

(*i*) We can focus on the "high consciousness" of Jesus. Historical evidence certainly seems to suggest that, even if the human Jesus of Nazareth wouldn't have been inclined to articulate a developed incarnational account of his own identity, he spoke reflexively with a remarkable kind authority.[2] And we might judge that Jesus's claim

---

[1]On history and Christology, see, *e.g.*, James D. G. Dunn, *Christology in the Making: A New Testament Inquiry into the Origins of the Doctrine of the Incarnation*, 2d. ed. (Grand Rapids: Eerdmans 1996) 253-4; Bruce Vawter, *This Man Jesus* (Garden City, NY: Doubleday 1973); Larry W. Hurtado, *Lord Jesus Christ: Devotion to Jesus in Earliest Christianity* (Grand Rapids: Eerdmans 2005); Richard J. Bauckham, *God Crucified: Monotheism and Christology in the New Testament* (Grand Rapids: Eerdmans 1999); Richard J. Bauckham, *Jesus and the Eyewitnesses: The Gospels as Eyewitness Testimony* (Grand Rapids: Eerdmans 2006); Murray J. Harris, *Jesus as God: The New Testament Use of* Theos *in Reference to Jesus* (Grand Rapids: Baker 1992); Oscar Cullmann, *The Christology of the New Testament*, trans. Shirley C. Guthrie and Charles A. M. Hall, rev. ed. (Philadelphia: Westminster 1963) Raymond E. Brown, *Jesus: God and Man* (New York: Macmillan 1967) 1-38; J. C. Fenton, "Matthew and the Divinity of Jesus," *Studia Biblica* 1978, ed. Elizabeth A. Livingstone, *JSOT* Supp. Ser. 11 (Sheffield: Sheffield 1980); James D. G. Dunn, *The Christ and the Spirit* 1: *Christology* (Grand Rapids: Eerdmans 1998); Turner; Christopher Rowland, *Christian Origins: From Messianic Movement to Christian Religion* (Minneapolis: Augsburg 1985) 174-87; Martin Hengel, "The Son of God," *The Cross of the Son of God* (London: SCM 1986); C. F. D. Moule, *The Phenomenon of the New Testament: An Inquiry into the Implications of Certain Features of the New Testament*, Studies in Biblical Theology—2d. ser., 1 (Naperville, IL: Allenson 1967); C. F. D. Moule, *The Origin of Christology* (Cambridge: CUP 1977); Eduard Schweizer, *Lordship and Discipleship*, Studies in Biblical Theology (Naperville, IL: Allenson 1960) 56-60.

[2]See, *e.g.*, David Abernathy, *Understanding the Teaching of Jesus* (New York: Seabury 1983) 155-67; E. P. Sanders, *The Historical Figure of Jesus* (London: Lane-Penguin 1993) 236, 238, 248; Joachim Jeremias, *New Testament Theology: The Proclamation of Jesus*, trans. John Bowden (New York: Scribner 1971) 249-55; Ben F. Meyer, *The Aims of Jesus* (London: SCM 1979) 152; Raymond E. Brown, *An Introduction to New Testament Christology* (New York: Paulist 1994) 70-89; Marinus de Jonge, *Jesus, the Servant Messiah* (New Haven: Yale UP 1991) 68-72; Reginald H. Fuller, "The Clue to Jesus' Self-Understanding," *Christ and Christianity: Studies in the Formation of Christology*, comp., ed., and intro. Robert Kahl (Valley Forge, PA: TPI 1994) 37-46; Ben Witherington, *The Christology of Jesus* (Minneapolis: Augsburg/Fortress 1990) 51-3, 55, 222-3, 227, 232-3, 248, 274-5; Seeyoon Kim, "The

to authority left us with no choice to regard him as simply a good man—that he must either truly *be* entitled to this authority or else prove to be a charlatan, a mad-man, or a fool.[1]

(*ii*) We might begin with the robust evidence that Jesus's disciples really did encounter him alive after his death.[2] A *fully persuasive* account of divine action, ruling out, of course, a miraculous understanding of these encounters, might judge that they were evidence of Jesus's spiritual distinctiveness (since ordinary people are not encountered postmortem as Jesus was).[3] A *mixed* view that treated the evidence of the appearances and the empty tomb as evidences of an immediate divine act, a *miracle*, might well see the miracle as placing a divine *imprimatur* on the career of Jesus, *including his distinctive claim to authority*.

(*iii*) The narratives of Jesus's postmortem appearances, and the early Christian theological reflection on Jesus's identity we find in the New Testament, suggest that Jesus was experienced, when encountered by his disciples after his death, as *exalted*, as *worthy of worship*. And this quality of the experiences might, for proponents of a

'Son of Man'" as the Son of God (Grand Rapids: Eerdmans 1985); Richard Bauckham, "The Sonship of the Historical Jesus in Christology," *Scottish Journal of Theology* 31 (1978): 245-60; I. Howard Marshall, "The Divine Sonship of Jesus," *Interpretation* 21.1 (Jan. 1967): 87-103; Robert H. Stein, *The Method and Message of Jesus' Teachings* (Philadelphia: Westminster 1978) 127-32; Eduard Schweizer, *Jesus Christ—The Man from Nazareth and the Exalted Lord*, ed. Hulitt Gloer (London: SCM 1987); John Riches, *Jesus and the Transformation of Judaism* (New York: Seabury 1982) 188.

[1]This argument has received contemporary currency through the work of C. S. Lewis; see *Mere Christianity* (New York: Macmillan 1952) 55-6. Cp. Richard Sturch, "Can One Say 'Jesus is God'?," *Christ the Lord: Studies in Christology Presented to Donald Guthrie*, ed. Harold Rowden (Leicester: IVP 1982) 337; Charles Gore, *The Incarnation of the Son of God* (London: Murray 1896) 238. Gore attributes the argument to Victorinus Afer, writing against Candidus the Arian.

[2]Pannenberg, *Jesus* 88-105; Gerald O'Collins, *The Easter Jesus* (London: Darton 1980); Gerald O'Collins, *Jesus Risen: An Historical, Fundamental, and Systematic Examination of Christ's Resurrection* (New York: Paulist 1987); David Brown, *The Divine Trinity* (London: Duckworth 1985) 126-45; Vawter 33-51; Pheme Perkins, *Resurrection: New Testament Witness and Contemporary Reflection* (Garden City, NY: Doubleday 1984); Ethelbert Stauffer, *Jesus and His Story*, trans. Richard and Clara Winston (New York: Knopf 1967) 143-53; John C. O'Neill, "On the Resurrection as an Historical Question," *Christ, Faith and History: Cambridge Studies in Christology*, ed. Stephen Sykes and John P. Clayton (Cambridge: CUP 1971) 205-19; William Lane Craig, *The Historical Argument for the Resurrection of Jesus during the Deist Controversy*, Texts and Studies in Religion 23 (Lewistown, NY: Mellen 1985) 528-46; N. T. Wright, *The Resurrection of the Son of God*, Christian Origins and the Question of God 3 (London: SPCK 2003); William Lane Craig, *Assessing the New Testament Evidence for the Historicity of the Resurrection of Jesus*, Studies in the Bible and Early Christianity 16 (Lewiston, NY: Mellen 1989).

[3]Cp. John A. T. Robinson, *The Human Face of God* (London: SCM; Philadelphia: Westminster 1973) 138-40; Chögyam Trungpa, *Born in Tibet* (London: Allen 1966) 95 (cited by Robinson).

mixed view, be seen as vouchsafed by the miraculous nature of the experiences, and so used correctly to understand Jesus's premortem life.[1]

(*iv*) While one might, then, think of the specific content of Jesus's resurrection appearances as validating his claims about himself, as in (*ii*), or as justifying the understanding of Jesus as God incarnate by disclosing Jesus as exalted and worthy of worship after death, as in (*iii*), one might also think premortem and postmortem characteristics together in a related but slightly different way, judging that (*a*) the evidence we have for Jesus's high consciousness premortem makes it more likely than would otherwise be the case that his ministry might be endorsed as revelatory by a divine miracle, (*b*) the evidence we have for Jesus's being encountered alive postmortem makes it more likely than would otherwise be the case that he was the sort of person who would have engaged in a revelatory ministry including claims of authority, and that therefore (*c*) the independent evidence we have for *both* a high consciousness premortem *and* what, on a mixed view, we might read as a miracle postmortem tend to reinforce each other, with both more likely together than either would be separately, and both taken together providing especially robust support for understanding Jesus as God incarnate.[2]

(*v*) We might, alternatively, begin with the interpretation of Jesus as God incarnate which in some cases we may simply adopt on say-so, perhaps because we have been taught to read the events of Jesus's life in this way.[3] We might treat this way of looking at things as a presumption—no doubt a rebuttable one, but one with which we can begin, continuing to retain it because we can see plausible responses to the challenges it confronts.

(*vi*) We might embrace an incarnational understanding of Jesus on the basis that it is both attractive and illuminating in multiple respects.[4]

[1] The best defense of this view is Brown, *Trinity* 101-58.

[2] For this argument, see Richard Swinburne, *The Resurrection of God Incarnate* (Oxford: Clarendon-OUP 2003); Richard Swinburne, *Was Jesus God?* (New York: OUP 2008) 114-27. I assess *The Resurrection of God Incarnate* in Gary Chartier, ["Reason and the Resurrection,"] *Conversations in Religion and Theology* 2.1 (May 2004): 11-28.

[3] See, *e.g.*, Morris, *Logic* 201-2. Cp. John Knox, *Christ the Lord: The Meaning of Jesus in the Early Church* (Chicago: Willett 1945) 1-56; Rahner 230-2; Peter Hinchliff, "Christology and Tradition," *God Incarnate: Story and Belief*, ed. A. E. Harvey (London: SPCK 1981).

[4] See, *e.g.*, Brian Hebblethwaite, "The Appeal to Experience in Christology," Sykes and Clayton 268-75; Brian Hebblethwaite, *In Defence of Christianity* (Oxford: OUP 2005) 110-22; Brian Hebblethwaite, "The Moral and Religious Value of the Incarnation," *The Incarnation: Collected Essays in Christology* (Cambridge: CUP 1987) 27-44; Ward, *Religion* 242; John Milbank, *The Word Made Strange: Theology, Language, Culture* (Oxford: Blackwell 1997) 145-68; Ronald F.

None of these approaches offers a knock-down, drag-out proof. There is, unavoidably, risk involved in embracing and acting on belief in incarnation, or any other aspect of Christian doctrine. In the ambiguous circumstances in which we unavoidably find ourselves, however, we must make choices, and it is perfectly reasonable for us to do so in light of the considerations available to us.[1]

## SOME POSSIBLE FUTURE DIRECTIONS FOR ADVENTIST SOTERIOLOGY

Many Christian views of salvation seem to fly in the face of the conviction that God is love. If we are to regard that conviction as the central element of Christian belief and life, we should shape our understandings of salvation accordingly. I want to focus here on three issues related to the nature of salvation. I will argue against the idea of atonement as penal substitution and in favor of a much more comprehensive and less problematic notion of atonement. I will suggest that evangelistic mission is good for lots of things, but not for saving people (in the sense of ensuring their embrace by divine love). and I will argue that, while we may hope for universal salvation, we should not regard it as guaranteed.

### Atonement and Divine Love

One common Christian view of *atonement*—of what God does to ensure right relations between God and God's personal creatures—maintains that salvation means deliverance from divine judgment. On this view, making bad choices renders people liable to everlasting punishment—on the standard Adventist view, therefore, to everlasting death. But people can escape liability to everlasting punishment and come to enjoy blissful life after death with God because God visits the punishment to which they ought to be subjected on God incarnate—on the crucified Jesus—rather than on them. Those who appropriate this graciously offered substitution by faith will receive everlasting life. Because this view involves the idea of judicial punishment assumed on our behalf by God incarnate, it is sometimes labeled the *penal substitution* view.

The idea of penal substitution has come in some Christian circles to be so closely associated with accounts of atonement that in

Thiemann, *Revelation and Theology: The Gospel as Narrated Promise* (Notre Dame, IN: U of Notre Dame P 1985); Hans Frei, *The Identity of Jesus Christ: The Hermeneutic Basis of Dogmatic Theology* (Philadelphia: Fortress 1975).

[1]See, *e.g.*, Rahner, *Foundations* 228-46; Joseph Runzo, *Reason, Relativism and God* (New York: St. Martin's 1986) 222; Gerald O'Collins, *Fundamental Theology* (New York: Paulist 1981) 158-9; Robert C. Roberts, *Faith, Reason, and History: Rethinking Kierkegaard's* Philosophical Fragments (Macon, GA: Mercer UP 1986) 140-3; Ward, *Religion* 232-58.

popular parlance "atone" is often treated as synonymous with "provide expiation." "Atonement" and "substitutionary atonement" are understood as effectively synonymous. But of course etymologically "atonement" is "at-one-ment," making one, the creation of community. And the fostering of community between God and created persons is not best understood through the lens of substitution, especially penal substitution.

There are two insurmountable problems with the idea of penal substitution. The first is that it is essentially retributive: it assumes that wrongdoing renders one liable to retributive punishment. And the idea of retributive punishment is, simply put, a bad idea. If I harm you, it makes sense to expect me to take responsibility for *remedying* the harm, for doing what I can for you to heal the damage I have done. But the idea of retribution assumes that, when I suffer retributively because I have injured you, I somehow do something *for you*: my suffering causes or constitutes a benefit to you (or, even less plausibly, to myself). The problem is that it doesn't do any such thing. As the wise old saying goes, "An eye for an eye makes the whole world blind." Punishing me, injuring me because I have harmed you, introduces a *new* bad thing, the harm to me, into the world. But it does not eliminate or reduce the bad thing I have done to you. When I have harmed you, rectifying the situation requires compensation and, where possible, reconciliation; doubtless, it would be a good thing, for me and for others, if I underwent rehabilitation of some kind, too. But there is no value in, no benefit conferred by, retribution. Retribution is itself an evil, as we are reminded by the challenge to the eye-for-an-eye principle recorded in the Sermon on the Mount.

So the substitutionary view is problematic because it presupposes that the human problem, or at least *a* key human problem, is liability to retributive punishment. Retributive punishment is a nonstarter, since it does nothing to improve the world or to deal satisfactorily with the harms that are supposed to occasion it.[1]

The substitutionary view of atonement is caught in even more tangles, though, because, having begun with the morally deficient notion of retribution, it then goes on to propose that retributive

[1]Vernon White explains various difficulties with the notion of retribution in *Incarnation and Atonement: An Essay in Universalism and Particularity* (Cambridge: CUP 1991) 91-106. I have criticized the idea of retribution in multiple contexts: see (in a theological context, with a focus on penal substitution) Gary Chartier, *The Analogy of Love: Divine and Human Love at the Center of Christian Theology* (Exeter: Imprint Academic 2007) 213-6; (in a pastoral context) Gary Chartier, "Farewell to Retribution," *Vulnerability and Community: Meditations on the Spiritual Life* (Ann Arbor, MI: Griffin 2015) 44-7; and (in a legal and philosophical context) Gary Chartier, *Anarchy and Legal Order: Law and Politics for a Stateless Society* (Cambridge: CUP 2012).

punishment can reasonably be *substituted*. If you think, however, that people *deserve* punishment for their wrongdoing, it is hard to see how justice is or could be served by subjecting *someone else* to the punishment they deserve. If *we* deserve retributive punishment, then it doesn't effect the good that retribution is supposed to effect to punish *anyone else*. Substituted punishment doesn't accomplish what retribution is supposed to achieve.

Someone might attempt to salvage the substitutionary view by suggesting that God is the ultimate object of wrongdoing and can therefore choose to forgive it. Of course, if this were so, God could simply forgive without any recourse to substitution. God wouldn't need any *entitlement* to forgive, any more than we do (and, of course, in the Newer Testament Jesus simply urges us to forgive, without any reference to any sort of special entitlement). Proponents of the "governmental" variant on the substitutionary view of atonement, a variant associated with the great legal theorist Hugo Grotius, might say that God needs to visit punishment on *someone* while forgiving in order not to appear to ignore wrongdoing or treat it lightly. But this framing of the issue still assumes what I think we should reject—the retributive assumption that wrongdoing merits *punishment*.

As regards the claim that God is the ultimate object of wrongdoing: God suffers when we harm ourselves or others.[1] And the existential structure of our wrongdoing is such that, when we do wrong, we often or always treat ourselves or some other aspect of the creation as absolute when it's actually relative, and so as an idol, as a substitute God. In addition, we may do wrong because we are not property grounded in an (implicit or explicit) awareness of God's love. So our relation to God matters as regards our wrongdoing in multiple ways. But doing wrong isn't a matter of violating some arbitrary divine edict which God, as a sort of law-maker, would be free to forgive. Doing wrong is a matter of unreasonably harming ourselves or other sentient creatures.[2] Whether something is wrong is a function of the way in which God has made us and made other creatures. Either our choices have unreasonably harmed others or ourselves or they haven't. As Will Campbell sums up the gospel in *Brother to a Dragonfly*, "We're all bastards, but God loves us anyway." But that love doesn't cancel or ignore or render irrelevant the harms we do to others. God loves us anyway because love is who God *is*; and God doesn't visit retributive punishment on us

---

[1]See Marjorie Hewitt Suchocki, *The Fall to Violence: Original Sin in Relational Theology* (New York: Continuum 1995).
[2]See Chartier, *Analogy* 97-128, for a defense of this potentially controversial view and an elaboration of related points.

because doing so is incompatible with love in principle—
retribution is evil.

So a substitutionary view of atonement won't work, both because retribution is itself a non-starter and because if retribution *did*
make sense it wouldn't make sense to substitute retribution.

Seventh-day Adventists have often been hospitable to an alternative view of atonement, a view that has been labeled "atonement
by revelation." This view, resonant with Adventism's theological
vision of God as love, has been embraced by figures ranging across
the Adventist ideological spectrum, including the conservative (as
he then was) Dick Winn,[1] the moderate-to-conservative Graham
Maxwell,[2] and the moderate-to-liberal (in contemporary Adventist
terms) Jack Provonsha.[3]

On this view, the human problem is not that we are liable to
retributive punishment but that we lack solid ground on which to
stand, a stable sense of who we are, confidence in our own worth
and in the meaning of our lives. It is the fact that we suffer from
this deficiency that accounts at a deep level for the poor choices we
make in relation to ourselves and others. We don't need the removal of legal guilt; we need *healing*. We need (implicitly or explicitly) to know ourselves loved by God, to recognize that the universe is, at root, a friendly place, to experience and act out of a
sense of basic trust.

This position is a descendant of Peter Abelard's "moral influence" view. But it is much broader than traditional moral influence
views, since it emphasizes that God heals us, gives us the grounding
and the basic trust we need, in a diverse array of ways. It is not
simply through our encounters with God as revealed in Jesus but
also through what God does everywhere in the world, through parents and friends, through societies and cultures, through legal institutions and religious communities, that God offers the sense of
groundedness we need. To speak of atonement by revelation is to
speak of the way in which God's love is conveyed through divine
action in every district of human experience, in every nook and
cranny of human history and culture.

[1]See Dick Winn, *God's Way to a New You* (Mountain View, CA: Pacific
1979); Dick Winn, *If God Won the War, Why Isn't It Over?* (Mountain View, CA:
Pacific 1982); Dick Winn, *His Healing Love* (Washington, DC: Review 1988).
[2]See A. Graham Maxwell, *Can God Be Trusted?* (Redlands, CA: Pine Knoll
2002); A. Graham Maxwell, *Servants or Friends? Another Look at God* (Redlands,
CA: Pine Knoll 1992).
[3]See Jack W. Provonsha, *You Can Go Home Again: An Untheology of the
Atonement* (Washington, DC: Review 1982); Jack W. Provonsha, *God Is With Us*
(Washington, DC: Review 1974). The phrase "atonement by revelation" is
Provonsha's.

The sense that the human predicament is *existential* rather than *judicial* is a huge step in the right direction. The judicial approach embodied in ideas of penal substitution (and related governmental and satisfaction-oriented views) is a non-starter.[1] But I think it is worth emphasizing that the human problem can hardly be seen as *exclusively* existential. It is also cultural, and political, and perhaps even biological. And atonement in the broad sense, what God has done and is doing, especially but not exclusively in and through the story of Jesus, to remedy our multifold predicament can be seen as responsive to all of these aspects of humanness.

Culturally and politically, the current of activity initiated by Jesus's ministry, death, and life beyond death has transformed and continues to transform history. We can identify at least two aspects of this transformation.

(*i*) The Christian community is a universal community, a community in which divisions based on ethnicity, nationality, and class, and increasingly also divisions based on gender and sexual orientation, are relativized. So much human conflict and violence reflects the drawing of clear boundaries separating *us* and *them*. But the church, rooted in the inclusive practice of Jesus,[2] is an institutional rejection of the destructive business of boundary-making. This matters for those who form the church, of course, since they are given the opportunity to experience a truly welcoming community. But it also matters for the rest of God's world, the part of God's world not incorporated in the church. For through the inclusive community that is the church God can model for the world, even if (given human finitude, fallibility, and sin) imperfectly, the possibility of a kind of community life strikingly different from the sort to which so many political and legal and cultural institutions aspire.[3]

(*ii*) The Christian community tells and retells the story of Jesus as the story of an innocent victim, murdered by the powers that be. In so doing, it challenges at a deep level two of the most persistent dynamics of human history. It challenges the tendency to justify victimization and to claim that victims deserve the harms they suffer (a tendency vital to the cohesion-fostering process of scapegoating).[4] And it also challenges the tendency to assume that those in

---

[1] See Edward Farley, *Good and Evil: Interpreting a Human Condition* (Minneapolis: Fortress 1990) 140-4.

[2] See Marcus J. Borg, *Conflict, Holiness, and Politics in the Teaching of Jesus* (Harrisburg, PA: TPI 1998).

[3] Cp. Stanley M. Hauerwas, *The Peaceable Kingdom: A Primer in Christian Ethics* (London: SCM 1983).

[4] See René Girard, *Violence and the Sacred*, trans. Patrick Gregory (Baltimore, MD: Johns Hopkins UP 1979); *The Scapegoat*, trans. Yvonne Freccero (Baltimore, MD: Johns Hopkins UP 1986); *Things Hidden since the Foundation of the World*, trans. Stephen Bann and Michael Metteer (Stanford, CA: Stanford UP

power act legitimately and reasonably.[1] The repetition of this story has led over time to an increasingly (and appropriately) critical attitude toward social authority and toward the denigration of the marginalized and the victimized—so that today, ironically, victimization can become a means of claiming social power. (This tendency itself requires critical scrutiny, of course.)

In addition to the existential and the political-cultural aspects of atonement, it is possible that there is also a biological aspect. Echoing what some of the earliest Christian thinkers hypothesized regarding the work of Christ as including the transformation of human nature itself, we can consider, in full awareness of the limits of our knowledge, the possibility that God's activity in Jesus might be thought to exert a ripple effect capable of altering human biology itself, perhaps in so doing fostering love and community to a previously absent level. Whether the highly controversial biological theory that might ground such a view will finally survive scientific criticism is an open question; if it did, however, it would provide a modern way of framing a very ancient conception of Jesus's work.[2]

Adventists of multiple ideological persuasions have embraced the idea of atonement as revelation. This idea is vastly superior to the idea of atonement as penal substitution. But it should be augmented by complementary understandings of atonement. Such understandings should include ones emphasizing (*i*) the church's contribution to crafting a new kind of community life that challenges the *status quo*, (*ii*) the Christian story's resistance to victimization and positional authority, and (*iii*) the intriguing possibility that the early Christians who envisioned a global change in human nature resulting from the work of Jesus might have been right.

*Evangelistic Mission and the Reach of God's Presence and Activity*

Evangelistic mission is good for multiple things. One thing it is not good for is saving people from eternal damnation.

On one popular conception of Christian, and so of Adventist, mission, the purpose of evangelism, of mission, is to get people to

1987); *I See Satan Fall Like Lightning*, trans. James G. Williams (Maryknoll, NY: Orbis 2001). Cp. Gil Bailie, *Violence Unveiled: Humanity at the Crossroads* (New York: Crossroad 1997).

[1]Cp. Pannenberg, *Jesus* 263; Jürgen Moltmann, *The Way of Jesus Christ: Christology in Messianic Dimensions*, trans. Margaret Kohl (London: SCM 1990) 160-70.

[2]See Rupert Sheldrake, *A New Science of Life: The Hypothesis of Formative Causation* (London: Paladin-Granada 1983); *The Presence of the Past: Morphic Resonance and the Habits of Nature* (New York: Vintage 1988); "The Laws of Nature as Habits: A Postmodern Basis for Science," *The Reenchantment of Science: Postmodern Proposals*, ed. David Ray Griffin, SUNY Series in Constructive Postmodern Thought (Albany: SUNY 1988) 79-86; *The Rebirth of Nature: The Greening of Science and God* (London: Century 1990).

take up the right stance in relation to God (and so, typically to embrace the right beliefs and the right lifestyle) so that God won't subject them to eternal punishment. Thus, for instance, according to
one Adventist essay in the theology of religions: "In spite of the
hundreds of missionaries today, there are literally millions living in
heathen darkness, in spiritual night. Unless the gospel reaches them
soon, they too will end in Christless graves"[1]

Though this book was written by an Adventist and published
by an Adventist press, I am not surprised that its endnotes include
no references to the work of Ellen White. For, at least in her later
years,[2] she clearly voiced her conviction that God was at work to
heal and deliver beyond the bounds of institutional Christianity.
She praises non-Christians who "have revealed in manifold ways
the working of a divine power on mind and character," who have
obtained "knowledge of God . . . under the operations of divine
grace." She maintains that people outside the bounds of institutional Christianity "have done the very things the law required,
because they have heeded the voice speaking to them in the things
of nature," and that "Christ implants his grace" in the hearts of
such persons.[3] "Heaven's plan of salvation is broad enough to embrace the whole world," she declares;[4] this basic recognition is a
useful beginning-point for our reflection on God's activity beyond
the walls of our community of faith.

We might consider using traditional trinitarian categories to
shape our thinking about the reach of revelation and salvation.[5]
(*i*) The activity of God as creator underlies the order and structure
of the world, shaping the basic dynamics of human existence and
experience in every culture and context. (*ii*) God the Word is the
"true light, which enlightens *everyone* . . . ."[6] That is to say, wherever there are insight and discovery, there is God's grace; wherever
there are reason and wisdom, there God is present and active. Thus,
the great Christian advocate Justin Martyr could write that Christ "is
the Word of whom every race of men were partakers; and those

---

[1] R. Rubin Widmer, *Jesus the Light of the World: A Study of Contemporary Views* (Nashville: Southern 1967) 122.

[2] For a catalogue of Ellen White's attitudes to the question of God's presence and activity outside Christianity, see Borge Schantz, "The Development of Seventh-day Adventist Missionary Thought: A Contemporary Appraisal" (PhD diss., Fuller Theological Seminary 1983) 714-24.

[3] Ellen G. White, "'Upon the Throne of His Glory,'" *Advent Review and Sabbath Herald* 75.38 (Sept. 20, 1898): 598.

[4] Ellen G. White, "Hope for the Heathen," *Advent Review and Sabbath Herald* 92.31 (June 24, 1915): 4.

[5] The best recent discussion of trinitarian theology: Nicholas Lash, *Believing Three Ways in One God: A Reading of the Apostles' Creed* (London: SCM 1992).

[6] Jn. 1:9a; my italics.

who lived reasonably are Christians, even though they have been thought atheists . . . ."[1] (Justin likely had in mind by "atheists" those who denied the reality of the traditional gods, rather than those who denied the reality of all gods, but there is no reason to think the latter would be in a different position from the former in relation to the divine Word.) (*iii*) God the Spirit blows everywhere, moves across the waters everywhere, touches every life with vitality and grace.

So we can see divine providence, divine inspiration, as in touch with every life everywhere. No one is without the presence of God, without the presence of the divine Word or the divine Spirit, because we're talking about *God*, who is omnipresent, universal. We don't need mission to enable people to interact with God, because God is omnipresent and universally active. We don't need mission to enable people to be loved and embraced by God, because God already loves the whole world. We don't need mission to enable God to enlighten people if the divine Word is "the light that enlightens everyone." And if that is the case, if Justin Martyr is right that those who live reasonably are living out the enlightenment of the divine Word, then we can expect not only that God's healing and enlightening and inspiring presence should be discerned everywhere but also that we will have things to learn from those who do not share our beliefs, and that we certainly need not fear their influence as contaminating.

It's worth emphasizing that what I've said here does not depend on my critique of the idea of penal substitution. A substitutionary view of atonement does not require conscious awareness of Jesus's activity to be effective. God would, that is, be entitled to forgive, as the substitutionary view suggests, whether or not people are aware that the *reason* they are forgiven is what God has done in Jesus. But of course I think that this is an unhelpful way to look at things. We should talk about divine love and acceptance, rather than forgiveness—since (*i*) God isn't a petulant and offended deity who needs to be propitiated and (*ii*) forgiveness as understood here (and, often enough, elsewhere) is taken to involve relinquishment of a putative right to engage in retribution; but this must be a nonsensical notion, given that there is no such right, since retribution is an unequivocally bad thing. And we should understand divine love and acceptance as predicated on who God is essentially rather than on any sort of contingent transaction.

If we confess that God is *love*, and so see God as accepting and embracing everyone, then we will not see the purpose of mission as

[1]Justin Martyr, *The First Apology*, trans. Marcus Dods and George Reith, *Ante-Nicene Fathers*, ed. Alexander Roberts, James Donaldson, and A. Cleveland Coxe, 10 vols. (Buffalo, NY: Christian Literature 1885), ch. 46, http://www .newadvent.org/fathers/0126.htm (ed. Kevin Knight); cp. Clark, *Awakening* 59-87.

saving people by keeping God from judging and condemning
them. And we will not see mission as a matter of making people acceptable (to God or to us), since we will see that they are God's
creatures just as we are and that, as enlightened by the divine
Word, they have things to teach us. Does that mean that mission
has no value? Not at all. I suggest that the broad enterprise of mission includes at least three elements that make it important and
worthwhile.

(*i*) People can be loved and accepted by God, and healed by
God's providential grace, whether they know this or not. Even if
they lack adequate understanding, they can be "rightly related by
faith to the God of Jesus Christ."[1] But understanding more clearly
who God is and what God is up to in the world is valuable in its
own right and can increase people's ability to live well by integrat-
ing various aspects of their lives and insights regarding those lives
and helping them to see more clearly how and why to seek healing
and growth. And it can connect them with a community in which
they can learn to read the world as the theatre of God's grace in
which they can be challenged to continue growing and healing and
assisted in the growing and healing process.

(*ii*) Mission can involve direct challenges to religious ideas that
are deeply destructive—ideas calling for the subordination of particular groups, encouraging fatalistic acceptance of the social *status
quo*, prompting submission to human authorities, or generating fear
and self-abnegation.[2] Challenging these ideas and replacing them
with healthier ones can lead to improvements in institutions and
patterns of interacting and so in people's lives.

(*iii*) Mission need not involve a focus on conveying *ideas*. Mission activities can involve sharing God's healing grace through economic development, health care, and education, which are tremen-

---

[1]Paul Griffiths, *Problems of Religious Diversity*, Exploring the Philosophy of Religion 1 (Oxford: Blackwell 2001) 164; cp. 158. See also Germain G. Grisez, *The
Way of the Lord Jesus* 1: *Christian Moral Principles* (Chicago: Franciscan Herald 1983)
744; Hauerwas 101; Karl Rahner, "Atheism and Implicit Christianity," *Theological
Investigations* 9: *Writings of 1965-67* 1, trans. Graham Harrison (New York: Herder
1972) 153; Keith Ward, *Images of Eternity: Concepts of God in Five Religious Traditions* (Oxford: Oneworld 1993) 177-8; John Baillie, *The Sense of the Presence of God*,
Gifford Lectures 1961-2 (London: OUP 1962) 79-87; Karl Rahner, "Anonymous
and Explicit Faith," *Theological Investigations* 16: *Experience of the Spirit: Source of
Theology*, trans. David Morland (New York: Crossroad-Seabury 1979) 55-6.

[2]See Max L. Stackhouse, *Creeds, Society, and Human Rights: A Study in Three
Cultures* (Grand Rapids: Eerdmans 1984) 269; John Milbank, "The End of Dialogue," *Christian Uniqueness Reconsidered: The Myth of a Pluralistic Theology of Religions*, ed. Gavin D'Costa (Maryknoll, NY: Orbis 1990) 184-7; Arthur C. Danto,
*Mysticism and Morality: Oriental Thought and Moral Philosophy* (New York: Columbia UP 1988 [1972[) 22-45; Charles Scriven "When the Jailhouse Rocks: In Defense of Evangelism for the Church of Today," *Spectrum* 18.3 (Feb. 1988): 22-8.

dously valuable whether or not those whose lives they touch improve their cognitive understanding of God and the world.

Evangelism, sharing the grace that is, in fact, good news, can take multiple forms. It need not be designed to enable God to like people or to keep them from being damned, as if God needed excuses to avoid rejecting and punishing people. Rather, we can share the good news as a way of helping people understand and integrate their lives more fully and experience personal and institutional healing, and by means of our transformative actions with regard to their bodies, minds, and institutions.

## Divine Grace and Universalism

Fritz Guy has offered a powerful and persuasive Adventist case for universal salvation—for the idea that we should at least hope that everyone will ultimately be saved.[1] And it seems to me that we ought to take this case very seriously indeed, given the all-embracing nature of divine love and the idea of salvation as effected through and on the basis of grace rather than performance.

How we ultimately evaluate universalism will depend on how we understand salvation. It will be important to distinguish multiple senses of this crucial term. Salvation in some senses is entirely up to God, and salvation in these senses can be guaranteed to be universal by divine love. Salvation in some other senses depends on the proper behavior of personal and sometimes nonpersonal elements of the creaturely world, and so cannot be guaranteed to be universal.

Salvation is *not* best understood as deliverance from divine condemnation, because the God who is love is not best conceived of as being in the condemnation business. Instead, in the broadest sense, salvation is whatever answers at a deep level to the human predicament. Thus, within the broad ambit of salvation, we can include, at least, (*i*) divine acceptance, (*ii*) awareness of this acceptance, (*iii*) personal meaning, worth, and security, (*iv*) personal healing from moral and spiritual brokenness, (*v*) deliverance in this life from oppressive or debilitating historical circumstances, (*vi*) personal life beyond death, and (*vii*) ultimate fulfillment in conscious relation to God.

It will be apparent that category (*i*) salvation is entirely up to God. To affirm that God is love is to affirm that God wills the good of every creature and desires communion with every creature. And, whether because, as I argue, retribution is a deeply objectionable concept and God cannot thus be thought to seek or desire or intend retributive justice, or because, as on a view like Karl Barth's, God incarnate is judged on behalf of all humanity so that no one need suffer divine condemnation, we ought not to expect retribu-

[1]Fritz Guy, "How Inclusive is Our Hope?," *Spectrum* 33 (Spring 2005): 16-25.

tive punishment from God. So divine love, divine acceptance, might be supposed to embrace all creatures without distinction.

It also seems to be the case that (*vi*) is up to God, too, whether on a mixed view of divine action or on a view of divine action as fully persuasive. There are at least two different ways in which God could offer people life after death—either (*a*) miraculously embodying them in the new life of the resurrection (an option for a believer in a mixed view of divine action) or (*b*) creating them, and creating the world, in such a way that they come to experience new life after death (this would be the only option available, of course, on a fully persuasive view of divine action, though of course a believer in a mixed view could also embrace this option). It is worth noting that, while we might talk about this latter view as a matter of what is "natural" for persons, the point would be that the intention and activity of God underlay these processes at every point in a way that made them possible.[1]

It would appear that, pre-mortem, God could facilitate, inspire, empower through persuasive providence the work of those testifying to God's love and those features of the natural world and human experience that foster awareness of that love. God can thus make (*ii*) more likely, though, given that the occurrence of (*ii*) involves both the actions of the creatures God uses to increase the likelihood of awareness of divine love and the free responsiveness of those God seeks to make aware of divine love, God cannot guarantee the occurrence of (*ii*). The same seems likely to be true post-mortem, though perhaps (we of course know too little to be certain) there might be fewer impediments to divine persuasion post-mortem. And perhaps, on a mixed view of divine action, God might ensure that post-mortem existence featured experiences that effected unequivocal direct awareness of divine acceptance. Category (*iii*) salvation similarly depends on changes in understanding which involve the actions of free creatures and, at least pre-mortem, the cooperation of orderly physical processes, and so cannot be guaranteed by divine providence. To find myself grounded and meaningful and valuable, I must, whether or not I am consciously, thematically, aware that God's love is the ground of my existence, grasp that love, rely on it. The point is not that I need to understand this properly; even if I don't, I still must take the existential risk to accept the love I sense at some deep level, and I may not, out of fear or for some other reason, fail to do so.

Category (*v*) is concerned with this-worldly events. The occurrence of salvific events in this category fairly clearly depends on the

---

[1]See John B. Cobb, Jr., "The Resurrection of the Soul," *Harvard Theological Review* 80.2 (1987): 213-27.

activity of persuasive divine providence (even on a mixed view of divine action, immediate divine acts will obviously be rare, and large-scale historical change doesn't seem to be drive by such acts) and is therefore a function of the free choices of creatures and the behavior of physical processes. Divine action alone will not guarantee the occurrence of the kind of salvation with which this category is concerned.

If I have come to experience category (*iii*) salvation, at least to some degree, this will facilitate category (*iv*) salvation—personal healing, character development, personal growth into wholeness. And a mixed view of divine action would leave room for some miraculous divine acts that shaped people's environments in ways that might prompt them toward growth and away from self-absorption. But facilitating growth doesn't guarantee it. I might well know myself grounded to a significant extent without feeling ready to embrace the full implications of loving divine acceptance and the meaningfulness of my existence. I might resist because of the comfort of old responses or the persistence of a fear that makes believing that I am truly loved difficult. I might truly believe in God's love and acceptance and in the groundedness of my existence but still instinctively view other creatures with fear and suspicion. Healing is not an all-or-nothing matter. And so category (*iv*) salvation might not be evident in all its fullness.

Even more troublingly, I might simply not experience divine acceptance or the meaningfulness of my existence at a deep level. And I might continue, defensively, self-protectively, to curve in on myself, to refuse to let myself experience real openness to the world because I fear that openness will mean, not a loving embrace, but domination or destructive dissolution. If I fear this, I will be deeply mistaken, of course, but persuasive divine providence, and even a miraculous transformation of my environment, cannot guarantee that this kind of turn away from reality will not continue. It might even be that continued self-absorption of this kind might lead, post-mortem, to a continued self-contraction leading finally to disappearance from existence. Divine action on a fully persuasive view cannot guarantee that this will not occur; divine action on a mixed view might keep me in existence despite my slide toward dissolution, but it could not respect my freedom while simultaneously compelling me to change course. Even on a mixed view, one would, I think, have good reason to reject the direct, miraculous transformation of people's attitudes, the performance of what Guy has characterized, in a different but related context, as "spiritual lobotomies." For such miraculous transformations would violate the integrity of persons and turn them into automata.

This means that the occurrence of category (vii) salvation will not be something that divine action could guarantee unilaterally, either. This kind of salvation depends on continued personal openness to growth and flourishing. While, on a mixed view of divine action, God could offer various personal powers and opportunities to each creature consistent with that creature's ultimate potential for flourishing and fulfillment, fully embracing those powers and opportunities and making appropriate use of them would be a matter of decision for each free creature. And of course some powers and opportunities would not be desirable for, might not even be options for, creatures who had not experienced some level of healing and personal growth. Since healing and personal growth depend on creatures' free choices, experiencing these powers and opportunities would not be possible absent the right sorts of free choices.

We may reasonably assume that creatures are made for flourishing and fulfillment and so for communion with God. This means that creatures ought to be susceptible, in general deeply susceptible, to divine wooing. And to affirm that God is love is to affirm that God intends and desires ultimate fulfillment and flourishing for all persons (indeed, all creatures). This means that there will be no barrier on God's side, as it were. God is not stingy with grace, and will seek to woo creatures toward wholeness and fulfillment. In short, we ought to expect God to be no less loving than we ourselves ought to be. As John Greenleaf Whittier puts it, in a poem first brought to my attention by Jack Provonsha:

> Not mine to look where cherubim
> 　　And seraphs may not see,
> But nothing can be good in Him
> 　　Which evil is in me.
> The wrong that pains my soul below
> 　　I dare not throne above,
> I know not of His hate,—I know
> 　　His goodness and His love.[1]

A hopeful rather than dogmatic universalism, one like Guy's, is well worth affirming. We can and should hope and pray for universal salvation.[2] But we must also recognize that some kinds of salvation, those that depend on creaturely responses, cannot be *guaranteed* by

[1]John Greenleaf Whittier, "The Eternal Goodness," *English Poetry* 3: *From Tennyson to Whitman*, Harvard Classics, ed. Charles Eliot, 51 vols. (New York: Collier 1909-14) 43: no. 792; Bartleby.Com 2001 (http://www.bartleby.com/42/792.html; last visited January 19, 2007).

[2]Cp. Thomas B. Talbott, "On Predestination, Reprobation, and the Love of God," *Reformed Journal* 33.2 (Feb. 1983): 11-5; Thomas B. Talbott, "The Doctrine of Everlasting Punishment," *Faith and Philosophy* 7 (1990): 19-42; Thomas B. Talbott, "Providence, Freedom, and Human Destiny," *Religious Studies* 26 (1990): 227-45; Thomas B. Talbott, *The Inescapable Love of God* (Boca Raton, FL: Universal 1999).

divine action (or by ours).[1] Further complicating matters: these sorts of salvation are matters of degree: even if they occur to some extent, it cannot be guaranteed that they will occur *in toto* in any individual life.

On the attractive view that people are created, at root, for communion with God, it is reasonable to expect divine wooing to be successful, and both fully persuasive and mixed accounts of divine action allow for such wooing to occur both pre- and post-mortem.[2] But regard for freedom means that there cannot ever, I think, be a guarantee that no one will opt finally for self-absorption over reality, or that people will opt for partial healing and growth while remaining stuck at something less than their full potential. So there can be no guarantee that everyone will experience the fullness of salvation, though we should hope not only that this will not occur but that it is not even possible because of an inherent bent toward God. So we can and should hope and pray. for universal salvation, but that, I suspect, is the most we can do.

## CONCLUSION

An attractive Adventist Christology and soteriology would focus, I believe, on love. This means that they would emphasize the importance of freedom, with consequences for how we think about God's presence and activity in Jesus, how we think about God's self-communication, and how we think about the nature and extent of God's saving activity and our role in facilitating it.

Such a Christology and soteriology might build on an account of divine action as fully persuasive. Or they might build on a mixed account of divine action. Either way, however, they would need to take seriously the fact that a credible account of divine action must begin with the recognition that God's will is frequently not done, God's love frequently not realized, in the world. Thus, if we want

---

[1] One could perfectly well disagree about the merits of the idea of penal substitution, affirming this idea while judging, as Karl Barth seems to have done, that God incarnate is judged on behalf of all humanity, which is, accordingly, saved. And one could embrace universalism while supposing that conscious encounter with the Christian message *was* required for divine acceptance and personal healing to take place, thus rejecting my account of the universality of divine grace, divine revelation, and the divine presence, as long as one also supposed that this encounter could occur post-mortem; cp. George Lindbeck, "*Fides ex Auditu* and the Salvation of Non-Christians: Contemporary Catholic and Protestant Positions," *The Gospel and the Ambiguity of the Church*, ed. Vilmos Vajta (Philadelphia: Fortress 1974) 91-123.

[2] Cp. David Brown, "No Heaven without Purgatory," *Religious Studies* 21.4 (1985): 427-56. Such a view would obviously need to be separated sharply from the embrace of works-righteousness that seems to dog traditional accounts of purgatory.

to say that God is love, then we must affirm, as well, I think, that there are serious moral or metaphysical constraints on the realization of God's will in the world. In turn, taking these constraints seriously means thinking carefully about divine action and, in light of what we conclude about divine action, thinking carefully about what we say about Jesus and salvation.

The Adventist Christology and soteriology of the future could obviously take many directions other than those I have suggested. There will obviously be disagreement about much of what I have said here. I welcome the discussion that I am sure will be occasioned by my proposals. But whatever we ultimately say as a community about Jesus and salvation, our message should be marked by at least one fundamental conviction: that God is with us.[1]

The doctrine of the Incarnation points us to a God whose tabernacling in our midst is expressed in the story of Jesus of Nazareth, a God who is present to and with us in the midst of the vulnerability and contingency and pain and joy that are our lot. An adequate Christian understanding of salvation will give voice to the same essential belief—that the God who has been revealed as love in and through the histories of Israel, Jesus, and the church is now—and always has been—at work in and through the processes of nature and history to offer acceptance and healing, empowerment and liberation, to human beings and communities everywhere.

That God is truly with us is the most powerful and reassuring belief to which we can give voice. Our ongoing existence as a community of faith will be justified only to the extent that this belief forms the center of our mission, our proclamation, and our corporate life.[2]

---

[1] To employ the title of what is still, I think, Jack Provonsha's finest book.

[2] I am grateful to David Larson and David Gordon for comments that have improved this chapter at multiple points, and to Fritz Guy for conversation regarding the lecture that preceded it.

# 7

# Sanctuary

## Roy Adams

L et me say at the outset that, notwithstanding my very good intentions, this chapter does not include all I could have wished. I
wanted, for example, to include an overview of Adventist publications on the doctrine of the sanctuary since 1980—to gauge the
trends, to sense more accurately the current mood in the church.
But time and space prevented me. I wanted to include an up-to-
date section of what's happening in our college and university religion classrooms at the moment. In fact, I sent out a brief question-
naire and received some answers. But when I looked at the length
of the draft I already had, I knew I couldn't include that. Besides I
did not want to come to hasty (written) conclusions about my colleagues and their curricula.

What I share with you comes from inside me. You will not find
a multitude of technicalities or scholarly jargon here. And the fundamental question you should bring to the material is: Does it make
theological sense?

### FROM THE PERSPECTIVE OF THE PAST

We cannot discuss adequately the future of Adventist sanctuary
theology without at least a brief consideration of where we have
been, and where we are today.

That, in part, was the task before me years ago as I prepared to
write my doctoral dissertation.[1] And here, by way of laying the
foundation for the assignment at hand, I fall back, in summary, to
the findings of that study.

I think we can say that Adventist sanctuary theology was born
the morning following the October 22, 1844, disappointment, as

---

[1] I published this dissertation as *The Sanctuary Doctrine: Three Approaches in the
Seventh-day Adventist Church*, Andrews U Diss. Series 1 (Berrien Springs, MI: Andrews UP 1981).

Hiram Edson walked across a cornfield in Port Gibson, New York. It was during that historic stroll, as Edson reported years later, that a vision (or something close to it) came to him, indicating "distinctly and clearly that instead of our High Priest coming out of the Most Holy of the heavenly sanctuary to come to this earth . . . at the end of the 2,300 days, He for the first time entered on that day (October 22, 1844) the second apartment of that sanctuary; and that He had a work to perform in the Most Holy before coming to this earth."[1] This is the basic understanding that lies at the foundation of Adventist sanctuary theology. All that has followed in succeeding decades has had reference, directly or indirectly, to the insight received by this Adventist pioneer that October morning.

The trauma of October 22 shook the Millerite camp; and by May of 1845 at least four separate groups had formed.[2] For the one that eventually came to be known as Seventh-day Adventists, Edson's early morning vision (I use the word loosely) provided the key that unlocked for them the mystery of what happened at the end of the 2,300 days of Dan. 8:14. And the doctrine of the sanctuary that grew out of that vision came to be regarded by them not only as fundamental in itself, but also as a bulwark of defense for the other vital tenets of their faith.

One of the first ones to use the doctrine of the sanctuary in this auxiliary role was a young convert by the name of Uriah Smith (1832-1903). Only twenty years of age when he joined the Advent group in 1852, Smith produced, less than one year later, a small "epic"[3] ("The Warning Voice of Time and Prophecy") extolling the group as

> . . . "a faithful few" . . .
> Whom Treason cannot move, nor unbelief,
> Nor Doubt corrupt . . . .

This 35,000 word poem, serialized through nine issues of the *Review and Herald*,[4] sought, at its core, to establish confidence in the

---

[1]Hiram Edson, ms. fragment, Heritage Room, James White Library, Andrews University, Berrien Springs, MI.

[2]"One group rejected the validity of their past experience, believing it was all a mistake. A second group saw the 1844 failure as evidence that the 2,300 days had not yet ended, a conclusion that led to further time setting. Yet another group, not rejecting their former experience outright, nevertheless became afflicted with doubt. A fourth group expressed confidence in the integrity of the Millerite calculations and believed that the prophecy in Daniel 8:14 had been fulfilled" (Adams, *Sanctuary* 20).

[3]So John O. Waller considered it. See "Uriah Smith's Small Epic: The Warning Voice of Time and Prophecy," *Adventist Heritage* 5.1 (Sum. 1978): 53-61.

[4]From March 17 to August 11, 1853.

integrity of the Millerite movement and the validity of 1844 as the termination of the 2,300 days.

With the passage of time it was to be seen that this poem was a programmatic expression of Smith's basic theology, a theology centered on three overriding concerns:

- the salvation-historical significance of 1844;
- the perpetuity of the law and the Sabbath; and
- the imminence of the Advent.[1]

Smith saw the doctrine of the sanctuary as the hub around which the entire framework of biblical truth revolved,[2] "the key to the interpretation of some of the most important prophecies pertaining to the present time," "the grand and radiant nucleus around which cluster the glorious constellations of present truth!"[3]

Remarkably, then, the sanctuary doctrine—itself to come under fire from many quarters in succeeding decades—had become so quickly entrenched among our early believers that its various aspects could be used in defense of other, seemingly even more fundamental, points of faith.

Smith's dogged insistence on the literalness of the heavenly sanctuary and its appurtenances, for example, served to defend the validity of the law and the Sabbath. For if a literal ark resides in the sanctuary, then this must mean, *ipso facto*, that the tables of the Decalogue, containing the ten commandments, are also there. And thus the law stands solid. Likewise, there must be two apartments in the heavenly sanctuary, making a change of setting for Christ's ministry at a certain point in time (1844) a logical development.

And just as the service in the most holy place of the earthly sanctuary was some 360 times shorter than that in the holy place, so the work of Christ from 1844 to the end would be proportionately—chronometrically—shorter than that from the cross to 1844. This gave ever increasing urgency to Smith's lifelong emphasis on the imminence of the Advent.

There were certainly other early exponents of the sanctuary message—James White, Ellen White, and J. N. Andrews, among others. But Uriah Smith out-wrote them all, and his interest in the sanctuary doctrine never waned. Ironically, it is perhaps true to say that the themes in whose defense he marshaled it (the law, in particular) came thoroughly to dominate the Adventist theological landscape, eventually leading to the 1888 crisis over righteousness

---

[1] See Adams, *Sanctuary* 53.

[2] Adams, *Sanctuary* 31.

[3] Uriah Smith, *Looking unto Jesus* (Chicago, IL: Review 1897) 56-58; cp. Smith, *The Sanctuary* (Battle Creek, MI: Adventist 1877) 10-5; Smith, *The Sanctuary* (Battle Creek, MI: Adventist 1863) 71; see also Adams, *Sanctuary* 31-35.

by faith, a crisis in which the church came close to being crippled by its own apologetic success in defense of the law.

The perceived trend in the church toward legalism in the wake of, and in the years following, 1888 perhaps had much to do with the theological focus of Albion Fox Ballenger (1861-1921).

Latching on to the last of Smith's major emphases (an imminent eschaton), Ballenger apparently came to the conclusion that at least three things must happen to bring about the end of history:

• There must be a return to righteousness by faith among us.
• We must gain the victory over every sin.
• We must receive the "latter rain."[1]

What I find interesting in Ballenger's almost total reinterpretation of the sanctuary doctrine was that it was done in the interest of weeding out from it those aspects that, in his view, led inevitably away from righteousness by faith and toward legalism.

Thus, for example, according to his version of the sanctuary doctrine, Christ ministered in the heavenly sanctuary from the fall to the cross, thereby removing from view the Levitical priests, ("shadowy middlemen," as he called them) and squelching what he saw as the "Adventist idea" that the only throne of grace accessible to us from Moses to the cross was "a 1 1/2 by 2 1/2 [cubit] golden plated wooden box which men carried about on two poles."[2]

Ballenger spent much time fighting this idea. Pardon, he urged, has always been administered from the heavenly sanctuary, all the way back to the fall. The Levitical priesthood was an institution of purely temporary significance, designed (out of concession) to point ignorant former slaves to the heavenly sanctuary already then in operation.[3]

We must leave alone much of the specifics of Ballenger's (precarious) sanctuary theology—such as, for example, the notion of angel priests in the heavenly sanctuary before the cross and the concept of a heavenly Melchizedekan priesthood, separate from that of Christ.[4] Suffice it to say that it was in an effort to correct what he regarded as a near total eclipse of Christ in traditional Adventist sanctuary theology that he undertook an almost complete reinterpretation of the doctrine. And it was his concern for righteousness by faith and Christian assurance that eventually led him to repudiate completely what he considered the most offensive aspect of the sanctuary doctrine—the notion of an investigative judgment.[5]

[1]Adams, *Sanctuary* 105-6.
[2]Adams, *Sanctuary* 117.
[3]Adams, *Sanctuary* 115-8.
[4]See Adams, *Sanctuary* 113-5.
[5]See Adams, *Sanctuary* 135-40.

When Ballenger was eventually called by church leaders in 1905 to answer for his views on the sanctuary, Milian Lauritz Andreasen (1876-1962), too young to be a participant in the resulting hearings, nevertheless eavesdropped on the pre-dawn proceedings through an open window along with his colleague, L. H. Christian (the two took turns standing on each other's shoulders).[1]

When he himself came to write on the theme of the sanctuary, he differed in emphasis from both Smith and Ballenger. Unlike Ballenger, he held fast to the traditional Adventist positions on the doctrine. And unlike Smith—or perhaps *because* of Smith—he did not, for example, give much space to traditional sanctuary themes like the 2,300-day prophecy and its 1844 terminus, an area on which Smith had been rather exhaustive. Nor did he dwell at any length on the notion of a literal heavenly sanctuary.

Andreasen had a good deal to say, however, about the defilement and cleansing of the heavenly sanctuary; about the locus of Christ's ministry after the Ascension; about the investigative judgment; and about the atonement. Through it all, his overriding concern, and the conviction in whose defense he marshaled the doctrine of the sanctuary, was the absolute perfection of God's last day remnant people, a development he believed would bring about the *parousia*.[2] Andreasen's passion for the perfection of the final remnant is much alive today among his contemporary followers, causing frictions, tensions, and divisions in some sectors of the church.[3]

The sanctuary doctrine as formulated by Uriah Smith basically became the officially accepted position of the church, while Ballenger's attempted reinterpretation has been largely discredited and rejected. The response to Andreasen's emphases has, on the whole, been mixed.

## WHERE WE ARE

The year 1980 turned out to be a pivotal one for Adventist sanctuary theology. That was the year in which the challenge to the church's position on this question by Australian theologian Desmond Ford came to a head. The ensuing controversy led the church to convene (at Glacier View, a mountain camp in Colorado) what was perhaps the largest committee of Adventist theologians, educators, pastors, and administrators to address a single theological question. Ford had openly called into question the validity of certain fundamental aspects of the church's sanctuary theology.

[1]Adams, *Sanctuary* 165.
[2]Adams, *Sanctuary* 179-80.
[3]See Roy Adams, *The Nature of Christ: Help for a Church Divided over Perfection* (Hagerstown, MD: Review 1994) 37-54.

In a massive document prepared in defense of his position, he, like, Ballenger before him, concluded, flatly, that the investigative judgment is not defensible from the Bible.[1]

As it turned out, the Sanctuary Review Committee (as the gathering was called) did not accept Ford's conclusions, voting instead a consensus statement reaffirming the church's historic position.[2]

During this period, sanctuary theology was a focus of intense controversy. Churches split in the wake of Glacier View, and a few ordained ministers surrendered their credentials.

The dust eventually settled, and (whether from fatigue, or fear, or apathy) an ear-splitting silence followed, with both "traditionalists" and "progressives" keeping a low profile. Feelings still run deep, however, and attitudes remain entrenched on the subject. The stalemate has everything to do with the future of sanctuary theology in the Adventist church.

I got an inkling of this when I read the evaluations of the manuscript of my 1993 book on the sanctuary.[3] Several of the comments from the various evaluators (whose identities I do not know, of course) intrigued me. Let me share a few of these here as a way of pointing out some things that may have to change if we are to move forward theologically on this question.

1. In the original draft of my introduction for the book, I had indicated that as a matter of procedure, I had purposely refrained from consulting Ellen White's position on any major aspect of the sanctuary doctrine. I was taking that approach, I explained, in an effort to demonstrate that the doctrine was able to stand independently of White's support, notwithstanding the charges of critics to the contrary.[4]

In the end, although I proceeded to do precisely that, I backed away from making the statement in the introduction of the book because of the following comment from one reviewer: "Adams puts this forth as a strength of the current manuscript, but a large portion of the [Adventist] reading audience will see this not as a strength but as a weakness. Many will see this sentence as tantamount to a disbelief in E. G. W."

[1]Desmond Ford, "Daniel 8:14, the Day of Atonement, and the Investigative Judgment" (unpublished ms. 1980) 14.
[2]Published in *Ministry*, Oct. 1980: 16-8.
[3]Roy Adams, *The Sanctuary: Understanding the Heart of Adventist Theology* (Hagerstown, MD: Review 1994).
[4]I have included the sentiments expressed in the section below in Roy Adams, *Beams of Heaven Guiding Me: Looking Back on God's Hand in My Life* (Parker, CO: Outskirts 2014) 85-7.

I rather doubt that there could be many Adventists more appreciative of the writings of Ellen G. White than I am. But I have to confess that there are days when I could almost wish that those writings never existed, as I see the misuse and abuse to which they are subjected. Too many of us in the church have come to use them as a crutch, as a way of avoiding serious Bible study, as a way of stifling discussion on every issue. But on numerous occasions, Ellen White herself admonished us to substantiate our beliefs from Scripture. In my 1993 book, I attempted to do precisely that, but ironically, however, was dissuaded from saying that I had done so because of a widespread hang-up among us on this issue.

2. With no further identification, the *Review and Herald* described the comment that follows as coming from "a well respected SDA scholar." It read: "Adams implies there is no literal furniture in the heavenly sanctuary. I read[, however,] about all sorts of objects seen there in the book of Revelation." According to this same scholar—or another reviewer (I could not be sure)—"Adams ignores E.G.W.'s literal references to the heavenly sanctuary."

3. And this comment from another reviewer: "Adams needs to preserve more physical movement on the part of God the Father and Christ in the heavenly sanctuary and not leave it with a statement that Christ began a new ministry."

4. And one more: "Adams should weigh the language carefully so as not to unnecessarily offend conservative readers. If published as is, is Adams ready for the possible fallout? I hope I am wrong, but I can foresee a terrible firestorm of reaction to this book. I have not been so fearful about publishing a book in (all) my years of publishing work. Is Adams willing to go to another Glacier View meeting—this time with himself at the center of the discussion?"

Fortunately for me, that last comment has turned out to be a false prophecy. But, every so often, my mind reverts back to its message, and I wonder. . . .

- I wonder if its author ever pondered the statement that the path of the just is as the light of dawn that shines ever brighter until the perfect day.
- I wonder if this was a comment written out of concern for my well-being, or out of an effort to scare me into silence.
- I wonder if it implies or presupposes that the positions we have held on every doctrine or theological issue should remain frozen in formaldehyde forever—never to be examined again, never to be modified, never to be refined.
- And I wonder how widespread this attitude might be in the church and what danger it might pose to future theological progress.

The comment surprised me. Because if I know myself at all, I have, I think, a fairly decent respect for delicate things, with no stomach whatsoever for playing bull in a China shop. But I also know that from time to time even the most delicate, the most precious things, may need polishing, may need adjusting, may need retuning. It doesn't become us, as a church, to take the view (to quote Ellen G. White) that "there is no more truth to be revealed, and that all our expositions of scripture are without error." Says White: "No true doctrine will lose anything by close investigation"[1]

What challenges face us, as a church, on the question of the sanctuary! Is there a future for this doctrine in the Adventist church? That's the question now before us.

On the one hand, I think we need to ask whether the doctrine of the sanctuary is an untouchable—something which must not be investigated for any reason; something on which the last word has been spoken, the last argument made, the last plank established; something on which there can be no new discussion, no new finding, no fresh insight. Is it a fragile ornament to be kept permanently locked in a padded box, never to be removed for dusting lest we shatter it?

On the other hand, we need to grapple with the limits of the historical-critical method, with which we can bog down the doctrine in fruitless technicalities. As valid as that method is (and I believe in its validity), is it adequate for the determination of every biblical truth or affirmation? Indeed, is it capable of dealing with the most fundamental truths of all: creation, incarnation, conversion, resurrection, advent? Do not all these point to suprarational phenomena, completely beyond the parameters of the historical-critical method?

As Seventh-day Adventists, we should have no qualms about the integrity of the sanctuary message. There is no need, I think, to apologize for this aspect of our faith. We have sufficient evidence in Scripture for it, evidence that runs clear through the sacred writings.

The wilderness tabernacle was the first manifestation on earth of the heavenly sanctuary. At its completion, God's presence and power were tangibly demonstrated. As the work finished, Scripture says, "a cloud covered the Tent of Meeting and the glory of the Lord filled the tabernacle." And even Moses found himself unable to enter the place "because the cloud had settled upon it and the glory of the Lord filled the tabernacle."[2]

[1]Ellen G. White, *Counsels to Writers and Editors* (Nashville, TN: Southern 1946) 35.
[2]Ex. 40:34-5.

In this way, and for a long time, Israel had the unique privilege of God's "tangible" presence in their midst and the assurance of God's personal protection and guidance. As they traveled through a trackless wilderness, the cloud and the fire stayed with them. "Whenever the cloud lifted from above the tabernacle, they would set out; but if the cloud did not lift, they did not set out-until the day it lifted." This signal manifestation of divine presence was with them "during all their [wilderness] travels."[1]

As they prepared to cross over into the promised land, the waters of the Jordan divided before them at the presence of the ark, the most sacred symbol of the tabernacle. And all through the time of the judges, beginning with the miraculous fall of Jericho, the surrounding nations, and Israel itself, learned to appreciate the power represented by that sacred emblem.

At the dedication of the Jerusalem temple, God's powerful presence was manifested again. As the service reached its high point with the performance of the choir and the blowing of the priestly trumpets, "the temple of the Lord was filled with a cloud . . . for the glory of the Lord filled the temple of God."[2] And in the great prayer of dedication that followed, Solomon clearly identified the temple as the central focus of Israel's worship.[3]

Years later, in the midst of an impious banquet in Babylon, in which Belshazzar made sacrilegious use of the sacred vessels captured from the Jerusalem temple, a bloodless hand appeared to write the doom of an arrogant kingdom.

What we're seeing here is a divine concern for the sanctuary/temple running through the Old Testament, a concern that continues into the New:

• Jesus is taken to the temple as a baby, where his parents hear predictions of his mission and destiny.
• At the age of 12, he delays on God's business in the temple.
• Near the beginning of his ministry—and again at the end— Jesus cleanses the temple, stressing its identity with God: "It is written," he says at one of these cleansings, "My house shall be called the house of prayer; but ye have made it a den of thieves."[4]
• As he concluded pronouncing his seven woes against Jerusalem at the beginning of Passion Week, Jesus cited two godly figures (Abel and Zechariah), both killed in the line of sanctuary duty, so to speak. Then, in a clear reference to the end of Israel's probation as a nation, he said, referring to the coming

[1]Ex. 40:3-38; cp. Num. 9:15-23.
[2]2 Chron. 5:12-4.
[3]See 2 Chron. 6:12-42.
[4]Matt. 21:13 KJV.

crisis: "Look, your house [your sanctuary] is left to you deso-late."[1]

• Finally, in the most dramatic event of all, the veil of the tem-ple supernaturally rips asunder at the death of Jesus,[2] by all ac-counts signifying the radical and irrevocable shift from the temporal, earthly entity to the heavenly.

It is possible, then, to draw a horizontal line running from the wilderness tabernacle clear through the First Testament into the Se-cond. And we are able to pinpoint the precise moment when that horizontal line changes into a vertical—at the death of Christ—with the arrow turning upward toward the true sanctuary where, as the author of Hebrews affirms, Jesus, our Great High Priest, minis-ters at the right hand of God.[3]

I am absolutely convinced about the theological veracity of the-se things. It would be theological negligence to ignore them.

But all of us need to develop a clearer understanding as to what constitute the fundamental components of the sanctuary doctrine. Over the years, we have wasted much time, horns locked in com-bat over non-essential matters, well removed from the doctrine's central core.

The notion of a two-part heavenly sanctuary, for example. Or the mobility of the throne of God. Or the presence in heaven of showbread and candles and incense. We have engaged in heated debates about whether blood cleanses or defiles. Some have pontifi-cated on the meanings of the multitudinous paraphernalia and ac-tivities associated with the ancient Hebrew tabernacle seeking to in-terpret how each piece and each detail corresponds to the antitype.

I do not wish to denigrate the study of Old Testament sanctu-ary details, as such. Many have found comfort and inspiration in this exercise. I myself have listened to homilies on these themes that I've found intriguing, spiritually challenging, and beneficial. But how I wish we could develop perspective. How I wish we could find a way of distinguishing between the essential and the peripher-al, a way of zeroing in on the essence!

Scripture provides its own models of this essence targeting. All the laws and regulations of the Pentateuch, for example, are cap-tured and summarized in one short document: the Decalogue. Faithfully to observe it is to fulfill, automatically, all the rest. That's divine wisdom for you!

When his detractors asked him to identify the greatest com-mandment in the law, Jesus tightened that summary even further—this time reducing both the Decalogue and the entire legal corpus

[1]Matt. 23:35, 37.
[2]Matt. 27:51.
[3]Heb. 8:1, 2.

of the Pentateuch into just two sentences: "'Love the Lord your God with all your heart and with all your soul and with all your mind' [and] 'Love your neighbor as yourself.'" "'All the Law and the prophets,'" he said, "'hang on these two commandments.'"[1]

A whole section of my 1993 book deals with this issue of summary and contraction—in regard to prophecies, parables, and other literary genres in Scripture.[2]

Understanding this, we need to look beneath the literal categories that define the Old Testament manifestation of the sanctuary to the sanctuary's antitypical essence. Using this approach, we may, for example, understand the three main divisions of Old Testament sanctuary services (the outer court, the holy place, and the most holy place) as pointing, respectively, to Christ's death on the cross, to Christ's intercession (from the cross to the end), and to judgment.[3]

To express it in this way makes our position more defensible from Scripture. Such reformulations ought not to be accompanied by any theological arrogance on our part—as if we now have superior knowledge that our pioneers did not have. Rather, there should be a straight-forward recognition that our pioneers, like we, were finite mortals—unable, as are we, of perceiving at any one point all God wished to show them. So they, beginning with Hiram Edson, expressed the truth as best they could.

But shame on us if we are content to advance no further than they. How can we, in the face of all the evidence that has emerged during 150 years of study and reflection, doggedly hold on, for example, to the notion of a two-part heavenly sanctuary? The rending of the veil at Jesus' death was meant to convey the message of an open sanctuary. No more barriers! Our great High Priest is absolutely unrestricted.

The point is critical. God's presence could not be manifested in the earthly sanctuary without a veil. Even Moses needed to veil his face when he emerged from the living presence of God.[4] An open earthly sanctuary would have been fatal for the ministering priests. The veil existed for their protection.

But how can we credibly make the same case for the heavenly sanctuary when the High Priest is the risen, spotless Christ? That's why I said in my 1993 book that for us to maintain today, after 150 years of reflection, that "our spotless High Priest was confined to one section of the heavenly sanctuary—assuming there was literally

---

[1]Matt. 22:36-40 NIV.
[2]Adams, *Understanding* 61-7.
[3]Adams, *Understanding* 55-6.
[4]Ex. 34:29, 30.

such a place—for 1,800 years would be theologically incongruous and intolerable."[1]

But if the message of the sanctuary is to receive the hearing it deserves in our time, we will have to move beyond the perennial arguments and debates over issues such as those, and bring the sanctuary's central core into contact with the real problems of contemporary society.

Whether we like it or not, the mood of our time is *relational*. People are concerned about community, about relationships, about how to cope. And if the doctrine of the sanctuary is to remain strong and relevant, it must somehow make contact with this mood, addressing both its longings and its problems.

## SCRATCHING WHERE THEY ITCH

What do people around us—and we ourselves—long for most? I would suggest the following, among others:[2]

- justice;
- forgiveness;
- reconciliation;
- peace;
- community;
- renewal;
- security.

And what problems face us all? These:

- tribalism;
- estrangement;
- loneliness;
- boredom;
- stress;
- alienation;
- hopelessness;
- futility;
- ennui.

Does the message of the sanctuary have any relevance to this catalogue of contemporary concerns? I think it does. I think the more we come to understand the broad parameters of the doctrine, the more we will see it as present truth for our times.

Take the contemporary longing for justice, for example. Would this not be the natural context in which to explore the notion of judgment? Isn't justice the most fundamental goal of judgment? Then does not the innate longing or concern for justice naturally

---

[1] Adams, *Understanding* 113.
[2] I express the same or similar sentiments in "The Cry for Justice . . . and the Answer from the Heavenly Sanctuary," *Ministry*, Aug. 2014: 10-13.

open the way for a consideration of this fundamental aspect of the sanctuary theme—both in its pre-advent and post-advent aspects?

Bad news for tyrants and despots, the notion of judgment culminating in justice should be good news for the abused, the oppressed, the victims of injustice.

In this connection, I've always been intrigued by Psalm 73, with its depiction of the fate of evil and the destiny of its perpetrators. Asaph (to whom the psalm has been attributed) confesses that he had almost lost his way, puzzling over the prosperity of the wicked. These arrogant people did not have to struggle, he said. In spite of a dissolute lifestyle, "their bodies are healthy and strong. They are free from the burdens common to man . . . [and] are not plagued by human ills."[1]

Swollen with arrogance, they threaten and coerce the less fortunate, "lay claim to heaven" and earth and, in the process, even question the wisdom of God.[2] "Carefree, they increase in wealth" while the humble and the godly suffer harassment and derision.[3]

The very thing that puzzled Asaph was also a concern for the patriarch Job. "Why do the wicked live on, growing old and increasing in power?" Job asked. "They see their children established. . . . Their homes are safe and free from fear. . . . Their bulls never fail to breed: their cows calve and do not miscarry. . . . They spend their years in prosperity and go down into the grave in peace."[4]

Comparing the final disposition here on earth of the wicked rich and the godly poor, Job says, "One man [the wealthy wicked] dies in full vigor, completely secure and at ease, his body well nourished, his bones rich with marrow. Another man [the godly poor] dies in bitterness of soul, never having enjoyed anything good. Side by side they lie in the dust, and worms cover them both."[5]

This is the great puzzle, the great conundrum, of the ages. Is life fair? Is there justice? It almost drove Asaph to agnosticism, and, in a million ways, it still plagues the thinking of many of our contemporaries.

How did Asaph resolve it? The significant observation (for our purpose) comes in verses 16 and 17 of Psalm 73: "When I tried to understand all this, it was oppressive to me till I entered the sanctuary of God: then I understood their final destiny."

Whatever else Asaph's words might mean, they certainly present the sanctuary as the place where our vision enlightens, where

[1]Ps. 73:4-5.
[2]Ps. 73:6-11.
[3]Ps. 73:12-15.
[4]Job 21:7-13 NIV.
[5]Job 21:23-6.

the puzzle of life unravels, where we get a concept of ultimate justice.

Justice. We see it in the Exodus, as well—the Old Testament watershed of God's salvific judgment. Throughout history, this great story has lighted the way of both reformers and liberators. Oppressed people have taken fresh courage from it, recalling it to help keep hope alive. And it was in the shadow of the Exodus that the Hebrew sanctuary emerged. As if God was saying: True worship follows freedom, and freedom is the child of justice.

The point is far from theoretical. How different would have been the image of the church if from our inception we had fully appreciated the implications of the element of justice—including social justice—embedded in the concept of judgment, in the concept of sanctuary! Born in New England while slavery was still entrenched in American society, our church might have become a leader in the struggle for freedom. The long term effect of such an image for our world-wide mission today could have been enormous.

To be sure, the church was not totally silent. And, interestingly, it was sanctuary language that Ellen White employed when she excoriated the nominal churches of her day for their tolerance of slavery. "The tears of the pious bondmen and bondwomen, of fathers, mothers, and children . . . are all bottled up in heaven [where else, but in the sanctuary?]," she said. "Angels have recorded it all; it is written in the book."[1] "'Justice and judgment have slumbered long,' she heard the angel say, 'but will soon awake'. . . . The fearful threatening of the third angel are to be realized. . . ."[2]

If God is "the habitation of justice,"[3] Ellen White seemed to be saying to the nominal churches of her day—and to us—then the place where God dwells, the church, cannot continue to be a citadel of injustice.

How is it with us today? Is our church a model of the just society? If this fundamental question does not emerge from our doctrine of the pre-advent judgment, then we are dealing simply in doctrinal theories and pious superficialities.

- A student experiences delays in the completion of a doctoral dissertation resulting from a deliberate and willful effort on the part of an advisor to frustrate the student's progress. That is not justice.

---

[1] Ellen G. White, *Early Writings of E. G. White* (Washington, DC: Review 1945) 275.
[2] See White, *Writings* 274.
[3] Jer. 50:7.

- A student receives a low grade on a paper simply for arriving at a conclusion that conflicts with the position of the teacher. This is not justice.
- A person is passed over for employment or promotion because of race, or gender, or place of origin. That is not justice.
- A person is condemned and humiliated before family, friends, and colleagues without a hearing or due process. That is not justice.
- People are promoted or appointed to boards or committees, not because of ability or competence, but because of their surnames, because of the clout of their parents or relatives, because of the contents of their bank accounts. That is not justice.
- Certain people in the church, regardless of their ministerial calling and competence, cannot expect the hand of ordination to be laid upon them, just because of gender. That is not justice.

All of the above, as you might suspect, refer to actual cases inside the Adventist church.

Is our church noted for justice? If you stood accused of doing something terrible, something evil—and you were innocent (or even guilty), how many people in the church could you confidently select as individuals from whom you'd receive a fair and impartial hearing? People of integrity, people who would not waffle, people who'd not be afraid to come down on the side of justice, even if they had to stand alone? How many?

The doctrine of the sanctuary should mark us out, I think, as God's special people—a people in whose midst the God of justice dwells, and who, as a consequence, constitute a just society, a model for an observing world.

We live in a world that cries out, on every hand, for peace, to mention another of the contemporary longings listed above. There are few things more desirable than peace. But, as one of my colleagues never tires of saying, there can be no peace without justice.

Civil wars persist throughout the world. These conflicts may come to an end with a truce. But there will be no lasting peace if justice is not done. Today, a thousand trouble spots lie dormant, but not dead—because justice has not been done. Revolting genocide and other crimes against individuals and society go unpunished. That is not justice. And it comes back again and again to haunt us.

There is no peace, there can be no peace, without *justice*. Justice is the essential thing, and lies at the very foundation of the concept of sanctuary. Contrary to the theological pabulum of our time, a whole catalogue of Old Testament saints, and the "souls" under the altar in the heavenly sanctuary, cry out for judgment, for justice. If this is not one of the most basic concerns of contemporary society, then I must be living in another world.

I have visions of what could happen if our church, amidst the widespread cynicism of contemporary society, were truly to model the just society.

But my vision is not original. Thousands of years ago, Isaiah wrote down his own, from which I copy: "In the last days the mountain of the Lord's temple will be established as chief among the mountains; it will be raised above the hills, and all nations will stream to it. Many peoples will come and say, 'Come let us go up to the mountain of the Lord, to the house of the God of Jacob. He will teach us his ways, so that we may walk in his paths.' The law will go out from Zion, the word of the Lord from Jerusalem. He will judge between the nations and will settle disputes for many peoples. They will beat their swords into plowshares and their spears into pruning hooks. Nation will not take up sword against nation, nor will they train for war anymore."[1]

Let me briefly take another example.

It occurred to me that we might even couch the doctrine of the sanctuary in terms of the environmental concerns of our day—sneaking in, at the same time, the contemporary longing for community and security, and the church's concern for mission. All of this together!

Here's how.

We might begin with the command that brought the wilderness tabernacle into being in the first place: "And let them make me a sanctuary; that I may dwell among them."[2]

In our contemporary context, sanctuary has come to mean a place of refuge, of safety, of protection. I think we can make the case that this concept is completely at home with the text just cited. Without disrespect, we might think of comparing God with an endangered species.

Do we not see a trend today to X God out of the world? To live and function as if there were no God? To pursue our human paradigms without reference to God? How about our boasted technological advances today? How about our attempts at genetic manipulation? How about issues of active euthanasia? How about abortion for convenience or as a means of birth control? How about the development and amassing of weapons of mass destruction? How about the criminal destruction of the environment and the planet itself? Do we think we own this place? Do we think

[1]Isa. 2:2-4 NIV.
[2]Ex. 25:8.

there is to be no accountability? That we are masters of our own fate? That there is no God out there?

Has not God become an endangered species in a world created and sustained by divine power?

Our concept of sanctuary should proclaim to all and sundry that as a people, we make room, we make sanctuary, for God. That we invite God to take up residence in our midst. That God is "safe" with us.

And the flip side of this divine asylum in our midst provides the answer to our deepest yearnings—for forgiveness, for peace, for community, for security.

Think of the enormous sense of security the following phenomenon would have brought to ancient Israel: "On the day the tabernacle, the Tent of the Testimony, was set up, the cloud covered it. From evening till morning the cloud above the tabernacle looked like fire. That is how it continued to be; the cloud covered it, and at night it looked like fire. Whenever the cloud lifted from above the Tent, the Israelites set out; wherever the cloud settled, the Israelites encamped."[1]

This spectacular manifestation of God's presence, emphasized by way of repetition no less than 10 times in the passage,[2] involves two distinct, but interlocking, realities: 1) God graciously comes to dwell (to take up sanctuary) in our midst, and, 2) we draw near to the divine presence, ourselves to find sanctuary, to find reconciliation, to find security, to find peace. This mysterious symbiosis is the answer for the estrangement, the loneliness, the alienation of contemporary society.

These are just ideas—still undeveloped, thrown out at random to show the potential buried in this beautiful message to meet the longings, to address the problems, of our times. The sky's the limit, and it's deeper than we can ever go. But the singular power of this approach will derive from its currentness, its "present-truthness," from its ability to make authentic contact with the deepest longings of the human heart.

## Summary and Conclusion

As a convert to Seventh-day Adventism, shaped by an educational tradition characterized, among other things, by dispassionate objectivity in research, I wanted to settle for myself the issue of the sanctuary and get at the bottom of the whisperings and innuendoes that had come to my attention since joining the church. Hence my decision to do my dissertation on the doctrine of the sanctuary.

[1]Num. 9:15-7 NIV.
[2]See vv. 15-23.

In the midst of this effort, as chance (or was it Providence?) would have it, the entire mood in the Adventist church took an ominous turn with the theological crisis over this aspect of our faith in the early '80s. These were nervous times for me. What if my findings suggested that as a church we had been mistaken? It was, of course, never a question of what that would mean for the church, but rather what it would mean for *me*. I would have to follow the evidence wherever it led, and would have to make the appropriate personal decisions.

I am pleased—and relieved—to state that after some eighteen months of study, much of which could not be reported in my dissertation, I arrived at the conclusion that "no evidence to which . . . [my] study had access was considered fatal to any fundamental area of . . . [the sanctuary] doctrine as developed by Seventh-day Adventists."[1]

That is my position still. I consider our fundamental teaching on the sanctuary to be both biblical and sound.

But the statement with which I opened that final chapter of my dissertation still challenges me today: "Great philosophical or theological issues," it said, "are seldom resolved to the satisfaction of succeeding generations."[2]

By any definition, the doctrine of the sanctuary clearly falls into that category. And the question that faces us as a church is whether, after more than 170 years of study and reflection, we possess, as I put it, "the theological and emotional sangfroid"[3] that would give us freedom to explore, freedom to move, freedom to grow. Is the conception of a broader, more comprehensive understanding of this doctrine anathema to us? Do we have the resilience to combine the wisdom of the past with the vision of the future?

In my view, we would make shipwreck of all theological common sense if we failed to appreciate the fundamental importance of the core elements of our sanctuary teaching. But we will smother the very life we're trying so desperately to preserve if we fail to lift the thick blanket of needless tradition covering its nose and preventing it from breathing in the atmosphere of the contemporary world. We must get rid of our historic nervousness on this question. If the doctrine of the sanctuary is from God—and I have come to my own conclusion that it is—then it is stronger than any one of us or all of us combined, and will hold its own. All we have to do is let it loose!

---

[1]Adams, *Sanctuary* 283.
[2]David R. Mason, "What Sense Does It Make to Say, 'God Knows Future Contingent Things'?" *Religious Studies* 6-7 (Fall 1978/Spring 1979): 2. Cp. Adams, *Sanctuary* 236.
[3]Adams, *Sanctuary* 283.

Letting the sanctuary "loose" should not, of course, imply any abandonment of the past. We cannot make genuine progress without establishing appropriate continuity with the past. The fundamentals must be clear: *We have a Great High Priest, Jesus Christ, in the heavenly sanctuary. His intercessory ministry spans the period from the ascension to probation's close, running coterminously(since 1844) with a special final phase of judgment, typified in the Old Testament economy by the Day of Atonement. That (pre-advent) judgment constitutes the last event in salvation history this side of eternity. When it ends, Jesus will return.*

That's it!

This is no reductionism. Of course, it does not spell out the entire theology of the sanctuary. But it means to get at the central core, to define the essence. Only as we clearly identify the essence will we know when to dig in our heels in the face of challenge, and when not to. And only as we understand and feel comfortable with the essence will we effectively and authentically apply its message to the issues and problems of contemporary society.

Can we break out of the siege mentality that has gripped us as a church on this question over the years? Can we rid ourselves of the fear that the doctrine is so brittle that it would crumble upon close examination and scrutiny? That's the urgent question that will determine the future of the church's sanctuary theology.

If the doctrine of the sanctuary is to remain alive and healthy in our time we must be prepared to subject it to the deepest scrutiny so that it may emerge free of non-essentials—fresh as the dawn, and as powerful as the rising tide.

# 8

# Church

## Paul J. Landa

The respected baseball philosopher Yogi Berra once said: "Predictions are mighty difficult to make, especially if they're about the future!"

Regardless of how keen we are to know the future, none of us possesses the gift of foretelling, which means that no matter how long and hard we peer in our crystal balls, those of us who dabble in futurism had better be prepared to eat a lot of broken glass! And few understand this better than the descendants of Millerites who still have to deal with shards of broken dreams as we recall a great disappointment resulting from a faulty prediction.

Having said that, I'll still venture to think about the future, and I invite you to do so with me because I believe that it is both useful and needful—it forces us to get out of our rut, it forces us to become creative and constructive, it forces us to confront change and to think and act proactively as we anticipate where our church "market"—people—will be and how we ought to position ourselves to meet their needs in the most effective and efficient manner.

I'm proposing to think futuristically about some aspects of our church against a backdrop of unprecedented global changes and clearly identifiable trends. These unprecedented global changes— changes which have occurred for the most part over a single generation—include:

- the end of the industrial age and the emergence of the age of information;
- the end of Western dominance and the emergence of a new world disorder;
- the end of the capitalist era and the emergence of the free market era;
- the end of Communism and the cold war and the triumph of democratic ideals; and

- the end of traditional religious beliefs and the emergence of
  new religious Gnosticisms.

Further, we are in the throes of a global population explosion, a
global crime explosion, and a resurgence of the ugliest forms of
primitive nationalism.

The trends which are most likely to have an impact on Christianity in general and on our denomination in particular include
widespread secularization, urbanization, the fragmentation of personal relationships, and the resurgence of various forms of religious
fundamentalism. As you will see, there is an interconnectedness
among these trends. And there is yet one additional trend which
has to do with the way organizations are restructuring themselves
and choosing to offer their services which will quite likely influence
the way our church will choose to fulfill its mission in the next
century.

## THE WORLD OF THE CHURCH OF THE FUTURE

One of the principal characteristics of the world of the church
of the future will be secularization—an "umbrella term" which encompasses several clearly identifiable components.

1. *Contingency*—the view that everything in the sensate world
happens and can be explained through cause and effect linkages.
Thus, if I'm prone to anger, it is not because God made me that
way, but more likely because of the way my parents raised me or
because of a particular combination of chemicals in my brain, or
both. What used to be explained in terms of supernatural intervention or taken to God for resolution can now be explained, predicted, manipulated, controlled, and often resolved by scientific and
technological means. In the words of Alan Gilbert, ". . . a new . . .
order has emerged in which there are no mysterious incalculable
forces that come into play," for this is an age in which "one can, in
principle, master all things by calculation."

2. *Autonomy*—the belief that rational beings are quite capable of
formulating answers to their most difficult questions, of making responsible choices and decisions for their own lives, and of providing
solutions for their own problems without reference to God, religion, or a church. Each person is able to be the master of her or his
fate and the captain of her or his destiny, and does not need God
for any direction. In a very real sense, secular persons have created
their own gods and their own schemes of salvation. Instead of biblical salvationism, which proposes supernatural aid at the limit of
human capability, secular persons have redefined salvation by limit-
ing it to psychological and social needs and provided human means
and remedies to meet these needs.

3. *Relativity*—given the absence of the supernatural and the presence of autonomy, values and moral and ethical standards are matters of personal individual choice arrived at with one eye to prevailing societal norms and the other to the dynamics of a particular situation. In the absence of a dominant religious consensus, there is no longer a common morality which informs persons about the way life should be lived. All values are relative and any moral system can be viable for the person or group that creates it. Rather than seeking what is absolutely true or right, a secular person prefers to go along with whatever is "right for him or her" at a given point in time.

4. *Temporality*—human existence is limited to this life. The notion of an afterlife, although attractive, is regarded by secular people as mere wishful thinking conjured up by those who cannot face up to the finality of death. Since this is the only life they expect to live, secular people are determined to make the most of it, to experience it and enjoy it to the full. They are very much into self-actualization programs that promise a healthier, happier, sexier, more prosperous life.

5. *Materialism*—Secular persons are "thing-oriented," convinced that material possessions are almost as important as human relationships for the achievement of a happy life. Unlike the previous generation, however, which was intent in acquiring as much stuff as possible, the new secular types are more discriminating; they are interested in just *the best* stuff.

Contributing to the spread of secularization is the worldwide phenomenon of urbanization, which is affecting quite dramatically the way people think, feel, and act. In 1900, there were only twenty cities with populations of over one million—most of them in the First World. By the year 2025, there will be 546 such cities, many of them in the Two-Thirds World.

What is of significance here are the radical changes that urbanization is bringing to human existence for so many: educational opportunities, upward mobility, wealth, leisure time, and a choice of amusements as well as overcrowding, lack of personal space, violence, carelessness, apathy, survival behavior, depersonalization, and alienation. All of these factors feed a profound hostility towards religion and accelerate the process of secularization as well as the fragmentation of human relationships, which is the next trend characterizing the world of the church of the future.

The depersonalizing impact of urbanization, coupled with the increasing isolation of people in the workplace as a result of the cybernetic revolution, will increase the expectations placed on relationships—especially marriage and the family—by secular people longing for companionship and intimacy. But the persisting secular

tendencies towards autonomy, relativity, and temporality will viti-
ate all relationships and will make marriage and family life deeply
frustrating and disappointing. Having failed to develop and maintain
the relational skills required to make long-term relationships work,
people will marry over and over and over again. And friendships
will be mostly casual and ephemeral, given the narcissistic tendency
of the secular culture with its focus on the self, cutely expressed in
Fritz Perls's "Gestalt Prayer":

> I do my thing and you do your thing. I am not in the world to live up
> to your expectations and you are not in this world to live up to mine.
> You are you and I am I and if by chance we find each other, it's beauti-
> ful. If not, it can't be helped.

Finally, secularity with its moral relativity, its lack of certainty
and assurance, and its rejection of God and religion will continue to
feed a reactionary resurgence of religious fundamentalism, catering
to those looking for direction, for clearer definitions of right and
wrong, for simple answers to complex problems, and for spiritual
norms to provide some stability and constancy in their lives. They
will be receptive to a broad spectrum of ideas and ideals—both
Christian and non-Christian. And the ideas they will buy will most
likely come from those groups or individuals who speak with the
authority of deeply-held convictions—regardless of whether their
ideas are good or thoroughly bad!

In addition to the philosophical, religious, and sociological
trends I have just summarized, there is yet another "cluster" of
trends which have emerged from the corporate sector of our society
that will influence all organizations—including churches. This cluster of trends can be characterized as a shift away from vertical
command hierarchies and toward decentralized structures that function and thrive through more horizontal, collaborative networking.

The traditional hierarchical, vertical organizations (such as our
own church) are being replaced by collaborative, horizontal ones.
Within these new structures, leadership is information-based, visionary, and future oriented. It proceeds through consultations with
those who have to share in the implementation of decisions, seeking creative input, welcoming dissent, and enabling everyone involved to develop a sense of common direction. It is collegial, participatory, consultative, and open. And it is not fearful of accountability.

Policies are not developed *in abstracto* but in response to known
needs and with a keen sense of what others are doing, both near
and far, to maximize effectiveness and efficiency in the use of human and material resources. Information age methods and technologies which can link any number of entities together in all sorts of
networks are making all this possible.

What is and will be the impact of these trends on the SDA church and on the way it is perceived by boomers and members of what is commonly referred to as Generation X? This is an enormously broad, two-part question with lots of possible answers. I will limit myself to some key areas. But before I begin, let me generalize by saying that secularization has already had and will continue to have a profound impact on Christianity, the Christian church, and Christian people because of the ways it undermines the most basic, core assumptions undergirding Christianity, the Christian church, and the Christian life. Its persuasiveness and pervasiveness have made and will continue to make Christianity and the church seem irrelevant to most of humankind. Australian historian Alan Gilbert may well be right when he suggests that "secularization is a much deadlier foe than any previous counter-religious force in human experience," gradually eroding the standing of the Christian church in society from one of importance to one of impotence.

There has to be a better way. But before we consider that, let us consider the impact of our five major trends on our church and its members, both now and in the near future.

## TREND IMPACT

In an age that worships at the shrine of the scientific method, many Adventists are reassessing, reinterpreting, and even abandoning traditional church teachings about origins, the nature of persons, sin, the uniqueness of the Christian gospel, lifestyle issues (including homosexuality), the inspiration of Ellen G. White, etc., which cannot be supported by reliable, scientific evidence and, to a lesser extent, their own experience. "Thus saith" the church, or the Bible, or Ellen White doesn't cut it anymore.

As a church, we are always willing to engage in vigorous debate about what is truth, but we are less able to demonstrate how possessing the truth *makes much difference* to the quality of our lives. Recent noisy debates about biblical interpretation, the integrity of Ellen White, charismatic worship styles, the ordination of women, or pre-advent judgment have left two impressions: (*a*) ultimate truth may not be knowable after all and (*b*) to have arrived at truth doesn't seem to matter very much because it has so few existential, behavioral consequences. To debate about doctrines seems to be like engaging in a game of theological trivial pursuit which ignores the real issues of contemporary life. As one former Adventist put it to me: "While the world is going to hell, the church is arguing whether the temperature down there is measured in Celsius or Fahrenheit! Who cares!"

As persons and as an organization, we seem to feel less dependent upon God and the power of the Holy Spirit and more confident of our own abilities, methods and technologies to resolve most of our problem. Sit on any church committee at any level and you will know what I mean. *Spirituality* seems to be eroding. We're spending less time in Bible study and prayer and in reflecting about how we might apply Bible principles to various life situations. Think how unpopular the series of Sabbath School lessons on the books of the Bible have been to so many of our members! We find it difficult, almost embarrassing, to talk about spiritual things with people outside the church. Our appreciation for the sacredness of the Sabbath is being eroded by the secular weekend. Quality sacred time tends to be equated with periods of personal pleasure rather than spiritual reflection. Traditional Adventist standards of behavior, dress, diet, and recreation are being abandoned by members who do not appreciate being told by anyone—least of all by pastors and church administrators—what to do in these personal areas of their lives. Relativity and autonomy are having an impact

By surprise and, as a denomination, we are losing our foothold in some of the great cities of the world. We are not being helped by our traditional and pervasive negative attitude towards cities and the evils within them, and we remain poorly equipped—both culturally and theologically—to respond to the challenge posed by *urbanization.*

*Fundamentalism* is alive and well among SDAs, many of whom believe that the church has become too worldly and no longer represents "historic Adventism." They are dismayed by uncertainty about what used to be fundamental beliefs, by slipping behavioral standards, by the loss of mission and commitment, and by a proclamation which lacks "that certain Adventist prophetic ring." And on every continent, latter-day reformers and self-appointed prophets are coming forward bearing "the straight testimony" to members and administrators alike who are leading the church into a great apostasy by condoning all sorts of heresies and worldly practices. And thousands are responding to their convincing mix of criticism and piety.

The new style of *leadership* in flattened administrative structures with collaborative networking has not yet made it into the Adventist church, although there are signs that it may be on the way, forced upon us by dwindling resources, uneven expansion patterns, large membership losses, the disaffection of women and young people (especially in the First World) and the demands for greater accountability and involvement by laity.

*The Churches as Outdated*

Perceptions of our church by baby boomers and members of Generation X are partly shaped by what the church says and does as

well as by the way these ideas and actions are reported by the secular media and studied and interpreted by a wide array of scholarly
and non-scholarly commentators. The perceptions that are being
created tend to apply somewhat indiscriminately to all Christian
bodies—ours included. While they may not always be accurate they
do provide insights which ought to be taken seriously by the Adventist church of the future in setting some of its goals and priorities.

Christian churches tend to be perceived as belonging to an old
social order. They seem to be out of place in a society where work,
wealth, relationship, and leisure are dominant concerns. For all
their collective experience, the churches' views on the significant
issues on our political and social agendas—the economy, matters of
war and peace, world hunger, the environment, the poor, health
care, the rights of women, violence, and crime—are ignored because they are perceived as somewhat irrelevant. To be sure, the
churches' humanitarian efforts are always appreciated and frequently
reported on by the media. But such actions are not viewed as addressing the root causes of humankind's most pressing problems.
When churches use terms such as the Bible, original sin, Satan,
greed, or lust, when they speak of the need for conversion, for
*agape* love, and so on, they seem to be perpetuating the thinking of
another era, thinking the world has left behind long ago.

The fact that so many churchgoers have adopted for themselves
secular views regarding matters of conduct and character seems to
prove that the moral norms propounded by the Christian churches—including our own—are outmoded, impractical, and out of
touch with real life. Indeed, the churches are viewed by some as re-
tarding the moral maturation process of individuals by imposing
upon them ready-made inflexible standards instead of allowing
them to develop their own through education, experience, and
critical reflection.

In a consumerist society, the churches are viewed as offering
optional services, often placed under the umbrella of the leisure industry, as offering leisure options which some may choose in lieu of
or along with sports, the theater, travel, and so on.

To societies that have labored long and hard to achieve a margin of leisure, churches come across as wet blankets and spoilsports.
As Martin Marty put it: "The most common objection of the ordinary American to the church is that it spoils his fun." Churches are
perceived as always siding with restriction, repression, and prohibition. They seem to find it difficult to be able to give arms and legs

and smiles to the words of the Jesus who proclaimed: "I have come so that they may have life and have it to the full."[1]

To a generation brought up in front of TV screens and all too sensitive to the difference between a dazzling show and a mediocre one, church rituals and services are for the most part unattractive, uninteresting, and uninspiring—in a word, *boring*. And to make matters worse, churches are always asking for money to keep these boring shows afloat.

## The Churches and the Cities

Churches often seem irrelevant to the concerns of contemporary urbanites. Among other things, they divide people into classes. Most suburban churches seem to appeal to members of society's privileged class (which many aspire to join some day). They seem to function as exclusive private clubs, serving the interests of their members. They often appear insensitive to the economic, cultural, racial, and social diversity which is so characteristic of modern urban agglomerations. Inner-city churches, on the other hand, are appreciated for helping to cluster people together in more or less homogeneous groups and for making genuine efforts to meet people's needs. Unfortunately, in many cities, downtown churches are being forced to close their doors because they lack financial resources.

Churches offer little help with city living. The fact that so many church-goers do not exhibit a quality of life that is markedly different from that of non-church goers seems to prove that churches have little to offer to assist people in coping with the stresses of city life. More might believe the churches' claims if more members could model a more viable urban lifestyle.

## The Churches and Personal Relationships

As far as human relationships go, the fact that church-goers experience the same rate of family failures and divorce as non-churchgoers seems to prove once again that churchgoing does little to enhance relationships and that Christian moral norms are impractical, outmoded, and out of sync with modern life. Many so-called "church people" appear inauthentic and superficial; it is easy to conclude that such people are not likely to have much to offer to fill the emotional and relational longings of their non-churchgoing contemporaries. Moreover, belonging to a church does not seem to do very much to relieve the feelings of acute loneliness and emotional emptiness experienced by single people.

[1]Jn. 10:10.

## Organizational Structure

When it comes to ecclesiastical organizations and structures, many people do not get that close to a church to know or to really care. Church for them is a congregation and its pastoral staff. They rarely bother to go beyond the local organization. For those who do, however, the perception of churches with hierarchical structures is one of "imperialistic remoteness." Such entities appear to be concerned primarily with preserving organizational integrity and maintaining uniformity of belief and practice in the name of Christian unity.

Unlike many modern corporations, churches with centralized governance structures appear unwilling to involve lay members with professional expertise in such fields as planning, financial management, marketing, human resources, and development in their policy development and decision-making process. They also seem to possess a congenital inability to tolerate dissenters, visionaries, and other creative people.

## Where Do We Go From Here?

So what are we to make of all this and where do we go from here?

In the face of the trends and perceptions just presented, the church could decide to take what Jon Paulien calls the "lean and mean" approach of doctrinal and lifestyle purity, restricting its membership to a small "remnant" group, fully committed to a statement of beliefs and a corporate mission to really "finish the work" and thus bring about the long-awaited second advent. Such a church would certainly satisfy the demands of Adventism's fundamentalist wing. But it would cut off a majority of members and it would greatly diminish the denomination's impact on society and the world at large.

A second and far easier option is to disregard trends and perceptions altogether and continue to do what we've always done, buoyed up by our past successes and by the assurance that this is God's church and that, in the words of Ellen White, divine providence will "carry the noble ship which bears the people of God safely into port."

This option is tempting. As we look at our experience over the past century and a half, there is so much to rejoice over and to praise God for. Think of it—from a handful of disappointed Millerites in 1844, we have become the most widely spread Protestant denomination in the world, operating in over 200 countries and 619 languages. We are really a church of all nations! Our educational system is the envy of many other churches. The same can be said for our international network of medical institutions, our publishing houses and our humanitarian endeavors. We continue to operate the largest Protestant missionary organization in the world, with the greatest number of missionaries out in the field serving in many different professional specialties. And the Advent people continue to provide strong financial support for the operation of the church's programs and institutions.

The really thrilling part of the Adventist story, however, is found beyond what is expressed by numerical growth, by geographical spread, by institutional strength, and by financial resources. Our church has changed people's lives and influenced society for good through the love, compassion, and healing it has brought; by the hope and strength and meaning it has given; by the fellowship it has created; and by the service it has rendered to humanity. Millions of people have been affected by the persuasive power of our ministry and mission. Constitutions have been rewritten to guarantee religious freedom for all; new national health care programs have been developed along with new systems of disease prevention.

In many areas in which Adventist missions have been established, a new work ethic has brought new economic growth and prosperity. In other areas, the Adventist presence has led to social and moral reform, fostering justice for minorities, equality for men and women, and a more equitable distribution of land and wealth. Seventh-day Adventists have led out in agricultural development, stimulated national school reform, brought improvement to nutritional habits, and contributed to community development. Yes, the Seventh-day Adventist church has been used mightily by God to help restore the divine image and character in God's creatures.

But the *status quo* option, tempting as it is, is dangerous as well because it ignores the reality that the world in which the church operates is changing very rapidly, that people are no longer as receptive to what we have been offering as they used to be, and that Adventists themselves have been profoundly impacted by secularization, urbanization, the fragmentation of human relationships, the lure of fundamentalism, and the promise of more effective and efficient ways of accomplishing our tasks. To ignore the impact of these trends upon us as a church is to choose to ignore a few other truths about ourselves which we have not yet mentioned:

*Truth 1*: Our membership statistics do not tell us that probably less than 50% of Seventh-day Adventists attend church every Sabbath and even fewer contribute anything to the work and mission of their local congregations. The percentages vary from location to location, but there seems to be a predictable operative pattern which divides "first generation" churches from "second generation" ones. "First generation" churches, comprising converts from non-Adventist backgrounds, are growing rapidly. Their members exhibit an enthusiastic, contagious faith in the Advent message, a zeal to share it, and a love and loyalty to the church. "Second generation" churches grow very little—or not at all. Their members no longer seem excited by the Advent message and their commitment to the church is formal, devoid of passion and profound conviction.

*Truth 2*: Our growth patterns are very uneven. The church is growing rapidly in the countries of the Two-Thirds World and of the former Soviet Union, but it is stagnant in the countries of the First World. Moreover, while we claim almost universal presence, our spread is also very uneven and spotty, with large concentrations mostly around church-owned institutions. And we are very thinly represented in the mega-cities of the world. Since the 1960s, the Adventist church's "center of gravity" has shifted from the American-European hemisphere to the countries of Africa, Asia, Latin America, and Oceania—again a First World to Two-Thirds World shift. From a generational perspective, churches in the Two-Thirds World are largely made up of young people open to new ideas, to diversity, to new ways of doing things. Churches in the First World are graying churches, basically conservative and not too receptive to new ideas and methods. The implications of Truth 2 are plain for all to see: quite apart from the very real generational differences between First World and Two-Thirds World Adventists, there are even greater social and cultural differences. Even more critical are the economic disparities and the enormous strain it creates on the church's financial situation where a distinct minority of the world membership supports the clear majority.

*Truth 3*: Our traditional evangelistic emphasis has not made us good nurturers. We have presumed that an understanding of Adventist doctrines would protect our members from the corrosive influence of secularism—and we have presumed wrong! Secularism has already impacted our lives as well as our institutions. We have also presumed that attending church on Sabbath and participating in an occasional church-sponsored social activity would satisfy both the spiritual and the relational needs of our members—and once again, we have presumed wrongly. We are losing a huge number of members, and the result is not a purer church but a poorer one because most of those who leave us are young (under 45), well-educated professionals on fast tracks to becoming the thought-shapers and the movers and shakers of society. Their loss diminishes our impact and our influence; it also accelerates the graying of the church and makes it unattractive to many.

*Truth 4*: The business of running the church has developed a life of its own and is siphoning key talent and resources away from where the action should really be—at the level of local congregations and in service and evangelistic outreach. A large percentage of our budgets are earmarked to support administrative functions and many of our most effective members are getting lost in the many layers of our hierarchical organization. Church members have noticed this and don't like it. This may explain, in part, why giving patterns have shifted away from general, centralized programs and towards more specific local or mission needs. These truths about ourselves are telling us quite clearly that to carry on business as usual is not a very good option for the Adventist church of the future. Can we find a better way? Yes—if we are prepared to begin by asking whether our mission, our goals, our priorities and our methods are consonant with what we understand the church to be.

## THE IDENTITY OF THE ADVENTIST CHURCH OF THE FUTURE

We must begin by looking at our identity, by asking the question, "What is the church?" How we answer this question—from Scripture and not on the basis of an alien corporate model—will help us understand what we are meant to be, and in light of that, what we are meant to do, and the dynamics that ought to be operative between leaders and members.

What I'm suggesting here seems obvious, almost simplistic to most of us today, but we haven't traditionally thought about our ecclesiology in light of our identity. From the very outset, we have paid more attention to what the church does or should do than to what it is, more attention to the function of the church than to its essence or being.

We can thank our Millerite forebears and the American nineteenth-century ethos for that. The former regarded the very idea of a church, with a name of its own, as a thoroughly "Babylonian" notion. The latter enabled the United States to become the world's industrial giant, exalting before all else the "can do anything" spirit. So we became a movement, rather than a church.

There is both an advantage and a disadvantage in this. On the positive side, we have not been bound by the strictures of a narrow ecclesiology. We have been somewhat free to accommodate to circumstances in a world in which, until the middle of the last century, our "WASPish" values were highly influential. That world, as we know, no longer exists. But the quality of adaptability in our past—even if it was somewhat one-sided—should work to our advantage as we face up to the enormous diversity of the world of tomorrow.

On the negative side, the absence of an ecclesiological center (anchored in Scripture) has led us to elevate structure and administrative functions and equate them with the church. A rapidly expanding movement in an increasingly complex and threatening world elicits protective reactions from those responsible for the well-being of the organization. And these responses tend to pull everything towards the center (as they should), towards uniformity, towards rigid conformity to established policies and procedures.

What, then, is the church? It is not merely a human organization like the Rotary or the Garden Club, a group a people drawn together by common interests—although it is both human and an organization. It is not merely a social institution—like the government or the public school system—although it is a social entity. It is not merely a corporation—a task-oriented business, producing or selling something or offering certain services—although it does have a corporate reality and it does offer services.

1. *A Called People.* The New Testament word for church is *ekklesia*—literally "the called out ones"—not a self-constituted group but a community of people divinely called out from the world into a special relationship with Christ and with one another. It is a community of people who have heard the invitation "follow me" and who have consciously chosen to respond to the call to become "come outers" and "followers."

2. *Related to Christ.* The church is a community of people who derive their identity from Jesus Christ, whose call each member has heard and answered. To be called out and to choose to join Jesus' band of disciples is to acknowledge him as Lord and Savior.[1] To belong to the church is to belong to a community of people committed to being Christ's people, committed to living in harmony with his teachings and to apply his principles in all relationships. This allegiance supersedes all other allegiances[2] and provides a bond that unites the members of the community so intimately with Christ that the church can be identified in the New Testament as the "spouse of Christ[3] and as the "body of Christ."[4] The church is a community of people among whom the Holy Spirit is active, producing repentance and inner transformation of life (*metanoia*),[5] bringing people together in unity of spirit, purpose and fellowship (*koinonia*),[6] and empowering them for proclamation (*kerygma*)[7] and service (*diakonia*).[8] Thus, the church helps to mediate God's grace

---

[1]Rom. 10:9; Phil 2:9.
[2]Luke 14:26; 20:20-25; 9:23
[3]Ephesians 5.
[4]I Cor. 12:27; 2 Cor. 11:2; Rom. 7:4.
[5]John 3:5-8; I Peter 1:2, 12
[6]Acts 2:42-47.
[7]Matt. 28:18-20.
[8]Eph. 4:11-15, Rom. 12:6-7.

to the world: it is an instrumentality of salvation, which is ultimately God's work. And therefore, the church is a community which
no human beings, no human organizations, and no human methods
can produce.

Because of this dual nature, it is not always easy to talk about
the church. Indeed, it is difficult to think about the church in a way
that does not distort both of its dimensions. The Adventist church
of the future will have to make a deliberate effort to keep both in
healthy tension, recognizing that to overemphasize the divine dimension at the expense of the human will make the church inac-
cessible and irrelevant and will diminish its sense of involvement in
and responsibility for God's world. To overemphasize the human
dimension at the expense of the divine will continue to perpetuate
our traditional way of thinking about the church as an institution,
an organization, a creation of our own making whose ultimate fate
is our responsibility.

To keep the duality of the church's nature in proper tension
and to help us understand better what the church was originally
meant to be, the Bible uses a variety of models and metaphors—the
church as God's new creation, as the people of God, as the body of
Christ, and so on. The one metaphor to which I hope the Adventist church of the future will want to return often is the model of the
church as a *family*. Like all metaphors, it has its limitations, but it is
more helpful than the others.

1. The concept of family is helpful because it is accessible to so
many of us. Christians, according to Paul, are members of the
"family of God."[1] They are sons [and daughters] of God.[2]

2. The image of the church as God's family correlates well with
the primary Christian way of thinking about God—namely as "Father"—the source of our being, whose loving, caring, nurturing
and disciplining ways also correlate with those of the best conceivable mother.

3. The family metaphor also speaks of continuity: a family always looks in three directions—to the past, to ancestors who gave it
its name and its uniqueness; to the present, as it expands with the
addition of spouses whose extended families bring diversity in all
sorts of ways; and to the future, as it expands even further with the
arrival of children born in the family or adopted from other families, who will carry on the family's name as well as some of its
unique traditions (while abandoning others). The church family also looks to the past for its identity, which is grounded in the incarnation of God in the person of Jesus Christ and the transmission of

[1]Eph. :19
[2]Gal. 4:5, 6; 1 Jn. 3:1- 2

the knowledge and experience of the Gospel through the centuries. The church in the present continues to proclaim the good news as it makes disciples around the world. (Their response to the call to become disciples confirms that the Gospel is still the "power of God to save all who have faith."[1]) And the church looks to the future as it educates each new generation to own the core principles of its understanding of the Gospel while at the same time providing enough freedom for the reinterpretation of those principles in order to keep them meaningful and relevant in new times and new settings.

4. This inevitably brings us to the issue of diversity and unity, in connection with which the metaphor of the church as "family" is again helpful. In a family, each member possesses uniqueness and a separate identity signified by a first name. Yet the individual person is also related to the head of the family and shares a common family identity signified by a family name derived from a father or (these days) a mother. Despite their unique, separate identities, the family members are, and know themselves to be, related. Thus, in addition to diversity, there must also be a measure of commonality to ensure unity. Similarly, in any church—and especially a world church—there will always be a great deal of diversity—diversity of perceptions, of understandings, and of practices. Yet the church will not lose its identity, neither will it fragment on account of this diversity, as it continues to articulate clearly certain central, unifying affirmations. In our church, the Statement of Fundamental Beliefs constitutes that central, unifying core. All the members of the church family can be expected to affirm it in order to be Seventh-day Adventists, though not necessarily to relate to it in the same way.

What is important to recognize here is the difference between affirmation and application. To belong to the church family means to affirm certain core, unifying principles which are constitutive of the church. But it does not mean to interpret or to apply them in exactly the same way, at all times, and everywhere.

5. Again, the family metaphor is useful in drawing our attention to the principles of trust and respect which are absolutely vital to maintain happy interdependence, collaboration, and relations within a family, in the face of all sorts of disagreements and crises. And once again, what pertains to the family also pertains to the church: it is faithfulness to the principles of trust and respect among members which enable the church to do more than tolerate diversity, but actually embrace it without fear of disintegration and chaos because of its marvelous potential for fostering enrichment and growth and for providing an attractive witness before the world of

[1]Rom. 1:16.

the transformational and unifying power of Christian love. We must also recognize that families—even Christian ones—are prone to dysfunctionality. The family metaphor reminds us that families are made up of imperfect people who get on each other's nerves, take advantage of each other, and even betray each other's trust Such painful experiences call for a willingness to forgive and become reconciled, although this is not always possible—separation does occur. The same dynamics also operate in the church. The analogy with family life reminds us that we need not become disillusioned with and bitter about the church but instead, do all in our power to act as agents of reconciliation and healing.

6. The family metaphor also provides helpful correctives to our proclivity as Seventh-day Adventists to think of the church only in terms of impersonal organization or bureaucracy. I'm indebted to Fritz Guy for pointing out that, when applied to the church, the idea of family acts as a safeguard against four dangers: (a) the danger of *professionalization*—assigning all the most important work of the church to full-time, paid employees, leaving the rest of the members uninvolved beyond the level of paying the bills; (b) the danger of *centralization*—concentrating authority in the interest of efficiency and unity instead of its dispersal in the interest of responsibility and competence; (c) the danger of *bureaucratization*—the ever-increasing number of people involved in support services—which, more often than not, hinders progress, kills creativity and stifles local initiatives; (d) the danger of *quantification*—defining success strictly in terms of numbers without regard for the more elusive yet very tangible manifestations and expressions of the fruits of the Spirit in the church which defy all quantification.

Because the church needs to be an organization to carry out its mission, it is subject to these dangers like every other organization. But because it is also, and more fundamentally, the family of God, it can resist these dangers. The family does not need "professionally trained" parents or children to be a good family! It functions more happily and more efficiently when decisions are made and tasks are done collaboratively, and its successes is not measured by its adjusted gross income or the number of its children!

Because the advantages of thinking about the church as "family" are so obvious, the Adventist church of the future will want to return to this metaphor in order not to lose its proper sense of identity. The metaphor of family will remind the church of its unique, dual nature—pointing to Christ, its head, the source of its being. But it will also remind the church that it is a community of people and not an abstract, faceless organization. This should also result in a kinder, gentler church in which people issues will have priority over the more theoretical matters of structure. It will enable the church to be more winsome as it is continually nudged to model and not merely talk about openness, inclusiveness, diversity, creativity, and unity. It will enable us to do more with the ministry of listening, to take seriously the concepts of servant leadership, dialogue, compassion, and forgiveness. It will shift our attention from our preoccupation with quantity to a greater appreciation for quality. It will lead us to recognize and affirm the gifts of the Holy Spirit found in all our members, regardless of gender, race, ethnicity, or age It will convince the church to invest more of its resources in those endeavors that have the greatest potential for bringing and keeping people together in the church. And it will go a long way toward counteracting the destructive effects of secularization and the persisting negative perceptions of organized religion.

## THE MISSION OF THE ADVENTIST CHURCH OF THE FUTURE

A clearer sense of identity will enable the Adventist church of the future to define its mission more precisely and to fulfill this mission more effectively. My second proposal for the future Adventist church is that it will want to keep a better balance between its outreach and its inreach—between its proclamation of the Gospel to all the world and its service to humanity and its nurture of members through worship, education, and fellowship. (There is, of course, crossover between outreach and inreach at more than one level.) In striving to achieve this balance, the church will find its blueprint once again in Scripture, helpfully illuminated by the metaphor of church as "family."

*Outreach*

*Proclamation.* The church's very existence is a response to the Gospel—the good news of what God has done for humankind in Jesus Christ, which forever reminds us that in spite of our sin, our rebellion, and our secularity, God loves us. The church exists because of this Gospel. It is to live by the love expressed in this Gospel. And the proclamation of this Gospel is central to its *raison d'etre* in the world because this is what brings redemption, healing and hope in the face of alienation and brokenness.

In *The Apostolic Preaching and Its Development*, C. H. Dodd summarized the Gospel proclamation of the earliest Christians: (*a*) Jesus came from God (Old Testament prophecies foretold his coming). (*b*) When you killed him, he died for human sin—including yours. (*c*) God raised him up. (*d*) The Holy Spirit is present with us now. (*e*) Jesus will come again. (*f*) Therefore, repent and believe. This was the apostolic message. It was and remains the Gospel. It should still be the heart of the church's proclamation, and we should never forget it!

To be sure, Seventh-day Adventist teaching has much to say that is important about the Sabbath, the law, the state of the dead, tithing, healthful living, and so on. But these tenets should not overshadow or eclipse the centrality of the Gospel from our proclamation. It was this Gospel which had a powerful impact upon the secular world of the first century, not only because of what it revealed about God, but also (and perhaps more importantly) because of the obvious way it transformed the lives of men and women everywhere, prompting pagans to exclaim: "Look at the way they love each other, and how they are ready to die for each other!" Will the apostolic Gospel make any kind of impact upon our society? Will the secular generation stop long enough to hear it and consider it?

(*a*) Some will when we enlist our best talent to do the job of communicating it engagingly and imaginatively, using all the media available to us. (We basically know what to do on this score already).

(*b*) Many more will stop and listen when more members of the family of Christ take seriously the business of modeling what it means to believe and to live the Gospel. Secular people have judged the Christian Gospel to be irrelevant largely because of the impression left by Christians who have failed to demonstrate its relevance in their lives, who have been prone to forget that "we are ambassadors for Christ, God making his appeal through us,"[1] Christians have not taken to heart Christ's new commandment to "love one another even as I have loved you . . . [because] everybody will know that you are my disciples if you have love for one another."[2] Modern pagans will stop and listen to the Gospel when Seventh-day Adventist Christians model its transformational power in their lives, as they relate with one another in love, and especially with those who are different from them, those who are indifferent to them, those who disagree with them, those who give them a hard time, and those who betray their trust or maliciously take advantage of them. Ellen White was profoundly right when she wrote: "The strongest argument in favor of the Gospel is a loving and lovable Christian."

(*c*) Yet even more will stop and listen to the Gospel proclamation when Adventist Christians take seriously the ministry of *dia-konia*—service—following in the footsteps of their Lord who said: "The Son of Man came not to be served but to serve."[3] Servant-

[1] 2 Cor. 5:20.
[2] Jn. 13:34, 35.
[3] Matt. 20:28.

hood was at the center of the Incarnation—consider the self-humiliation involved in God's becoming human—and it was central to the witness of the early Christians, causing pagans, as Eusebius noted, to praise "the God of the Christians, and confess[] that they alone were the truly pious and God-fearing people, because they gave proof of it by their deeds." "Lowering oneself to serve" is still arresting because it runs so counter to the human proclivity to exercise power and control over others. It stands over against the secular ethos with its self-centeredness, its fixation with taking care of "Number One," its admiration of success, of winning all the time at any price. Adventists have had a hard time in recent years with the concept of servanthood because of our emphasis on education and professionalization which have contributed to the upward social mobility of our members. Along with other Christian groups, we too have institutionalized the ministry of *diakonia* and made it a department of the church: we have Dorcas societies, ADRA, 5-Day Plans, etc. If our Gospel proclamation is to have a real impact on the world of the future:

(1) We will have to bring service back where it belongs—as the central quality of the Christian life which is to be an "existence-for-others" after the One who was the "Man for Others." One does not engage in service if one is not a servant to begin with.

(2) To be meaningful, service will have to remain largely spontaneous—not programmed—capable of responding to any human need, anywhere and at any time—both inside the church as well as outside it.

(3) The concept of "Service" will have to inform the priorities of the church and permeate all of its functions at every level—and especially in the area of administration. It will need to shape our planning and the execution of our plans. And the church will have to resist the temptation to compartmentalize it and institutionalize it, for when we do so, *diakonia* tends to become impersonal, to ride roughshod over human feelings, and to co-opt local initiative and involvement, thus making Christians passive and lazy; and it often becomes inefficient as well as ineffective.

(4) Despite the Adventist proclivity to be separate and inbred and to shy away from the political process, the church's mission of *diakonia* will require us at times to stand up and move quite explicitly against the structures, the policies, and the persons who are responsible for creating injustice, oppression, and abuse. It isn't good enough for us to operate an ambulance service at the foot of the cliff—we must go after those who push people off the cliff! In this sense, service is prophetic, even political. It is an open challenge to the *status quo* and it never misses an opportunity to affirm freedom from servitude to other people, to institutions, to oppressive sys-

tems, and to sexism, racism, and all other abusive "isms." An authentic ministry of *diakonia*, based upon authentic caring and modeled before the world, should be central to the outreach of the Adventist church of the future.

*Inreach*

I suggested in my second proposal that there will need to be a better balance in the church between outreach and inreach. Inreach is a dimension of the Adventist church's mission that traditionally been relatively neglected; it simply has not received as much attention as outreach. Our budgets tend to tell us that, and so do the statistics on worship attendance, divorce, and defection from the church.

Since inreach is primarily a local affair which cannot be programmed from the top down, it stands to reason that a hierarchical, bureaucratic church would have more difficulty addressing this matter than one with a congregational polity. There are signs of change all around, however, as pastors and members join together creatively to address this aspect of the church's mission, which encompasses worship, learning, and fellowship.

*Worship.* The words used for worship in both Hebrew and Greek mean "to bow down" or "to prostrate oneself." When we gather together to worship on Sabbath, we are taking a pause to recognize our proper place, to realign our perspective, as it were, by figuratively "bowing down" before God—acknowledging that God is God and that we are not. It is an affirmation of who God and who we are in relation to God. The focus of worship then is God—not the preacher or the worshippers,.

This is quite different from the more utilitarian understanding that many Adventists presently have of worship. Søren Kierkegaard's analogy of worship and the theater is quite helpful here. Kierkegaard's nineteenth-century Danish Lutheran contemporaries tended to treat worship as entertainment: the congregation was the audience, the preacher was an actor, and the Holy Spirit was the prompter who whispered lines to the actor. People came, sat, watched the show, and went home. Kierkegaard turned this model on its head. God, he suggested, was the audience to whom the worshippers "play" as actors, prompted by the pastor who, prompted in turn by the Holy Spirit, tells the congregation how to bow down. The point is: the *responsibility to* worship, to bow down, to pray, to praise, to listen, to learn is our own. And the *object of* our worship is to be God and not ourselves and our own good ends. This means that Seventh-day Adventist worshippers in the church of the future will have to learn how better to engage themselves in the expression of worship—how to offer praise and thanks to God for the Gospel, for the gift of the Holy Spirit who empowers us to live the Christian life, for opportunities to love and serve, for the strength to hope and say "Nevertheless" in the face of chaos, tragedy, and sorrow.

*Religious Education.* There is also an educative or learning element in our Sabbath worship when we hear the proclamation of the Word of God—which unfortunately is too often eclipsed by pop psychology with a bit of sociology thrown in. Good biblical preaching will engage the congregation in a spiritual conversation with God through the Bible, enabling the saints to achieve insights that will assist them in making moral judgments and decisions, in achieving wider horizons for the expression of their love and service, and so on. But the best learning on Sabbath will occur in the more intimate setting of the Sabbath School (something which rarely takes place any more because what goes on in today's Sabbath School has become either trivial or terribly formal; on both counts the learning opportunities have almost vanished).

What will be the purpose of religious education or learning?

(1) It will be about growing Christians, not only in grace, but also "in the knowledge of our Lord and Savior Jesus Christ."[1] In other words, it will be intellectual—enabling members to enlarge their understanding of religious truth, helping them to see meanings, implications and applications of truth never seen before. It will also enable them to change their minds, to discard unwarranted prejudices and notions as they are led by the Holy Spirit into a fuller understanding of the ways of God.

(2) Learning will also enable Adventist Christians to outgrow any childish, elementary religiosity and to go on to maturity,[2] developing "to the measure of the stature of the fullness of Christ; so that we may no longer be children."[3] Learning therefore will be more than expanding intellectual knowledge—it will also consist in Christian formation, helping to shape and form persons into more authentic disciples of Christ, members of an alternative society whose values are different and superior to those of the secular society in which they invest so much of their lives. It will help members to question their secular values, to shed some of them and to replace them with the values of Christ, enabling them to become more like Jesus and less pagan.

(3) Religious learning will also be about "equipping the saints for the work of ministry for building up the body of Christ."[4] Each congregation will become a seminary in which the members are

[1] 2 Pt. 3:18.
[2] Heb. 6:1.
[3] Eph. 4:13-14.
[4] Eph. 4:12.

trained for ministry, in which their spiritual gifts are recognized, perfected, and applied for the good of other members and for service in the wider world as well. This is the point at which the classic Protestant doctrine of the priesthood of all believers ceases to be a nice ideal and becomes instead a practical reality, fulfilling the injunction of Ellen White: "Ministers should not do the work which belongs to the church, thus wearying themselves, and preventing others from performing their duty. They should teach the members how to labor in the Church and in the community."

I don't need to remind you that the best learning does not occur in a large group where people listen passively to a lecture or a sermon. It occurs in small groups where genuine dialogue can take place, where people can interact, where they can be more open, where they can ask any question without feeling stupid and, most importantly, where modeling and mentoring can actually take place. As the old saying goes: "Christianity is caught, not taught." People "catch" living like Christ by being around those who live like Christ. Disciple-making, like learning ballet, or the violin, or painting happens most effectively in a master-apprentice relationship.

> Being Christian is more like learning to paint or dance than it is like having a personal experience or finding out something about oneself. It takes time, skill, and the wise guidance of a mentor. Discipleship implies discipline—forming one's life in congruence with the desires and directions of the Master.[1]

Christians are best formed and equipped for ministry in small groups where they are known and know others, where they are encouraged and supported, where the master-apprentice model is real, where respect and love between persons can grow, where problems can be faced, analyzed, and solved, where strength can come and where the disciplines of the Christian life—Bible study, prayer, and preparation for ministry—can grow into life habits. The Sabbath Schools of the Adventist church of the future will hopefully serve as settings in which this goal can be achieved, becoming centers of genuine Christian *koinonia*—fellowship.

(4) Fellowship is a word used by Paul to mean "a sharing with someone in something." He uses the concept to describe both believers' sharing or participating in Christ, and also the mutual sharing of spiritual life among believers. What he has in mind is more than friendship. It is a spiritual union in a shared faith. And here, once again, the metaphor of church as "family" resurfaces. As in the

---

[1]Mark A. Lamport, "Unintended Outcomes, Curious Inventions and Misshapen Creatures: Juxtapositions of Religious Belief and Faith-Formed Practice and the Renewed Case for the Educational Mission of the Church," *Asbury Journal* 63.1 (2008): 109.

family, the church is the place where bonding occurs among members through the shared experiences of study, conversation, questioning, praying, involvement in meaningful activities, serving, and caring. In a world of fragmenting relationships, it is this *koinonia* that will keep people in the church and will attract people to the church (as did in times past). What we are describing here is not something that any group of people—in a therapy session for example—can conjure up. It is part of the fruitage of the Holy Spirit in the Christian family.[1] This is what Ellen White must have had in mind when she described how, in the church, God "is making experiments of grace on human hearts and is affecting such transformation of character that angels are amazed, and express their joy in songs of praise. They rejoice to think that sinful, erring human beings can be so transformed." The Adventist church of the future will learn, after years of experimentation with all sorts of gimmicks, that successful inreach is the one indispensable component of successful outreach.

## STRUCTURE AND LEADERSHIP IN THE ADVENTIST CHURCH OF THE FUTURE

Having caught a glimpse of the character and the mission of the Adventist church of the future, we can now conclude with a brief consideration of the master principle that will most likely shape the structure and the leadership of that church. Here I would like to suggest that *servanthood* become the model in all matters of organization and leadership, so that church structures can really become servants of the church's mission, church leaders servants of the church's members.

*Servanthood* as a leitmotif for organization and leadership seems especially appropriate for the church because (*a*) it is fundamentally Christian, (*b*) it makes good administrative sense, given that it is responsive to people issues yet not indifferent to issues of efficiency, cost, and order, and (*c*) it provides the church fresh opportunities to model before the world the practical values of the kingdom of Christ which—in this particular instance—are not altogether dissimilar from modern corporate values, thus enhancing the relevance of Adventism among secular people.

Before applying the concept of servanthood to administrative structures, however, it is proper to acknowledge certain "givens" about the Adventist church of the future: (*a*) It will continue to be an international church. (*b*) Its greatest growth will continue to be in countries of the Two-Thirds World. (*c*) It will continue to operate a vast network of educational, medical, publishing, and philan-

[1]Gal. 5:22, 23.

thropic institutions and organizations. (*d*) It will continue to sponsor a large foreign mission enterprise.

(1) As an international body, the Adventist church of the future will retain a centralized administrative structure consisting of a General Conference with world divisions and church federations organized into newly constituted conferences. In keeping with the normative concept of "servanthood," however, the structure itself will be less hierarchical and vertical and therefore flatter and more horizontal, with many collaborative networks providing input and increasing responsiveness, efficiency, and productivity while at the same time reducing operating costs. Indeed, openness, flexibility, adaptability, and greater independence will characterize all the administrative entities of the church. They will be less autocratic and more democratic, less traditional and more innovative, less unilateral in their operations and more multilateral, less remote and more accountable, less uniform and more pluriform, less bureaucratic and more efficient, less directive and more coordinative, less controlling and more advisory. Strategic planning and contingency planning methods will be utilized widely in order to prevent costly and often frustrating crisis interventions.

More specifically, a "servant" General Conference will be clearly international in composition and thus truly representative of the world church. Its primary functions will be to articulate and promote a global vision arrived at with considerable input from all the segments of the church, to deal with global church issues consultatively, to coordinate the allocation of resources, and to foster unity in the essential core areas of beliefs and values while promoting diversity in the more peripheral areas of interpretation and application. The present centralized, hierarchical structure will be replaced by a multilateralization of relationships in which world divisions will be much more involved in planning, the development of doctrine, and the process of decision making not only with regard to their own segments of the world field but also with regard to the work of the church in other parts of the globe. The new thinking and the new methods emerging from younger and more innovative churches and institutions anywhere in the world will be able to influence the church in positive, constructive ways everywhere else. In this way, every administrative entity will be able to serve every other administrative entity and the international General Conference will come to play a crucial information-gathering and disseminating role. It will become more coordinative than directive, more enabling than controlling, somewhat like the International Federation of Red Cross and Red Crescent Societies.

(2) In light of my earlier projections related to the inreach and outreach aspects of the church's mission, the administrative struc-

tures of the Adventist church of the future will do everything possible to enable local congregations (and to a lesser extent educational and medical institutions) to become the primary action centers of the church. It is these sites at which the members of the family of God are equipped and interface most directly with the secular world. Adventist churches will not be places where members are passive spectators. Instead, they will be centers where members will be able to discover, develop and exercise their spiritual gifts, where they will be nurtured and taught to nurture others, where they will be inspired and shown how to serve others so that, in the words of Martin Luther, they will become "as Christs" to one another and to society at large.

(3) What will facilitate all of this will be a genuine openness at all levels of the church to the manifestation and the guidance of the Holy Spirit,[1] who will bring visions to the church of new missions, new responsibilities, and new methods.

- This openness to the Holy Spirit will result in a genuine appreciation of the *charismata*—the gifts of the Spirit—in all the members of the family of God, regardless of gender, race, ethnicity, or age.[2]
- Openness to the Holy Spirit will also result in a deeper understanding of the Biblical and Protestant doctrine of the priesthood of all believers,[3] which will move church leaders and pastors to look upon lay members not merely as sources of revenue but rather as "fellow pastors"—partners in different forms of the very same ministry in which they themselves are engaged.
- In this context, the church will encourage the continuing development of independent, innovative, supportive parachurch organizations which will provide more opportunities for lay members to use their spiritual gifts and become involved in the local as well as the international ministry of the church.
- Openness to the Holy Spirit will also protect the church from the rigor mortis which accompanies Institutionalitis, Bureaucratitis, and Proceduralitis.

(4) Servant leadership in the Adventist church of the future will be oriented primarily to "followership," by being more open, more willing to listen, to dialogue, to learn, to share, to be accountable, and to ask for forgiveness. Servant leaders will realize that followers cannot be expected to support goals and objectives which they have had little or no role in shaping. They will realize that followership is based on trust—and trust cannot be commanded. "Great leadership

[1] 14:16-18
[2] 1 Cor. 12:4-31
[3] 1 Pet. 2:9; Rev. 1:5,6; 5:10

is not a zero sum game. What is given to the leader is not taken from the follower. Both get by giving. This is the mystery of great [leadership]."[1] Servant leaders and servant followers will learn over time how to give to each other respect, trust, visions, goals, talents, energy, commitment, and the ability to somehow put it all together and bring it off for the benefit of society and to the glory of God.

## CONCLUSION

Time will tell whether or not I would have done better to stick to history instead of dabbling in futurism. I will probably end up having to eat a lot of broken glass. And when I do, I shall do so un-repentant for having tried to be hopeful about the Adventist church of the future. I realize that living an interim existence between dis-appointment and fulfillment can be terribly frustrating for any indi-vidual or organization. As Adventists, we have tried to cope by em-bracing the Gospel commission and by getting busy. And our fre-netic efforts have yielded impressive results. There are signs, how-ever, that, in the words of the old hymn, we are getting "weary, faint and sore." What seems to add to our weariness is the realiza-tion that we are trying to move against an overwhelming current of secularity.

Additionally, there is the realization that our experience is not unique. It has been the experience of the universal Christian church for almost two millennia, during which it has tried to cope with the tension of living between the already and the not yet, and it has not been too successful. This scares us into thinking that we too may have to be around for a long time and that we may be doomed to repeat the long and frustrating saga of our Catholic and Orthodox and Protestant ancestors.

In this chapter, I have tried to suggest that, while the Adventist church may be around for a bit longer, there are reasons to be hopeful about its future.

1.  As a church, we have the benefit of hindsight from which we can draw helpful lessons. All we need to do is to look back.

2.  We are an honest people, capable of genuine self-criticism and willing to change. And we have access to the most in-credible human resources imaginable. All we need to do is look within.

3.  We can still see the power of the Gospel at work, transform-ing human lives, and empowering them for ministry and service. And we still have countless opportunities to make a

[1]Gary Wills made this point in article in the *Atlantic Monthly*.

difference for good in the world. All we need to do is look around.

4. Given the dual nature of the church, we have access to unlimited divine resources, assured that the church remains, in Ellen White's words, "the only object on earth on which Christ bestows his supreme regard . . . constantly watching it with solicitude and . . . strengthening it by his Holy Spirit."

5. Again, given the dual nature of the church, we have the promise from the Lord of the church that the gates of hell will not prevail against her[1]—a promise the first installment of which has already been given in the resurrection of Jesus. And we also have his additional promise, "I will come again."[2] These reasons are good enough to look forward and to remain hopeful for the Adventist church of the future.

[1] Matt. 16:18.
[2] John 14:3.

# 9

# Ellen White's Ministry

## Arthur N. Patrick

### INTRODUCTION

Christianity offers a saving knowledge of God through Jesus Christ,[1] taught of the Holy Spirit.[2] Libraries of books can be consulted about the process of disclosure (revelation), its trustworthy communication (inspiration), and the help of the Spirit for those who seek to understand and apply the message (illumination).[3]

Christianity has witnessed creative and destructive battles over these doctrines, few more intense than those within the United States during the first three decades of the twentieth century as fundamentalism[4] and modernism[5] engaged each other. Seventh-day Adventists belong in neither camp.[6] However, with a valid concern about Modernism and an ambiguity with reference to Ellen White, many Adventists aligned themselves with the fundamentalists. Especially since 1970, when Ellen White studies entered a new phase, this lack of clarity has threatened the unity and mission of Adventism.

---

[1]Jn 17:3; 1 Jn 5:20.

[2]Jn 14-16.

[3]I acknowledge the formative influence of Raoul Dederen on my thought in these areas while I undertook MA and MDiv studies at the Seventh-day Adventist Theological Seminary, 1970-1972.

[4]Fundamentalism has many positive elements; the verbal inerrancy of the Bible is not one of them. Such other fundamentalist doctrines as dispensationalism, secret rapture, Keswick holiness, immortality of the soul, and an eternally-burning hell do not cohere with Adventism.

[5]Some observers suggest that "modernism is dead," and the present threat to Adventism is "the pluralistic, postmodern world view." See the *Adventist Theological Society Newsletter* 8 (September 1997): 1-2.

[6]For a North American perspective on evangelicalism, see Leonard Sweet, ed., *The Evangelical Tradition in America* (Macon, GA: Mercer UP 1997).

Unrealistic concepts of inspiration caused many Adventists to adopt extreme positions with reference to Ellen White's ministry,[1] including reversionist attitudes. The Adventist of fundamentalist inclination, confronted with a massive amount of new information, tends to elevate an idealized past as normative for the present, requiring a strong continuity (even identity) with that past. Therefore, historical data may be seen as the cause of unnecessary problems; primary sources may appear to initiate doubt about the leading of God; probing questions may seem threatening, with even their asking categorized as evidence of lack of faith. Thus judgmental groups tend to form on the edges of the church and mount a guerrilla war, firing salvos at people and institutions.

The polar opposite to reversion is a rejectionist stance, which declares the past is so unreliable in view of present knowledge or so irrelevant to present needs that separation from it is essential. Historical data may be grasped as a weapon with which to attack the church (as in the writings of Gregory Hunt and Wallace Slattery); primary sources may be used by the rejectionist in an attempt to discredit claims about God's leading. During the resultant confusion some people quietly slip out of the church because they perceive the church as dishonest, or congregations may divide when the advocacy of opposing ideas fragments relationships, or militant individuals may leave Adventism in anger and direct long-range missiles back at the body of Christ.

Meanwhile, the church and its institutions experience turmoil. At a time when there is an enormous need to comprehensively support creationism, great effort may be expended to prop up a peripheral idea—the chronology of Archbishop James Ussher (1581-1656). When health and educational institutions need creative help to express Adventist values to patients and students, they may be threatened by well-meaning authors and administrators responding to negative reports which often turn out to be rumors. With unity under threat, bewildered leaders may grasp promising solutions offered in books like *Omega* and *Receiving the Word*, only to witness intensified conflict and a tarnishing of the church's credibility.[2] Adventist ministers, historians, scientists, and religion teachers at times find hazardous the professions for which they prepared with great effort and outlay. Accountability is essential, as is a creative tension between academic freedom and academic responsibility. But to be

---

[1] I am indebted, for a way to name these three categories, to Robert M. Johnston, "Orthodoxy and Heresy in the Biblical Period: Reflections on an Elusive Category," address to the Andrews Society for Religious Studies (Dec. 1981) 10.

[2] *Omega* is skillfully written, but is based on grossly inadequate historical research. *Receiving the Word* has a penchant for naming people and placing them in negative categories without due care as to their actual position.

effective, these professionals and their institutions also need accurate understanding from laity and leaders if the church is to proceed coherently with the fulfillment of its mission.

Consensus on the role of Ellen White would go a long way toward resolving many such tensions within Seventh-day Adventism. All the evidence needed to facilitate this objective is on the church's corporate desk; in fact, it has been there for fifteen years. A need remains in the church for a more faithful, informed, and unifying application of the writings of Ellen White. To that end the church needs to understand the reversionist and rejectionist options, and consciously adopt and promote a transformationist stance.

During her seventy-year ministry Ellen White developed a symbiotic relationship with the Seventh-day Adventist Church. From 1915 to about 1970, partly because of unresolved issues in the conflict between fundamentalism and modernism, many Adventists came to use Ellen White's writings as an all-encompassing and authoritative encyclopædia of faith and practice. The years 1970 to 1982 brought to light a wealth of fresh information which, lacking adequate interpretation/application, created a "Great Bereavement" in Adventism. Therefore, from 1982 to the present, diversity has marked the Adventist understanding and application of the writings of Ellen White. Thus it seems appropriate to seek to enhance the church's future by a more consistent and unifying approach to this crucial subject.

I have tried to understand and apply Ellen White's writings during forty years of ministry—as pastor, evangelist, religion teacher, director of an Ellen G. White/Seventh-day Adventist Research Center, academic administrator, historian, and hospital chaplain. Nothing in this paper claims qualitative newness, only urgency. Surely all who lead the church want to find common ground on which to press forward together, fulfilling the mission given us by Jesus Christ.

## ELLEN WHITE STUDIES SINCE 1970

Ellen Gould Harmon White was born in a Maine farmhouse on November 26, 1827, and died in her California home (Elmshaven) on July 16, 1915. Between 1844 and 1863 she "helped the sabbatarian Adventists to keep their Advent hope alive and coalesce as a group; between 1863 and 1888 she expanded Adventist understanding of religion to include health, education, and missions, among other things; and between 1888 and her death in 1915 she turned Adventist attention toward Christ and prevented the church from pursuing several theological aberrations that had arisen in its midst."[1]

Historians are wary about "what if" questions, but it is useful to meditate on what might have happened to the early sabbatarians without Ellen White's first vision; her counsels on publishing, organization, health, and education; her mediation on the issue of salvation during the 1888 crisis and thereafter; and her stabilizing counsel in the first difficult decade of the twentieth century. Furthermore, the church has been deeply influenced by the "great books" in which Ellen White revised and expanded her earlier writings on such themes as the war between Christ and Satan (*The Conflict of the Ages* series, 1888-1917), Christian education (*Education*, 1903), and the health message (*The Ministry of Healing*, 1905).

Although her voice was silenced in 1915, Ellen White's writings continued to speak powerfully to the movement of which she was a co-founder. Currently more than 100 of her book titles are in print; over 4,600 periodical articles have been republished; near 60,000 typewritten pages of letters and manuscripts are available in a chain of research centers serving the major geographical areas of the world. More recently, computer technology has made most of Ellen White's writings readily available for research in institutional libraries and individual homes; thus the process of discovery has been democratized. At the present time some people claim that this little lady (Ellen White was a mere five-feet-two inches tall!) should be dismissed from any significant role in the Adventist movement. Others still contend that her writings are a definitive encyclopedia on every topic that is essential for last-day Christians. Neither of these views is adequate. A wealth of research impinges so dramatically on our understanding of Ellen White's life and ministry that there is an urgent need to reassess and present her role coherently in the light of facts largely unknown before 1970.

The unprecedented developments which occurred during the 1970s and 1980s relating to Ellen White were influenced by a cluster of powerful forces. Too often Adventists assumed, when they spoke of "the truth" or "the message," that their church's beliefs formed a fixed body of doctrine. It is important to list for consideration some of the factors which initiated or sustained the processes of change which have occurred in recent years:

1. The development of accredited educational institutions in the early decades of the twentieth century, and particularly the provision of graduate education beginning in the 1930s, played a crucial role in driving these processes.

---

[1]Gary Land, writing in the *Student Movement,* May 6, 1982: 4

2. The graduate education of ministers and teachers by persons who had themselves undertaken university programs became a significant factor by the middle of the twentieth century.

3. After the publication of the *SDA Bible Commentary* between 1954 and 1957, the church at large began to interpret the Scriptures more faithfully in the light of the meaning and syntax of the Hebrew, Aramaic, and Greek languages in which they were written, and to demonstrate a growing respect for the context and historical setting of the biblical statements which were quoted in Sabbath Schools, sermons, and church publications.

4. Two missionaries from the United States to Africa (Robert Wieland and Donald Short) were among those who forced the church from 1950 to begin a reassessment of its presentation of the gospel.[1] Further, during a long series of discussions with evangelical Christians in the 1950s Adventists accelerated the process of honing their self- understanding and their expression of cardinal doctrines about Christ and salvation.

5. During the early 1970s the General Conference moved to establish an archival center at its headquarters and to create a chain of research centers to serve the various geographical areas of the earth. Thus, for the first time, primary sources for the study of SDA history become quite widely available. This new reality was bound to have a creative influence on the thought and practice of the church.

6. By 1970 these developments were becoming influential in a number of spheres, not least in the maturation of Adventist historiography. The need for a comprehensive reassessment of Adventist history would become apparent from the writings of a group of well-trained historians: Jonathan Butler, Everett Dick, Ron Graybill, George Knight, Gary Land, Don McAdams, Ron Numbers, and Richard Schwarz, to name a few. The work of biblical scholars, scientists, and systematic and historical theologians would have similar importance.

7. However, the church was not welcoming to those who saw a need to revise certain aspects of its self-understanding.[2] More than any other organization, the Association of Ad-

---

[1] This process came to a constructive climax with the publication of the "Dynamics of Salvation" statement in the *Adventist Review,* July 31, 1980:3-8.

[2] Jonathan M. Butler, "The Historian as Heretic," introduction, *Prophetess of Health: A Study of Ellen G. White,* by Ronald L. Numbers, 3d ed. (Grand Rapids: Eerdmans 2008) 1-41 illustrates some of the perils inherent in the vocation of the historian of Adventism.

ventist Forums took responsibility for publishing the studies which impinged on Ellen White and her ministry. By presenting a variety of perspectives, *Spectrum* informed the ongoing discussion. Although it was blamed for some articles which seemed experimental or even rejectionist, time has shown that the church greatly needed to keep at the forefront of the dialogue and be involved in the processes of discovery and interpretation which were occurring.[1] Between the Great Disappointment of 1844 and the time of Ellen White's death, a mutually beneficial relationship developed between the church and its prophet, marked by a remarkable degree of consensus in the church's understanding of her ministry. The following seven statements suggest some of the important ideas on which this symbiotic relationship was based. As a minimal commitment, any well-informed, loyal Adventist might be expected to believe and teach that:

1. Ellen White's writings make a striking appeal to timeless truth.
2. They contain many unique elements.
3. Her writings on health placed Seventh-day Adventists on vantage ground by relating bodily health to basic spiritual well-being and by pointing out numerous paths to right living.
4. She made copious and effective use of the Bible in her writings.
5. She often helped the church develop and express its theology.
6. She retained control over her literary output.
7. Her writings reveal a remarkable literary beauty.[2]

During the first century of the church's existence, difficult questions were posed about the life and ministry of Ellen White, often by people outside of or on the fringes of Adventism. By 1951, Francis Nichol had gathered these questions and appended answers in a large volume entitled *Ellen G. White and Her Critics*, to the general satisfaction of the church. Nichol's book renewed an earlier wall of defense around Ellen White, built by Uriah Smith during

---

[1]Seventh-day Adventists, despite the excellence of *Ministry* and the transformed *Adventist Review,* must still depend on such publications as *Spectrum* and *Adventist Today* for some vital aspects of the information they need about the church they love and support.

[2]For a discussion of these points in the context of Adventist history, see my article, "Does Our Past Embarrass Us?" *Ministry,* April 1991: 7-10. Note that one correspondent stated this article was "dangerous" and "deceptive"; the editor suggested that "Credibility is enhanced when the church is candid about the problems it faces." See *Ministry,* August 1991, 2; December 1991, 4. Cp. *Ministry,* June 1992: 27.

the 1860s through articles in the *Second Advent Review and Sabbath Herald* and republished in a similar book, entitled *The Visions of Mrs. E. G. White*. But Nichol's wall, which seemed adequate in 1951, crumbled in the 1970s. Why? A few illustrations of the new questions, this time mainly asked by people within the church, show how some of the factors noted above impinged on the church's understanding of Ellen White and her ministry.

1. Richard Lewis looked exegetically at Rev. 14:12 and 12:17, questioning our use of the expression "Spirit of Prophecy" with exclusive reference to Ellen White and her writings.[1]

2. Frederick Harder suggested that Ellen White "was not writing history, she was interpreting it," and that she learned history "by ordinary means, but the activity of God in the historical situation was seen by revelation."

3. Roy Branson and Herold Weiss called for Adventists to "discover the nature of Ellen White's relationship to other authors" and to "recover the social and intellectual milieu in which she wrote."

4. William Peterson highlighted the reality of problems in Ellen White's selection and use of historical materials relating to the French Revolution.

5. Ron Graybill, after a careful analysis of primary sources, concluded that Ellen White did not engage in historical research on the French Revolution; instead she followed one major source, Uriah Smith.

6. Donald McAdams carefully evaluated manuscripts which revealed how Ellen White constructed sections of *The Great Controversy*, noting that she made extensive use of historical sources.

7. Ronald Numbers, after an exhaustive investigation of Ellen White's writings on the theme of health, concluded that she derived important health reform ideas from contemporary health reformers. The strong contrary opinions which Numbers' book evoked did not invalidate this major conclusion from his research.

8. Late in the 1970s, Walter Rea began to press upon the church substantial but sometimes exaggerated claims of Ellen White's literary dependence. In a 1957 thesis, Ruth Burgeson noted in some detail the literary relationship between John Milton's *Paradise Lost* and Ellen White's depiction of the same events. Later, in 1971, Raymond Cottrell wrote a long paper on historical conditioning in the Bible and the

---

[1] For a fuller discussion and documentation of this and the following six points, see Donald R. McAdams, "Shifting Views of Inspiration: Ellen G. White Studies in the 1970s," *Spectrum* 10 (March 1980): 27-41.

writings of Ellen White. Because we failed to observe the warnings which were implicit in such studies as those by Burgeson and Cottrell, we were not prepared for the more extensive revelations which Rea broadcast in the late 1970s and early 1980s.

These presentations and others similar to them uncovered a large quantity of data previously unknown even to serious students of Ellen White's life and writings. Indeed, by early 1982, when the first International Prophetic Guidance Workshop convened at the church's world headquarters, it was as though a huge basket of new information cards had been dumped on the church's corporate desk. These cards required careful sorting and interpretation so that the new information could be fitted into coherent patterns, a process which remains to some extent as a challenge for the immediate future.[1]

During the last two decades, many in the church have experienced a form of bereavement due to the breaking of their long-held and cherished picture of Ellen White and the consequent attenuation of a pervasive yet valued source of authority in their personal lives and in the church. All the classic symptoms of grief have been painfully evident in the church, including, in particular, denial, anger, and depression.

The history of this period demonstrates our slowness as a church to create a coherent alternative to the traditional picture of Ellen White; thus we have prolonged the problems associated with the "Great Bereavement." There was an urgent need to provide sensitive pastoral support to ministers, teachers, and other members. For those of us who led the church to provide this, we needed to quickly grasp the implications of the evidence and give constructive leadership in the discovery and adoption of viable new patterns of thought. The lapse of time allowed the already-mentioned extreme responses to flourish: *reversion* and *alienation/rejection*. The first of these responses claimed that the new research and discussion were evil, that they raised questions which should not be asked, and thus such investigations should be prevented or discontinued. Alienation/rejection, on the other hand, claimed that the new evidence exposed Ellen White and her ministry as a great deception, a cause for disregarding her writings or leaving the church entirely.[2]

---

[1] One of the issues is whether or not Ellen White is "canonical." See Arthur N. Patrick, "Ellen Gould White and the Australian Woman, 1891-1900" (MLitt thesis, U of New England 1994) 120-1; Roy Adams, "A Prophet for Our Time," *Adventist Review,* June 4, 1992: 8-11.

[2] These responses are placed in an historical context by my unpublished paper, "The Minister and the Ministry of Ellen White in 1982."

Clearly the far better response, *transformation*,[1] needed to be adopted with energy, involving a comprehensive reassessment of Adventism in general and Ellen White in particular.[2] Of course, every generation must reformulate its religious tradition for itself if it is to adequately take ownership of its faith. However, a cluster of factors made this process more urgent than usual, beginning in the 1970s. But the need to actively lead the church toward a comprehensive new picture of Ellen White and her ministry was given such a low priority that for many the church seemed either uncaring or dishonest, factors which in part account for the loss of 180 ministers in the South Pacific Division alone. There needed to be an open dialogue in the church in which lay people and specialists participated in the task of redrawing a composite and comprehensive picture of Ellen White and her ministry, a need which remains as a priority for the twenty-first century. Church leaders can facilitate but they cannot control this process. Our hesitancy to give active leadership in this process thus far has allowed the understanding and consequent benefit of Ellen White's prophetic ministry to decline markedly. To lose an understanding of our heritage is to lose a clear sense of our identity.

The summary of what a loyal Adventist might be expected to believe and teach before 1970 is no longer viable for any well-informed person who tells the truth. Modification of the seven statements along the following lines is essential in order to fit now well-known facts.

1. Ellen White's writings make a striking appeal to timeless truth even though they are historically conditioned to a significant degree.
2. They contain certain unique elements even though they are related in an evident way to both the Adventist and the non-Adventist literature of her time.
3. Her writings on health placed Seventh-day Adventists on vantage ground by relating bodily health to basic spiritual well-being and by pointing out numerous paths to right living, even though she reflected some of the inaccurate ideas of her Adventist and non-Adventist contemporaries.
4. She made copious and effective use of the Bible in her writings even though she employed Scripture in a variety of ways, not all of which express the meaning and intent of the Bible.

[1] See Fritz Guy "The Future of Adventist Theology: A Personal View" (unpublished paper, 1980).

[2] For a constructive early attempt, see George R. Knight, *Myths in Adventism: An Interpretive Study of Ellen White, Education and Related Issues* (Washington, DC: Review 1985).

5. While she often helped the church develop and express its theology, her doctrinal understandings underwent both growth and change during her seventy-year ministry.

6. She retained a position of control over her literary output, but her literary assistants and advisers had more than a minor, mechanical role in the preparation of her writings for publication.

7. Her writings reveal a remarkable literary beauty, but her use of sources and the role she assigned her assistants/advisers indicate that this literary excellence should not be used as a proof of her divine inspiration.

The need for such adjustments rings a death-knell for Adventist fundamentalism.[1] We cannot proceed effectively as a movement without Ellen White, nor can we retain her credibility and ours without addressing the known evidence. Clearly, the past informs the present, thus continuity with it is essential. Historical information is to be welcomed as a basis for accurate understanding. Primary sources may enable the believer to search for a better understanding of the interaction between the human and the divine. Hence, the church needs to prize research into its heritage as a means for effective growth in knowledge and faith.

In April 1982 I flew across the United States. For the first time in my flying experience there, visibility was excellent. From the warm sky above Los Angeles I saw the serene Pacific Ocean and the vast sprawl of the City of the Angels hugged by mountains. I saw the blot of Las Vegas; the life-giving waters of the Hoover Dam; the huge scar of the Grand Canyon; the Rocky Mountains wrapped in white; ribbon-like rivers; billiard-table prairies; the stain of Chicago whitened with snow; the vast waters of Lake Michigan; the confused land-forms of Pennsylvania. So upon this journey I saw a panorama of a vast continent bounded by ocean, contoured by mountains, watered by lakes and rivers, enriched by plains, scarred by human technology.

You may ask me to draw a street map of Las Vegas; to state the depth of the Grand Canyon; the location of the John Hancock Center in Chicago; the types of trees in the Appalachian Mountains. In response, my mistakes would be numerous.

You might ask a thousand other simple questions about the continental United States which I could not answer. You might, therefore, be tempted to deny my experience. You might discount

---

[1] When these revisions were discussed by the Spirit of Prophecy Resource Committee of the South Pacific Division in 1982-3, consensus was reached that they were accurate, but (after a statement by a Union Conference president) it was decided that no one outside the Resource Committee should have access to them.

my claim that I saw a panorama of a great country absolutely beyond the vision of a surface traveler. You might, therefore, discredit
the fact that through the miracle of jet transport I was shown a useful vista of *landmarks* and can now better interpret a vast *landscape*.

I believe that, for the benefit of Seventh-day Adventists, Ellen
White was given a jet-aircraft vision of crucial realities in an age of
spiritual surface travel. She saw landmark truths: God as the One
whom to know is to love;[1] health as the right arm of the third angel's message;[2] education as having to do with the whole person
and "the whole period of existence possible to man";[3] history as
moving toward a supreme confrontation between good and evil
that will climax in the universal declaration that God is love,[4] as
well as other distinctives precious to Seventh-day Adventists. She
was shown these features of truth so that she could encourage and
guide the Advent people in charting their journey heavenward.

It is a tragedy that some Seventh-day Adventists are either claiming too much or too little for Ellen White's ministry. Those who
claim she gives us an authoritative, detailed, surface survey in all respects have no way to handle certain data clearly present in her writings. Those who deny her spiritual gift and assess her as a fraud and a
false prophet forfeit the enduring value of her prophetic vision. Either way there is a conflict and disillusionment at the end of the road.

Ellen White ever wrote with an attitude of urgency, with a
sense of an imminent end for all things earthly. Since her death,
Seventh-day Adventists have benefited from many attempts at surface exploration: into the historical background of Scripture: the
causes of volcanic eruptions; the principles of genetics; the history
of the Albigenses; the causes of cancer, cholera, tuberculosis, and so
on. Adventists have had over 170 years to reflect on the Shut Door
in relation to their mission; on the identity of the law of Galatians;
on the biblical doctrine of salvation. While responding to the detailed insights of painstaking investigation, we must remember the
abiding usefulness of Ellen White's direction-setting, panoramic vision, and those instances in which she maps in a detailed way segments of our spiritual journey. To deny a role to either her panorama or our detailed investigation is to reject part of God's gift of
knowledge to humanity.

[1]Ellen G. White, *The Desire of Ages: The Conflict of the Ages Illustrated in the
Life of Christ* (Mountain View, CA: Pacific 1947) 22.
[2]Ellen G. White, *Testimonies for the Church*, 9 vols. (Mountain View, CA: Pacific 1948) 1: 486.
[3]Ellen G. White, *Education* (Mountain View, CA: Pacific 1903) 13.
[4]Ellen G. White, *The Great Controversy between Christ and Satan: The Conflict
of the Ages in the Christian Dispensation* (Mountain View, CA: Pacific 1911) 678.

## THE CONTINUING RELEVANCE OF ELLEN WHITE
## FOR SEVENTH-DAY ADVENTISTS

If *to be relevant* is *to be connected with, to have bearing upon* or *to be pertinent to*, then Ellen White has had a profound relevance for Seventh-day Adventists. She was the church's most notable thought-leader from 1844 until her death seven decades later.[1] During the first half-century following her death, her perceived relevance for the church tended to increase.[2] Not only did her writings accompany the church's geographical spread and numerical growth; they were reprinted in new editions, compilations and devotional volumes: they were made more accessible by a one-volume index (1926) and a three-volume index (1962-3).[3] During this period, the mood within the church maintained and, at times, increased the acceptance of Ellen White's writings as authoritative with regard to all the many subjects upon which they touched briefly or which they covered in detail. Consequently, it is necessary to look long and hard to compile a list of other authors who have as many pages in print eighty years after her or his death.[4]

However, it is evident that about 1970 the relationship between Ellen White and the church began a new phase, especially in Western societies such as North America, Europe, Australia, and New Zealand. The beginning of this phase may be identified with the publication of the June 1970 issue of *Spectrum*.[5] Thereafter, the processes of change were imperceptible at times, but a vast difference is apparent when the 1960s are compared with the present decade. Ellen White's writings are cited less often in Sabbath School discus-

---

[1] Or, to use the words of *The New Encyclopædia Britannica*, "the most powerful single influence on the church during her lifetime"; *Micropædia*, 15th ed. (Chicago: Encyclopedia Britannica, 1976) 10: 651. However, it should be kept clearly in mind that sometimes Ellen White's role was to endorse the ideas of others, including both Adventist and non-Adventist authors.

[2] See Jaroslav Pelikan, *Jesus Through the Centuries: His Place in the History of Culture* (New Haven: Yale UP 1985) for the way in which Christian theology has been shaped to meet the exigencies of widely-varying circumstances during Christian history. Pelikan's observations can be applied fruitfully to Adventist interpretations of Ellen White since 1844.

[3] More recently, sophisticated computer technology has given efficient access to any given expression in Ellen White's entire corpus of perhaps 25,000,000 words.

[4] The 1926 index covered 28 Ellen White books. By 1958 (my first year in the ministry), the number had increased to 51 volumes. It topped the 100 mark during the 1980s.

[5] Included was William S. Peterson, "A Textual and Historical Study of Ellen White's Account of the French Revolution," Spectrum 2.4 (Aut. 1970): 57-69, along several other articles relating to Ellen White. For a cogent later perspective, see Benjamin McArthur, "Where Are the Historians Taking the Church?" *Spectrum* 10 (November 1979): 9-14.

sions, sermons, periodicals, and books; fewer ministers, teachers, and members seek them avidly or read them regularly. Currently there is a lessened desire among Adventists to participate in discussions about Ellen White's role, or to allow her the former level of authority in the corporate affairs of the church, or to accept her advice as normative over individual thought and practice. But, at the same time, some Adventists lament what they identify as a fulfillment of Ellen White's prediction that Satan's "very last deception" would be to nullify her work.[1] Some church-sponsored publications still give no hint that their editors are aware of the vibrant discussions of the late twentieth century, and some independent Adventist publications constantly advocate ideas which seem absurd or dishonest to any person who has kept abreast of the relevant information.

## The Noonday of Ellen White's Relevance

It is not difficult for Adventists to remember when Ellen White's writings were accepted more-or-less as a definitive encyclopædia of truth and duty for the faithful church member.[2] Her writings treated the full lexicon of issues in which Adventists had an interest: amusements, church organization, diet, dress, education, health, life insurance, Reformation history, sexuality, the use of time, vulcanology, and so on.[3] The words "Sister White says" could guarantee the effective termination of most discussions.[4] To cite examples is to note the pervasiveness and persistence of Ellen White's influence. For instance, the church's stance on theatre-attendance was vintage nineteenth-century Methodism as mediated to it through Ellen White,[5] and (rather than focusing on the need to enhance discriminatory judgment) it maintained that position until almost all its youth were attending theaters. The pattern which was adopted often forced young people to ignore or challenge Ellen White and the church as represented by parents, local church officers, pastors, and educators. A comparable struggle has occurred over a plethora of similar issues: card-playing, checkers, chess, competi-

---

[1]See Ellen G. White, *Selected Messages*, 3 vols. (Washington, DC: Review 1958-80) 1: 48; 2: 78.

[2]Some may remember the mental gymnastics which were necessary to explain how Melbourne could be in New South Wales, or how "the moon and the stars of the solar system shine by the reflected light of the sun." See *Testimonies* 8: 158; *Desire* 465; *Education* 14; Ellen White, *Gospel Workers* (Washington, DC: Review 1948) 50.

[3]The "Question and Answer File" in any Ellen G. White/SDA Research Center illustrates both the queries raised by the world church about Ellen White, and the most official responses given.

[4]See Alden Thompson, "The Scary Lady of Adventism Learns to Have Fun," *Insight*, October 2, 1993: 2-4.

[5]The church seldom differentiated between live theater and cinema.

tive sports, cricket, dancing, tennis, and more. Thorny issues such as adornment (hats, make-up, jewelry) could be cited as other examples, as could a range of health issues. Thirty years ago, if committed Adventists wanted to know whether or not cheese was suitable for human consumption, they were likely to go to Ellen White for the answer, as some did when they needed to know whether or not to eat mushrooms, or whether red clover was an effective cure for cancer. Similar examples could be multiplied, but it is clear that a decreasing number of Adventists think in those terms today.

Of even greater importance, Ellen White defined doctrine for Adventists in a less ambiguous way than the Scriptures were able to do. For instance, the intense debate in Australia, New Zealand, and the United States during the 1950s and 1960s over the human nature of Christ during the incarnation focused on Ellen White statements, not Bible texts. The church's costly struggle to support the chronology developed by Ussher has been motivated by Ellen White's statements rather than by biblical data.[1] A similar comment can be made about the interpretation of "Adventist" passages of Scripture.[2] Hiram Edson's insight initiated a principal Adventist interpretation of Hebrews on October 23, 1844; his view was given normative authority by Ellen White. Thus, for more than a century, Hebrews was interpreted mainly as a tract written for Adventist times. Only since 1980 has it been recognized by many Adventists

[1]The Geoscience Research Institute was established in 1958; its activities have included study tours for administrators, ministers and teachers in the United States, Australia, and New Zealand. The church was told plainly, in 1979, by the Adventist best equipped at the time to comment on the matter, that there is no biblical basis for any date preceding the birth of Abraham. Thus, the Adventist who wants to believe in Creation about 4,000 B.C. "would be better to say that he bases his defense on the several statements of Ellen White." Siegfried H. Horn, "Can the Bible Establish The Age of the Earth?" *Spectrum* 10 (November 1979): 19. It is clear that we have not "heard" well Gottfried Oosterwal's message in "Crossing a Chasm: The Adventist Believer Between Faith and Science," *Andrews University Focus,* Summer 1982: 14-7.

[2]It should be noted that, in common with some other Christian groups, Seventh-day Adventists developed a sense of ownership with respect to certain biblical passages or ideas. See Arthur N. Patrick, "Christianity and Culture in Colonial Australia: Selected Catholic, Anglican, Wesleyan and Adventist Perspectives, 1891-1900" (PhD diss., U of Newcastle 1991) 86-87. In 1974 the church was made aware of a dozen different uses of Scripture made by Ellen White. See Raymond F. Cottrell, "Ellen G. White's Use of the Bible," *A Symposium on Biblical Hermeneutics,* ed. Gordon M. Hyde (Washington, DC: Biblical Research Committee 1974) 154-161. It is of interest that the editor excised important material from the article, but the piece remained ground-breaking for its time.

as a New Testament tract which has particular relevance for the last days.[1]

The word *relevance* defines a major concern of this chapter. The connection with, and the bearing or pertinence of Ellen White for the church is now different from how it was perceived three decades ago. This fact gives the church a challenge and an opportunity to better reassess the ministry of Ellen White constructively in view of changed knowledge and new circumstances. Stark alternatives are apparent. One of these is to deliver Ellen White into the control of fundamentalist minds who might increasingly isolate her ministry (and themselves) from reality. Another is to allow her relevance to be actively denied or to quietly die amongst informed members.[2] If a viable alternative to these extremes is to be promoted successfully, it will require more painstaking care and transparent integrity than has generally been manifested since 1970.

*The Nadir of Ellen White's Relevance*

It is essential to understand why the relevance of Ellen White for Seventh-day Adventists has so diminished. While a range of contributing factors could be explored more fully than is possible here, the most important determinants are identified in Donald McAdams's review of trends which became apparent during the 1970s. McAdams pointed out that it took 55 years from Ellen White's death for Adventist scholars to begin "for the first time to examine critically her writings and to share their conclusions."[3] McAdams observed that three points were clearly established during

[1] Even in 1979 when Desmond Ford asked a *biblical* question, the church's first impulse was to give an *Ellen White* answer. See A. N. Duffy, "The Heavenly Sanctuary: Not One Pillar to be Moved," *Record*, December 10, 1979: 6-7.

[2] It is painfully apparent that in the 1980s the church in the South Pacific Division tended to lose people with brighter intellects and it has not attracted a comparable number of replacements with similar capacities. We were too diffident about sharing information with our people. Morris L. West, one of Australia's most influential authors, suggests "that honest error is a step toward a greater illumination of the truth, since it exposes to debate and to clearer definition those matters which might otherwise remain obscure and undefined in the teaching of the Church." See *The Shoes of the Fisherman* (1963) in *The Vatican Trilogy* (Port Melbourne: Heinemann 1993) 174; cp. 140: "He had never been afraid of error since all his experience had shown him that knowledge was self-corrective and that a search honestly pursued might bring a man closer to the shores of revelation, even though their outline remained for ever hidden from his view."

[3] See McAdams 27. In the 1970s the church was made aware that crucial issues had been known and discussed in 1919, but then put aside. Such actions were no longer possible in the age of photocopiers, audio-cassettes, and ham-radio networks, let alone (more recently) email. For an insightful account of a leading Adventist who nurtured a realistic understanding of Ellen White's ministry, see Gilbert M. Valentine, *The Shaping of Adventism: The Case of W. W. Prescott* (Berrien Springs, MI: Andrews UP 1992).

the first ten years of this process: "Ellen White took much material
from other authors"; "Ellen White was a part of late nineteenth
century American culture and was influenced by contemporary
health reformers, authors and fellow Adventist church leaders"; and
"Ellen White was not inerrant." He suggested that the significance
of these conclusions could hardly be overemphasized because "Ellen White is so central to the lives of Seventh-day Adventists that
her words impinge on practically every area of Adventist teaching
and practice both institutionally and individually." Thus he warned,
"[t]o consider her words as possibly derived from someone else and
not necessarily the final authority introduces an element of chaos
into the very heart of Adventism that makes all of us uneasy."[1]

Uneasiness was only one of the outcomes resulting from the
discoveries of the 1970s.[2] As already noted, some Adventists adopted a *reversionist* stance—being deeply threatened and wishing to stop
the process of inquiry they retreated into the safety afforded by a
denial of evidence. Others moved into an *alienationist* or *rejectionist*
position—being unready or unable to incorporate the new facts
about Ellen White into a coherent system, they were alienated from
her ministry altogether. Some abandoned the Seventh-day Adventist Church as well;[3] and a number of those who left Adventism for-
feited Christianity and their belief in God. The median position was
a *transformationist* stance which required the reformulation of ideas
to accord with the new data. Because that response is, in many
ways, more difficult than either of the others, the need for it still
beckons us through circumstances in the church. That need to is
the motivation for this paper.[4]

[1]McAdams 39, 40.
[2]For an analysis conditioned by its historical context, see Patrick, "Ellen
Gould White and the Australian Woman" 112-125.
[3]See, for example, Wallace D. Slattery, *Are Seventh-day Adventists False Prophets? A Former Insider Speaks Out* (Phillipsburg: Presbyterian and Reformed 1990).
[4]My conviction is that to understand Ellen White in the light of Scripture
and history will enable us to perceive and present an ongoing relevance for her
ministry. The constant process which is required to maintain truth as "present
truth" was well described by Guy in "Future" 2. In dealing with "the activity of
theological reflection and construction" within the Adventist community of faith,
Guy says: "This activity consists of an ongoing consideration of the bases, definition, and implications of beliefs such as those listed above, and may include
(1) reformulation, as eternal truth is understood afresh in the language of each
different culture and each new generation; (2) clarification and specification, as
new questions arise and require a more careful investigation and more precise answers; (3) elaboration, as the church enlarges its thinking by probing deeper and
looking farther; (4) application, as the ongoing course of human history produces
new situations; (5) reinterpretation, as further study and the witness of the Holy
Spirit indicate that the Biblical revelation means something slightly different from
what it has been understood to mean."

*"An Element of Chaos"*

As noted above, McAdams used a strong expression to portray the effect of the new information relating to Ellen White when he suggested that to lose her as the final authority in the church was to "introduce an element of chaos into the heart of Adventism." Chaos can be beneficial if it leads to a better ordering of reality. But some earnest leaders and members still expect Ellen White to be used in the pre-1970 mode. Let us test the viability of this fundamentalist expectation in the light of a series of possibilities suggested in the following scenes (or scenarios), constructed so as to be *realistic* even though they are not *real* (actual).

*Scene 1.* A student, researching a graduate thesis on religious factors in the French Revolution elects to use *The Great Controversy* as a major source. The student gives a work-in-progress report to the graduate students and faculty members of the university's department of history, affirming Ellen White's skill in choosing and using historical materials.[1] Subsequently, the departmental chairperson receives a letter from the European History professor questioning whether the student should be allowed to proceed with graduate study. The ensuing debate is aired on a *Sixty Minutes* program. It becomes clear that one of the most important Adventist books is "not usable as an independent source of authority on matters relating to time, place, or details of an historical event."[2]

*Scene 2.* A local conference family ministries director is assisting a young couple who are experiencing sexual incompatibility. He loans them *A Solemn Appeal Relative to Solitary Vice, and the Abuses and Excesses of the Marriage Relation,*[3] encouraging them to follow the counsels written by Ellen White. The wife is a relative of the state president of the Association of Marriage and Family Counselors, with whom she shares the information. After reading *A Solemn Appeal*, the state president leads the association of marriage and family counselors to strongly oppose a conference application to open and maintain a family crisis center.

---

[1]For relevant sources, see McAdams.

[2]Ronald D. Graybill, "Historical Difficulties in *The Great Controversy*" (unpublished paper 1978) 7.

[3]Ellen G. White, *A Solemn Appeal Relative to Solitary Vice, and the Abuses and Excesses of the Marriage Relation* (Battle Creek, MI: Adventist 1870). Key Ellen White materials from this book were later made available to Australasians under the title *A Solemn Appeal*, but, like other Ellen White statements which seemed to have diminishing relevance for the church, the latter book has been allowed to go out of print. Some of its ideas are included in more recent compilations, however. For an historical treatment, see Ronald L. Numbers, *Prophetess of Health: A Study of Ellen G. White*, 3d ed. (Grand Rapids: Eerdmans 2008) 76-219; Malcolm Bull and Keith, Lockhart, *Seeking a Sanctuary: Seventh-day Adventism and the American Dream*, 2d ed. (Bloomington: Indiana UP 2007) 162-81.

*Scene 3.* A systematic theologian from one of the church's tertiary institutions presents a paper at a international conference of theologians on the truth of Ellen White's earliest writings about the closure of the door of mercy in 1844.[1] The paper is passed on to the referees of the association's journal. One of the referees of the journal is a member of the team which is reviewing the college's accreditation and reporting on this matter to government funding agencies. The referee rejects the article and protests the continuance of accreditation.

*Scene 4.* A conference of medical specialists hears a paper by an Adventist colleague on the need for contemporary medical practice to adopt as normative all the counsel given in the writings of Ellen White.[2] The specialist is accredited to practice at a church-related hospital which is subsequently featured on a radio program entitled *The Investigators.*[3] The patient clientele of the hospital drops dramatically.

*Scene 5.* At an international conference of geologists, an Adventist scientist distributes a 63-page compilation, *Ellen G. White Statements Relating to Geology and Earth Sciences,*[4] as supplementary reading for his lecture on the importance which these truths have for professionals. He subsequently lodges a request to present a paper at the next conference of the same society, and questions why his request is declined.

*Scene 6.* An Adventist academy teacher discusses Ellen White's statements on wigs and wasp waists over lunch with her hairdressing and dressmaking students.[5] Subsequently, she is disappointed

---

[1]See Robert W. Olson, comp., *The "Shut Door" Documents* (Washington, DC: White Estate 1982).

[2]Note both the presuppositions and the content of *Medical Science and the Spirit of Prophecy* (Washington, DC: White Estate 1971). The deepest problem with the booklet is that it claims an inerrant Ellen White, failing to recognize that an extended list of inaccuracies could be cited from her writings. Cp. Robert W. Olson, *Inerrancy in Inspired Writings* (Washington, DC: White Estate 1982). Note also the way in which studies by Graeme Bradford and others indicate that the church has long lived with a false expectation that the gift of prophecy implies an inerrancy which is not to be tested by the community of faith.

[3]Think of how the Australian Consumers' Association might handle this situation in *Choice* magazine!

[4]Ellen G. White, *Ellen G. White Statements Relating to Geology and Earth Sciences* (Washington, DC: White Estate 1982). Cp. Paul A. Gordon, *The Bible, Science, and the Age of the Earth: The Testimony of Ellen G. White*, rev. ed. (Washington, DC: White Estate, 1981).

[5]See, for instance, "Words of Christian Mothers," *The Health Reformer,* Oct. 1871: 121; Nov. 1871: 154-7. Ellen White links "artificial braids and pads" to a range of difficulties including "recklessness in morals." She also notes that "wasp waists may have been transmitted to them [young women] from their mothers."

when none of them accept her invitation to attend the screening of a film, *Ellen White: Prophetic Voice for the Last Days.*

*Scene 7.* A local conference church ministries director is approached by a young person who is deeply concerned about an impulse to masturbate. The counselor loans the young person a compilation of Ellen White's writings which highlight the extensive list of diseases caused by masturbation (in the case of both males and females) including the "inward decay of the head."[1] A few days later, the youth expresses a deepened anxiety and confusion to the conference president. Soon after this conversation, the young person commits suicide. The church ministries director and the president are called to give evidence at the coroner's inquest, an event which provokes national publicity.

*Scene 8.* An English student presents an essay contending that the literary beauty of Ellen White's writings is an evidence of divine inspiration.[2] The essay discusses a number of examples, noting Ellen White's use of the phrase "the greatest want of the world" and highlighting choice excerpts from *The Desire of Ages.* The professor who is marking the essay has on file articles[3] about Ellen White's relationship with other authors, plus "How *The Desire of Ages* was Written," and "The Family Bolton Story."[4] The essay is presented to academic referees who advise that it should not receive a passing grade. Several young people drop out of the local Adventist church during the ongoing debate.

*Scene 9.* A group of geneticists is discussing the place of humans amongst mammals, especially hominids. An Adventist presents as needed truth Ellen White's statements about "the amalgamation of man and beast," urging his colleagues to read Uriah Smith's interpretation of her statements as published in *The Second Advent Review and Sabbath Herald,* and then put into book form and sold widely at Adventist camp meetings with James White's endorsement.[5] The Adventist subsequently is disappointed when the geneticists do not

---

[1]See *A Solemn Appeal* as placed in an historical context by Numbers 184-95. Contrast the counsel given by Robert Schwindt in *Insight,* Oct. 21, 1980: 11.

[2]See Gladys King-Taylor, *Literary Beauty of Ellen G. White's Writings* (Mountain View, CA: Pacific 1953). Many times this argument has been extended to "prove" divine inspiration, in that a person with only a few years of formal education could not write as well as Ellen White did without supernatural aid.

[3]Roger W. Coon has collected many relevant articles; see Roger W. Coon, comp., *The Writings of Ellen G. White: Anthology of Recently Published Articles on Selected Issues in Prophetic Guidance,* 3 vols. (Berrien Springs, MI: SDA Theological Seminary 1992).

[4]See also Warren H. Johns, Tim Poirier, and Ron Graybill, *Henry Melville and Ellen G. White: A Study in Literary and Theological Relationships* (Washington, DC: White Estate 1982); note also the Fred Veltman research reports.

[5]For sources, see Patrick, "Past"

support his application for a teaching appointment in their branch of science.

*Scene 10.* An Adventist presents a paper demonstrating the claim that Ellen White's life bears remarkable evidence of the supernatural. The examples cited include the Big Bible, visions as sources for the section of *The Great Controversy* dealing with John Huss, and the Furrow Story. The writings of A. G. Daniells, Ron Graybill, Donald McAdams, and Milton Hook have been read by the scholar who rejects the paper for publication.

*Scene 11.* An Adventist ministerial association secretary presents a paper to an evangelical history association on the biblical truth about perfection as portrayed in the pre-1888 writings of Ellen White.[1] The president of the association subsequently advises that an article on Ellen White should not be included in the association's dictionary of nineteenth-century evangelical thinkers.

Clearly, neither Ellen White nor Adventism would emerge from these encounters as either winsome or credible. The unease which we feel about projecting our prophet into such dilemmas indicates our need to address the issue of her relevance with great care.

## A New Morning for Ellen White's Relevance

A community of faith cannot prosper over time unless it values the truth To suppress or to deny facts is not constructive. In their heart-of-hearts, many Adventists know that the traditional picture of Ellen White is at best a distortion of truth, or, at worst, a complicated fabrication of fact and fiction.[2] Some of them see the administrators of the church as sometimes still giving ambiguous signals. White Estate personnel were brought to the South Pacific Division to share information in the early 1980s, but few key administrators attended their meetings, nor did they encourage those who

---

[1]During the first four decades of their denomination's existence, Adventists sought to correct an imbalance in Christian thought. However, in so doing, they often seemed to speak as though all Scripture orbited the truth of the Second Advent. Since 1888 they have more adequately recognized that Scripture forms an elliptical orbit around the two comings of Christ.

[2]It is worth noting with sadness that a number of former Adventists are currently undertaking professional therapy to "recover" from their experience in Adventism. Central to the dilemma of some is the former authority of Ellen White as mediated through what they now perceive as a harsh educational system. One former member has kept a daily diary since childhood, including a day-by-day record of his canings and "hard labor" sentences, and noting the times when he was caned above the limit of six strokes. For some current attitudes toward caning, see *The Sydney Morning Herald*, March 5, 1994: 23. Observe the comments by Lowell Tarling, Norman Young, Robert Wolfgramm and Genna Levitch in *On Being*, June 1993: 20-21; Sep. 1993: 57, Oct. 1993: 65; Nov. 1993: 63; Dec. 1993: 68.

sought to understand and interpret the data which was presented.[1] The same Division sent representatives to the first International Prophetic Guidance Workshop held in 1982,[2] but then prevented the data presented at that important gathering being made available. A Spirit of Prophecy Resource Committee was established to disseminate information, but minimal new data were disseminated. Thus the information which became available in the era of discovery (1970-1982) was not shared effectively with the church at large.[3]

This allowed rumor to burgeon and confidence in the church and its leaders to plummet. Perhaps similar patterns were duplicated in other parts of the world. Thus, deep-seated but unacknowledged cognitive dissonance has troubled the church, with some members charging the administrators with being "soft" in their support of Ellen White, and others charging them with telling less than the truth about Ellen White. A church whose historic concern is to discover and share "the truth" cannot afford to be grudging in its admission of evidence, or to be seen as willingly ignorant or carelessly duplicitous. Therefore, I would like to think that discussions like the ones I would like this chapter to stimulate might offer hope to those who want the church to make a more constructive attempt to reassess the significance of its heritage.

To highlight a few of the opportunities for Adventists to affirm an ongoing relevance for Ellen White with reference to issues which are important for the church and its mission today, let us present eleven scenes (or scenarios) which in some ways parallel those given above, but which open up the possibility of quite different outcomes. While only a few topics can be touched upon here (history, sexuality, biblical interpretation, health, science), and

[1]In fact, because I offered the solutions since published in "Does Our Past Embarrass Us?," the South Pacific Division President and Secretary had me dismissed without trial as Director of the Ellen G. White/SDA Research Center at Avondale College in 1983. It seems that no informed person in the church now questions the essence of the article.

[2]This was the high point in the entire history of the church, insofar as the availability of data for Ellen White studies is concerned. It marked an essential consensus on the basic facts which were relevant for Adventists to know about Ellen White. No significant new information has emerged since that time. Much detail has, however, confirmed conclusions of which the keenest researchers were aware by that time.

[3]Thus in today's polarized context, it is more difficult to unite the church constructively. The substance of part one of this paper was well received by the Sydney Adventist Forum in 1991, and repeated by request at an interdepartmental council at the South Pacific Division headquarters during 1992. The substance of parts two and three was presented at Trans-Tasman Union Conference seminars in 1994 and 1995. Pastor Graeme Bradford has been particularly effective, with the support of his administration, in updating the church through seminars.

even then only in a brief way, the principles advocated could be applied widely.

*Scene 1.* A student presents a paper to the graduate students and faculty members of a university on the way in which Ellen White developed the "Great Controversy" theme in books published under her name between 1858 and 1917. The professor of European History subsequently writes a letter to the departmental chairperson recommending the student be advanced to candidacy in the department of history. The ensuing discussion leads to a renewed interest in Ellen White amongst members of the association of Adventist university students.

*Scene 2.* An Adventist marriage counselor reviews the development of family theory amongst Seventh-day Adventists, giving specific attention to Ellen White's influence. The review is accepted as meeting one of the requirements for membership in the association of marriage and family counselors, and engenders support for the family crisis facility being planned by the local conference.

*Scene 3.* A systematic theologian reads a paper at an international conference of an association for theological studies dealing with the way in which the development of a Seventh-day Adventist theology of mission has been influenced by Ellen White. The paper is subsequently published in the association's journal and initiates a series of letters on the biblical basis for cross-cultural missionary endeavors.

*Scene 4.* A conference of medical specialists receives and approves for publication in its proceedings a paper by an Adventist specialist on the symbiotic relationship between mind, body, and spirit as portrayed in the writings of Ellen White. Subsequently, a State Minister of Health shows an interest in the way in which holistic health-care shortens the length of hospital stays.

*Scene 5.* An Adventist geologist presents a professional paper at an annual conference of Christian geologists on the search for meaning in nature, making reference to creationist ideas as expressed by Ellen White. The Adventist is subsequently accepted as a presenter for the next annual conference.

*Scene 6.* An Adventist academy teacher discusses the way in which Ellen White's ideas have influenced the dietary habits of North Americans, Australians, and New Zealanders. Several students accept her subsequent invitation to view the film, *Ellen White: Prophetic Voice for the Last Days.*

*Scene 7.* An Adventist counselor assists a ministerial student who is deeply disturbed about an impulse to masturbate, outlining relevant principles from Ellen White's writings and emphasizing the way in which peace-of-mind can come from following her advice to focus on Jesus and Scripture. The student's adjustment is enhanced by participation in a fellowship group and by reading *The Desire of Ages* as background for an essay entitled "To Know God is to Love Him." Not only does the student graduate, he proceeds to an effective youth-oriented ministry.[1]

*Scene 8.* A graduate student presents a paper (in a seminar series on nineteenth-century literary figures) on Ellen White's method as author of the major volumes which bore her name between 1851 and 1917. The paper is subsequently accepted for publication in a professional journal.

*Scene 9.* After a conference paper entitled "Time, Charles Darwin, and the Ascent of Man," an Adventist presents a paper on "Time, Ellen White, and the Descent of Man." Both papers are accepted for publication in a symposium on the response of Christianity to nineteenth-century anthropology.

*Scene 10.* An Adventist delivers an address entitled "Toil and Charisma in the Life of Ellen White: 1891-1900" to a conference sponsored by scholars devoted to the study of colonial Christianity. The address analyzes the combination of hard work and supernatural influences which can be documented in Ellen White's colonial experience. The center accepts the text of the address for distribution as one of its occasional papers.

*Scene 11.* The referees of an evangelical history association's journal accept, with only minor editing, an article by an Adventist which contends that Ellen White meets the fundamental criteria for inclusion in the association's forthcoming evangelical dictionary of biography.

Clearly Ellen White and Adventism could emerge from these encounters as winsome and credible. The relative ease which we feel about projecting our prophet into such contexts indicates that she can have an ongoing relevance for our movement and its mission.

## The Core of the Matter

A number of conclusions may be drawn from this discussion. If the church's mission is to be fulfilled, Ellen White cannot be secreted from the realities of the contemporary world as a private concern of Seventh-day Adventists. The long list of theses presented in many parts of the globe to credible institutions of higher learning demonstrates that her children are becoming adults.[2] We need to carefully evaluate a whole range of issues impinging on her ministry.

[1] I have more experience as a chaplain supporting dying persons than as a counselor dealing with this dimension of living.

[2] See Gilbert Abella and Vera May Schwarz, "Dissertations, Theses and Major research Papers Related to the Seventh-day Adventist Church" (Loma Linda: Loma Linda Research Libraries 1988) 207-18.

There is a great need to proceed with modernizing her language if we expect many of our youth to have any interest in reading her writings, or if we want more than a few new converts to actually read her books. Her writings must be interpreted in their historical and cultural contexts: to give a young person *Messages to Young People* will usually be counter-productive, to give a young couple *Adventist Home* will often destroy their openness to Ellen White, to distribute *Counsels on Diet and Foods* will stop many Adventists from further reading of Ellen White. In other words, Ellen White's counsel on the need to consider the "time and place" of her counsels is increasingly pertinent. We would do well to take the essence of her counsel and follow her method; for instance, being aware of the link between health and religion we must go beyond her writings to Scripture and science, distilling and then implementing the best that is known on how to live. In place of our backwardness in recognizing the spiritual giftedness of all God's children, including women, we might note the significance of Ellen White's ordination which was so apparent that no Adventist man dared lay hands upon her.[1] We ought to ask how Ellen White responded to the issues relating to human values and human rights, including the treatment of individuals and groups by churches and governments.[2] Instead of engaging in endless controversies about music and worship, we should focus on *worship* of our Creator and celebration of the divine handiwork combined with a healthy ecological concern. Further suggestions of constructive emphases we might explore are given later in this presentation.

The Apostle Paul's warning about dispensing with childish things may be applied to the Adventist experience. The time-honored patterns of authority which held the church together until the 1960s would totally destroy it if used in Western cultures in the present. Therefore, in the providence of God, the church since 1970 has been engaged in a crucial process of maturation. It now has the potential for a new approach to its mission, flowing from a different relationship with its prophet. Our impetus must be to implement the great emphases of her nurture rather than to bore her spiritual children to death with matters which are irrelevant to

[1]Cp. Steven G. Daily, "The Irony of Adventism: The Role of Ellen White and Other Adventist Women in Nineteenth Century America" (DMin project, School of Theology at Claremont 1985).

[2]In mooting this point in a letter dated March 16, 1994, Eric Magnusson observes: "I see this as one of the major issues for religion today and I think it was a sufficiently big issue for EGW for that to be one of her continuing areas of influence. Churches, ours included, are being judged by society on their performance as they deal with and treat human beings. They're not all getting the verdict they want."

them. (Few things are as irrelevant to the young as the total recall of the old!)

If Ellen White were present today, she might enjoin Adventists to leave behind some of their favorite controversies—How accurate was James Ussher? What fires volcanoes? Is bedroom drama compatible with the drama of salvation?—and be faithful to the big picture. That is one of the powerful messages which we can derive from the way the Lord has led and taught us through her ministry.[1] But what *is* the big picture as far as Ellen White is concerned? What is the panorama she has given the Second Advent Movement?

It is not easy to summarize the contribution of her fruitful life in a few words, but we must try.

Seventh-day Adventist faith is enveloped by two expressions in Revelation 14, "the everlasting gospel" and "the faith of Jesus." We live near the conclusion of the great war between righteousness and sin, identifying with Jerusalem over against Babylon. Ours is the faith of Israel: we are to worship the God of creation and exodus with the openness of the psalmists and the faithfulness of the prophets. But all the promise of the Old Testament meets fulfillment in the New. Thus, ours is the faith of the new Israel, centered in Christ and faithful to the eyewitness testimony of the apostles. We are, therefore, to be catholic in an authentic sense: our message is for every nation, kindred, tongue, and people. Not only is it shaped by an understanding of those who first spread the faith, it is taught by those who preserved the truth during ages of darkness, reformed it in the sixteenth century, and revived it in the eighteenth. In addition, behind us is the glow of Millerite Adventism; before us is Jesus, Author of our guidebook and Finisher of our faith.[2]

To be God's remnant in Ellen White's terms is to be eclectic in relation to both Jewish and Christian faith, to be reformist in relation to our culture, and to be mission-focused in all that we do.[3] To be faithful to her nurture is to orient ourselves by the timeless landmarks of truth which guide God's pilgrim people from Eden

---

[1] Essentially, the more we get the big picture in focus, the more likely our constituents will be to listen when we affirm an ongoing relevance for the mother of the church. However, for our people to "own" Ellen White, we must invite them to process the relevant information and express their consequent understandings—that is, we need to reactivate the process which formed Seventh-day Adventism in the beginning, what Fritz Guy calls "the dialogue and dialectic of a community."

[2] This paragraph is a frail attempt at interpreting Revelation 14:6-12 in the light of "the conflict of the ages," the controlling idea in Ellen White's writings from 1858-1915. This was her over-arching concern, her emphasis on faith, that is, *truth*.

[3] This is the principal purpose of her testimonies, her exhortations which emphasize Christian practice, that is *duty*.

lost to Eden restored: creation (the Sabbath), covenant (Sinai), Calvary (redemption), Olivet ("Go ye into all the world"), and Mount Zion (the Kingdom of God). It is to make truth more precious than life, as did the faithful souls of past ages,[1] yet to identify with the "present truth"—that Jesus is the Lamb slain, the Mediator of the tabernacle which God pitched, and the Advocate to which all judgment is committed. Our life-quest is "the truth as it is in Jesus,"[2] our life-style is to be one of "disinterested benevolence"[3] in this needy world as we pray, "Come, Lord Jesus."

## How, Then, Shall We Use the Writings of Ellen White?

John and Charlotte Pocock,[4] earnest Sunday-keeping Christians, migrated from England to Australia late in the 1880s. During 1892-3, an evangelistic series conducted in Parramatta (a suburb of Sydney) by Robert Hare and David Steed astonished them with the truth that the seventh day is the Sabbath, and they commenced keeping Saturday immediately. The 1890s were difficult enough for parents with a growing family, given the country's pervasive problems with a depressed economy. Sabbath-keeping created a serious employment problem for John Pocock: Saturday was the busiest day of the week for his trade, coach maintenance and repair; all his skills as a cabinetmaker, coachbuilder and wheelwright now seemed useless. John Pocock built a small home on a rocky hillside north of Sydney, meanwhile eking out a meager living and evangelizing his neighbors with the help of Ellen White's books.

The Pococks' relationship with Ellen White was strengthened while the Avondale School for Christian Workers was being pioneered at Cooranbong. As one of the tradesmen working on the college buildings, John Pocock lived in Ellen White's "Sunnyside" home for about seven months. At that time Ellen White was busily writing about the life of Jesus and supporting the mission of the

---

[1]Note Ellen White's use of the expression "faithful souls," some thirty-one times. See especially Ellen G. White, *Acts of the Apostles* (Mountain View, CA: Pacific 1911) 11: "From the beginning, faithful souls have constituted the church on earth."

[2]There are many names for our Lord, perhaps seventy in the Old Testament and 170 in the New. In her writings, Ellen White uses "Jesus" 47,114 times and "truth" 53,144 times. In 776 instances she juxtaposes the words "truth" and "Jesus." She employs the word "present" some 13,830 times, and speaks of "present truth" 2,452 times. Thus it is safe to say that she gives emphasis to both "present truth" and "the truth as it is in Jesus."

[3]Ellen White's use of this term enjoins us to pattern our ministry after the selfless example of Christ Jesus.

[4]See Mary Pocock-Stellmaker and Joan Minchin-Neall, "The John Pocock Story," *Adventist Heritage* 15 (Spring 1992): 15-25.

Seventh-day Adventist church in Australasia and overseas with constant testimonies. According to John Pocock, by breakfast time (7:00 AM), she had up to 40 handwritten pages ready for her secretaries to transcribe. His memory may have inflated the number of pages, but perhaps not, in view of the fact that sometimes Ellen White commenced writing before midnight, though more often about 3:00 AM. On April 2, 1899, the Pocock family moved from the Sydney region to Cooranbong so the husband and father could continue work on the college buildings, and the children could be educated there. On August 13, 1900, the Pococks wrote a page for the album which was presented to Ellen White as she embarked for North America after nine years in the Antipodes.

Amelia Patrick and her three young sons, Charles, Sydney, and William, met Ellen White at the 1898 Brisbane camp meeting. Amelia, a widow and a recent convert nurtured in the faith by A.G. Daniells, was encouraged by Ellen White to transfer to Cooranbong for the education of her sons. After being a neighbor of Ellen White and the Pococks, Amelia Patrick also wrote an entry in the album of 1900.

Hence my mother, Bertha Emma Pocock (1902-1986), and my father, William Nelson Patrick (1892-1972), were profoundly influenced by their parents' accounts of Ellen White's ministry. To this early nurture was added the vigorous emphasis given to Ellen White's prophetic gift during my years at Avondale College. These two influences were reinforced immediately after my graduation in 1957 by the first-ever Seminary Extension School in Australasia, at which Elder Arthur L. White offered a course entitled "Prophetic Guidance." It is understandable, then, that one of my goals as a young minister was to have in my library a copy of everything which Ellen White ever wrote, to read all the comments she had penned on any passage of Scripture on which I proposed to preach, and to determine every issue of Adventist faith and practice in harmony with her counsel.

Four decades later I still have a passion to understand and apply Ellen White's prophetic testimony, to benefit my own spiritual journey and that of the church. But it is essential to recognize the research in Adventist heritage and the writings of Ellen White which has been undertaken by Seventh-day Adventists during the past three decades. My purpose in the final section of this chapter is to ask, *In view of all we now know, how shall we use responsibly the writings of Ellen White to equip ourselves and our church for the mission God has for us in the twenty-first century?* Toward this end, we shall contrast two symbols: that of *the all-encompassing encyclopædia* and that of *the pioneer explorer.*

*Ellen White's Writings as an All-Encompassing Encyclopædia*

You can imagine the eagerness with which I greeted the 1962-3 publication of the three-volume *Comprehensive Index to the Writings of Ellen G. White.*[1] We now had a better way to find published references to a given Bible text or subject. Further, the treasure-trove of Ellen White's writings was being augmented by new compilations, then by collected volumes of articles, and (much later) by the publication of manuscript releases and sermons. Thus, increasingly, her encyclopedic coverage of Adventist thought and practice was being extended, and, as even more comprehensive indexing was developed, it was becoming more and more accessible to Adventists worldwide.

Let us explore, then, the viability or otherwise of using Ellen White's writings as an all-encompassing, authoritative encyclopedia.

*Amalgamation of Man and Beast.* Ellen White often proclaimed God as the Creator of life and beauty, and Satan as the destroyer of life and loveliness. In 1864, within a discussion of those larger themes, she told the newly-organized Seventh-day Adventist Church:

> Every species of animal which God had created were preserved in the ark. The confused species which God did not create, which were the result of amalgamation, were destroyed by the flood. Since the flood there has been amalgamation of man and beast, as may be seen in almost endless varieties of species of animals, and in certain races of men.[2]

This understanding of amalgamation, implying the interbreeding of humans and animals, created a vibrant debate during the 1860s. Uriah Smith weighed in on Ellen White's side, dealing with this and 51 other issues in a series of articles in *The Second Advent Review and Sabbath Herald.* Smith's series was soon collected in a book which James White endorsed strongly and sold widely at camp meetings.[3] Smith not only defended the notion that interbreeding between animals and humans had occurred—he went on to affirm that the results could be clearly seen amongst nineteenth-century people-groups. Such an explanation of racial characteristics is unthinkable to us, by reason of what we now believe to be scientific fact. But as late as 1870, the paragraph from *Spiritual Gifts* was grammatically adjusted, yet it was essentially unchanged as it was

---

[1]*Comprehensive Index to the Writings of Ellen G. White* (Mountain View, CA: Pacific).

[2]Ellen G. White, *Spiritual Gifts, 3: Important Facts of Faith, in Connection with the History of Holy Men of Old* (Battle Creek, MI: Adventist 1864) 75; cp. 64.

[3]See Uriah Smith, *The Visions of Mrs. E. G. White* (Battle Creek, MI Adventist 1868).

republished in the first volume of *The Spirit of Prophecy: The Great Controversy between Christ and His Angels and Satan and His Angels.*[1]

*Geology and Earth Sciences.* Ellen White often commented on the Genesis accounts of Creation and the Flood. Sixty-three pages of these comments have been collected under the title, "Ellen G. White Statements Relating to Geology and Earth Sciences."[2] Most scientists with a knowledge of the scientific subjects treated would be unwilling to seriously consider some of Ellen White's remarks as sustainable. Note, for instance, the problems inherent in her statements about earthquakes and volcanoes.

> God causes large quantities of coal and oil to ignite and burn. Rocks are intensely heated, limestone is burned, and iron ore melted. Water and fire under the surface of the earth meet. The action of water upon limestone adds fury to the intense heat, and causes earthquakes, volcanoes and fiery issues.[3]

*Health Sciences.* Ellen White, from 1863 onward, demonstrated a deep interest in the subject of health. Partially response to her counsels, Seventh-day Adventist have developed a worldwide system of clinics and hospitals which in most instances win a profound respect from the communities they serve. What would be the effects if we literally followed Ellen White's ideas with reference to the causes of certain diseases, the influence of heredity, or the application of such nineteenth-century ideas as vitalism? For instance, observe the following quotation which infers that acquired characteristics are transmitted from one generation to the next.

> Some women have naturally small waists. But rather than regard such forms as beautiful, they should be viewed as defective. These wasp waists may have been transmitted to them from their mothers, as the result of their indulgence in the sinful practice of tight lacing, and in consequence of imperfect breathing.[4]

*History.* From 1858 to her death, Ellen White's literary efforts concentrated more often on the cosmic war between Christ and His angels and Satan and his angels than upon any other theme. As an eager student in History I at the University of Queensland in the 1950s, I wrote an essay on the development of religious toleration in Europe, using *The Great Controversy* as a major source. At the next residential school I was perplexed when essays were returned

---

[1]See Smith 78, 69. For further documentation, see Patrick, "Past." Note the way in which the term "amalgamation" is used by Ellen White in *Review and Herald*, Aug. 23, 1892; Ms. 65, 1889; and *Manuscript Releases*, 16, 247. See also W. C. White, letter to L. E. Froom, Jan. 8, 1928, White, *Messages* 3: 452.

[2]White, *Geology*; cp. Gordon.

[3]See *Spiritual Gifts*, 3, 79-83.

[4]See *Review and Herald*, 31 October 1871; "Words to Christian Mothers," *Health Reformer*, Oct. 1871: 121 and Nov. 1871: 154-157; *Healthful Living*, 1897: 58.

to all the other students, but mine was not handed back. Rather timidly, I approached the lecturer, to be told my essay had already been reproduced and mailed to everyone else in the class as an example of how the assignment should be handled. I had taken Ellen White's philosophy and fleshed it out with the help of other historians. However, back then, we Adventists were also likely to settle detailed historical questions on the basis of what Ellen White said, something we now know we must avoid. Twenty years after I wrote that essay the Adventist church learned that *The Great Controversy* was not useable as a source for the details of history. Notice this account from the historian who most carefully researched this issue.

> . . . [T]he historical portions of *The Great Controversy* that I have examined are selective abridgments and adaptation of historians. Ellen White was not just borrowing paragraphs here and there that she ran across in her reading, but in fact following the historians page after page, leaving out much material, but using their sequence, some of their ideas, and often their words. In the examples I have examined I have found no historical fact in her text that is not in their text. The hand-written manuscript on John Huss follows the historian so closely that it does not even seem to have gone through an intermediary stage, but rather from the historian's printed page to Mrs. White's manuscript, including historical errors and moral exhortations.[1]

It would be decidedly perilous today to use Ellen White's writings in a way which appeared viable in earlier times.

*Scripture.* Ellen White was a lifelong, devout student of the Scriptures, with a remarkable breadth in her knowledge of the Word, a fact amply proved by looking at an index of the Scripture passages which are used in her writings. During the 1970s, major Bible conferences were held in various locations, including North America and Australia. One of many important issues which came to light at that time was the fact that Ellen White approached Scripture in a variety of ways, a dozen of which were identified.[2] A conclusion from this research is evident: we stand on very slippery ground if we give her writings exegetical control over our understanding of the intent and meaning of the Bible.

*Doctrine.* Between 1844 to the end of her ministry seven decades later, Ellen White developed a symbiotic relationship with the Seventh-day Adventist Church. She was present with the struggling groups of believers during the seven years when the "Shut Door" idea was a dominant explanation of 1844. She toiled with the movement as it came to terms with the identity of the law in Galatians, with a definition of clean and unclean meats, with the mys-

---

[1]Cp. McAdams 27-41; Ronald D. Graybill, *Historical Difficulties in* The Great Controversy , rev. ed. (Washington, DC: White Estate 1982).
[2]See Raymond F. Cottrell, "Ellen White's Use of the Bible," Hyde 154-161.

tery surrounding the nature of Christ, and with the necessity to refine its understanding of righteousness by faith. It is now clear that
our earlier concepts of continuity and change in the Seventh-day
Adventist movement must be updated to incorporate the fact that
not only did our community of faith grow and change in its understandings, Ellen White also grew and even changed as well.[1]

*Education.* Ellen White gave a great deal of attention from the
1870s onward to the matter of "true education." This has been
enormously fruitful in its effects. But Adventists have long debated
a host of issues which arise from her comments, such as the age at
which children should begin schooling, variously hoping or denying that Ellen White could give us a definitive answer. The nature
of these debates has frequently been destructive. Often it has been
claimed that she gave us a "blueprint" for Christian education, but
this symbol has proved less and less adequate as time has pro-
gressed.[2] In many such instances, our expectations of Ellen White
have created a problem, rather than the problem being inherent in
her statements.[3]

*Inerrancy.* Therefore, an important observation needs emphasis
at this point. As the Seventh-day Adventist Church has come to a
fuller understanding of both the content of Ellen White's writings
and the religious and social context in which they were penned, we
have found it necessary to stress that her writings are not inerrant.[4]
Further, in view of the traditional ways in which so many of us had
used Ellen White's writings, it became necessary for the church to
make and publish a specific list of affirmations and denials.[5]

There is truth which lies behind each of the seven illustrations
cited above. Smith noted that Ellen White's concern in her "amalgamation" statements was to illustrate "the deep corruption and
crime into which the race fell."[6] The message that God is Creator is
vastly more important than any nineteenth-century notions about
the earth's crust. Ellen White has influenced, profoundly, the health
of millions of people, despite the specific limitations of her health-
related counsels. Since she learned history largely by ordinary
means, and we have access to better sources on which to establish

[1]Cp. Olson, *Shut Door,* and Ronald D. Graybill, *The Development of Adventist
Thinking on Clean and Unclean Meats* (Washington, DC: White Estate 1981).
[2]I have attempted a constructive elaboration of this theme in my unpublished
paper, "Does Ellen White Have a Crucial Testimony for Avondale in 1995?"
[3]In *Reading Ellen White* (Hagerstown: Review 1997) George Knight offers a
comprehensive set of principles and methods for the effective interpretation of
Ellen White's writings.
[4]See Robert W. Olson, *Inerrancy.*
[5]See "The Inspiration and Authority of the Ellen G. White Writings," *Adventist Review,* Dec. 23, 1982: 9.
[6]Smith, *Visions of* 103.

our historical understandings, she cannot help us with the basics of history. But, on the other hand, she can help us in the far more important task of finding God in the mazes of history. We can rightly affirm her devotion to the Scriptures, and be challenged to go to the Bible with a desire similar to hers to learn the truth. We need to be as open to constructive change as she was, knowing we too have "many things to learn, and many, many to unlearn."[1] Further, we do well to avoid claims which her writings neither encourage nor sustain.

It is clear that Seventh-day Adventism would become an anachronism were we to adopt the writings of Ellen White as the definitive and authoritative encyclopædia of our faith and practice. In the process, we would destroy her credibility as a prophetic witness, and damage the mission of the church which was so precious to her. If the symbol of the all-encompassing encyclopedia is no longer an adequate way to depict the writings of Ellen White, is there not a more appropriate way for us to portray her writings?

*Ellen White: Pioneer Explorer*

Little was known by Westerners about continental Australia at the end of the eighteenth century, but by 1862 intrepid explorers had pioneered an understanding of the country's mountains, plains, and deserts. To use the maps of these explorers to find the way to the center of Sydney, the popular automobile racetrack over the Blue Mountains in New South Wales, or the internationally-known monolith in the Northern Territory would involve us in considerable frustration. Yet, without the orientation provided by the explorers, contemporary life would be impaired, if not impossible.

Seventh-day Adventists were uniquely helped by Ellen White's prophetic gift during their first seventy years. Her writings will continue to speak to us as long as time shall last,[2] but the longer time lasts the more challenging it will be to constructively apply them in the ongoing journey of the church. At this point, let us remind ourselves, again, of the importance of the direction-setting ideas with which section one concludes and those stated at the end of this paper, concepts which have a continuing and powerful significance for the church's thought and mission.

But there are other ways to symbolize Ellen White's work which merit exploration. Ellen White is, of all Adventist women, best fitted to be called the mother of the church. We need to recog-

---

[1] Ellen G. White, *Counsels to Writers and Editors* (Nashville: Southern 1946) 37.

[2] Ellen G. White, *Selected Messages*, 3 vols. (Washington, DC: Review 1958-80) 1: 55.

nize that in the providence of God we owe a great deal to her and that we will never outgrow the values which she has deeply embedded in our corporate psyche. The fact that her writings do not qualify as a comprehensive, all-encompassing, authoritative encyclopædia of Seventh-day Adventist thought and practice means that we, her children, are called to a measure of adultness which increases constantly as we move further from the historical matrix of her seventy-year ministry. An adult attitude which accepts individual responsibility, and wisely employs her writings and the spiritual gifts presently manifested within the church, will most fully appreciate her role as the foremost explorer in our movement, one uniquely used of God to determine the essential directions of our pilgrimage in this last segment of time. That metaphor accords well with the notion that Ellen White is the mother of Seventh-day Adventism.

My mother's parents were, as I mentioned earlier, personal friends and neighbors of Ellen White. They were able to give my mother only about the same amount of formal education as Ellen White herself received. My mother nurtured me lovingly and set my direction decidedly on a long road of discovery that caused me to finish the primary schooling she did not complete, plus high school, and academic programs at Avondale College and four other tertiary institutions. The longer we lived, the less my mother and I saw and understood things in the same way.[1] But our mutual love and respect were not impaired by that reality. Often, faithfulness to the spirit of my mother's nurture demanded a radical revision of what she had taught me and what she still believed. I can never dismiss the importance of her influence upon my life, nor can I be true to her and remain bound by her categories of thought. The application to Ellen White as a spiritual mother of the church is obvious. The Christian life is (according to Proverbs 4:18) like the light of dawn that shines more brightly until that noonday when (according to 1 Corinthians 13) we put childish things behind us and the smoked glass of this life is taken away.[2]

For some Seventh-day Adventists it may be appropriate to symbolize Ellen White as giving "a jet-aircraft vision of crucial realities in an age of spiritual surface travel."[3] Others may identify with her

[1] We do well to remind ourselves just how different our culture is from that in which Adventism developed. See Jonathan Butler, "From Millerism to Seventh-day Adventism: 'Boundlessness to Consolidation,'" *Church History* 55 (March 1986): 50-64.

[2] It is salutary to reflect on the fact that the landmarks of early Adventism are seen by us from a different perspective 150 years later.

[3] Arthur Patrick, "Landmarks or Landscape," *Adventist Review*, Oct. 27, 1983: 4.

best as the church's mother.[1] Indeed, it could be useful for each of us to give that symbol a personal application in that none of us can accomplish such a task effectively for our colleagues, due to the limitations of our knowledge about each other.

A further symbol also invites exploration. In an insightful reference to paradigms, Claire Monod Cassidy uses a metaphor which she notes has been popular since the 1940s, "The map is not a road."[2] Ellen White has given us a sketch map for the spiritual journey of the Advent movement. God did not give us through her a *road*, nor *a contour map* with all the details for which some of us long. What God *did* give us was, however, a map of profound significance. We must neither undervalue nor overdo the relevance of that map.

*Some Priorities for the Immediate Future*

There is a continuing need for a more comprehensive approach by the Seventh-day Adventist Church if we are to respond adequately to the issues raised in this paper. Several points appear to be worth consideration with reference to the church's understanding of the life and writings of Ellen White. I suggest that the church might give careful study to a range of constructive plans, including the following.

1. What steps may be taken to develop a more informed and resilient relationship between thought leaders and administrative leaders so that the kind of dialogue and dialectic which benefited the church in its early years—for example, during the Sabbath Conferences of 1848-50 and the US Civil War of 1861-65—might be re-experienced? This might benefit scholars, save administrators some of the painful investigations of institutions and ministers which they deem to be necessary at present, and build a greater sense of community and partnership in fulfillment of the church's mission.

2. Are there ways to enhance participation in the process of discovery and experimentation by White Estate personnel

---

[1]See my article "Ellen White: Mother of the Church in the South Pacific," *Adventist Heritage* 16 (Spring 1993): 30-40. Such symbols, like others the church developed earlier (for instance, a telescope, a pilot) may need redefinition over time to accord with the increasing understanding about Ellen White. Richard Rice, "Ellen White's Writings as Religious Classics: A Response to the Current Predicament" (unpublished essay, Feb. 1984), offers creative suggestions for the use of Ellen White's writings by Adventists who have (by training and/or experience) philosophical/theological interests. Bert Haloviak, "Ellen White and the SDA Church" (unpublished essay, Oct. 1980), gives a masterful treatment of some of the ways in which Ellen White's writings were understood during her lifetime.

[2]"Unraveling the Ball of String: Reality, Paradigms, and the Study of Alternative Medicine," *Advances: The Journal of Mind-Body Health* 10 (Winter 1994): 5-31.

and the staff of the Ellen G. White/SDA Research Centers around the world?[1] This might help to better identify both the problems and the promise of the discussion about Ellen White in relation to matters now on the church's agenda, and renew a sense of trust in the church.[2]

3. Would it be constructive to monitor such processes by a carefully-structured "think-tank," a group inclusive of the church's talent in administration, biblical studies, systematic and historical theology, mission, history, science, anthropology, sociology, psychology, medicine, literature, and pastoral care? This group could also generate and receive suggestions as well as explore and field-test ways to raise the level of awareness about Ellen White in the church at large.

4. Are there ways in which the church might profitably nurture (worldwide) its editors and publishing committees so it can be sure the magazines, journals, and books it supports are accurate and unifying in their content relating to the Adventist heritage and Ellen White?[3]

5. Could the Biblical Research Institute lead the church in an open, frank discussion of the ways in which fundamentalism has impacted the Seventh-day Adventist Church? Could this study explore the incompatibility between fundamentalism and the prophetic gift as known in the experience of Ellen G. White? Then, might the church consider how these findings should influence its activities, the way it understands related issues (including the inspiration as manifested in Scripture and Ellen White's writings), and the way it treats people?

6. Might it be fruitful for the Adventist Society for Religious Studies and the Adventist Theological Society to consider participating in an open, collegial dialogue on these issues in a search for ways in which their members might better support the unity and mission of the church with reference to Ellen White's ministry?

---

[1] Observe some of the constructive proposals offered in *Spectrum*. Note, for instance, the implications for creation science, Ellen White studies, and historiography in the following issues: 16 (April 1985): 67; 16 (Aug. 1985: 2-31; 18 (Dec. 1987): 58-9; 18 (February 1988): 36-42; and especially James W. Walters, "Ellen White in a New Key" 21 (Dec. 1991): 12-7. Walters calls for "an already discredited authoritarian Ellen White to be replaced by a revered, authoritative Ellen White."

[2] A first principle of business management is to listen to consumers, a starting-point for all quality" studies. Perhaps the ministry of White Estate could be enhanced by the equivalent of a market survey as it forms plans for the future.

[3] It would seem to be pastorally irresponsible to allow the Two-Thirds World to drift into the kind of crisis which occurred in the South Pacific and North American church late in the 1970s and onward.

7. How might the church mount a sustained effort to find and
foster apt symbols which will accurately encapsulate the
meaning and value of the ministry of Ellen White for Seventh-day Adventists? The symbols suggested herein—a jet-
aircraft panorama, a pioneer explorer, a mother, a sketch
map—might all be discarded in favor of better ones, but the
importance of the task demands that serious attempts be
made to find and foster adequate metaphors without delay.[1]

One of the great challenges which the church faces in the
twenty-first century is to understand the attitudes within the present generation of young Adventists, including those who have
grown up estranged from the church's mother. These young people
are potential recruits for the army which, rightly trained, may well
complete the task at which those who presently lead the church
have toiled so earnestly. Step-by-step the church has laid a foundation for a more comprehensive and accurate picture of Ellen White
and her ministry; we need at this time to judiciously continue this
endeavor.[2] Perhaps we can say with a Christian leader who was appointed to an important post recently, "Our greatest challenge is to
live as the modern-day Christians that we are—and as those who
are faithful to our founders' vision."[3]

As we proceed with this important agenda, we need to rise
above controversy and highlight the constructive spiritual ministry

---

[1]Men and women from a range of disciplines and perspectives have read
drafts of this chapter and shaped its development by their comments. For this
help I am grateful, even though I alone take full responsibility for each statement
made. It is clear that so short a treatment may raise more questions than it answers in the minds of some. Steve Daily notes the need to better explore three
ideas. First, Ellen White's self-understanding of her prophetic role given the
views of prophecy that characterized nineteenth-century America inside and outside Adventism. Second, how such views fit with a biblical understanding of
prophecy in the New Testament and post-New Testament eras. (See Wayne
Grudem, *The Gift of Prophecy in the New Testament and Today*, rev. ed. [Wheaton,
IL: Crossway 2000] and Graham Houston, *Prophecy: A Gift for Today* [Downers
Grove, IL: IVP 1989]. Thirdly, what the implications are for us as Adventists today if we are to continue as a prophetic community and properly understand and
model the gifts of the Spirit so as to fulfill our prophetic destiny. This latter issue
is rather fully explored in several of Daily's published volumes.

[2]In planning a video to highlight the centenary of Ellen White's arrival in the
South Pacific, it was decided to aim the production at this group rather than the
older generation in the church. The result is the Adventist Media Center production entitled "One Hundred Year Recall," released in 1991.

[3]A remark by Robert K. Johnston upon his installation as Provost of Fuller
Theological Seminary, March 7, 1994. In *Embracing the Spirit: An Open Letter to the
Leaders of Adventism* (Takoma Park, MD: Columbia Union College 1997), Charles
Scriven has well depicted the forces which are "at this moment, pulling Adventism
toward the maelstrom" (3), including "flat, mechanical readings of the Bible,"
"theological rigidity and arrogance," and "reactive, inward-looking separatism" (16).

of Ellen White for ourselves as individuals and for the church we
love. I shall conclude this paper by listing a few of the many constructive emphases which we may choose to stress in light of the attention given them in the writings of Ellen White. Such a list could
be expanded readily; these suggestions are given as hints of possibilities inviting exploration.

1. *The link between the cosmology and eschatology, first things and
   last things.* The doctrine of creation has powerful environmental implications. Prophet though she was, with a compelling sense of mission, Ellen White exemplified a mature
   delight in the entire world of nature, even to pansies, peach-
   es, and potatoes. A recovery of her comprehensive interest
   in this theme would speak powerfully to our age.

2. *The connection between health and religion, spiritual and physical
   well-being.* We are currently allowing our culture to edge ahead
   of us in some aspects of this endeavor; to recover the authentic
   voice of Ellen White could make us the head and not the tail.[1]

3. *The "great controversy" theme, the controlling idea in Ellen
   White's entire corpus of writings.* According to Herbert
   Douglass, a focus on this theme would help us to better understand Ellen White and Adventist distinctives, since it is
   "the golden thread which binds all her writings together,"
   and in which "she breaks out of conventional theological
   paradigms that cause all our internal divisions and lifts us into
   a new dimension of dealing with the plan of salvation."[2]
   This emphasis would also offer us perhaps the most positive
   way to present Ellen White's ministry, faithful to her objectives and the major findings of the research conducted since
   1970.

4. *The interpretation of history.* Christianity is a teleological religion; it is directed toward a specific goal. All history is moving toward that end, and Ellen White can help us to discover
   and articulate the way in which the past reveals the purpose
   of God for the present and the future.

5. *The primacy of Scripture in the formation of doctrine.* We have yet
   to fully implement Ellen White's counsel by making the Bible our sole rule of faith and practice.

6. *The dynamic nature of Adventism.* We have not yet maximized
   the significance of our heritage. The *life* and *writings* of Ellen
   White are inextricably linked with the *history* and *thought* of

---

[1]This conclusion was reinforced as I attended a number of presentations at a
session of the American Academy of Religion in San Francisco, Nov. 23-25, 1997.
[2]Eletter to Arthur Patrick, received December 1, 1997.

the Seventh-day Adventist Church. We are still in the early stages of making this relationship understood in the church.[1]

7. *The winsomeness of God.* In my first wide-margin Bible there are copious notes made with a mapping pen in India ink, detailing the way in which Ellen White's writings on the life of Christ assist our understanding of the Gospels. Were there two demoniacs or one at Gadara? What was the sequence of the events in the life of Jesus? Did a specific miracle occur on the way *into* or the way *out of* Jericho? I asked countless questions on that level, some of which are quite irrelevant in the light of now well-known facts.[2] I now believe that the main theme of *The Desire of Ages* is clearly stated on page 22: Jesus came to reveal to us the God whom to know is to love. Many of the questions which I asked of this masterpiece were no doubt important, but too many of them were outside of its purpose or what might be expected of it.

8. *The ultimacy of Jesus Christ.* Probably most Adventists would not claim that they have fully implemented Ellen White's far-reaching injunction that "of all professing Christians, Seventh-day Adventists should be foremost in uplifting Christ before the world."[3]

[1]I regard it as a great privilege to journey through Adventist history with students. My basic aims in this process are suggested by seven principal terms. The responsible study of Adventist history is an exciting quest for *truth,* including historical accuracy; *insight,* an understanding of how the past illumines the present and the future; *stability,* a sufficient grasp of the relevant data so that new items of information do not threaten our belief system; *identification,* a pervading sense that Adventist history is our personal heritage, and hence precious; *commitment,* a conviction that the Adventist church has a mission worthy of our best talents and energies; *awe,* faith that the God of Scripture and Jesus Christ have led and continue to lead the Second Advent Movement through Word and Spirit; *celebration,* a desire to commemorate the integrity, achievements and faith of the past—and thus to inform and inspire present.

[2]See Robert W. Olson, "How *The Desire of Ages* Was Written" (Ellen G. White/SDA Research Center shelf doc., May 23, 1979). Olson shows that Ellen White did not claim to know the order of the events in the life of Christ (32). If she did not claim a revealed understanding of such chronological matters, is it fair for us to claim her support of Ussher's chronology resulted from divine revelation? In exploring this issue, we would do well to consult all the relevant studies on biblical chronology, including the Andrews University doctoral dissertation by Colin House.

[3]Ellen G. White, *Evangelism* (Washington, DC: Review 1946) 188. When we show other Christians the extent of Ellen White's agreement with cardinal Christian doctrines, they are more open to heed her distinctive convictions. For one attempt in this direction, see my article, "An Adventist and an Evangelical in Australia? The Case of Ellen White in the 1890s," *Lucas: An Evangelical History Review* 12 (Dec. 1991): 42-53; rptd. (in edited form) as "Are Adventists Evangelical?" *Ministry,* Feb. 1995: 14-17.

# 10

# Health and the Healing Arts

## Roy Branson

On October 25, 1984, almost 140 years to the day after the Great Disappointment of 1844, Loma Linda University surgeon Leonard Bailey transplanted the heart of a baboon into a human infant, Baby Fae. The procedure drew worldwide attention to Adventists. Some months after the operation, the American Academy of Religion invited Bailey to participate in its annual convention. The Academy drew some 10,000 members from across North America to Anaheim, California. Bailey drove from Loma Linda to participate in a public session discussing the ethics of innovative surgeries.

I remember locating the large ballroom provided for the meeting and finding a chair next to my brother, Bruce Branson, chair of the University's Department of Surgery. He was going to see what yet another ethicist was going to say about his colleague. The speaker was Kenneth Vaux, well-known for his work in medical ethics, and the author of a volume called *Health and Medicine in the Reformed Tradition*. While Vaux raised familiar points about informed consent and the allocation of scarce resources, Bailey and my brother remained quite composed.

Then Vaux launched into a broader topic. Bailey, Vaux said, seemed unable to come to terms with death, with its inevitability. Bailey appeared to feel it his God-given mission to go to extraordinary lengths to snatch profoundly sick infants from death. All Christians—all humans, for that matter—of course valued life. But Bailey, Vaux said, never seemed to consider that death might, just possibly, be a part of the natural order. Next to me, my brother stiffened. On the platform, Bailey shifted in his chair.

Vaux then galvanized the audience by saying that not long before, he had had to face this issue directly. His infant son had developed a condition that was profoundly disabling. He had to decide whether to approve the use of every conceivable procedure to prolong a life that would be agonizingly painful. Vaux described his son's physical condition and said that, after much study and prayer, he and his wife had accepted the fact that they should not impose their will on God's. They had asked their son's physician to cease his efforts. Their son had died.

Vaux turned his gaze. "I believe you, Dr. Bailey, would never have made my decision and would have fought on against death."

By now, my brother, who considered the condition of Vaux's child treatable, was rigid with anger, muttering under his breath about Vaux implying God killed children. Bailey immediately confirmed in no uncertain terms that he most certainly would have treated Vaux's son; that was why he was a physician; that was precisely why he stayed up night-and-day performing operations others criticized. "Ken, I hope that you would have let me fight to save your son."

For Adventist physicians like Bailey and my brother—indeed, for almost all physicians—disease and disability are not to be accepted, but challenged—repulsed with every ounce of intelligence and will at their command. Disease must not be allowed to overcome the frail, must be beaten back from oppressing the young. While most physicians oppose disease and death, the apocalyptic consciousness of Adventists intensifies and expands the professional ethos of physicians. For physicians, death is grotesque, to be fought with every weapon in medicine's armamentarium. For *Adventist* physicians, disease, disability and death are nothing less than enemies in a cosmic battle between good and evil, opponents in the Great Controversy between God and Satan.

In 1991 the title of an article—"Why the Marlboro Man Wants Your Kids"—appeared on the cover of *Christianity Today*, the most widely circulated Protestant journal in America. Written by Charles Scriven, identified as the pastor of the Sligo Seventh-day Adventist Church, the article noted the over 400,000 deaths a year caused by tobacco in the United States alone. It referred to the ten million tobacco-related deaths worldwide, and the 200 million children now living on the planet who will eventually die as a result of taking up smoking. Citing the success of the Marlboro Man and Old Joe Camel advertising campaigns in persuading 6,000 children and teenagers each day to start smoking, Scriven charged American tobacco companies with deliberately adopting a strategy to hook youngsters "on an addictive product before they can give adult consent to the risks."

Scriven chastised the churches of America for not making "the fight against tobacco part of its witness." At a time when more and more church members are "recognizing that the biblical call to win converts is also a call to heal societies," too many denominations,

Scriven charged, continue to look on smoking as a private vice to be tolerated as a matter of individual choice. Many secular voices denounce smoking as a health problem of epidemic proportions, but it is also, Scriven said, a monstrous moral outrage. In the conclusion to his call for Christian America to rise up and act, Scriven expanded the scope of his condemnation. This "deliberate victimization of children for profit," is "not a question of merely private vice. It is a question of social evil and institutional wickedness." It is an affront to God.[1]

Adventists have done more than write articles. A graduate of Loma Linda University chaired the successful fight in California for a 24¢-per-pack tax on tobacco. Adventists, along with other tobacco-control groups, began agitating a few years ago for a tax on tobacco. Subsequently, when the Clinton Administration introduced its health care reform legislation, it included a significant increase in federal tobacco taxes. With the support of Loma Linda University, Adventists convinced sixteen large religious organizations—Muslim, Jewish, Catholic, and Protestant—to lobby the US Congress on behalf of a $2.00-a-pack tax on tobacco. A proposal for a similar per-pack tax is now before California's legislature. Past experience in other countries demonstrates that every dollar increase in the per-pack tax on tobacco will, over time, save one million lives. Adventists found themselves in the thick of one of the most dramatic public health battles of the twentieth century.

Health, disease, and healing can be understood in a variety of ways. Immediately after October 22, 1844, disappointed Millerites avoided filthy habits like smoking as a way to preserve the purity necessary for them to enter heaven—which they continued to believe they would see within a few days or weeks. Later, and to this day, most Seventh-day Adventists have regarded the pursuit of health as conformity to the laws of God's creation. The Adventist commitment to observing the natural laws of health is usually given credit for the fact that "Adventists are perhaps the longest-lived population that has yet been formally described."[2] So, for instance, in a study reported in 2003, the percentage of California Adventist men surviving from age 65 to age 85 was slightly over *twice* that of men in the United States generally.[3] "In the mid-1980s, . . . California Adventist vegetarian men and women lived 9.5 and 6.1 years longer than other Californians."[4] And "[f]or the common causes of

---

[1]Charles Scriven, "Why The Marlboro Wants Your Kids," *Christianity Today*, April 8, 1991: 33-5.
[2]Gary E. Fraser, *Diet, Life Expectancy, and Chronic Disease: Studies of Seventh-day Adventists and Other Vegetarians* (New York: OUP 2003) 50-5.
[3]Fraser 52.
[4]Fraser 58.

death, low-risk Adventist men die at ages about 13 years older and woman about 9 years older than other Californians."[1]

## SOCIAL REFORM AND
## THE CLIMACTIC BATTLE OF 1844

But well before there was a Seventh-day Adventist church, Millerite leaders, in addition to regarding health as purity and health as conformity to law, also looked on health as part of the great conflict between good and evil. Their apocalyptic fervor intensified their commitment to social reform, including health. The "evidence from ante-bellum America is overwhelmingly on the side of proving a connection between a belief in Christ's imminent return and energetic efforts to perfect this world."[2] David Arthur, the best known historian of Millerism, declares that participation in social reforms led some to embrace William Miller's apocalypticism as "the fulfillment of the reformer's humanitarian goals."[3]

One example of a group involved in social reforms that swelled the Millerite movement was the Christian Connection, sometimes known simply as the Christian Church. Later, it provided leaders for the Seventh-day Adventist movement—James White (as well as his father), Joseph Bates, and Uriah Smith. In the early part of the nineteenth century, preachers and congregations too radical for the Free-Will Baptists or Methodists—either in their theology or their social reform agenda—would become a part of the more loosely-knit Christian Connection. These "Christians exploited the potent themes of tyranny, slavery, and the Antichrist; they regaled their audiences with the latest chapter in the saga of the beast and the whore of Babylon."[4]

Elias Smith, one of the founders of the Christian Connection, preached that God had raised up Thomas Jefferson, like Cyrus of old, "to dry up the Euphrates of mystery Babylon." Smith believed that the foundations of Christ's millennial kingdom were laid in the American and French revolutions.[5] Reliance on the Bible as the only final authority created rebels against elites of all kinds, including purveyors of traditional medicine. Smith became a promoter for

[1]Fraser 58.
[2]R. Laurence Moore, *Religious Outsiders and the Making of Americans* (Oxford: OUP 1985) 132.
[3]David T. Arthur, "Joshua V. Himes and the Cause of Adventism," *The Disappointed: Millerism and Millenarianism in the Nineteenth Century*, ed. Ronald L. Numbers and Jonathan M. Butler (Bloomington: Indiana UP 1987) 36.
[4]Nathan O. Hatch, *The Democratization of American Christianity* (New Haven: Yale UP 1989) 76.
[5]Hatch 184.

Samuel Thompson, the founder of one the more prominent medical "sects," or health reform movements, of the time.

Joshua V. Himes, who later became the organizational leader of the Millerite movement, found his vocation as a preacher and reformer through the Christian Connection. As a lay "exhorter" for the Connection congregation in New Bedford, Massachusetts, he spent time once or twice a week working in the city's destitute neighborhoods.[1] At twenty-five, Himes moved in 1829 to Boston and turned his Clarendon Street Chapel into a meeting place for many of that city's reform groups. While continuing to pastor his Christian Connection congregation, Himes quickly became a temperance lecturer, established a school where boys learned trades that allowed them to work their way through the school, and participated in movements for women's rights and world peace. Himes was especially passionate and energetic in his opposition to slavery. Ignoring the popular idea of providing African colonies for American slaves, he was one of the earliest supporters of William Lloyd Garrison's more radical approach of abolishing slavery. Himes was elected to the board of the Massachusetts Anti-Slavery Society and served as president of the Young Men's Anti-Slavery Society.[2]

It was at a conference of Christian Connection ministers in 1839 that Himes first met William Miller. At Himes's invitation, Miller, also committed to temperance and a convinced abolitionist, gave a series of lectures on prophecy that December in Himes' Christian Connection Chapel. Within months, in the spring of 1840, Himes issued the first number of the *Signs of the Times*. That fall, in October 1840, Himes hosted at his church the conference that launched the Millerite movement. Through his network of reform associations and drawing on his incredible energy, Himes took a William Miller, accustomed to rural and small-town congregations and introduced him to America's major cities. Himes organized hundreds of meetings and arranged for the publication of thousands of books, periodicals, pamphlets, tracts, hymnbooks, and visual aids.

Though he expended an enormous amount of energy organizing and leading the most dramatic apocalyptic movement in America's history, Himes never severed his connection with other reform movements. In 1841, his Clarendon Street Christian Connection Chapel hosted conventions of the Friends of Universal Reform; the attendees included such famous Americans as Garrison, Bronson Alcott, Theodore Parker, James Russell Lowell, and Ralph Waldo Emerson. Himes's apocalyptic consciousness intensified his commit-

[1]Arthur 37.
[2]Arthur 38.

ment to social reform. The evils he fought stretched to cosmic dimensions. But Himes glimpsed in the visions of John the Revelator more than powerful institutional wickedness. To his famous Friends of Universal Reform, Himes spoke out against "those who are 'always pulling down, but know not how to lay a single brick in building the walls of Jerusalem.'"[1] The return of Christ would be the ultimate social reform, not only destroying evil institutions, but establishing the ideal city of God.

Until mid-1842, Himes continued to travel as a temperance lecturer, to serve as a counselor to the Massachusetts Anti-Slavery Society, and to fulfill his responsibilities as a member of the executive committee of the Non-Resistance Society. It was no doubt in large measure because of Himes that as late as 1843 William Lord Garrison declared that William Miller was one in whom "the cause of temperance, of anti-slavery, of moral reform, of non-resistance," found an "outspoken friend."[2] Even at an early 1844 conference in New York City, Himes declared that the poor of the city, "for whom no man seems to care," must be hunted out and comforted with the promise of a new heaven and earth. "At the same time," he challenged his fellow Millerites to do everything possible "to relieve . . . [the] pressing temporal wants" of the urban poor.[3]

After the Great Disappointment, Himes continued his commitment to social reform, including that of health. For two days he single-handedly held up an 1846 Evangelical Alliance conference in London, objecting to the seating of American delegates who were slave holders. In 1865, he was elected vice-president of the National Health Reform Association.[4]

While Himes did not live out his ninety years within the Seventh-day Adventist community, other Millerites, social reformers, and members of the Christian Connection did. Joseph Bates began his pilgrimage to the millennium by way of health reform. A sea captain out of New Bedford, Bates gave up "ardent spirits" in 1821 while returning from a voyage to South America. On subsequent voyages, he became increasingly abstemious, first swearing off wine, then tobacco, then beer and cider. In 1827, through a revival, he joined the Christian (or Christian Connection) Church. The day of his baptism he proposed the organization of a temperance society. On his final voyage, he announced to an astonished crew—after his ship had cleared port—that he was sailing an alcohol-free temper-

---

[1] See *Liberator*, Dec. 4, 1840: 113, qtd. Arthur 42.
[2] Ronald D. Graybill, "The Abolitionist-Millerite Connection," Numbers and Butler 140.
[3] Arthur 49.
[4] Ronald L. Numbers, *Prophetess of Health: A Study of Ellen G. White*, 3d ed. (Grand Rapids: Eerdmans 2008) 160.

ance ship. After his retirement from the sea, Bates became even stricter, following Sylvester Graham's admonitions on healthful living by giving up tea, coffee, meat, butter, cheese, greasy foods—even rich pastries.[1]

For Bates, as with others of the time, health reform was a part of social reform. In the mid-1830s, Bates organized an anti-slavery society. He devoted himself to fighting alcohol and slavery before embracing the all-powerful reform of the Second Coming of Christ. Bates regarded all reform, including the Second Coming, as intertwined. "All who embraced this doctrine would and must necessarily be advocates of temperance and the abolition of slavery; and those who opposed the doctrine of the second advent would not be very effective laborers in moral reform."[2]

While Joshua Himes and Joseph Bates were converts, James White, who married a visionary teenager named Ellen Harmon, had grown up in a Christian Connection home. His father was a member of the Christian Connection for forty years, holding the significant office of deacon for most of that time. James White was baptized into the Christian Connection at fifteen; he never smoked, and never drank alcohol, tea, or coffee. Millerite enthusiasm attracted him from school teaching to preaching. After the Great Disappointment of 1844, Bates, the retired sea captain, and the newly married couple of Ellen and James White—all steeped in both religious and social reform—became the most prominent leaders of the "Little Flock" of Sabbath-keeping former Millerites.[3]

## THE WAR AGAINST SLAVERY

During the late 1840s and 1850s, the disappointed Millerites, now Sabbath-keeping Adventists, refined their doctrinal core while remaining loyal to the social reform movements that had helped nurture them. The Disappointment did not interrupt Adventist involvement in the fight to free the slaves. Instead, it intensified their involvement in the work of meeting the health needs of black Americans.

Six years after the Disappointment, in 1850, when the US Congress passed the Fugitive Slave Act, Ellen White flatly told the Sabbath-keeping Adventists that, "the law of our land requiring us to

[1]Numbers 84, summarizing Joseph Bates, *The Autobiography of Joseph Bates* (Battle Creek, MI: Adventist 1868).
[2]Bates 262, qtd. Jonathan M. Butler, "Adventism and the American Experience," *The Rise of Adventism*, ed. Edwin Scott Gaustad (New York: Harper 1974) 176.
[3]I am indebted here to extensive unpublished research by Bert Haloviak.

deliver a slave to his master, we are not to obey."[1] When she learned that an Adventist defended slavery she wrote him, "you must yield your views or the truth. Both cannot be cherished in the same heart, for they are at war with each. . . . Unless you undo what you have done . . . . We must let it be known that we have no such ones in our fellowship, that we will not walk with them in church capacity."[2]

The Sabbath-keeping Adventists also devoted time to weaving the great cause of the day into the cosmic tapestry of apocalyptic interpretation. In an 1858 essay, "The Sins of Babylon," Ellen White cast the oppression of the bodies and souls of slaves into the cosmic conflict of John's Apocalypse.

> The cries of the oppressed have reached unto heaven, and angels stand amazed at the untold, agonizing sufferings which man, formed in the image of his maker, causes his fellow man. Said the angel, 'The names of the oppressors are written in blood, crossed with stripes, and flooded with agonizing, burning tears of suffering. God's anger will not cease until he has caused this land of light to drink the dregs of the cup of His fury, until He has rewarded unto Babylon double.'[3]

For Ellen White, America was the land of light at the center of God's concern, but Americans must be made to see that, by degrading their fellow human beings, they—and their economic and religious institutions—were at war with the all-just Creator Himself.

Sensing that the great public events of their time were part of a cosmic conflict energized the early Adventists. The roots of several Adventist leaders, such as James White, in "non-resisting" communities held most Sabbath-keeping Adventists back from rescuing slaves by taking up arms in the Civil War. Instead, Adventists did what American social reformers have always done—they fought with words.

Ellen White wrote in 1862 that Union setbacks at the First Battle of Bull Run and elsewhere were divine judgments against the North for endeavoring to save the Union without abolishing slavery. Furthermore, there were "commanding officers in sympathy with the rebels." Some Northern leaders continued to send slaves back to their masters. "They have deprived them of the liberty and free air which heaven has never denied them, and then left them to suffer for food and clothing."[4]

---

[1]Ellen White, *Testimonies to the Church*, 9 vols. (Mountain View, CA: Pacific 1948) 1: 202.
[2]White, *Testimonies* 1: 359-60.
[3]Ellen G. White, *Early Writings of E. G. White* (Washington, DC: Review 1945) 275-6.
[4]White, *Testimonies* 1: 264, 255, 257.

From the 1850s through Reconstruction, Adventists reprinted Radical Republican writings in their official church papers.[1] Even though Reconstruction, through the Freedman's Bureau established by Radical Republicans in the Federal Government, gave medical care from 1865-9 to a million people and constructed black schools and created special courts to protect the freedmen's civil rights, Ellen White was not satisfied. Later, in the 1890s, she chastised the government and "the Christian churches" for not doing more for the freed slaves. "Money should have been used freely to care for and educate them at the time they were so greatly in need of help."[2] In the vastly changed and inhospitable South of the 1890s, Ellen White urged her fellow Sabbath-keeping Adventists to take up the broad, uncompleted reform program of the Radical Republicans: expanded services to feed the hungry and clothe the naked; establishment of sanitariums; construction of schools; organizing of industries to employ freedmen; and introduction of crops other than cotton.[3] The scope of her proposed social reforms approached the expansiveness of her apocalyptic vision.

## THE FIGHT FOR WOMEN

After the Great Disappointment, Adventists continued to participate in other movements for social reform. Given the health-reform backgrounds of many prominent Millerite leaders, it is not surprising that, as early as 1848, Ellen White had a vision condemning tobacco, followed by one six years later attacking tea and coffee. In 1855 the *Review and Herald* launched the attack on tobacco that has persisted among Sabbath-keeping Adventists to this day.[4]

In 1863, Ellen White had a comprehensive vision on health. It was time to turn the attention of Adventists to how to live in the world. This vision picks up many of the themes found among the health reformers: regular physicians prescribe too many drugs, such as opium, mercury, calomel, and quinine; fresh air, clean water, and simple foods are more essential. An apocalyptic world view connects intemperance with injustice, including the oppression of women. "The present corrupt state of the world was presented before me," she says, leading men, and especially women, to become slaves to appetite. "Women spend a great share of their time over a heated cook-stove, preparing food, highly seasoned with spices to

---

[1] Butler, "Adventism" 186.

[2] White, *Testimonies* 9: 205; cp. Kenneth M. Stampp, *The Era of Reconstruction, 1865-1877* (New York: Knopf 1967) 16.

[3] White, *Testimonies* 7: 227-8; Ronald D. Graybill, *E. G. White and Church Race Relations* (Washington, DC: Review 1970); Ronald D. Graybill, *Mission to Black America* (Mountain View, CA: Pacific 1971).

[4] *Numbers* 84-8.

gratify the taste." Mothers, who should be educators in the home, are needlessly overworked. "Christians," she declares, "should not be such slaves to fashion and appetite."[1]

Ellen White was so determined to free women from the tyranny of unhealthy fashion she became involved in the agitation over a topic that for a while occupied both feminists and health reformers. Over a period of twelve years, she recommended the modified dress called "the bloomer," which first entered American public awareness through the pages of a women's temperance magazine. As early as the 1850s, feminists and health reformers both lauded the new costume because it struck a blow against the tight-waisted long skirts and dresses into which high fashion pinched and cinched women. From the time of her extensive health vision of 1863, Ellen White tried to free women from the tyranny of unhealthy fashion by recommending different forms of this reform dress.[2]

Many of Ellen White's comments about sexuality revolved around the maintenance of purity. In addition, however, she was also concerned that sexuality would be used as a tool for male domination. Women were not to understand themselves merely as means for fulfilling male sexual desires. Husbands who sought "excessive" sex were "worse than brutes" and "demons in human form."[3] Part of the Great Controversy between good and evil was the struggle to liberate women to develop their "reasoning faculties," to realize their full capacities as human beings.

During the 1860s, Adventists continued to expand their interest in health reform. Beginning in 1864, several leading Seventh-day Adventist families, including the Whites, spent weeks at a time at James Caleb Jackson's health reform institution, Our Home on the Hillside, in Dansville, New York. A long-time lecturer on temperance and slavery, Jackson brought together the teachings of various health reform groups. The two meals a day Jackson served at Our Home were vegetarian, along the lines recommended by Sylvester Graham of Graham Cracker fame—no white flour bread, butter, tea, or coffee. Each day included exercises and hydrotherapy treatments.[4]

Six months after the Whites' second visit to Our Home, Ellen White persuaded the May, 1866, General Conference of Seventh-day Adventists to approve the establishment a similar institution. Church leaders wasted no time. First, as was the habit of reformers and Adventists, a journal, the *Health Reformer*, began publication in

[1]Ellen G. White, *Spiritual Gifts* 3-4 (Hagerstown, MD: Review 1945) 4a: 131-2.
[2]Numbers 184-218.
[3]Numbers 216.
[4]Numbers 95-155.

August. The next month, the Western Health Reform Institute opened in Battle Creek, Michigan.

In the early 1870s, James White sent five young Adventists—including two of his sons and Merritt and John Harvey Kellogg—to train at the Hygieo-Therapeutic College in New Jersey, run by Russell T. Trall, America's best known hydropath. After completing Trall's twenty-week course, John Harvey Kellogg persuaded James White to give him $1,000 so he could spend two years attending the College of Medicine and Surgery of the University of Michigan (1873-75) and the Bellevue Hospital Medical School in New York City (1874-75), from which he received his doctor of medicine degree. While at Bellevue, Kellogg began editing the *Health Reformer*. A year after he returned to Battle Creek in 1875, at the age of twenty-four, Kellogg became superintendent of Adventism's Western Health Reform Institute; he was to remain its director for sixty-seven years.

## THE BATTLE AGAINST LIQUOR

With Adventism's own health reform institution and journal in capable young hands, Ellen White led her church into prominence in the national temperance crusade in the 1870s. Temperance was not simply a private virtue, but also a cause, like the abolition of slavery, that involved political advocacy. In the summer of 1874, Ellen White joined temperance forces in Oakland, California, making several public appearances that helped defeat the liquor interests by a margin of 276 votes in a key election. In 1876, Ellen White attracted perhaps 20,000 people to a lecture on temperance at a camp meeting in her home town of Portland, Maine. And she attracted 5,000 people to a rally co-sponsored by the Woman's Christian Temperance Union and the Battle Creek Reform Club.[1]

Adventists' apocalyptic consciousness never allowed them to think small. In 1881, Ellen White attacked intemperance as "a cause for the moral paralysis of society." Liquor endangered life and property, increased taxation, corrupted youth, broke up families, and crowded prisons. "The advocates of temperance fail to do their whole duty unless they exert their influence by precept and example—by voice and pen and vote—in favor of prohibition and total abstinence." Adventists expected Christ to return, but in the meantime they would attempt to do their part in the cosmic battle against evil. "We need not expect that God will work a miracle to bring about this reform, and thus remove the necessity for our exertion. We ourselves must grapple with this giant foe, our motto:

[1]Numbers 228-9.

No compromise and no cessation of our efforts till the victory is gained."[1]

The next year, 1882, the General Conference defended the election of an Adventist pastor, William C. Gage, as mayor of Battle Creek. After all, he was needed in the cause of temperance, which involved, the General Conference president said, "the safety of our youth, and the well-being of society."[2]

In New Zealand, just prior to an 1887 national election, future General Conference President A. G. Daniells led Adventists into weeks of public agitation in favor of prohibition. A few years later, in 1893, Ellen White introduced herself to New Zealanders with public lectures on temperance and prohibition. Adventists campaigned for specific pieces of prohibition legislation right up to the time of World War I.[3]

After the turn of the twentieth century, Seventh-day Adventists in the United States worked with the Woman's Christian Temperance Union and the Young Men's Christian Association to stage temperance rallies in the East and the Midwest. In 1914, Adventists testified before the House District Committee of the US Congress in favor of prohibition, and Adventist churches participated in a prohibition march on Washington, DC, sponsored by the National Temperance Convention.[4]

## THE REVOLUTION IN DIET

As the first Seventh-day Adventist to receive a diploma from a regular, nationally recognized medical school, John Harvey Kellogg was determined to bring up-to-date medical surgical practices to the Battle Creek Sanitarium. He conferred with some of the best-known physicians of his time, including the Mayo brothers; and he worked with Smithsonian Institution scientists to establish the field of physical anthropology in the United States. He also visited Ivan Pavlov in Russia, and brought one of Pavlov's research assistants to Battle Creek.[5] The medical director of the Johns Hopkins University Hospital, Henry Hurd, would publicly praise Kellogg for "hav-

---

[1]Ellen G. White, *Gospel Workers* (Washington, DC: Review 1948) 387, qtd. Butler, "Adventism" 197-8.

[2]G. I. Butler, "The Temperance Cause in Battle Creek," *Review and Herald*, April 11, 1882: 232, qtd. Butler, "Adventism" 198.

[3]Peter Ballis, "Early Adventists Plunged into New Zealand Politics," *Spectrum* 18.5 (June 1988): 40-57.

[4]Butler, "Adventism" 198-9.

[5]T. Joe Willey, "Kellogg and Pavlov: Portrait of a Friendship," *Spectrum* 14.2 (Oct. 1983): 16-9.

ing converted into a scientific institution an establishment founded on a vision."[1]

From the 1870s on, Kellogg became the voice of Adventism on health reform. He had not been a part of the generation that had awaited the imminent end of the world in 1844, but he remained fiercely committed to his Adventist heritage, and he never forgot his Adventist vision. The threats to the realization of an ideal society were powerful and must be challenged with thousands and thousands of pages of articles and books. Kellogg was to publish bestsellers exhorting Americans to repulse the forces dragging them into immorality and ill health. Kellogg also shared his fellow believers' sense that to be faithful to God was to share in God's work to change all of life. Like the leaders of the previous generation of Adventists who had experienced the Great Disappointment, Kellogg insisted that true religion included changing America into a healthy nation by teaching it the importance of exercise, fresh air, lots of water, and nutritious food.

Kellogg's transformation of America's eating habits grew directly out of health reform diet served at Jackson's Home on the Hillside. His predecessors as directors of the Western Health Reform Institute took a coffee substitute, Somo, that Jackson had developed from roasted bran and molasses, improved its taste (somewhat), and called it Caramel Cereal Coffee. Kellogg tinkered with the recipe and continued to serve it to patients. After leaving the Sanitarium, many would continue to order it by mail.

One released patient stayed in Battle Creek and poked around the Sanitarium's experimental kitchen, asking a lot of questions about the formula for Caramel Cereal Coffee. Employees shared their aroused suspicions with the superintendent, but Kellogg dismissed the problem. After all, he wanted America to reform as quickly and thoroughly as possible; the more cereal coffee people drank the better. The former patient went to the opposite end of Battle Creek and began marketing a coffee substitute named after himself. It was called Postum, and helped make Charles W. Post a fortune.

In the 1890s, John Harvey churned out one idea after another to improve America's diet and health. He thought of them not so much as commercial products but as means to change the country. Kellogg did not bother to patent even peanut butter, though he anticipated its wide popularity. It was something, Kellogg declared, that "the world ought to have; let everybody that wants it have it, and make the best use of it."[2]

---

[1]Numbers 183.
[2][Richard W. Schwarz,] "Granola, Postum, Corn Flakes, and Peanut Butter," *The Vision Bold: An Illustrated History of the Seventh-day Adventist Philosophy of*

Even Kellogg's greatest transformation of American diet ultimately came from improving one of Jackson's dishes at Our Home
on the Hillside. Jackson took Sylvester Graham's health reform
flour and water, and baked it into a grape-nuts-sized dish he called
granula, probably the first cold cereal breakfast food in America.
Kellogg added cornmeal and oatmeal until he found something he
called granola. Kellogg and his brother, W. K., persisted in experimenting, seeking versions of the health reform diet that would appeal to Sanitarium patients. They finally produced those crispy
wheat and corn flakes that decisively changed the breakfast habits of
an entire society.[1]

## BEACHHEAD IN THE CITIES

During the same decade in which Adventist social reformers
were improving America's health by revolutionizing its diet, they
were also tackling America's cities. Immigrants from Ireland, Germany, and Southern Europe had rapidly swelled the population and
taxed the resources of New York, Chicago, St. Louis and other
American cities to the breaking point.

At the National Museum of American History in Washington,
DC, is a permanent exhibit called "Parlor to Politics." In this story
of women who led reform movements in nineteenth and early
twentieth-century America, a major section is devoted to Hull
House in Chicago. America's most famous settlement house, Hull
House was established in downtown Chicago by Jane Addams in
1889. Addams' recruits to this city-block experiment in how to
challenge America's urban problems included many church-related
reformers, who helped pass pioneering laws, such as those mandat-
ing worker's compensation and the eight-hour working day for
women. Several of her recruits became the founders of sociology,
urban studies, social work, and urban architecture in America. Addams herself eventually received the Nobel Peace Prize.

Only four years after the establishment of Hull House, Seventh-
day Adventists also plunged into Chicago. The city became the
crucible out of which emerged both Adventist medical education
and the Adventist medical missionary. Kellogg led the charge. He
was inspired by visits to missions in New York City. In 1891, he
met George Dowkontt, and examined Dowkontt's combination of

*Health*, ed. Warren L. Johns and Richard H. Utt (Washington, DC: Review
1977) 79.
    [1]Schwarz, "Granola" 75-93.

religious services, medical clinic, and day nursery; the next year, he visited the famous Bowery Mission.[1]

Kellogg took action in 1893. Early in the year, he convinced General Conference president O. A. Olsen and the General Conference Committee that Chicago was a good center for the training of medical missionaries. He further persuaded them that the Seventh-day Adventist Medical Missionary and Benevolent Association should be created and given responsibility to manage the Chicago work and any similar activities that might develop. Kellogg was installed as president. The same year, new converts to Adventism in South Africa, Francis and Henry Wessels, asked Kellogg what he would do with $40,000, part of their share of the Kimberly diamond strike on their property. Kellogg answered that he would initiate medical mission work in Chicago, and they agreed to support it. By May 1, 1893 a building large enough for seventy paying patients had been purchased for the Chicago Branch Sanitarium.

A month later, Kellogg was ready to start working for the poor. He talked with Jane Addams about cooperating with her. At the time, she operated one of the two settlement houses in Chicago.[2] But she believed the Adventists would be too sectarian. Kellogg then went to the police chief of Chicago and asked to be directed to the "dirtiest and wickedest" place in the city; he ended up in the south end of Chicago's loop. On June 25, 1893, Kellogg started the Chicago Medical Mission, in a building shared with the Pacific Garden Mission.

Adventists offered a free medical dispensary, free baths, a free laundry, an evening school for Chinese, a visiting nurse service, and religious services. During the first month, an average of a hundred men and women per day came to the mission. Within six months, ten nurses and doctors were needed to care for the poor coming to the Mission. A free kindergarten for working mothers was begun, and that first fall penny lunches of bean soup, with zweiback crackers from Battle Creek, were served. For six months or so after the close of the 1893 World's Fair the program was expanded to a daily service for an average of five to six hundred people. Sometimes, as many as 1500 people were served. For years, Kellogg traveled from Battle Creek to spend every Sunday at the Mission. In its first three years the mission provided some 38,000 baths and 26,00 other treatments. Nurses connected with the mission had made 9,000 home visits, 75,000 penny dinners had been served and 13,500 tracts had been distributed.

[1]Richard W. Schwarz, "John Harvey Kellogg: Adventism's Social Gospel Advocate," *Spectrum* 1.2 (Spring 1969): 15-28.
[2]Richard Rice, "Adventists and Welfare Work: A Comparative Study," *Spectrum* 2.1 (Winter 1969): 53.

Kellogg was soon ready to start the first Adventist medical school. By the fall of 1895, he had admitted the first class of forty to the four-year curriculum of the American Medical Missionary College. Initial classes were taken in Battle Creek; the last third of the work would be in Chicago. The same year, Kellogg purchased a five-story building, the College Settlement Building in downtown Chicago. It served as a dormitory for medical students and nurses, who provided a full range of services: a day nursery, a kindergarten, a free laundry for women, and a school of health. First aid and home hygiene were taught, and a women's discussion club concentrating on methods of child training, healthful dress, diet and cooking was organized. At the building, students ran a free employment agency and a placement service for orphans and men and women reclaimed from skid row. Working out of the Settlement Building were eight visiting nurses who circulated in the low-income areas surrounding the building, and medical students organizing and running seventy-five clubs among the newsboys and bootblacks of the city.

In 1896, Kellogg began a fourth institution. He took over an old church in downtown Chicago that had been converted into a flophouse during the World's Fair. Christened the Workingmen's Home, its cleaned-up dormitory-style rooms housed 400 people a night. To be eligible for a bed, applicants had to take a bath and have their clothes fumigated. Meals were served for a pittance, and a portion of the building provided temporary work: weaving carpets or making brooms. There was also a hall for religious services. In its first year, the Workingmen's Home provided 70,000 individual night's lodgings and served nearly 600,000 meals.

Not far away was yet a fifth Adventist institution, the Life Boat Mission. This, in turn, spawned a maternity home, established in 1896, that could provide shelter to twenty girls at a time. It also operated a Life Boat Rescue Service. Four Adventist women would walk into the notorious red-light districts of Chicago at night, from 12:00 to 1:30 AM, and talk to the most destitute of prostitutes. During its first year of operation, the Life Boat Rescue Service persuaded seventy-five girls to leave the streets.

A Life Boat Rescue Home for girls was also established in the brothel district. On one occasion the Adventist Life Boat Rescue workers invited some of the most prominent women in Chicago's churches to the home, as well as prostitutes. Thirty prostitutes responded, two of whom changed their way of life as a result of the experience.[1] *The Life Boat*, a journal produced by the mission, became the voice of urban mission for the church, reaching at one

[1]Rice 57.

point a circulation of 200,000. It published articles on such social reform topics as juvenile delinquency, child-labor problems, and prison reform.[1]

Given all that had been done in three short years since Adventists had first joined the forces of reform in Chicago, it is not surprising that Kellogg was invited to speak at Northwestern University on October 11, 1896. On the same platform, among other civic leaders, were Jane Addams and C.R. Henderson, pioneer University of Chicago sociologist. There, Kellogg gave an comprehensive description of sickness and health. "The homeless, destitute man is always a sick man," said Kellogg. " He is sick morally, mentally, and physically. He needs the physical tonic of good food and cleanliness."[2]

Within two years, urban reform efforts similar to that in Chicago—though, of course, on a smaller scale—had been started by the Seventh-day Adventist Medical Missionary and Benevolent Association in seventeen American cities. By the turn of the twentieth century, the Association employed some 2,000 people, more than the Seventh-day Adventist Church itself.

The graduates of the American Medical Missionary College received *bone fide* medical degrees, recognized by several state examining boards and even the London Medical Council, which Kellogg claimed was the highest examining body in the world.[3] The Adventist medical school also uniquely combined regular medical education with enlistment in the vanguard of social reform in America. Its students were taught what were perhaps the broadest definitions of medicine and its mission on offer to any medical students in the country. That may be the reason that physician Stephen Smith, a founder of the American Public Health Association, called the American Medical Missionary College "the most important educational institution in the world."[4]

## REFORMING THE WORLD

Never, since Joshua Himes, had an Adventist been so prominent in social reform efforts in America. Like Himes, Kellogg challenged what he was convinced were powerful, widespread evils oppressing God's creatures; he worked to bring change as quickly as possible; and he did so inspired by a vision of a constructive ideal. And like Himes, Kellogg suffered a great disappointment.

[1]Butler, "Adventism" 199.
[2]Schwarz, "Kellogg" 16.
[3]Malcolm Bull and Keith, Lockhart, *Seeking a Sanctuary: Seventh-day Adventism and the American Dream*, 2d ed. (Bloomington: Indiana UP 2007) 304.
[4]Rice 5.

The withdrawal of denominational support from Kellogg at the turn of the twentieth century, and his disfellowshipping in 1907, came about for many reasons. One criticism related to the work in Chicago. It was said to be too non-denominational, too large and expensive an effort in comparison with the rest of Adventist activities. Perhaps church leaders believed they had to decide between grand visions: leading social reform in Chicago—even America—or dispatching medical missionaries throughout the world. They chose the world. But, of course, Adventism's medical missionaries turned out to be smaller reincarnations of John Harvey Kellogg, challenging not only disease itself, but the malnutrition, hunger, and poverty that undermined health.

In order to become the quintessential missionary doctor, Harry Miller, the most obvious re-embodiment of John Harvey Kellogg, had to defy the original. Harry and his wife Maude, entered the American Medical Missionary College in 1898. spent their junior and senior years at Rush Medical College in Chicago, passed the Illinois state medical examinations (Maude with a slightly higher average than Harry), and interned under the revered David Paulson at the Life-Boat Mission in Chicago. In short, they were John Harvey Kellogg products. But when he found out that Maude and Harry were planning to go to China, Kellogg traveled to Chicago to tell them they were silly to leave behind great futures as teachers in America's medical schools. Like the Seventh-day Adventist denomination, the Millers defied Kellogg to carry Kellogg's reforms to the world.

Maude and Harry Miller—along with another physician couple trained at Battle Creek and Chicago—traveled to central China in 1903, carrying with them a Chicago printing press. After arriving in China, they opened a dispensary and Harry started publishing tracts, thinning his ink with castor oil. When the Millers moved to Shanghai, they moved the printing press into a building owned by Charlie Soong, a Christian educated in the United States. The three became good friends, and just as Kellogg came to know the famous of America, Harry Miller, through Charlie Soong's daughters, came to know, treat and influence the emerging rulers of China. One daughter married H. H. Kung, a future minister of finance; another married Sun Yat Sen, the first president of China; and the third, became Madame Chiang Kai-shek.

Miller developed a reputation as a surgeon, built hospitals in China and Southeast Asia, established schools like the China Training Institute, and occasionally served as head of Adventism's entire China Division. Yet for much of his life, his greatest passion was experimenting with and developing healthful foods—in Miller's case not corn flakes, but cheap, nutritious soy products. His work drew the admiring attention of Unicef and the World Health Organization. Miller was never more an Adventist than when he pursued a vision of transforming the fundamental eating habits and the health of a quarter of the world's population, and then the entire world.[1]

Another legendary missionary couple, Fernando and Ana Stahl, followed an encompassing vision of change in the Altiplano of Peru, where they arrived in 1909. The couple proceeded to transform the physical, social, and economic culture of the Indians surrounding Lake Titicaca. Their approach was to improve the health of the entire society. The Stahls established not just chapels, but clinics, schools, and free-standing markets. The Indians learned how to read and write and throw off the tyranny of alcohol and other drugs—as well as the iron domination of town judge, village priest, and wealthy landowner. "For the first time," writes José Tamayo Herrera in his social history of the *Altiplano*, "the Indian acceded to letter, hygiene, and a consciousness of his own dignity."[2]

In the face of violence and death threats to themselves and their students, the Stahls also encouraged the Indians to send memorials to the central government. This led, in 1920, to a formal government commission to investigate local abuses and the need for reforms. The greatest tribute to the Stahls' eleven years of transformative mission is the fact that the children of their students now represent their people in the halls of the national parliament and the country's universities.

At their finest, Adventist medical missionaries have been global circuit riders of the Apocalypse, embodying the luminous society.

## The Future of Health as Cosmic Struggle

Seventh-day Adventists can look at their past and future health practices and focus on the need to preserve the body as a temple of God. We can also look on the past and future of Adventism and see health care as a form of moral education for individuals, training them to conform to the laws of health

But there is a third stream of Adventist concern for health that I have attempted to trace here—a stream that throws Adventist engagements in healing against a cosmic sky, that can say with Ellen White that the liquor-trafficker is a part of "the mystic Babylon of

[1]Raymond S. Moore, *China Doctor: The Life Story of Harry Willis Miller* (Mountain View, CA: Pacific 1969).

[2]Jose Tamayo Herrera, *Historia social e indigenismo en el Altiplano* (Lima, Peru: Trentaitre 1982) 95, qtd. Charles Teel, "The Radical Roots of Peruvian Adventism," *Spectrum* 21.1 (Dec. 1990): 9.

the Apocalypse . . . dealing in 'slaves and souls of men'."[1] This third stream of Adventism and health believes with Joshua Himes, James White, and Ana and Fernando Stahl, that the health of individuals is directly related to the quality of freedom and justice in society, that healers must work with God peacefully but vigorously to over-throw those who oppress the weak and the impaired.

After the death of Ellen White and the onset of World War I, the Adventist tradition of health as cosmic struggle went under-ground, at least in America, until the 1960s and '70s. With further research, we may find that, during this period, in Africa, Latin America, and Asia, there were medical missionaries and indigenous physicians striding across a cosmic tapestry, leading their people out of hunger, poverty, and disease. But in the United States, from 1915, through a depression and two world wars, into the '60s, health care as a dimension of social reform was kept safely under wraps.

For fifty years, Adventists pursued theological and professional orthodoxy. Theologically, the *Advent Review and Sabbath Herald*—then read every week in virtually every American Adventist home—told Adventists that they were fundamentalists of the fun-damentalists; people who believed in the Bible and did not believe in something called the Social Gospel. The Social Gospel, Advent-ists were told, was really the church in politics, which violated the principle of separation of church and state.

It was not until an increasing number of voices claimed that their theological training entitled their differing theological views to be heard, and avenues were found for their ideas to be circulated beyond the good but gray, monochromatic *Adventist Review*, that a ferment of theological discussion could break out. Then Graham Maxwell and Jack Provonsha, for example, advanced new interpre-tations of Adventism, including its health message. Edward Hep-penstall, at La Sierra and the SDA Theological Seminary, re-emphasized righteousness by faith. Very gingerly, especially after Waco, Adventists are revisiting those strange apocalyptic books that may say a whole lot more about social reform than the *Adventist Review* did after 1915.

Professionally, enormous energy went into securing accredita-tion for the medical school and ensuring the education of its faculty in order to increase its institutional respectability (and, incidentally, qualify for reimbursement). Adventist hospitals around the country became, in their various communities, pillars of the establishment,

---

[1] Ellen G. White, *The Ministry of Healing* (Mountain View, CA: Pacific 1905) 338.

increasingly operated by managers similar in profile to their corporate counterparts in other hospital systems.

It was not until well after the College of Medical Evangelists had became Loma Linda University in 1961 that, with a growing sense of academic security, Adventists dared to burst on to the national scene with such highly innovative, controversial procedures as baboon-to-human heart transplants and the initial hospital-based uses of proton accelerators.

The Adventist past we have traced suggests that Adventists have contributed most to health care when they have been most Adventist; that is, when they have had the confidence to believe that there is in scripture a usable future. Adventists are rather boring, invisible, and quite useless when they are interchangeable with other denominations, other professional groups, other institutions in society. Adventists have been of most help to their fellow human beings when they have been willing to see the problems of their time against an apocalyptic screen; when they regard apocalyptic as a moveable feast, served up in the present moment.

Evils should be seen as more than individual peccadilloes to be dealt with as purely pastoral problems. It is not enough to counsel and forgive a repentant drug dealer. Those with an apocalyptic consciousness will first see evils as complex, structural, institutional, and massive; they may focus, for example, on the reliance of some nations on income from death-dealing drugs to keep their people fed. For those with an apocalyptic consciousness, the appropriate response is assumed to be encompassing—not just getting individuals off drugs, but confronting corporations and governments that depend, directly or indirectly, on drug dependency.

In addition to being rooted in a sense of the power of evil, an apocalyptic consciousness is, secondly, confident that God values our participation in the battle against principalities and powers. Such a God can take "a little flock," a "remnant," and transform it into a vanguard that can effect changes out of proportion to its numbers. No minority steeped in apocalyptic can rest, certain that it is hidden safely in the vast processes of creation. An apocalyptic consciousness expects the remnant to be pivotal in God's plan of action.

Thirdly, those with an apocalyptic consciousness are sure that the outcome of the cosmic struggle is more than the destruction of the beasts and Babylon; it is the establishment of the New Jerusalem. They look for ways in the present to do more than confront evil. They seek out opportunities actively to do good.

SOLUTIONS?

What, concretely, might an Adventism with such a lively apocalyptic consciousness do in the future? First, Adventism might pursue scientific medicine and through research develop powerful medicines, technologies and procedures to confront disease, disability and death. Thus, innovative physicians at Loma Linda University do the work of God by hurling potent forces for good at the enemies of human existence—a Leonard Bailey developing innovative heart transplantations, a Larry Longo exploring the effects of destructive gases on fetal life, a James Slater creating healing treatments out of nuclear technologies of destruction, a Gary Fraser demonstrating the life-extending benefits of a vegetarian diet.

Secondly, in its attempt to battle fundamental evils and build communities that are glimmerings of a new Jerusalem, Adventism might draw from the periphery to the center of its life the kinds of projects the Adventist Development and Relief Agency sponsors—well-drillings and water-reclamation projects in the Philippines or the development of small enterprises to improve the incomes of village women in Mali, now able to purchase adequate food, clothing, and medicines for their children.

Thirdly, Adventism might accept the challenge to alter the health of the nations. Adventists might mobilize its network of health-care institutions to engage in a struggle against the self-serving, bestial lobbies protecting the use of easily purchased automatic weapons that send hundreds of victims to emergency rooms and morgues; the foul, but powerful petrochemical conglomerates whose pollution endangers generations of lives yet unborn; and the principalities and powers targeting women and children through tobacco advertising.

Understood as participation in a cosmic struggle, health care cannot be undertaken only through individual ritual purity or conformity to law. Healing is gained through victories over the forces that cause injury and disease. The task is cosmic. "We are all," wrote Ellen White, "woven together in the web of humanity. The evil that befalls any part of the great human brotherhood brings peril to all."[1] Suffering is a setback in the controversy between God and God's rebellious principalities, an outrider for more powerful evils, a warning of more profound defeats. Death is an enemy to be fought. Life is to be lived in all its fullness. The Adventist tradition most certainly revitalizes itself as a force in society and the world when it takes seriously its most distinctive motif: an apocalyptic vision of a dramatically transformed cosmos.

[1]White, *Ministry* 345.

# 11

# Mission

### Charles Teel, Jr.

I never told you about that letter Jane Crofut got from her minister when she was sick. He wrote Jane a letter and on the envelope the address was like this: It said: Jane Crofut; The Crofut Farm; Grover's Corners; Sutton County; New Hampshire; United States of America; Continent of North America; Western Hemisphere; the Earth; the Solar System; the Universe; the Mind of God—that's what it said on the envelope . . . . And the postman brought it just the same.

—Rebecca in Thornton Wilder's *Our Town*, Act I

When Rebecca recognizes that her home, her neighborhood, her community, and her nation are parts of a reality that far exceeds the spit of sand that is Our Town, her universe at once expands and explodes. In viewing herself as a part of a much larger whole, Rebecca participates in an existential discovery that is fraught with both peril and promise. She may feel herself imperiled because the security that is Our Town seems to have been shattered. Is Our Town not special, peculiar, unique? Could Our Town be but one among many towns? Do towns exist in which there is no clapboard Methodist Church? Can the mind of God be apprehended through such contrasting forms as Gregorian chants, Black Gospel music, Zulu dances, Islamic calls to worship, Quaker solitude, Chichicastenango incense rituals, Jewish chants, and Zen meditation? Are our ways of doing, believing, and being in Our Town merely relative? How can God be named by many names? Can God be named at all?

Marshall MacLuhan's term *Global Village* reminds us that Rebecca's parochial world is with us no more. Mass communication daily forces us to leap over the boundaries of our safe havens; and when parochial Our Town meets Global Village, we of Our Town can never be as snug and comfortable as we once were. Yet the citizens of Our Town and Home Church have been commissioned to "Go ye, therefore . . ." into the Global Village. Hence the challenges posed by Christian mission. "Home Church" and "mission band" engage Global Village.

For the purposes of this paper, "mission" refers to the process by which individuals contextualize and incarnate the Gospel in the Global Village—a task which calls for crossing many boundaries, including those imposed by time no less than by rivers and oceans and mountains and borders.

Apart from offering a review of our mission roots, this paper argues a modest thesis: that as "mission band" carries the Gospel across boundaries, the "home church" is renewed in profound ways. Said negatively, if the "mission band" ceases to exist, the "home church" loses this built-in opportunity for renewal, the home church loses—if not disintegrates.

## A REVIEW OF MISSION ROOTS

In examining the challenges of Adventist mission, it will prove instructive to engage in a selective review/overview of missiological hurdles faced by our spiritual forbears at the time of the primitive church, the Millerite adventists, the sabbatarian adventists, and the early Seventh-day Adventists.

Some near-idyllic descriptions of the primitive church notwithstanding, New Testament scholars are increasingly footnoting the "no small dissension and disputation" in social and theological matters which resulted as diverse culture groups evangelized by "mission bands" forced the primitive Christian "home church" through the work of mission bands.[1]

*Fostering Cultural Diversity*

Chief among those to be credited for goading the New Testament home church squarely to face the implications of Christian mission is Saul of Tarsus cum Paul the Apostle. Paul's mission band crossed territorial boundaries, radically revised gospel form and content, contextualized the good news, and forced the home church in Jerusalem to face the perils and promise of Christian mission and cultural diversity. Accordingly, this has resulted in the examination of Paul's ministry in recent years using such anthropological themes as "inculturation," "ethnocentrism," and "cultural forms" no less than such traditional theological themes as "law," "grace" and "faith." The apostle's vision of Christianity's future was of an inclusive and diverse religious community not limited by the cultural

---

[1] See Robert Banks, *Paul's Idea of Community: The Early House Churches in their Historical Setting* (Grand Rapids: Eerdmans 1980; Robert Jewett, *Christian Tolerance: Paul's Message to the Modern Church* (Philadelphia: Westminster 1982); and Ralph Winter, "Two Structures of God's Redemptive Mission," *Missiology* 2.1 (January 1974): 121-139.

forms and traditions of orthodox Judaism. Thus, New Testament scholar Günther Bornkamm, among others, views the Jerusalem Council recorded in Acts 15 as a watershed event in which Paul's mission-band vision moved Christianity from a mono-cultural home church (represented by those referred to in the New Testament text as the Judaizers, the circumcision party, or—quite simply—the weaker) to a multi-cultural movement that left the constraints of home-church Aramaic Palestine behind and became rooted in the scattered and diverse provinces of the Roman world.[1]

Paul's inclusive and universal gospel cast a wide net and, accordingly, reaped wide-spread confusion—as compared with the relative order of the monocultural religious system of his forbears. In embracing the task of communicating the gospel across cultural boundaries, Paul drastically pared down theological essentials by distinguishing between gospel essence and cultural custom; he led the church in refashioning—even discarding—symbols previously thought to be central to the faith; he entered into dialogue with other movements; he opened the door to heterogeneous multitudes from throughout the Roman Empire; and he encouraged the employment of local forms in shaping congregational life and practice.

It is not surprising, then, that lauded missioner Roland Allen—writing at the beginning of the twentieth century and chafing under what he deemed to be the untenable controls which his mission board exerted over indigenous congregational life—would pen a work with the rhetorically fashioned title: *Missionary Methods: St. Paul's Or Ours?* In this book Allen opines forcefully that Paul

> refused to transplant the law and customs of the churches in Judea into the Four Provinces. He refused to set up any central administrative authority from which the whole church was to receive directions in the conduct of local affairs. He declined to set up *a priori* tests of orthodoxy which should be applicable for all time under all circumstances everywhere. He refused to allow the universal application of particular precedents.[2]

Allen moved from generalizations to specifics by citing the congregational life and practices at Corinth as a particular example:

> The Jewish Christians in Corinth must have thought the church there given over to unbridled license. Uncircumcised Christians attended the feasts of their pagan friends in heathen temples. Every letter of the ceremonial law was apparently broken every day without rebuke. Even in the meetings of the church, preachings and prayers were built on a

[1]Günther Bornkamm, *Paul*, trans. D. G. M. Stalker (New York: Harper 1971) 31.
[2]Roland Allen, *Missionary Methods: St. Paul's or Ours? A Study of the Church in the Four Provinces*, Library of Historic Theology (London: Scott 1912) 68.

strange system of thought which could hardly be called Christian, and there was a most undignified freedom of conduct.[1]

## An Ethic of Tolerance

In his book, *Christian Tolerance: Paul's Message to the Christian Church*, Robert Jewett suggests that it is precisely in the context of conditions described by Allen that a creative tension emerges within which Paul's tolerance ethic of mutual acceptance is given opportunity to flourish. Jewett concludes this timely work by contrasting how Saul the Pharisee cum Paul the Apostle responded to the cultural diversity he encountered. Pharisaism was based on teaching and enforcing conformity with tradition as the means of world redemption, a stance which called for the eradication of alien laws and customs. Conversely, the encounter with the risen Lord on the Damascus road alerted Paul to the fact that the "very outsiders excluded by his former message should now receive the good news of their inclusion."[2]

Jewett sees Paul developing this ethic of tolerance most tightly in the letter to the Romans, giving special reference to the extended passage in Rom. 14:1 to 15:3 in which the conservative wing and the liberal wing are counseled to remain true to their diverse doctrinal understandings (regarding holy days, diet, etc.) while accepting one another as sisters and brothers in Christ. The apostle calls for the left wing and the right wing to affirm their commonality through the act of giving thanks even though they may be giving thanks in light of radically different understandings: "The one gives thanks for the meat and the wine, the other for the vegetables. . . ."[3]

Paul's appeal to the congregation in Rome—an appeal not lost on the Jerusalem home church—is that the "weak" and the "strong" wings be united not by their methodological approaches or their doctrinal formulations but by the mutual tolerance evoked in understanding that both wings are offering thanks to God who is Parent of them all.

Nineteenth-century Millerite adventists sounded both the cry, "The bridegroom cometh," and the call "Babylon is fallen, come out of her my people" as an integral part of their self-perceived mission.

## "The Bridegroom Cometh"

Self-educated upstate New York farmer and biblical expositor William Miller heralded the bridegroom's return with this positive

---

[1] Allen 129.
[2] Jewett 146.
[3] Jewett 34.

and inclusive call beginning in 1839. Armed only with Bible, concordance, and a wooden literalism that summoned the prophetic and apocalyptic works of Scripture to interpret themselves, Miller voiced an inclusive missionizing cry that was broadly embraced by clergy and lay persons who remained members of various Protestant communions. In addition to their shared commitment to the advent movement, the Millerite leaders one and all were activists who had cut their teeth on such broad-based reform endeavors as the anti-slavery and temperance movements. In sum, the proclaimers of this inclusive cry viewed their call to mission as explicitly rejecting sectarian divisiveness and inviting those in diverse religious communities and reform groups to join hands in proclaiming the positive news of the bridegroom's soon return.

*"Come out of Her."*

As these proclaimers of the "Advent near" became more singular in their cause, the broad-based movement which had eschewed sectarianism took on the baggage of an exclusive organization. In 1843 Charles Fitch's widely circulated apocalyptic sermon, "Come Out of Her, My People!" declared that the saved remnant would consist only of those who embraced the Advent movement: Babylon was made up of those who would not—including Catholics and "all sects in Protestant Christendom."

Miller did not wish to support this fracturing and exclusiveness: "I have not ordained anyone to separate from the churches to which they have belonged unless their brethren cast them out," he wrote as late as January of 1844. "I have never designed to make a new sect, or to give you a nickname." But with this new exclusivist cry the movement was gaining a momentum of its own, a momentum which Miller "feared." Shrinking from the brethren giving "another cry, *'Come out of her, my people,'*" Miller confided his fear: "I fear the enemy has a hand in this, to direct our attitude from the true issue, the midnight cry, *'Behold the Bridegroom cometh.'*"

With the latter cry, the Millerite mission had been radically refocused, as the inclusive Bridegroom cry was drowned out by the exclusive Babylon cry. The celebrative and inclusive call to welcome the bridegroom had been replaced by the negative and exclusive declaration of Babylonian judgment. What had begun as a broad-based mission assumed an embattled, indeed embittered, position. Only the separated Millerite remnant remained to usher in the Coming—and they were disappointed.

To those missioners engaged in calculating the Coming with Newton's precision and not yet out of the nineteenth-century woods, the Millerite experience serves as a blunt reminder of what can happen when the forest becomes obscured by the trees. In this state of "wooden literalism" individuals and communities are pushed further and further out on the proverbial limb. And when the end comes, it is an end informed less by Newton's numerical calculations than by his law of gravity.

But might the Millerite experience hold meaning for those who have long since wandered out of the nineteenth-century woods and who now bask in the enlightenment of the modem—even post-modem—age? Ernest R. Sandeen, a student of American and British millenarianism, suggests that twenty-first-century humankind still experiences some of the basic ambiguities which haunted the Millerites and their ilk. The metaphor shifts from woods to rivers:

> Nineteenth-century society was very much like its most famous me-chanical invention, the steamboat. Many millenarian newspapers in that day carried a column entitled "Signs of the Times," which contained news of ominous events and portents of the end of the world. One of the most common items in those columns was the notice of the explo-sion of a steamboat harnessed new power and moved with unprece-dented rapidity. It was exciting, but it was also dangerous. The passen-gers knew that their voyage might possibly end by their being blown to smithereens. In such a world, millenarianism was not out of place, nor will it ever disappear while men still yearn for deliverance from immi-nent destruction.[1]

Where does a Millerite go once the symbols that shape her or his mission, purpose, and destiny have been shattered? The three options reported by one believer writing in the aftermath of 1844 suggest that territorial loyalty survived the Disappointment intact: some believers in the Advent near, noted this New England broth-er, struggle on in hope, others had turned to strong drink, and oth-ers had gone to California! Eschewing both strong drink and Cali-fornia—for the time being—a sabbatarian wing of the Millerite band emerged. This group of believers went beyond Miller by in-fusing the calculated end year with new meaning: 1844 had ushered in the beginning of a final era of divine judgment. They also would go beyond Miller as they interpreted the apocalypse blessing which defined their mission: "Here is the patience of the saints; here are they that keep the commandments of God and the faith of Jesus."

*Commandments of God*

In identifying the commandments of God with the Ten Com-mandments of the Mosaic Decalogue, special attention was focused upon the fourth commandment, which demanded the keeping of the seventh-day Sabbath. In light of this emphasis, a remnant of Sabbath-keeping adventists emerged which had found its place in

---

[1]Ernest R. Sandeen, "Millennialism," *The Rise of Adventism: Religion and So-ciety in Mid-Nineteenth-Century America*, ed. Edwin S. Gaustad (New York: Har-per 1974) 117.

cosmic history: all bodies that had preached the imminent advent had pronounced the first angel's message of Revelation 14 ("Judgment is come!"); the Millerites had sounded the second angel's message in 1844 ("Come out!"); and they, the Sabbath-keeping adventists, were now to proclaim to the world the message of the third and final angel ("Keep [all of] the [ten] commandments[—[especially the fourth one]!"). If such an urgent call to keep the Decalogue took on legalistic overtones, it must be remembered that these missionizers perceived the time to be short and their message focused.

## The Faith of Jesus

While self-claimed responsibility for saving the world would have daunted more ecumenically-minded believers, the biblical understandings of this parochial group pared its mission task down to size: the world population to be reached was limited to those on whom the door of salvation had not already shut—Millerites who had prepared to receive the bridegroom and who had "come out" in 1844. With the door shut to all but the remnant of a Millerite remnant, world mission was confined to the world of the Boston/New York corridor. (It should be noted that these Millerites once removed were neither the first nor the last in the history of the republic to equate the Boston/New York corridor with the center of the world or with the hub of the universe!)

When the Shut Door was pried open at mid-century, as individuals who had never heard of the Millerite Disappointment sought entrance to fellowship, the world of these Sabbath-keeping adventists enlarged—as did their exegetical and missiological tasks. Exegetes invested increased vigor in defining the parameters of remnant and world, branding the beasts of the apocalypse, and pronouncing God's judgment upon the world and its institutions. The call to a now-enlarging remnant to "come out" of worldly Babylon did not entail total ignorance of the world's social and political institutions; rather it urged hearers to rebuke unjust Babylonian structures in the severest of terms. Castigating the American Republic for tolerating the social sin of slavery, for example, Ellen White declared that "God's anger will not cease until he has rewarded Babylon double."

By drawing upon the apocalyptic imagery of universal history in articulating this mission, these Adventists could employ the rhetoric of the radical reformers, but their apocalyptic perspective kept them from participating in active efforts on behalf of reform. Precisely because the controversy between good and evil was cosmic in scope and the mid-nineteenth century was the end time, these believers left it to angels and winds and vials and plagues unleashed by

God to reward Babylon double. The mission of the church which existed "between the times," then, was less to engage in action than to proclaim truth. The slave would be freed not by human engineering but by divine intervention when Jesus would come—soon. The slave was freed not by the battle of Armageddon, but rather by the battle of Appomattox. As the Disappointment receded into the past, as months became years and years became decades, the sabbatarian remnant cautiously prepared to put down roots and to settle in for the long haul. They, the come-outers of the come-outers who had eschewed all human structures and who had equated any form of organization with Babylon, now embraced "gospel order" (James White's euphemistic substitute for the term *organization*), "took a name" (organizing the Seventh-day Adventist Church explicitly as a business organization, and not as a religious institution), and geared up for expanded mission (first to the United States and—later—to the world).

*Home Mission*

The opening of the Shut Door did not immediately result in an understanding of Adventist mission that was world-wide in scope. Rather—as the United States was a land of immigrants drawing uniquely from every nation, kindred, tongue, and people—the early Seventh-day Adventists insisted that the Gospel Commission could be fulfilled within the confines of this country. Evangelization expanded the Adventist presence west from New England to the Allegheny Mountains, to Michigan and the Northern Great Plains, to the border states and the former Confederacy, and on to California and the Pacific Northwest.

Given that the log cabins and sod houses of the mid-west prairie states boasted millions of immigrants primarily from Scandinavia and Germany, grass roots home-mission initiatives by foreign-language-speaking individuals nudged the church toward the evangelization of these peoples. The early lay leadership of mission bands was followed by the training and appointment of foreign-language ministers and the publishing of foreign language periodicals. It is estimated that, by the late 1870s, one tenth of all church members communicated exclusively in a language other than English.[1] These believers brought diversity to the fledgling church in the United States and also helped to broaden the definition of world mission as they grew anxious to share their newfound faith with their European relatives. Further, the emphasis on foreign-language missions in the United States provided a precedent for

---

[1]See Emmet K. VandeVere, "Years of Expansion, 1865-1885," *Adventism in America: A History*, 2d ed., ed. Gary Land (Berrien Springs, MI: Andrews UP 1998) 70.

specialized mission activity—often of an "independent ministries" and mission band nature—elsewhere on the continent, including an outreach to urban centers, the evangelization of freed slaves in the latter part of the nineteenth century,[1] work for such groups as the Poles and Italians around 1920, and outreach to Spanish-speaking, Japanese, and Native American groups in the following decade.[2]

## World Mission

It fell the lot of one Michael Belinda Czechowski, a United States-based Catholic priest from Poland who converted to Protestantism and then to Adventism, to organize the first Sabbath-keeping adventist groups beyond the borders of the United States. Against the explicit direction of the church leadership, which viewed evangelization beyond America's borders as unhelpful in fulfilling the gospel commission, Czechowski struck out on his own in 1864, secured sponsorship elsewhere, and preached the Adventist message in independent mission band fashion in Switzerland, Italy, Germany, and Rumania—where he spent the last days of his exciting, if less than predictable, life.

In response to requests from Czechowski's Swiss believers for pastoral assistance, the soon-to-be "world church" leadership reversed its stance against overseas mission and sent J. N. Andrews to Switzerland in 1874 as the first church-sponsored foreign missionary. A letter from Andrews at the outset of his Switzerland endeavors indicated that he understood his mission mandate to be three-fold: preaching the Sabbath command, calling attention to God's law, and proclaiming the imminent judgment. Commenting on Andrews' somewhat narrow understanding of what constituted the essence of the good news that is the gospel, Gottfried Oosterwal acknowledges that "the Advent Movement in those days tended toward legalism and self-righteousness" and goes on to note that "Christ and his love for sinners were not sufficiently prominent. . . ."[3]

With the election of A. G. Daniells to lead the world church in 1901, its organizational structure was radically overhauled—an overhaul which was, some argue, hastened by the critical review of home church operations from the vantage point of mission bands. Adventist foreign mission skyrocketed under Daniells's leadership of two decades: nearly one hundred missioners set sail annually for overseas posts, a dramatic increase over earlier mission commitments. Daniells's administrative experience in Australia had en-

[1]See Richard W. Schwarz, "The Perils of Growth, 1886-1905," Land 92-3.
[2]Richard W. Schwarz, *Light Bearers to the Remnant* (Mountain View, CA: Pacific 1979) 343n17.
[3]Gottfried Oosterwal, *Mission: Possible* (Nashville: Anvil-Southern 1972) 26.

dowed him with a global view of mission and a sensitivity to the demands of contextualization as is evident from a letter he wrote to a church worker in Africa during the first year of his presidency. "All we can do in this country is to make suggestions for consideration and study," he wrote. "When you come to deal with the situation face to face, you must use our suggestions just as far as they prove to be wise."[1]

It is clear that Daniells' successors did not uniformly share his openness to contextualizing gospel form and content. Yet it is equally clear that as Adventist mission moved from Takoma Park to Europe to Australia and to Africa and the uttermost parts of the earth, it has set a record: no single Protestant mission group is as widely represented on the face of the earth. The far-flung presence of Adventist adherents—ranging from the Aluts of Alaska to the Laps of Norway to the Aymara of the Andes to the aborigines of Australia to the Maasai of Africa to the Samoans of the South Seas has led more than one observer of the international scene to place our church (for better and/or for worse) in the company of the world's most active and visible multinational corporations. Although the initial observation was made during the colonial era and before synthetics had replaced much of the rubber industry, the generalization still holds: wherever one goes on planet Earth, one is sure to encounter three entities—the Goodyear Tire and Rubber Company, the Coca Cola Bottling Company, and the Seventh-day Adventist Church!

This international community of believers now boasts a world membership of nearly twenty million. Worldwide, Adventists operates over one hundred colleges and universities, nearly 6,000 primary schools, nearly 2,000 secondary schools, nearly 200 hospitals, and striking numbers of dispensaries, clinics, retirement homes, orphanages, and publishing houses in countries around the globe. In short, "seldom, while expecting a kingdom of God from heaven, has a group worked so diligently for one on earth."[2]

## A PREVIEW OF FUTURE CHALLENGES

Pressing challenges—some sighted and others yet to be sited—abound. Indeed in our brief overview of mission history we have seen hints of challenges that are ecclesiological, ecumenical, cultural, sociological, and methodological.

---

[1] Qtd. Schwarz, "Perils" 105.
[2] Winthrop S. Hudson and John Corrigan, *Religion in America: An Historical Account of the Development of American Religious Life* (Englewood Cliffs, NJ: Prentice-Hall 1998) 336. This passage is intended to express the position of Edwin S. Gaustad, *Historical Atlas of Religion in America* (New York: Harper 1962) 115.

Like St Paul, today's missioners and missiologists must identify theological "essentials" and in turn contextualize these essentials in new cultural settings. Consider three culture interface models for mission: colonization, cohabitation, and contextualization.

*Colonization*

This model, at base, calls for the missionized culture to adapt to the missioner culture. Beginning with the "civilizing" efforts fostered by New England Puritans on behalf of their indigenous neighbors, historians of mission ruefully recognize that the colonization model came to inform much of Protestantism's missionizing efforts. The slogan "Civilization and Christianity" is cited as fostering mission approaches which were informed by a two-pronged fallacy: indigenous culture is "primitive," as well as "heathen," and—therefore—"anti-gospel." One need not read exhaustively in missiology texts, indigenous diaries, anthropological studies, or novels to document the perception of Protestant mission as fostering the mentality of colonial dependency. In short, mission is a one-way street: the colonized adopt from the colonizers.

*Cohabitation*

Cohabitation is, simply put, the opposite of colonization. Where the colonizer uncritically imposes Western culture on her converts, the cohabiter uncritically accepts the host culture as equal or superior to that of the West. Proponents of cohabitation have "gone native" in ways that prevent them from challenging less-than-ideal features of the cultures they confront in mission. Where the colonizing missioner refuses to learn from non-Western cultures, the cohabiting missioner rejects the whole idea of mission—replacing it with "dialogue" or "coexistence"—for fear of disrupting traditional cultures, or adopts a romanticized view of such cultures that renders criticizing or seeking to change them inappropriate. The cohabiter would prefer to leave hierarchies of gender, age, and class in place, to avoid opposing slavery or clitoridectomy, than to appear like the "ugly American." The cohabiter is the mirror image of the colonizer, and is equally insensitive, naïve, and unhelpful.

*Contextualization*

This model is the paradigm hailed by evangelizing bodies as diverse as the Mennonite Mission Board and the Catholic Missionary Society of America (Maryknoll Order). While contrasting definitions are advanced by respective groups, common themes appear.[1]

---

[1]See, *e.g.*, Ruy O. Costa, "Introduction: Inculturation, Indigenization, and Contextualization," *One Faith, Many Cultures: Inculturation, Indigenization, and*

These include: the need in all cultural contexts to affirm traditional forms and symbols that implicitly or explicitly bear witness to the truth of the gospel; the need to differentiate between the theological "essence" of the gospel and the socio-cultural forms of the missioner; and the need in turn to translate and implant this distilled gospel in the linguistic and cultural forms of the host people.[1] Citing the Incarnation as the ultimate example of contextualization, adherents of this model call for a similar emptying to be attempted with regard to cultural sets as sending culture interfaces with the host culture. In contrast to the demeaning dependence required by the colonization model or the detached independence encouraged by the cohabitation model, the contextual model aims to foster interdependence between missioner and host and between missioner culture and host culture. It is claimed that such interdependence is encouraged when, among others, the evangelizer and the evangelized come to recognize that each holds a partial perception of the eternal Truth that is God.

Max Stackhouse praises such advocates of contextualization as Charles Kraft and Robert Schreiter for their efforts in nudging gospel communicators to understand the significance of context, and for acknowledging that we have no direct pipeline to divine truth. At the same time, however, Stackhouse wonders whether it's possible to isolate the core of a tradition from its context, and how we might even begin to identify a context? In short, Stackhouse contends that to be about the matter of contextualizing before these hard questions are grappled with produces two equally disturbing heresies: "soft contextualism," which he brands as today's new form of polytheism (everything could become so contextualized that we end up with nothing that is "transcontextual"); and "hard contextualism," which he brands as today's new fundamentalism of the left (if you don't embrace my contextual reading you are not a believer).[2]

In fact, the contextualization of Christianity by the Christian Church has been with us since Paul quoted Greek poetry to the Greeks as the word of God. Stackhouse reminds us that we are in the company of saints and apostles and prophets as we look to the future and call for the contextualization of the Gospel. Adventist

---

*Contextualization*, ed. Costa, Boston Theological Institute Annual 2 (Maryknoll, NY: Orbis 1988) xiii; and Wilbert R. Shenk, "The Changing Role of the Missionary: From 'Civilization' to Contextualization," *Missions, Evangelism, and Church Growth*, ed. C. Norman Kraus (Scottdale, PA: Herald 1980) 33-58.

[1]See Charles Kraft, *Christianity and Culture: A Study in Dynamic Biblical Theologizing in Cross-Cultural Perspective* (Maryknoll, NY: Orbis 1981); and Robert J. Schreiter, *Constructing Local Theologies* (Maryknoll, NY: Orbis 1985) are the most significant evangelical and Catholic works on this subject.

[2]Cp. Max L. Stackhouse, *Apologia: Contextualization, Globalization, and Mission in Theological Education* (Grand Rapids: Eerdmans 1988).

mission of the twenty-first century must be willing—indeed able—to be about the hard tasks of developing a transcontextual apologia for "the faith" we wish to affirm. Are we willing—indeed able—to trust the Spirit to speak through sisters and brothers from both the traditionally "missionizing" and "missionized" lands who together seek to define that faith and to operationalize it in different ways and in different contexts? Are we willing—indeed able—to envision an Adventism that takes on a more distinctly indigenous character in its liturgical forms, its theological formulations, and its methods of outreach?

The nature of the church (what it is, theologically) and how it organizes itself for mission (how it frames its polity to incarnate what it claims to be) are of one piece.

In his highly acclaimed *Models of the Church*,[1] Avery Dulles argues that no contemporary form of church polity ought to be presumed to be based on biblical precedent. Rather, just as form is intended to serve function, so polity is intended to serve evangelization, a task which Dulles suggests may be undertaken effectively through any and all of the varied forms of church polity operative today. In short, it may well be that the spreading of the gospel is less advanced or inhibited by the form of ecclesiastical polity than by the administrative style of ecclesiastical politicians. (Is the system open or closed, participatory or autocratic? Does a climate of trust exist that permits risk-taking and mistake-making? To what extent have structures and policies become so hardened and brittle that the maintenance of the organization itself becomes the end?

Adventism's central jurisdictional polity has much going for it, and it is hailed as a model for mission by such analysts as Dutch missiologist J. B. A. Kessler.[2] The *Seventh-day Adventist Yearbook* reveals an impressive world church order. Yet structure, organization, and form are intended to serve content, message, mission: the structures exist for mission. Sadly, as anticipated by our Adventist pioneers, the tendency is for structures to become the end, at which point they become hardened, inflexible, and brittle—and thus incapable of adjusting to diverse needs and expressions of varied portions of the world church. Perceived inflexibility of the central jurisdiction is translated at the local level into congregationalism, with the local unit operating independently from the world church. When such inflexibility is perceived at the national level, the result

[1]Avery Dulles, *Models of the Church* (Garden City, NY: Image-Doubleday 1978).
[2]Jean Baptiste August Kessler, *A Study of the Older Protestant Missions and Churches in Peru and Chile, with Special Reference to the Problems of Division, Nationalism and Native Ministry* (Utrecht: Goes 1967)

tends toward schism or, depending upon negotiations, national churches.

It should come as no surprise that a church which is increasingly experiencing burgeoning membership growth in the "Two Thirds World" will experience increased indigenization and demands for greater flexibility in the administration and definition of geographical sectors which will inevitably take on local, national, or continental characteristics. Will the church emerge as strengthened or weakened if it encourages form to follow function (say, at the division level) as it goes about the task of fashioning the earthen vessel? What benefits/deficits may accrue if the status quo is mandated from an international headquarters? What benefits/deficits may accrue if greater initiatives may be encouraged in experimenting with matters of form and function? Will issues in the "First World" be able to be addressed in ways which differ from the ways in which they are addressed in the "Two Thirds World?" And vice versa. Adventist mission of the future will make increasing demands for greater flexibility in church polity.

Because the Adventist Church is not the only Christian church, its service in the global village requires it to consider how best to interact with the various Christian organizations committed to similar objectives and operating in similar fields of endeavor. And just as Adventism is not the only Christian church, so Christianity is not the only world religion; and, as other Christians increasingly find themselves compelled to reassess their relationship to non-Christian religious movements, Seventh-day Adventists would be well served to do the same. In short, taking a page from the tolerance ethic advanced by Jewett, via Paul, how tolerant can we be of diverse theologies and still be faithful to the Christian/Adventist teachings that we cherish?

Gavin d'Costa[1] has identified three principal responses to the reality of religious diversity that a Christian theology of the religions might make. He labels them exclusivism, pluralism, and inclusivism. For the exclusivist, people can be saved and God can be known only through the agency of the Christian gospel as proclaimed by the visible Christian church. The pluralist, by contrast, maintains that all—or nearly all—religions are equally adequate responses to ultimate reality, and that the claims of each are equally valid. For the inclusivist, by contrast, Christianity's claims are distinctively adequate and God is specially revealed in the history of Israel and the church and uniquely in the Incarnation. Salvation and revelation are available to all, whatever the nature of their contact with Chris-

---

[1]Gavin D'Costa, *Theology and Religious Pluralism: The Challenge of Other Religions*, Signposts in Theology (Oxford: Blackwell 1986).

tianity, but acceptance of Christian convictions enriches human experience, action, and understanding.

An Adventist response to the problem of religious diversity—which is obviously intimately related to the problem of Adventist mission and cultural diversity—cannot, it seems to me, be either an exclusivist or a pluralist one. The pluralist option too easily concludes that all faiths are alike and that one can understand the religious tradition from outside the experience of its members as well and as easily as they themselves can from the inside. The "pluralist" option is an imperialistic attempt to homogenize all of humankind's religious experience. In an important sense, then, this option is not really pluralist at all. Pluralists in this sense are not serious about diversity, as they claim to be; instead, they refuse to take it seriously. Further, and most importantly, pluralists fail to recognize that religions differ as social projects. Differing religious convictions issue in sometimes widely-differing social and cultural strategies. Religious traditions differ not only about theological esoterica but also about the ways in which human societies should be organized and human lives shaped. Religious disagreements force us to make difficult ethical choices that cannot be avoided by declaring all religious options equally acceptable.

On the other hand, Adventism cannot afford to take exclusivism seriously, either. Can we really say with straight faces that thousands of "heathen" are going down to Christless graves each day with no hope and only fiery annihilation to look forward to? Can we really believe that those we live and work with, those we love and employ, those with whom we socialize and our children marry, are damned because, for various reasons, Christianity is not a live option for them? Is such a conviction remotely compatible with the divine love encountered in the Incarnation? Can we proclaim the damnation of the heathen at the same time as we blithely recite John 3:16?

Not only is the love of God compromised by the claim that God can save only those who are consciously confronted in this life with the word of the Gospel, the creatorship and providential efficacy of God are compromised by the claim that God's nature and will cannot be known at all apart from the history of revelation, from salvation history. Christians must affirm that there is something special about this history, that in the experience of Israel and the Christian church, and pre-eminently in the Incarnation, God's self-gift to humanity is experienced uniquely.[1] Nevertheless, to affirm the decisiveness of God's salvific action in and as Jesus of

---

[1]Karl Rahner, *Foundations of Christian Faith: An Introduction to the Idea of Christianity*, trans. William V. Dych (New York: Crossroad 1978); Wolfhart Pannenberg, *Jesus: God and Man*, trans. Duane A. Priebe (Philadelphia: Westminster 1967).

Nazareth, and to affirm the distinctive adequacy of Christian images and language, cannot be to deny God the power to work in and through the created order and the natural order to touch the lives of others outside the stream of revelatory history or unlearned in the language of the Christian community. It is to insult God to suppose that, as Creator and Sustainer and Provider, God is not at work everywhere in the world. Further, Christians may rightly perceive that, in some instances, God may have been capable of achieving in other communities things God has not been able to achieve in their own. This need not be cause for jealousy; it can instead inspire thankfulness for the divine largesse—a humble gratitude for the grace of a God who patiently continues to tabernacle with humankind.

Christian mission has continuing validity in a context of religious diversity. But it will not be carried on with insensitivity to the reality of God's work outside the Christian community. Nor will it deny the possibility that Christians may have something to learn, as well as to give, from those among whom they live in mission.[1]

What is the nature of society and what is the nature of the relation of the individual to the larger social whole? No question is more basic than this as people hammer out a social contract in anticipation of how they shall live their individual and collective lives. How individuals engaged in Adventist mission answer this question will be basic to the form of Adventist mission in the twenty-first century.

*Communalism*

The primal human reality in traditional cultures is the tribe, the community, the group. In this view, the greatest good is the good of the social unit, for without the tribe the individual cannot survive. Individual self-identity is achieved solely in the context of identity with the social whole, and in this primal context individuality will ever be subsumed to that whole. John Taylor's *The Primal Vision* offers an overview which aids modern and individualistic humankind to perceive the manner in which tribal individuals define themselves vis-à-vis the social unit. Humankind, Taylor says,

is a family. This living chain of humanity, in which the tides of world energy ebb and flow most strongly, stands at the heart of the great totality of being and bears the secret of creativity.

The act of individuality may often clash with the demands of this collective humanity, just as conflict often arises between father and son, and the occasions for this are far more numerous in these days. Yet the underlying conviction remains that an individual who is cut off from the communal organism is a nothing. . . . As the glow of a coal depends up-

[1] Cp. Jon Dybdahl, *Missions: A Two-Way Street* (Mountain View, CA: Pacific 1986).

on its remaining in the fire, so the vitality, the psychic security, the very humanity of a man, depends on his integration into the family.[1]

To sum up this position: from the standpoint of communalism, "the individual cut off from the group is a nothing."

### Individualism

An elitist form of individualism, what Mennonite missioner and scholar Norman Kraus terms "aristocratic individualism," takes root in the Greco-Roman tradition. A reaction against self-definition on the basis of tribal affiliation alone, this individualism demands that the individual—at least the free, male individual—demonstrate his individuality by responsibly husbanding the spark of divine reason entrusted him. What the individual *knows*, then, becomes the prime basis for self-identity rather than the manner in which the individual is incorporated into the tribe.[2] Buttressed by the classical teachings of its Judæo-Christian heritage, Western thought has come to proclaim that society is bound to covenant in a manner which grants basic, inalienable rights of personhood to the individual self. The French Revolution's cry of "Equality, Liberty, Fraternity"— anticipated some years earlier by the revolution of their American cousins—called for an end to calculating an individual's worth solely on the basis of status in hardened structures which demanded that one be defined by her or his class or intelligence quotient.

While much creative energy is unleashed as the individuality of the self is expressed and developed, the creative potential of individuality is ever to be differentiated from the self-centeredness of individualism. This extreme reaction against communalism perpetuates the myth of the self-made person, lifted up by her or his own boot straps, the "Lone Ranger," the person who—in the words of my maternal grandmother—"never asks no one for nothing." Robert Bellah's *The Broken Covenant* and *Habits of the Heart* both argue eloquently, if less than perfectly, for a critical review of this "cancerous" development: individuality gone amok.

### Individual-in-Community

A key challenge to Christian mission in the twenty-first century will be to proffer a safe haven to individuals and tribes of peoples whose identity has been ravaged by the onslaught of Western culture and rugged individualism. Whether we speak of the Guerini on the banks of the Amazon, the Maasai of the Serengeti Plain, the hill peoples of Thailand, or the Native American tribes of the Southwestern United States, modern Western civilization will continue to dismantle tribal Gods, lay to rest tribal symbols, and make

[1]Qtd. Kraus 79n6.
[2]Kraus 97.

nonsense of tribal cosmic stories—myths which no longer serve to engender meaning, purpose, and destiny. The role of Christian mission and Adventist mission at this point, I propose, is to offer such peoples a place to land, to be, to become. Those whose traditional worlds have been shattered by the onslaught of "progress" are people in whose social worlds Durkheim's *anomie*—normlessness—emerges full blown: people bruised, shattered, and void of meaning. Will the Christian churches and the Adventist church find ways to incarnate the good news, to mediate healing, and to offer hope to those whose lives have been disrupted by the enforced mobility and social dislocation that are the inevitable consequences of untrammeled capitalism? Will the Adventist community come to define the Sabbath rest and the Advent hope in ways that truly offer rest and hope to people shorn of both? Will the common life of the world church and of local communities of faith provide a place for those left rootless by the onslaught of transnational capitalism to discover their individuality while becoming integrated into a hope-filled community which has embraced—but not uncritically embraced—the culture of the post-Enlightenment west? Or, to push the issue even further: is there a place in Christian Adventist mission for lobbying against the disruptions wrought by capitalism—the disintegration of social networks and families, the rape of the land that leaves people and their crops rootless. the introduction of sweatshop labor practices illegal in the West but still permitted elsewhere? The church has no reason uncritically to endorse traditional forms of life, which may depend on repressive hierarchies of race, gender, class, or age. But it also has no reason to accept as legitimate the depredations effected in the name of commerce—in the West as much as in the "Two-Thirds World." Its protests may make its task more difficult; instead of ensuring that everyone speaks its—Western—language, they may lead to the preservation of cultures in whose unfamiliar idioms the church may find it difficult at first to communicate its message. It will no doubt learn and grow, however, as it grapples with the challenge of doing so.

Christian mission and Adventist mission have been roundly criticized for having advanced a less-than-adequate balance between "orthodoxy" (right doctrine) and "orthopraxy" (right practice). Accordingly, as I invite diverse missioner groups to address students while engaging in field study beyond North American cultural contexts, I invite presenters to define not only such terms as "church," "salvation," and "evangelization," but also the term "word"—for one's understanding of the nature of word and of how word is heard is basic to one's understanding of how a religious community gears up for mission. Models for method in mission thus may be reviewed through yet another triune formulation: word without flesh, flesh without word, and enfleshed word.

*Word without Flesh*

How is the word heard? The most uncomplicated and direct—if uninformed and inadequate—answer our student group of learners has received to date was given by a young evangelist who offered a schematic in which word began as personal word (God) and ended as written word (Bible). The word is absolute; it is one; it is infallible; it is uniform; and it is simple. "Our students can be very direct in giving God's word to the masses," he told us. "They regularly take megaphones to city squares and quote from the Bible: 'Hear the word of God! Hear the world of God! I will heal this land.'"

For this evangelist, word and truth are exclusively propositional, informational, and intellectual. Such presuppositions can lead only to a cold legalism, a smug self-righteousness, and an arrogant triumphalism—my information is more correct than your information. Communicating word without flesh is an empty exercise.

The older Ellen White was wont to sound the alarm that word as doctrine alone leads to a dry and dead end, bluntly warning a church purporting to be engaged in mission that "There is danger of . . . dwelling too much on doctrines."[1] Rather, Christ is to be presented as one whose service and sacrifice empowers, and "when the people behold Christ as He is, they will not wrangle over doctrines."[2] Word alone is insufficient.

*Flesh without Word*

The church engages—indeed, it engages perpetually—in activity. Often enough, it engages in frenzied activity. But especially in the context of its self-conscious confrontations with culture (of which confrontational mission is a prime example) it cannot afford to act without reflecting. It cannot afford not to bring to bear its symbols and convictions and rituals on its action and experience. When the church seeks to do without thinking, to escape the messy and often disturbing consequences of inquiry and analysis, it tends all too quickly to lapse into uncritical endorsement of whatever ideology—"democratic capitalism," Marxism, "church growth" or other management-based techniques—its leaders happen to encounter. Only when it assesses the sociological, philosophical, economic, and political tools and strategies it considers employing *with*

[1]Ellen G. White, *Counsels to Writers and Editors* (Nashville: Southern 1946) 79.
[2]Ellen G. White, *Testimonies to Ministers and Gospel Workers* (Mountain View, CA: Pacific 1923) 49.

*both eyes open* will it be able to offer a distinctive response to the cultural issues with which it engages.

*Enfleshed Word*

The essence of the term "incarnation," of course, is that word/idea/concept becomes flesh/action/deed. The same incarnational language in the Gospels which has the Spirit hovering over Mary as she prepares to give birth to Jesus figures in the Book of Acts as the Spirit hovers in the Upper Room and empowers the primitive church to put hands and feet on the body of Christ and makes it walk. Adventist evangelization is replete with illustrations of missioners who from earliest times truly incarnated the good news of the Gospel in flesh and blood—making the Gospel walk in very real and material ways through clinics, hospitals, medical centers, schools, colleges, and universities. Yet it remained for the Adventist Development and Relief Agency (ADRA) International to lead the church on a grand scale to wrestle with the relation of the Gospel and materiality. And one of ADRA's key contributions has been that the service which it renders is broad and inclusive. ADRA ministers to all: Jew and Gentile, male and female, believer and unbeliever. From its modest beginnings in 1956 as Seventh-day Adventist Welfare Service, ADRA currently operates with an annual budget of $47,500,000 and, in 137 countries, manages such wideranging programs as well drilling, dam building, small enterprise development, AIDS education, health care, school and clinic construction, vocational education, literacy training, and income generation through agriculture, gardening, and small business projects, as well as providing emergency food, shelter, and medical attention.

Adventist mission in the twenty-first century will be bound to acknowledge a debt to ADRA for the manner in which it has led the world church in "incarnational evangelism."

## SUMMARY OF MISSION HOPES

1. *The Adventist future will be built on mission—or there will be no Adventist future.* Church exists in and through mission. The church is, by definition, the body of Christ—necessitating the task of being the hands and feet of that body and making it walk in human history. Unlike those who gather routinely in the names of such individuals of accomplishment as Shakespeare, Santa Teresa of Avila, or C. S. Lewis, Christians assemble not merely to remember one who died—or even one who rose from the dead and ascended to heaven. Rather, in its gathering and scattering the Christian church in mission engages in the audacious task of extending Christ's body as it walks and witnesses, hopes and heals, inquires and empowers in this time and in this place. The Adventist church will not have a fu-

ture without mission, for mission quickens, enlivens, and is a part and parcel of the business of being church. No mission band, no world church. The decision facing Christian mission, then, is not a question of "whether" but "whither." And "what." And "how."

2. *Mission of the future will be radical—demanding a review of belief, practice, and polity essentials.* When any part of the body of Christ crosses boundaries of time and/or space there is the necessity to ask of belief, practice, and polity: what is the "root," the essence, the irreducible core that we must carry across this boundary of time and/or this boundary of space? This is a revisionist act, a revolutionary act, a radical act. For when individuals and groups pare down the gospel and peel away layers of accumulated belief, practice, and polity by asking the crucial reformation question—what is core, essence, essential?—such endeavors naturally denude, expose, threaten, and renew. Adventist mission, the Adventist Church, has a future only as it continues re-forming itself. And precisely because Adventist mission has been so successful in raising up congregants in diverse parts of the globe, the Adventist mission of the future will have more diverse voices, not fewer, calling for a review, a reformulation, of belief, practice, and polity. More and more free-wheeling mission bands will be interfacing in creative ways with home church(es). And that is something to give thanks for! It is through this "no small disputation and dissension" that we participate in the reformulation and evolution that is life. The open question, I think, is how this "no small disputation and dissension" will be managed.

3. *Mission of the future will be contextual—requiring a refashioning of evangelization.* The act of paring down belief, practice, and polity by way of exposing the essence of the gospel is preparatory to the creative and adaptive process of communicating that essence across borders of space and time. And in that process of giving new expression to form and content of gospel, we may be certain that wondrous surprises lie in store: new sights, strange sights; new sounds, discordant sounds; new expressions, different expressions.

4. *Mission of the future will be ecumenical—inviting a redefinition of remnant.* There are signs that the Adventist church is moving from a remnant mentality of exclusivism and triumphalism to a more inclusive understanding of God and God's interaction with humankind. Indeed, it is precisely to those sensitive missioners who have engaged in service abroad that many of the rest of us are indebted for our exposure to a bigger picture of God, God's world, and God's invisible church. The present and future challenge will be to define, enact, and communicate to our portion of God's remnant that we are at once called to be Adventist and part of God's large and inclusive remnant—and that such is eminently possible and de-

sirable. In that process, Adventist mission will become more inclusive.

5. *Mission of the future will be incarnational—effecting a recommitment to action.* Adventist mission must increasingly articulate an "enfleshed word" as it enacts the Gospel. In teaming up with other humanitarian agencies—both governmental and non-governmental, both secular and religious—Adventism will eschew the extremes of word void of flesh and flesh void of word. To paraphrase missioner E. Stanley Jones: *Any gospel which proclaims word void of flesh is a soul without a body, and a gospel which proclaims flesh void of word is a body without a soul. The one is a ghost and the other is a corpse.*

*To conclude with our thesis:* engaging in mission across boundaries of space and time, the home church will be renewed in profound ways. Said negatively, if the home churches of the world lose this built-in opportunity for renewal, the world church loses—if not disintegrates. Just as Rebecca was stretched as she was challenged to at once celebrate her roots in Our Town and encounter the larger universe of the Global Village, so world mission has the capacity of stretching the Seventh-day Adventist church as it celebrates its roots and looks hopefully to the future.

# 12

# Higher Education
# and Theological Ethics

## Charles Scriven

Tony Campolo, the Philadelphia preacher and professor familiar on many Adventist campuses, often flies home tired from his speaking appointments. When his seatmate wants to know his name and what he does, the answer depends on whether Campolo feels like talking or not.

"Now when I want to talk," he says, "I say I'm a sociologist. And the person next to me says, 'Oh, that's interesting.' But if I really want to shut someone up I say I'm a Baptist evangelist. That generally does it."

Once, on a red-eye special, he told the man sitting beside him that he was a Baptist evangelist. But the man didn't retreat. "Well, do you know what I believe?" he said. "I believe that going to heaven is like going to Philadelphia."

Campolo was taken aback—Philadelphia?

The man explained that just as there are "many ways to get to Philadelphia," so there are many ways to get to heaven. You don't have to be a Baptist or even a Christian—"we all end up in the same place; how you get there doesn't matter."

Campolo was too tired to argue. He maneuvered himself out of the conversation as fast as he could and went to sleep. But several hours later, when the plane began its descent into Philadelphia, he woke up to gusting winds, heavy rains, and fog as thick as wool. The ride was rough and scary. Everyone was tense.

So Campolo, feeling pugnacious, turned to his seatmate and said, "I'm certainly glad the pilot doesn't agree with your theology."

"What do you mean?"

"Down in the control tower," Campolo replied, "someone is talking to the pilot: 'You're on beam,' the controller's saying, 'You're on beam,' and the message is: don't deviate from this." Campolo went on: "It's foggy outside, and I'm glad the pilot's not spouting off about how he can get to Philadelphia any way he pleases. I'm glad he's saying to himself, 'The controller knows the best path to the runway, and I'm going to stay with it.'"

As for how to live the best life you can—how to get to "heaven," how to walk the road to fulfillment—Campolo's seatmate was very like the modern educational establishment. From the viewpoint of conventional understanding, school is no place to take a strong position about morality and religion. On these matters the rule in school is, Don't be partisan and don't ruffle any feathers.

When Adventist education was developing in the second half of the nineteenth century, our pioneers were flat-out partisan feather-rufflers. In her first extended essay on education, Ellen White declared that the young can be trained "for the service of sin or for the service of righteousness." She said, too, that we should give them "that education which is consistent with our faith.[1] Percy T. Magan, describing the 1891 (and first-ever) Adventist education convention, said the reform participants envisioned was seen mostly in terms of making the Bible central to the curriculum.[2]

All the while the conventional secular orthodoxy, especially as regards higher education, was headed in another direction. The oldest colleges in the United States were sponsored by churches, but many were just then breaking their religious ties. Educational leaders were challenging, or even ridiculing, education that tries to instill in students a specific spiritual heritage with its own distinctive way of thinking and living.

At his inauguration in 1869 Charles Eliot, the Harvard president who cut the last links between the university and its original Christian patrons, mocked the teaching that tries to instill some *particular* set of beliefs about what is good and true. That may be "logical and appropriate in a convent, or a seminary for priests," he said, but it is "intolerable" in universities.[3]

Eliot perhaps gleaned his comparison from Cardinal Newman, who in *The Idea of the University* had declared more than a decade

---

[1]Ellen White, *Testimonies for the Church*, 9 vols. (Mountain View: Pacific 1948) 3: 131, 159.
[2]The description appears in *Windows*, ed. Emmet K. Vandevere (Nashville: Southern 1975) 172-3.
[3]James Tunstead Burtchaell, "The Alienation of Christian Higher Education in America: Diagnosis and Prognosis," *Schooling Christians*, ed. Stanley Hauerwas and John Westerhoff (Grand Rapids: Eerdmans 1992) 133.

earlier that the university is neither a convent nor a seminary.[1] In any case, the misgivings about religious training in higher education were taking an ever-stronger hold. In 1904 DeWitt Hyde, who studied at Harvard while Eliot was there and soon afterward became the president of Bowdoin College, called the "narrowness" he associated with church colleges "utterly incompatible" with responsible higher education. "A church university," he declaimed, "is a contradiction in terms. "[2]

To these educational leaders, in other words, teaching a general awareness was fine; teaching a specific religious heritage was suspect. Today, this sentiment still predominates. Partisan education, especially in matters religious and moral, is seen widely to be, at best, narrow, and, at worst, bigoted and victimizing. Responsible teaching does not inculcate a particular point of view or set of virtues; rather, it imparts knowledge and skills sufficient, as Mortimer Kadish writes, to enable the self to criticize its "social milieu" and to "form" its being and "determine" its wants.[3] Even a teacher at a Southern Baptist college echoes the conventional understanding: "It's not my job as a professor to tell . . . [students] what to think," the teacher told the *Chronicle of Higher Education* recently, "it's my job to make them think. "[4]

I will show here why the historic Adventist understanding is closer to the mark than secular modern orthodoxy. My claim, made with a view to secularization inside as well as outside the church, is that teaching and learning in the Christian setting, including the Christian college, should be, as Ellen White insisted, "consistent with our faith." It should display (in its own way) the church's true identity; it should be, indeed, a deliberate strategy for building and bracing the circle of disciples. Bland neutrality is a mistake, and it is a dangerous mistake.

## THE TOURNAMENT OF NARRATIVES

Let me begin by explaining a figure of speech I learned from my teacher and friend, Professor James Wm. McClendon, Jr. In *Ethics*, the first volume of his *Systematic Theology*, he remarks that

[1]Qtd. Jaroslav Pelikan, *The Idea of the University: A Reexamination* (New Haven: Yale UP 1992) 39.
[2]Pelikan 132.
[3]Mortimer Kadish, *Toward an Ethic of Higher Education* (Stanford, CA: Stanford UP 1991) 73, 79.
[4]Qtd. by Courtney Leatherman, "Southern Baptist College Enters Carefully Into Women's Studies," *Chronicle of Higher Education*, July 14, 1993: A13.

we humans exist "as in a tournament of narratives."[1] What does he mean by the arresting phrase "tournament of narratives"?

His point, first of all, is that whatever idea or possibility confronts us, any day or any hour of the day, the way we respond—the way we think and feel and act—depends on the stories we're attached to. The stories, or narratives, we know and identify with shape our whole lives, our whole ethos or ethics. Narratives, in others words, are bedrock—bedrock for both personal and communal frames of mind—for insight, for attitude, for conduct.

The second point of the phrase concerns conflict. The narratives women and men identify with are many—across the total human landscape, beyond counting. And frequently, like contenders in a tournament, these narratives clash with one another, one story feeding this loyalty or outlook and another that. The result is variety in human culture, often welcome and often winsome. But more than anyone would like, the conflict of narratives feeds strife as well, including violent strife. We are sadly aware, we who inhabit the world of Sarajevo and Rwanda and (for that matter) the United States, that differences of faith, politics, morality and custom occasion not only charm but also bloodshed.

These are the conditions we live in, and under these conditions, bland neutrality is, I repeat, a mistake. If uncharitable narrowness is also mistaken, that does not gainsay the point. Conflict is a fact, and bland neutrality leaves conflict, even violent conflict, unchallenged. Conflict is a fact, and bland neutrality puts blinders over people's eyes. Bland neutrality, in short, threatens society by feeding indifference—and then compounds the threat by feeding self-deception.

It is in this light that I want to advance my claim, namely, that *Christian education, including Christian higher education, should be partisan.* It should not be blindly or arrogantly partisan, but, without embarrassment and without apology, it should both build and brace the circle of disciples.

As we have seen, among the secular-minded, and to a surprising degree among the religious, antipathy to the partisan is widespread. The background to this antipathy is the Enlightenment. Kant declared that movement's ideal of the autonomous individual when he called his readers to thrust off dependence on others for direction. "'Have courage to use your own reason!'—that," he said, "is the motto of the Enlightenment."[2] And with the ensuing shift to the self-governing, or self-defining, individual, the meaning of respect for others veered toward non-interference, or even neutrality,

[1]James William McClendon, Jr., *Systematic Theology* 1: *Ethics* (Nashville: Abingdon 1986) 143.
[2]Qtd. James C. Livingston, *Modern Christian Thought* (New York: Macmillan 1971) 1.

with respect to differences of outlook and conviction. The partisan was now bad manners. Conflict was to be domesticated.

The motive was admirable. The Enlightenment grew into full flower on blood-soaked soil. The Thirty Years' War, religion stoked and staggering in its brutality and senselessness, ended (more or less) in 1648, endowing Europe with a need and a lively desire for peace, or at least respite. Blood-letting had failed to resolve the doctrinal discord from which it sprang. As Stephen Toulmin writes, circumstances called for a means of determining truth that "was independent of, and neutral between, particular religious loyalties."[1]

But truth, despite these hopes, could not be determined in total independence of particular religious loyalties. Consider the idea that the individual is self-governing and self-defining, with no need to depend upon others for direction. This idea subverts—indeed, it was meant to subvert—accountability to authority, whether religious, familial or communal. Autonomy was needed, so the thinking went, in order to fend off acquiescence to inherited prejudice and folly. But we each speak a human language, and every human language gives particular peoples, each with the particular narratives they have lived and told, the ability to communicate. What is more, every language bears the freight of stories past and so gives every user an inherited frame of mind. Thus no neutral vantage point exists from which the self may practice its alleged autonomy. In a world of many languages and histories, there can be no neutral point of view, no single pathway of knowledge available to everyone. How and what we think at all times reflects a storied past.

The point, despite conventional modern thinking, is not *whether* to be partisan but *how*. Even so, the narrative that shapes the dominant version of higher education continues to be that of the Enlightenment. The debate over "political correctness" sweeping the campus and the wider culture betrays growing uneasiness about standard educational assumptions. Still, the curriculum usually comes across as a kind of intellectual bazaar, catering, at least ostensibly, to autonomous selves in the process of forming their being and determining their wants without "direction" (as Kant put it) from others. Students are still said to be learning how to think, not what to think. It is still "narrow" and "sectarian" to inculcate a particular point of view, especially if the point of view involves religious or moral commitment. Except in defense of diversity itself, it is still bad manners, and bad education, to be partisan.

The deception—the self-deception—in all this is palpable. But antipathy to the partisan jeopardizes education in other ways as

[1]Stephen Toulmin, *Cosmopolis: The Hidden Agenda of Modernity* (New York: Free 1990) 70.

well. For one thing, it trivializes differences. When disagreements over faith, politics, morality, and custom flame up in violent strife, as they often do, it is disingenuous to speak, in the customary, bleached-out phraseology, of mere "competing value systems," as though students were consumers meant to pick and choose like shoppers in a marketplace. To be or feign to be impartial is to push the truth away, to keep it at a distance. It is a kind of indifference, and it communicates indifference.

Far from being innocuous, such indifference damages humanity. For when in matters of faith and morals education must be too open to contain conviction, it can no longer fight off the tendency to spiritual coma that seems in any case to bedevil contemporary culture. Differences trivialized by neutrality feed the trivialization of morality itself—and examples abound: this is an age when expert witnesses can make ethical judgments seem repressive even at an incest trial; it is an age when "standards" at media command posts consist in whatever the market will bear; it is an age when lawmakers wring their hands over teen violence and still cast votes for murder weapons. The situation recalls what Yeats, in "The Second Coming," declared of an age without conviction: "Mere anarchy is loosed upon the world, / The blood dimmed tide is loosed. . . ."

Suspicion of commitment in the classroom does not, of course, produce students with no biases at all; it rather favors their "assimilation," as Patricia Beattie Jung writes, to the "prevailing cultural ethos."[1] The fiction of neutrality tends to baptize the *status quo*, with its implicit morality or immorality, and to nullify the stark alternatives. Antipathy to the partisan turns out, then, not just to trivialize differences, but also to protect whatever now predominates. Despite the homage paid to criticism, antipathy to the partisan is fundamentally conservative.

What this entire criticism of liberal education displays is the emerging awareness that the modern era, heralded by Descartes and the Enlightenment, is now passing. We are entering what some now call "postmodern" era, with its key realization that outlooks are bequeathed to individuals, not discovered or created by them. How we see and live depends on the background—family, community, history—we each absorb growing up with our particular languages and cultures. Systems of thought and practice characteristic of particular communities may involve differences too deep to be adjudicated or even understood through simple conversation.

But does all this add up to irrationalism, to the tribalization, as one might say, of knowledge? This question is central to the issue

---

[1] Patricia Beattie Jung, "A Call for Reform Schools," Hauerwas and Westerhoff 117.

of ethics and education. If we are left with mere subjectivity, if everything comes down to mere personal choice, how is anyone accountable? How does ethics, with its assumption that some attitudes and actions are right and some wrong, even have a place?

Nietzsche, who in the nineteenth century anticipated the shift to the postmodern, believed that the ideas we consider true are fixed and binding merely from long usage and endorsement within particular groups. One may employ strategies to promote or subvert a point of view, but it is impossible to adjudicate among contending points of view. So-called "truths" are only fictions that further the expression of the "will to power," conventions whose conventionality has been forgotten.

But even if we accept the absence of a neutral viewpoint, it's still possible—and important—to make a vigorous argument for accountability, and thus for the importance of defending right against wrong. Sheer consent to rival truth claims, after all, is not just the embrace of charming or fertile disagreement; sheer consent is surrender to injustice and bloodshed, for these are what differences of faith, politics, morality, and custom all too often bring about. Writers such as Alasdair MacIntyre, James McClendon, and Nancey Murphy, who will figure prominently in what follows, argue that even though we see the world through our inherited frameworks, no framework must be a prison house. It is possible and important that conversation, both within and across the lines of human difference, should yield new increments of understanding and agreement. The shift to the postmodern does not, in other words, compel anarchy and resignation with respect to human knowledge.

## INTELLECTUAL ACCOUNTABILITY IN THE CHRISTIAN COLLEGE

In light of all this let me now suggest the outlines of a postmodern conception of intellectual *accountability* for colleges of explicit Christian *commitment*. How can higher education under the church's auspices contend responsibly—with no retreat of mind or heart—in the human tournament of narratives? How can it nourish post-adolescent minds with its own distinctive vision? How can it be partisan and still hold itself responsible to justify its partisan convictions?

*To begin, let me say unmistakably that the partisanship in question is countercultural.* From the biblical narrative this is obvious enough: solidarity with God and God's Messiah means dissent from the wider world. Nevertheless, the lure of respectability within the surrounding, dominant culture has always tantalized the Christian community. As McClendon writes,

The church's story will not interpret the world to the world's satisfaction. Hence there is a *temptation* (no weaker word will do) for the church to deny her 'counter, original, spare, strange' starting point in Abraham and Jesus and to give instead a self-account or theology that will world on the world's own present terms.[1]

What is true for the church is true for its colleges. Here, too, the endurance of distinctively Christian vision must be a matter of deliberate design. In its decisions about personnel, curriculum, and student life, the Christian college must renounce congenial neutrality, what is in any case artifice and self-deception, and embrace without apology its own heritage and discipline. In the tournament of narratives, anything less is a recipe for defeat. Anything less marks capitulation to "the unstoried blandness (and the mortal terrors) of late-twentieth century liberal individualism."[2]

In the college setting, learning takes place under the leadership of teachers. So if the countercultural, the embrace of distinctive vision, is crucial for responsible Christian partisanship, a corresponding view of the teaching function is also crucial. In the guidance and inspiration of students, intellectual accountability allows, and indeed requires, commitment to a particular point of view.

Being responsibly countercultural means acknowledging the self-deception and emptiness inherent in the platitude about teaching students how to think, not what to think. The platitude fits neatly with the Enlightenment antagonism toward authority and obsession with personal autonomy. It reflects as well the earlier Socratic form of moral education, which trained students for criticism of convention without offering a positive account of the good in human life. The overall impact of a purely negative approach was to leave students without reasons for preferring one way of life to another, and thus without reasons to fend off the blandishments of purely private satisfaction.

In his play, *Clouds*, the Greek writer Aristophanes made this point with his imagination. A father named Strepsiades has a son who is a spendthrift and idler, with hardly any conscience at all. The father, desperate for change, brings his son to the school of Socrates in Athens.

Socrates arranges for the son to hear a debate between one teacher who is a stern guardian of traditional values, and another who is a smirking, self-indulgent enemy of these values. In the end it becomes clear that Socrates himself, though courageous and serene compared to both debaters, has more in common with the smirking critic of traditional values. It turns out that he has nothing positive to teach about how to live. He is like the tradition-hating

---

[1]McClendon, *Ethics* 17.
[2]McClendon, *Ethics* 171-2.

debater in that his whole mode of teaching is to raise questions about traditional morality and to shoot it down. He ridicules inherited wisdom and those who try to instill it into the minds and lives of students. And it's all the worse because he offers virtually nothing to substitute for what he ridicules. He says nothing about what a person *should* aim for in life, nothing about the standards and convictions that *should* prevail.

Aristophanes is Socrates's critic; he thinks the situation is disastrous. So in his play, the fancy education at the fancy school in Athens leaves the son as selfish as ever. In the end he just doesn't care about anything but himself, anything but his own personal satisfaction. The wider world, and the people in it, don't meet any of his needs and don't even matter.[1]

In order to make advances in awareness and comprehension, the inquirer must first have been taught what to think, must first have been initiated into some actual way of life or type of practice. Knowing how to think presupposes some partisan account of the subject matter, some positive immersion into a tradition. Being partisan may, it is true, slump into narrow indoctrination. But it doesn't have to, and responsible partisanship is in any case fundamental: nothing positive can happen without it. The road to enlightenment requires advocacy as well as criticism.

*Responsible partisanship engages the whole person.* Yet another respect in which the learning environment at Christian institutions must swim against the current is in the attention paid to the total way of life—not just technical, calculating intellect but also feelings, imagination, habits, and virtues. The mere removal of ignorance— what the distinguished education writer Jacques Barzun reveres as the "prime object" of education[2]—calls for such attention, anyway, since study itself is a discipline involving virtues. Just paying attention and seeing clearly—traits important for scholarship as well as moral growth—require emotional involvement. As Martha Nussbaum argues, interpreting Aristotle, a person may know something as a fact—a connection as father or mother, say, to a child; or the benefit of unearned privilege relative to others in her or his society—yet fail to take in the fact "in a full-blooded way," fail to confront or acknowledge what it means and what response it calls for. When a person lacks "the heart's confrontation" with what lies open to view, the deficit narrows vision and foils insight. Percep-

---

[1]See Martha Nussbaum, "Aristophanes and Socrates on Learning Practical Wisdom," *Aristophanes: Essays in Interpretation,* ed. Jeffrey Henderson, Yale Classical Studies 26 (Cambridge: CUP 1980) 43-97.

[2]Jacques Barzun, *Begin Here: The Forgotten Conditions of Teaching and Learning,* ed. Morris Philipson (Chicago: U of Chicago P 1991) 54.

tion, to be complete, must involve "emotional and imaginative, as well as intellectual, components."[1]

But as with the bare noticing of facts, so with the emotion and imagination that deepen our perception: they, too, reflect personal experience over time. Emotion and imagination disclose stories heard and lived. They reveal communal ways of life. They make manifest the past and present habits, duties, and affiliations that constitute the evolving self. All this signals the need for attention to the whole person. Education must concern itself with character, with the student's total way of life. This matters, indeed, for the mere removal of ignorance; for positive enlightenment, it matters all the more.

That is why Parker Palmer, in *To Know As We Are Known*, his work on the spirituality of education, declares his opposition to "objectivism" in education. In this still-dominant classroom pattern, students learn the "facts" from an emotional distance, like bystanders. Mostly, the heart has no role; in accordance with the "objective" ideal, what is investigated remains at arm's length, an object and nothing more. Yet this detachment, this denial of the connection and interdependence of the student and the subject matter, "leaves the inner self unexamined." And without attention to the inner self, Palmer declares further, humans tend to scorn the common good and veer toward arrogant manipulation of the world outside themselves.[2]

If mere technical expertise—the mere removal of ignorance—were truly the prime object of education, then few could be said to have received better training than the scientists who produced the first nuclear bomb. Before the initial explosion their technical expertise smoothed the way toward the perfecting of their awesome creation. On the day after the first mushroom stained the sky, when the scientists stopped to agonize over what they had done, one said that "the glitter of nuclear weapons," had seemed "irresistible." The participants were overcome, he said, by "technical arrogance" that arose from their knowledge of what they could do with their minds.[3] They no doubt understood, at some level, that weapons with the capacity to lift a million tons of rock into the sky would bring unspeakable danger and death to humanity. But without confronting this fact "in a full-blooded way," through feeling and imagination as well as calculating intellect, they failed to see what it meant or what response it called for.

[1] Martha Nussbaum, *Love's Knowledge: Essays on Philosophy and Literature* (New York: OUP 1990) 79-81.
[2] Parker Palmer, *To Know as We are Known: Education as a Spiritual Journey* (San Francisco: Harper 1993) 33-9.
[3] Parker Palmer tells this story to introduce his argument (1, 2).

The story illuminates the point: education that plays down feeling and imagination, and pays no heed to training the entire self, including those habits, duties, and affiliations that give shape to feeling and imagination, is both indigent and undependable.

A third aspect of responsible partisanship is this: *it must acknowledge conflict, it must confront conflict, it must initiate students into conflict.* James McClendon writes about the school in Alexandria where Origen, the great Bible scholar and theologian, first gained fame as a teacher. He told his students that no topic or question or opinion was off limits, but at the same time took an unmistakably partisan position. By instruction and example, he sought to instill the theory and practice of Christianity and to model an alliance of piety and scholarship. To him, the school was a training ground; its goal was the formation of lives that would honor and reflect the church's narrative.[1]

The same spirit and goal must infuse the responsible partisanship of Christian colleges today. If all education, to be complete, must engage the whole person, Christian education must do so in a manner appropriate to its own struggle in the tournament of narratives. It must acknowledge, and deal constructively and honestly, with the challenges posed by other points of view. Masking over differences feeds apathy by pushing truth away, whereas the point is to nourish passion and involvement.

In the second volume of his *Systematic Theology*, McClendon says that Jesus enrolled his followers "as students in his school, his open air, learn-by-doing, movable, life-changing dialogue." The purpose was "training" for world-changing witness; the method was "costly apprenticeship." Then he alludes to blind Bartimaeus, said by Mark to have received his sight from Jesus and immediately followed him on his dangerous mission to Jerusalem. On the view suggested by the story, declares McClendon, "enlistment and scholarship are integral parts of one whole." Bartimaeus, occupied with Jesus' mission and immersed in its conflict, was "the paradigmatic Christian scholar."[2]

Alasdair MacIntyre, who himself suggests the need for "rival universities," says one task of responsible partisanship I s "to enter into controversy with other rival standpoints." This must be done in order to challenge the rival standpoint, but also in order to test one's own account against "the strongest possible objections" against it.[3] The pairing of enlistment and scholarship by no means

[1]McClendon, *Ethics* 42-4.
[2]James William McClendon, Jr., *Systematic Theology 2: Doctrine* (Nashville: Abingdon 1994) 32.
[3]Alasdair MacIntyre, *Three Rival Versions of Moral Enquiry* (Notre Dame: U of Notre Dame 1990) 231.

entails, in other words, a flight from challenges or a refusal to give reasons and make adjustments. Within limits required by the maintenance of basic identity, the Christian college or university, like a responsible partisan journal or newspaper, must tolerate— must, indeed, seek out—lively confrontation with other points of view. This can happen, not just in the classroom or library, but through the selection of students or even faculty. Postmodern awareness puts the difficulty of the knowledge enterprise in bold relief, but accountability is still vital. Convictions must still be justified. To be responsible, partisan higher education must provide, or better, be, a context for accountability.

In certain academic disciplines and certain aspects of collegiate bureaucracy, the Christian institution may find itself in virtual consensus with models dominant in the surrounding culture. Consider the natural sciences. Here the Christian setting may evoke a distinctive framework for instruction—it may, for example, lead teachers to discourage the use of scientific knowledge for violent purposes— but the course content will no doubt reflect what broadly respected authorities have had to say. At the points, however, of profound difference—in the human sciences and the humanities; in the administration of student life—the only responsible conduct in the face of challenge is honest conversation. And this means readiness "to amplify, explain, defend, and, if necessary, either modify or abandon" what one believes.[1]

In her book on *Theology in the Age of Scientific Reasoning*, Nancey Murphy argues that the right method for defending Christian convictions is exactly analogous to the scientific method. She writes from a postmodern point of view and relies on the distinguished philosopher of science, Imre Lakatos. Christian communities, she says, are "experiments" in a "research program." The program has to do with the claims of the Gospel. As in all productive science, the convictions central to the program must be held tenaciously. Secondary convictions may be held less tenaciously, but all—the central as well as the secondary—must be willingly subjected to testing. The testing is in the living out of Christian life, and in the meeting of objections to the beliefs and practices associated with that life. The objections are met either by displaying, through words or deeds, their deficiency, or by attempting to make adequate adjustments. Over the long run, evidence accrues that counts for or against the secondary or even the central convictions. The intent and hope, always, is that "new and more consistent models of the Christian theory" may emerge.[2]

[1]MacIntyre 201.
[2]Nancey C. Murphy, *Theology in the Age of Scientific Reasoning*, Cornell Studies in the Philosophy of Religion (Ithaca, NY: Cornell UP 1990) 196.

A paragraph gives short shrift to the nuance and complexity of Murphy's argument. She means to embrace the postmodern awareness of the limits and uncertainty of human knowledge while arguing for standards of evidential reasoning that defeat "total relativism" and reclaim accountability. Justifications cannot be absolute, even in the natural sciences. In the domain of moral and spiritual conviction, as in the human sciences, the difficulties are even greater. But when challenges are sufficiently understood to cause dismay—a common enough experience—they must be dealt with through honest, open conversation. The attempted justifications, as McClendon writes in his own discussion of these matters, may seem acceptable and effective only in the eyes of the person or community being challenged.[1] But the effort of justification, and the intent of framing new and more consistent models of the Christian theory, must be embraced. Otherwise, the partisanship so necessary for growth in knowledge becomes a barrier to growth and ceases to be responsible.

For colleges and universities of explicit Christian commitment, then, intellectual accountability requires a countercultural frame of mind, a willing dissent, that is, from the wider world and a deliberate advocacy of the church's distinctive belief and practice. In the exercise of such accountability, teachers should first of all be protagonists. Second, they should, in their teaching, engage the whole person, intellect and character alike. Third, they should acknowledge and participate in conflict; they should meet challenges with attempted justifications.

In these ways colleges that honor and reflect the church's narrative can address the "critical years" of post-adolescence when, as Sharon Parks writes, the emerging self is especially open to "life-transforming vision."[2] In these ways such colleges, following their particular purpose of education, can embody and refine the practices of teaching and learning and thus create standards for these activities that assist congregations and eventually the wider world.

The genesis of modernity was, substantially, a hope for peace. But the attempt to realize the hope proved self-deceptive and, all too often, oppressive, not just in its hostility to differentiation but also in its drift toward compelled uniformity. My argument for partisan education is an acknowledgment, as Toulmin puts it, "of the unavoidable complexities of concrete human experience."[3] But as a call for responsible partisanship, it is also an evocation of a humane

[1]James William McClendon, Jr., and James M. Smith, *Understanding Religious Convictions* (Notre Dame: U of Notre Dame P 1975) 182.

[2]Sharon Parks, *The Critical Years: The Young Adult Search for a Faith to Live By* (San Francisco: Harper 1986) 17.

[3]Toulmin 201.

approach to discord: honest partisanship, involving mind and heart alike, fused with honest conversation and shorn of the need to injure or coerce. Here higher education can be a beacon—and especially Christian higher education, whose narrative, in decidedly unmodern fashion, calls its partisans to peaceable and prayerful regard for those with whom it differs, including its mortal enemies. The point of the Christian narrative is not resignation, it is transformation. In a sometimes winsome but often violent tournament of narratives, colleges embracing such an approach to discord and such a hope of transformation may and must stand tall.[1]

---

[1]Different versions of this essay have appeared in print previously; see "Schooling for the Tournament of Narratives: Postmodernism and the Idea of the Christian College," *Theology Without Foundations: Religious Practice and the Future of Theological Truth*, ed. Stanley Hauerwas, Nancey Murphy, and Mark Nations (Nashville: Abingdon 1994) 273-88; "Schooling for the Tournament of Narratives: Postmodernism and the Idea of the Christian College," *Religious Education* 94.1 (1999): 40-57; "The Unembarrassed Adventist: Conviction and Truth in Adventist Higher Education," *Spectrum* 25 (Jan. 1997): 40-50; and "Conviction and Truth in Adventist Education," *Ministry*, Jan. 2001, 20-3.

# 13

# Bible Study

## Alden Thompson

One day, as this paper was taking shape, three advertisements landed back-to-back in my mailbox All three were rooted in Scripture. The first was Adventist in orientation, a notice for a Sabbath event to be held in the public school right across the street from what is now Walla Walla University. The topics included "National Sunday Law" and "The Latter Rain and the 144,000." Though no longer holding denominational credentials, the speaker was described as an "ordained SDA minister" and his name was prefixed with "Elder." The ethos of the meetings was clear: "What you will learn may shock you," read the notice, "but the SDA Bible message will move you with the love of Jesus." "These are solid SDA messages for Seventh-day Adventists! No Catholic, Charismatic, New Theology, Bee Bop Celebrations."

If the use of "bebop," a trendy word of the World War II era, suggested a nostalgic and insular SDA world of a half-century ago, the other two advertisements opened up the modern world in which Adventists now live. One was an eight-page announcement of the 18th Annual "Jesus Northwest" festival, planned for July 21-23, 1994, in Vancouver, Washington. No doubt my Adventist friends across the street would label this event as "Charismatic" and "Bee Bop." But the sponsors—the People's Church of the Assemblies of God in Salem, Oregon—were more sophisticated, billing their event as interdenominational and never using the term *charismatic*. Words like "fellowship" and "ministry" dominated the copy and described the thrust of the messages that would be presented by well-known Christian speakers. On the agenda would be relationships, prayer, and lifestyle evangelism. As for music, "pop" (not "bebop") was in—and unashamedly so. A stellar array of "Contemporary Christian Music Artists" had been scheduled. The sound system would operate "at acceptable decibel levels," possibly "reduced" at times in order to meet "state statute sound levels." Patrons were urged to enter the arena carefully when the gates opened, for "in the past, children and adults have been knocked down and hurt as people rush in." A "Fun Center" would offer amusement rides, with the proceeds going to missions.

The Bible was mentioned twice in the eight pages, once on page 3 in a blurb describing a seminar on "Intimacy with God," and again on page 7. There, under the heading, "What to Bring," the Bible was first on the list, followed by "Your pass"—available for as much as $52.00, amusement rides not included.

The third advertisement was another eight-page item, a catalog of scholarly publications from Polebridge Press. In one sense, it was more "biblical" than the other two, announcing books about Jesus, John the Baptist, and the Gospels. Two books in particular caught my attention. *The Five Gospels*, subtitled, *The Search for the Authentic Words of Jesus*, reflects the work of Robert Funk and the Jesus Seminar. It is a kind of contemporary New Testament echo of Paul Haupt's 1898 *Polychrome Bible*, a multicolored edition of the Old Testament that printed different authors or sources in different colors. In Funk's book, the sayings attributed to Jesus in the Gospels are reproduced in red, pink, gray, or black: red is for words "close to what Jesus actually said"; words in pink "less certainly originated with Jesus"; words in gray "are not his, though they contain ideas that are close to his own"; black is for sayings that have been "embellished or created by his followers, or borrowed from common lore."

While the book would no doubt unsettle the devout believer eager to see *all* Jesus' words in red, it would also be likely to irritate the newer generation of literary critics who are tired of linking the value and meaning of a text to the historicity of its contents. And the rainbow colors applied to reputed sources and authors simply don't want to stay put. In David Gunn's words, "It is no exaggeration to say that the truly assured results of historical critical scholarship concerning authorship, date and provenance would fill but a pamphlet."[1]

The other book that caught my eye was Robert Funk's revised *Jesus As Precursor*. An awareness of Funk's fundamentalist roots helps illumine such statements as: "Jesus' primary successors may not be Peter, Matthew and Mark, or even Augustine and Luther, but Franz Kafka and Jorge Luis Borges, two modern tellers of parables." The choices are remarkable. According to *The Columbia Encyclopedia*, the German-speaking, Prague-born Jew Kafka (1883-1924)

---

[1]David M. Gunn, "New Directions in the Study of Hebrew Narrative," *Journal for the Study of the Old Testament* 39 (1987): 66, qtd. Joyce Baldwin, *1 & 2 Samuel: An Introduction and Commentary*, Tyndale Old Testament Commentaries 8 (Leicester/Downers Grove: IVP 1988) 29.

"presents a world . . . in which individuals burdened with guilt, isolation, and anxiety, make a futile search for personal salvation."[1] The same source notes that the Argentine author Borges (1899–1986) was a supporter of the poetic movement *Ultraismo* which "advocated the use of bold images and daring metaphors in an attempt to create pure poetry, divorced not only from the past but from reality."[2]

"A futile search for personal salvation." "Divorced not only from the past but from reality." This is the heritage Funk links with the biblical story of Jesus? That would not be easy to explain to believers who read in the Bible that Jesus is Creator and Redeemer, the Lord of history who promises a future.

Only one of three advertisements was by Adventists for Adventists, even if the sponsors stood to the right of the mainstream church. But some Adventists will listen to the voices that speak through the other two as well, many finding them more congenial than the voices at the gathering across the street from Walla Walla University. Given these diverse attractions, what is the future of biblical studies in Adventism? Has the book that once united us on common ground become the book that divides us? Will Adventism fragment into liberal and conservative camps, into liturgical high church and charismatic low?

In this chapter, I will argue that a responsible return to our Adventist roots and to Scripture could allow the Bible itself to be the book that unites us again. All three advertisements identify potential threats to the community. But they also point to factors that Adventists must take seriously if we are to be a body united in Christ. Those across the street are the "structural conservatives" for whom stability is more important than emotion. Resisting change and fresh confrontation with Scripture, they are quick to label seeming innovations as "Catholic" or "New Theology." Yet they rightly remind us that we dare not neglect our Adventist roots. It's harder to know where you are going if you do not remember where you have been.

The "Jesus Northwest" people are the "experiential conservatives," those whose religious experience is dominated by the emotional and the social. Adventists have rightly worried that from such a perspective, the warm feelings of the moment can put at risk the faith once delivered to the saints. Nevertheless, Adventists need to be reminded that religion is of the heart as well as the head. Wesley's Aldersgate experience, that moment when his heart was

---

[1]"Kafka, Franz," *Columbia Encyclopedia,* 5th ed. (New York: Columbia UP 1993).
[2]"Borges, Jose Luis," *Columbia Encyclopedia.*

"strangely warmed," and Ellen White's alarm over "cold formality"[1] and "dry formalism"[2] should spark a certain sympathy for those who crave the religion of the heart.

Finally, the Polebridge Press offerings appeal to the academic community—in Adventism a relatively small but potentially influential group. Here the danger is two-fold: first, to react against the fundamentalist tendencies in Adventism in ways that might imply, Kafka-like, that the study of Scripture can only result in "a futile search for personal salvation"; second, perhaps more dangerous because less obviously sinister, to undermine Scripture as "sacred" text simply through the process of rational analysis. If some err by avoiding analysis, academics too easily overlook the implications of analysis for those who approach Scripture with reverence rather than curiosity. Analytical study of sacred texts is inevitable in our modern era and can bring fruitful results even to the lives of ordinary believers. And Adventist academics must lead the community's efforts in such study. But the power of Scripture for believers lies in their conviction that God speaks to us through his Word. The challenge for those of us who are academics is to make sure that our church hears us speak as believers not merely as scholars.

## Constructing a Center Position

In the theological spectrum, two of the items that landed in my mailbox originate with groups on the theological right: the dissident Adventists and the Jesus Northwest people, the Adventist group representing a sectarian fundamentalism, the festival crowd an evangelicalism that is very nearly fundamentalist, though not as strident as those who wear the fundamentalist badge with pride. The Polebridge group is on the far left, a scholarly perspective that is both ex-fundamentalist and anti-fundamentalist.

And the center? That is the challenge facing Adventism, for our secular age easily fragments the spectrum, leaving a lonely no-man's land between two warring extremes. My goal in this chapter is to suggest a unifying model for Adventism that encompasses all the essential impulses evident in Scripture—from those of a pained Ezekiel, sighing and crying over the abominations in Israel, to those of an exuberant Paul, admonishing us to rejoice in God's salvation and to keep rejoicing; from the probing skepticism of Ecclesiastes to the buoyant optimism of Proverbs.

[1]Ellen G. White, *Testimonies for the Church*, 9 vols. (Mountain View, CA: Pacific Press 1946 [1843]) 1: 48.
[2]Ellen G. White, *Counsels to Writers and Editors* (Nashville: Southern 1946 [1875]) 124.

In short, I am arguing that the Bible itself can bring us together. The diversity in Scripture sets the parameters for diversity in the church, while that which is clear and unequivocal in Scripture is the basis for our unity. While my model is based on Scripture, it takes its inspiration from our Adventist forebears, who by providential accident more than deliberate design, it seems, approached Scripture in a way that ensured unity while allowing diversity.

That early perspective was stated succinctly by James White in the *Review and Herald*, on August 11, 1853, in response to an inquiry from a Seventh Day Baptist:

> As a people we are brought together from divisions of the Advent body [the Millerites], and from the various denominations, holding different views on some subjects; yet, thank Heaven, the Sabbath is a mighty platform on which we can all stand united. And while standing here, with the aid of no other creed than the Word of God, and bound together by the bonds of love—love for the truth, love for each other, and love for a perishing world—"which is stronger than death," all party feelings are lost. We are united in these great subjects: Christ's immediate, personal second Advent, and the observance of all of the commandments of God, and the faith of his Son Jesus Christ, as necessary to a readiness for his Advent.[1]

The genius of James White's statement is its clear focus on a few key unifying elements while making room for differences of opinion within the community. When the first Seventh-day Adventist local conference was organized in 1861, the delegates moved along similar lines, adopting a simple written covenant to be used in the organization of local churches. Published in the *Review and Herald* on October 8, 1861, it reads:

> We, the undersigned, hereby associate ourselves together, as a church, taking the name, Seventh-day Adventists, covenanting to keep the commandments of God, and the faith of Jesus Christ.[2]

When, in 1872, it seemed advisable to provide an inquiring public with a "synopsis of our faith," the preamble stated pointedly that "we have no articles of faith, creed, or discipline, having any authority with our people, nor is it [the synopsis] designed to secure uniformity among them, as a system of faith. . . ."[3]

Our most recent statement of "Fundamental Beliefs," voted in Dallas in 1980, includes a preamble that preserves that sense of openness cherished by our Adventist forebears: "Revision of these statements may be expected at a General Conference session when the church is led by the Holy Spirit to a fuller understanding of Bi-

---

[1]Qtd. *SDA Encyclopedia*, rev. ed. (Washington, DC: Review 1976) 395.
[2]Qtd. *SDA Encyclopedia* 356.
[3]*Declaration of the Fundamental Principles Taught and Practiced by the Seventh-day Adventists* (Battle Creek: Adventist 1872).

ble truth or finds better language in which to express the teaching of God's Holy Word."

Significantly, the *Adventist Review* of January 6, 1994, commemorating the 150th year after 1844, features that 1980 preamble in a lead article by the editor, William Johnsson, an AnchorPoints piece on "Present Truth." Not all Adventists, however, seem to greet such a preamble with enthusiasm. The first printing of the Ministerial Association's commentary on the Dallas statement, *Seventh-day Adventists Believe: A Biblical Exposition of 27 Fundamental Doctrines* omits the preamble without comment.[1] Similarly, the first "official" statement of Adventist beliefs, published in 1931, included no qualifying preamble. And in 1888 at the peak of the battle over the law in Galatians, General Conference President G. I. Butler was ready to set Adventist thinking in concrete, declaring in a circular letter to Adventist ministers that Adventists had "never taken a stand upon Bible exegesis which they have been compelled to surrender."[2] Similar thinking surfaced at the General Conference of 1888 where some were convinced that a revised view of Galatians 3 would destroy Adventism. The argument is preserved in an Ellen White rebuttal:

> The remark was made, "If our views of Galatians are not correct, then we have not the third angel's message, and our position goes by the board; there is nothing to our faith." I said, "Brethren, here is the very thing I have been telling you. This statement is not true. It is an extravagant, exaggerated statement. If it is made in the discussion of this question I shall feel it my duty to set this matter before all that are assembled, and whether they hear or forbear, tell them the statement is incorrect. The question at issue is not a vital question and should not be treated as such."[3]

I am convinced that if we in fact return to our roots, discovering that Adventism rests on pillars so secure that we can afford to be absolutely open with Scripture, then Adventists can recover a genuine excitement for the study of Scripture. By a kind of sixth sense our Adventist forebears came to Scripture in a way that did not force every question to yield an either/or answer. Building on that foundation, I want to argue for a functional model that provides the

---

[1]See [P. Gerard Damsteegt, ed.], *Seventh-day Adventists Believe: A Biblical Exposition of 27 Fundamental Doctrines* (Washington, DC: Review 1988). By the third printing (1989), the preamble was included in the front matter. And when the revised edition was reissued in 2005 after the addition of the 28th belief (#11), the preamble takes center stage in the front matter as a justification for the inclusion of the additional belief.

[2]"A Circular Letter to All State Conference Committees and Our Brethren in the Ministry," qtd. George R. Knight, *Angry Saints* (Washington, DC: Review 1989) 15.

[3]Ellen G. White, *Selected Messages*, 3 vols. (Washington, DC: Review 1958-80) 3: 174-5 (1888).

stability desired by the conservatives and the flexibility desired by the liberals, a structure within which it is safe to explore the intricacies of Scripture while retaining the conviction that God speaks to us through his Word.

In contrast to the model that threatens to be dominant in Adventism, I propose one that is *motivational,* rather than strictly *informational; dynamic* rather than *static; adapted* to human needs rather than *absolute.* In my more playful moments, I illustrate the difference between the two models by contrasting *tug of war* and *soccer.* The tug of war model resists give-and-take and has no logical way of incorporating diversity, change, or adaptability. By contrast, soccer thrives on adaptability. The playing field and the goal are clearly defined, but the methods of reaching the goal are diverse. Skilled players readily kick the ball in the opposite direction, sometimes all the way to their own goalies, employing moves that might easily alarm an uninitiated observer. In my view, something like a soccer model allows the interpreter to be honest with the diversity in Scripture while maintaining its unity.

The stability of the interpretive structure I am proposing (the clear boundaries and the goal) is provided by the dominant ethical norms in Scripture: the One great principle of love, Jesus' Two great commands (love to God and love to fellow humans), and the Ten commandments. Key New Testament passages include Romans 13:8-10 and Matthew 22:35-40. In addition, Jesus' statement in Matthew 19:8 that the law of divorce was given only because of "hard-hearted" people, allows us to say that the additional commands in Scripture are more limited in scope, illustrating and applying the One, Two, and Ten in particular times and places. As Ellen White put it, "That the obligations of the Decalogue might be more fully understood and enforced, additional precepts were given, illustrating and applying the principles of the Ten Commandments."[1]

One of my students suggested the word "codebook" for the enduring One, Two, and Ten matrix, and "casebook" for the additional legislation. I have adopted that language and find it very helpful, though some readers of my book *Inspiration* see it otherwise. The real tension may be between the two models, tug of war and soccer. Based on my own observations, however, some of the critics actually do a good job of practicing what I preach. They just don't like to hear it preached!

In any event, the whole ethical corpus is refracted through a Christological prism, for Jesus came as the incarnation of God's law

---

[1] Ellen G. White, *The Story of Patriarchs and Prophets: The Conflict of the Ages Illustrated in the Lives of Holy Men of Old* (Mountain View, CA: Pacific 1947 [1890]) 310.

of love. In the words of Matthew 5:17, "I have not come to abolish the law or the prophets; I have not come to abolish but to fulfill."[1]

If the law pyramid of the One, Two, and Ten assures stability, then it becomes safe to recognize the remarkable adaptability to human need demonstrated throughout Scripture. In the Old Testament, for example, some laws protected Israel from threats posed by her neighbors. Thus eunuchs and illegitimate children were barred from the community, most likely to ward off participation in tempting fertility rites; the exclusion of the Moabites and Ammonites also served to preserve the integrity of the community. Though all four exclusions are stated clearly in Deuteronomy 23:1-6, in each case, notable exceptions appear within the Old Testament. No eunuchs? Isaiah 56:3-5 promises them a place "in my house and within my walls, a monument and a name better than sons and daughters." No illegitimate children? Jephthah, the son of a prostitute, was a judge upon whom "the spirit of the Lord" came when he went out to battle.[2] No Moabites? Ruth the Moabite was an ancestor of David and Jesus.[3] No Ammonites? The only one of Solomon's seven hundred wives to be mentioned by name was Naamah the Ammonite,[4] mother of Solomon's successor Rehoboam, also in Jesus' bloodline. Clearly, within the Old Testament itself, the additional laws beyond the ten were applied with remarkable freedom and flexibility.

That same tradition of flexibility winds through in Acts 15 at the Jerusalem Conference debate over circumcision. In the end, the conference made circumcision optional, while adding a prohibition against food offered to idols. The letter to the churches said it all happened because it "seemed good to the Holy Spirit and to us."[5]

And the give-and-take continued after the conference. Acts 16:3 reveals a Paul who was more conservative than the conference, insisting that Timothy be circumcised. But in 1 Corinthians 8 and 10, Paul moves in the other direction, articulating a position on food offered to idols that was more liberal than that adopted by the council.

In short, both Testaments reveal remarkable adaptation to human need as God pointed his people toward wholehearted love for him and for each other. And that need for adaptation continues. Some years ago when one of my colleagues quizzed a group of ministers in South Africa to determine which biblical laws they re-

---

[1]Unless otherwise indicated, all Scripture quotations are from the New Revised Standard Version.
[2]Judges 11:29.
[3]Matt. 1:5.
[4]1 Kings 14:21.
[5]Acts 15:28.

garded as temporary and which ones they thought were enduring, all the white South Africans said the prohibition against food offered to idols was temporary; by contrast, all the black South Africans said it was permanent. The black culture still perceived idols as a threat; the white culture did not.

In a world threatened by relativity, I believe Adventists can proclaim a sure and consistent standard. We are not faced with the awkwardness of proclaiming obedience to God's law while explaining away the fourth commandment. For us, structure, theory, and practice can all be consistent because we draw the line where Scripture does: the decalogue was engraved on tables of stone and went inside the ark; the additional legislation was written in a mere book and was placed beside the ark. In Deuteronomy 4:13-14, only the decalogue is "covenant"; the additional laws are simply "statutes and ordinances." The beautiful simplicity of the Adventist position means that ordinary people can read or hear and understand the key elements of God's law; they can see it lived out in Jesus; and to the extent that they can understand the rest of Scripture, they can see it further applied in time and place.

Now all Adventists everywhere have always agreed that the One, Two, and Ten are binding and that Jesus is the incarnation of the One. But we have not said clearly that the rest of Scripture is an adaptation of God's law in time and place. I believe we must now declare that distinction more clearly. With vigor and openness we must show what is enduring and universal in Scripture, then demonstrate how those enduring elements are applied in time and place, drawing on the rest of Scripture to provide examples. All this is in the spirit of 1 Corinthians 10:11: "These things happened to them to serve as an example, and they were written down to instruct us, on whom the ends of the ages have come." For Adventists, the same model places Ellen White's voluminous writings in proper perspective. They, too, are examples, illustrating how God's people have lived out the principles of the One, Two, and Ten in varied circumstances. But her counsels are helpful and instructive, not absolute and all-encompassing.

A model that shifts the emphasis from the informational to the ethical and motivational, also gives focus to the exegesis of Scripture, for everything in Scripture then points to the goal of whole-hearted commitment to God and mutual love for each other.

The concern of exegesis, then, is not just accurate information, but appropriate application for the purpose of motivation. It is at once more open to the text *and* more closely linked to human experience. The implications for the interpreter of Scripture are significant.

## A Motivational Model:
## Implications and Applications

The strikingly varied reactions of my students to portions of Scripture illustrate how a motivational approach allows a more open attitude to exegesis and a more practical application to Christian experience.

In an assignment that focuses on a cluster of Jesus' parables, for example, I ask each student to indicate which parable was most helpful and which was most troubling. Typically, the lost sheep and the lost boy in Luke 15 are favorites while the reluctant midnight friend[1] and the unjust judge[2] are troubling. In one class, though, a student actually said the parable of the unjust judge was her favorite, commenting, "I really admire the lady for standing up to someone infinitely more powerful than she." More instructive, however, was the response to the parable of the vineyard workers who all received the same pay regardless of time each spent in the field.[3] Out of forty-two students, six said that parable was the most helpful of all the ones we had studied. Six others, however, found it the most troubling one.

Immediately I thought of the classic tension between the Calvinist emphasis on God's grace and the sovereignty of God, and the Arminian emphasis on human freedom and responsibility. I suspect that if I had included the parable of the talents from Matthew 25, in which rewards correlate with effort and energy, the reactions would have been reversed. Now was one group wicked and the other righteous? One right and the other wrong? Possibly. More likely, however, the groups simply comprised people of different temperaments. Those who work best in secure, supportive environments reveled in a marvelous story of grace. Regardless of specific accomplishments, all willing workers in God's vineyard are rewarded equally. By contrast, those who love challenges were troubled by the lack of incentive.

To illustrate from everyday life, one could contrast the natural-born salesperson, working the customers in the showroom, with the faithful accountant, hidden away in a back room somewhere. The sales personality loves the exhilarating life on the knife-edge of pure commission. By contrast, the accountant craves the security of a regular salary. Putting the accountant on commission and the sales person on salary could destroy them both.

Looking at Scripture from a motivational perspective, then, allows us to evaluate each passage honestly and on its own merits. In-

---

[1]Luke 11:5-8.
[2]Luke 18:1-5.
[3]Matt. 20:1-16.

stead of the Calvinists twisting the Arminian passages to fit their mold, and the Arminians twisting the Calvinist passages to fit theirs, we may all simply let the chips fall where they may as determined by the text. On such a model, contradictions are not the problem, but the solution.

Another assignment asks my students to respond to three diverse psalms: Psalm 90 in which an awesome God towers above an impressed but cowering psalmist; Psalm 91, with its promise of protection from all harm; and Psalm 137, a wrenching lament from an exiled psalmist who concludes with these stunning words against his enemies: "Happy shall they be who take your little ones and dash them against the rock!"[1]

After comparing notes in small groups, the students come together again and each one indicates which psalm was most helpful and which was most troublesome. The results are all over the place. The last time I conducted the exercise, Psalm 90 was most helpful for two, but most troublesome for thirteen; Psalm 91 was most helpful for fifteen, but most troublesome for five; and remarkably, while Psalm 137 was most troublesome for four it was most helpful for four others. Never before had one of my students claimed the baby-bashing Psalm 137 as most helpful. Now, all of a sudden, there were four in one class.

I could share similar results on reactions to prayer (quiescent faith vs. aggressive confrontation), prophecy (divine control vs. human response), and the heavenly sanctuary (the concrete vs. the abstract). Class discussions have allowed us to understand each other, recognizing that not all of us respond with equal fervor to all parts of Scripture. If each one of us is to love God wholeheartedly, we must help each other find those passages of Scripture that light the fire.

Turning to a more specific exegetical illustration, the three biblical versions of the story of Moses' killing of the Egyptian show how a motivational approach can liberate the interpreter to be open with Scripture. Brevard Childs' monumental commentary on *Exodus*[2] first drew my attention to this cluster of stories. For Adventists who are tempted to let an inspired writer interpret the Bible for us, this cluster is particularly interesting because the original account in Exodus 2 is reinterpreted in one way in Acts 7 and in yet another way in Hebrews 11. In brief, the original story in Exodus 2 condemns Moses' pride; but in Acts 7, Stephen turns Moses into a hero, using the story to illustrate the ongoing history of Jewish rebelliousness; Hebrews 11 reinterprets the story as an illustration of en-

[1]Psalm 137.9.
[2]Brevard S. Childs, *The Book of Exodus,* Old Testament Commentary (Philadelphia: Westminster 1974).

during faith: "By faith he [Moses] left Egypt, *unafraid* of the king's anger,"[1] a sharp contrast with "Moses was *afraid*" of Exodus 2:14.

In my own experience, that contrast has greatly enriched my understanding of faith, suggesting that someone who is teeth-chattering afraid on the surface, can still cherish a deep confidence in God's plan and purpose. I was so moved by that insight that I wrote it up under the title, "Less Than a Grain of Mustard Seed," and sent it in to the *Adventist Review*. It was published in 1984.[2] Yet when I highlighted those differences in my book *Inspiration*, differences that were essential to the insights that had brought a blessing to my soul, some vivid objections appeared in print and in personal letters.

But I am increasingly convinced that the body of Christ needs to find a way to see such differences, not as necessary nuisance, but as divine gifts with the potential to bless the church. Let me illustrate in a very personal way, for I must admit that the contrast between my experience and my wife's has heightened my sensitivities to these differences. Wanda is a gentle person with significantly reduced energies because of Lyme disease; but she is married to a high-energy husband, one who is highly competitive and who thrives on challenge. As the limitations imposed by Lyme have reshaped our lives, we have drawn closer to each other, still aware of our own needs, but with heightened sensitivity to each other's needs as well. To cite one example: she looks forward to a restored world that is peaceful and free from conflict; I look forward to one that is free from hurtful pain but still throbbing with challenges. As you might imagine, our habits, interests, and joys in this world are shaped along similar lines. But because of the bond between us, she and I are finding meaning and joy, not just in meeting our own needs, but in seeing each other's needs met as well.

I understand better, now, why Paul talked about the church as the body of Christ and compared the bond between Christ and the church to the relationship between husband and wife. My heightened sensitivity to my wife's needs and hers to mine, has changed the way I teach my classes and has markedly affected what I write and how. Perhaps most surprising of all (and this will be a mystery except for those who know the jargon), my Myers-Briggs temperament profile has changed. A 1981 test pegged me as an ENTJ; eleven years later, in 1992, I tested out as an ENFJ. In Myers-Briggs jargon, that's a shift from "commander" to "catalyst," a shift from a logic-oriented approach to one that is more sensitive to feeling.

---

[1] Heb. 11:27.
[2] Alden Thompson, "Less than a Grain of Mustard Seed," *Adventist Review*, Dec. 6, 1984: 6-7.

But now let me be more specific about what that means for the interpretation of Scripture. Since our temperaments have much to do with how we relate to each other and to God, we should expect that a book like the Bible, written over a period of time by a variety of authors, could be an ideal way of meeting a wide variety of needs. And since the formation of the canon of Scripture was essentially a community effort, the diversity within the early church would be reflected in the diverse writings found in Scripture. That's why some like Paul, but others prefer James; why some like Proverbs and others Ecclesiastes; why some like John and others Jeremiah. Tragically, the whole fundamentalist mind set has forced a homogenization of Scripture, something like offering everyone a glass of room temperature 2% milk, instead of skim milk, 1%, 4%, half and half, whipping cream, ice cream, yoghurt, cottage cheese, cheddar—yes, and even something as ghastly as buttermilk.

If we can find a model that lets us see the Bible as a people's book, one designed to meet everyone's needs, then each of us can find what we need in Scripture as well as helping our brothers and sisters find what they need. Lacking such a model, we tempt the structural conservatives to meet by themselves and torment the church with their one-string version of the Adventist message; we tempt the experiential conservatives to meet their more emotional needs at the Jesus festivals of the world; and we tempt the academics to anger and frustration because the church doesn't want to see the rich diversity that they have found in our sacred texts.

As I have worked with this model, I have been encouraged by Ellen White's comments on the Bible teacher: Students should not have the same teacher year after year, she says. "Different teachers should have a part in the work, even though they may not all have so full an understanding of the Scriptures." Why so many different authors in Scripture, she asks? "It is because . . . [people's] minds differ. Not all comprehend things in exactly the same way." Her most striking statement has to do with unique insights: "Often through unusual experiences, under special circumstances, He gives to some Bible students views of truth that others do not grasp. It is possible for the most learned teacher to fall far short of teaching all that should be taught."[1]

Powerful support for such diversity is found in Scripture, especially in 1 Corinthians, a rich resource for exploring a biblical pluralism. The fact that the Corinthians had divided into at least four parties rallied behind four different leaders (Paul, Cephas, Apollos, Jesus), was not so troubling to Paul as was the fact that they were

---

[1]Ellen G. White, *Counsels to Parents, Teachers, and Students* (Boise, ID: Pacific 2011 [cf. Ms. 87, 1907]) 432-3.

quarreling. In fact, he actually spells out how his role differs from that of Apollos: "I planted, Apollos watered."[1] His metaphors of field and building in chapter 3 and the body in chapter 12, all suggest a cooperative pluralism, a unity in diversity. He even tucks in a blunt reference to the two classic forms of external motivation, carrot and stick: "What would you prefer?" he asks. "Am I to come to you with a stick, or with love in a spirit of gentleness?"[2] If we had been more sensitive to that diversity in Paul, perhaps we would have been less brutal in our use of Ellen White. And her work has diverse strands, too. To one brother she wrote, "You need to educate yourself, that you may have wisdom to deal with minds. You should with some have compassion, making a difference, while others you may save with fear, pulling them out of the fire."[3] To a brother who was being much too critical of his wife, she said: "Your wife needs your help . . . . She wants to lean upon your strengths. You can help her and lead her along. You should never censure her. Never reprove her if her efforts are not what you think they should be."[4] It would be interesting to know how Ellen White might counsel such a soul with reference to the reading of the *Testimonies* and certain portions of Scripture.

I am convinced that our Adventist heritage points us to a model for understanding Scripture that could make Adventism a remnant in the right sense of the word, a body of Christ for every nation, kindred, tongue, people, and temperament. The key elements that have always bound us together: Sabbath and Advent are ideally suited for uniting a diverse people in Christ. Whether one is brilliant or average, a concrete thinker or abstract one, the Sabbath is a day we can all cherish. When it comes to the Advent and the return of Jesus, however, I have discovered remarkable diversity in Adventism, even though Advent is central to the life of the whole. American Adventists are inclined to view the future world in quite literal terms: smell the flowers, hear the birds, munch an apple from the tree of life. But when we were in Germany, I was startled to see otherwise very devout and conservative European Adventists resist our Kodachrome version of the after life. Yet my German brothers and sisters have a deep-seated hope, expressed by a word that is hard to capture in English: *Sehnsucht*. It's something like the English word "longing" but with four or five O's to stretch it out— loooonging. Given all that they have endured in this century, one can understand. Restoration. It's terribly important for them, for me and for millions of my fellow Adventists around the world. We

[1] I Cor. 3:5.
[2] I Cor. 4:21.
[3] White, *Testimonies* 3:420 (1874).
[4] White, *Testimonies* 2:305 (1868).

may envision that restored world differently, but we all know that something is dreadfully wrong with this present one. We believe God can do better than this. So we wait and we hope.

And in that connection I want to speak candidly to the more sophisticated members of my church, including my academic colleagues, those who rub shoulders with sophisticated people who do not believe. The dominance of science in our modern secular world has threatened to push God to the fringes for some, making it more difficult for them to believe. Interestingly enough, the natural scientists are statistically more inclined to believe than are their academic colleagues in either the humanities or the behavioral and social sciences, even though we often perceive the greatest threat to our world view as coming from the natural sciences. One survey reported that 20% of natural scientists do not believe in God, compared with 36% of humanities scholars, and 41% of the social scientists.[1] I suspect that the marvelous complexity of nature makes it more difficult for many natural scientists to believe that our world "just happened" all by itself.

The model I am proposing, however, implies a stronger role for both the psychologists and the sociologists, the academics at the bottom of the belief heap. We must understand why we relate to each other and to sacred texts the way we do. Awe inspires worship. Traditional concepts of the sacred rely on awe in the presence of the mysterious. But understanding can also lead to worship and back to awe again. Though understanding is important in an age that relies on analysis and informed reflection, the Bible is also a mysterious symbol of God's presence for ordinary people. That's why we must deal with it and with them with a great deal of care.

Just to illustrate the nature of the challenge, I want to quote from a student's response to the chapter on "Manuscripts" in my book *Inspiration*. In that chapter I explain why some well-known passages in the King James Version are missing from modern translations: the last lines of the Lord's Prayer in Matthew 6, the story of the woman taken in adultery,[2] and the trinity proof text of 1 John 5:7-8. This was her reaction:

> I guess I really don't understand. If we teach our children the doxology part, wouldn't we want it in our Bible, too? The story of the adulteress—if it is not in the old manuscripts then how do we know that it is true? I guess that maybe I am one of those people that you talk about that have a hard time with the fact that you are raising up questions about the word of God.

---

[1] Robert Wuthnow, *The Struggle for America's Soul: Evangelicals, Liberals, and Secularists* (Grand Rapids, MI: Eerdmans 1989) 146-7, ctd. David A. Fraser and Tony Campolo, *Sociology Through the Eyes of Faith* (San Francisco: Harper 1992) 23.

[2] Jn. 7:53 - 8:11.

It is really starting to upset me the way you are making the Bible seem like it all might not be true. See, when I was a kid a lot of people turned out to be not true. They let me down and now I don't trust them. Well, you are making the Bible feel like I can't trust it. How do I know what really happened and what did not happen? I have always been able to feel security in the Bible. When I was scared or frightened as a kid I would sleep with it. I always felt safe then. But your class is bringing up questions that I don't like and can't deal with. Please help gain back the trust I am losing. Thanks.

We talked and prayed and she gave me permission to keep her assignment. By God's grace and with the help of Christian friends she will be able to grow and mature in her walk with the Lord. But her case hints at the enormity of our challenge. Recently, in one northwest Adventist church of several hundred members, no fewer than 78 people signed a petition to take out the New International Version pew Bibles and replace them with the King James Version. Though Adventist publications have been using modern versions for years, the battle is far from won.

Yet Adventism is and must be a church for all the people. In 1992 the US department of education published the results of a comprehensive literacy study, showing that 48% of American adults read prose at the lowest two of five levels of prose literacy.[1] That means they cannot read and comprehend the more challenging parts of the Bible. And that means we will have to keep our message simple, stressing that which is clear and certain.

If we can make clear that which is enduring and stable in Scripture, then I believe Adventist academics can also have the freedom and flexibility we need to interpret Scripture faithfully in our day and for our generation. If there is to be a future for Adventist biblical studies that is more than an echo of the past, we must have room to explore, freedom to propose new alternatives, and the privilege of differing with each other. But that will not happen unless the church knows that the pillars are secure.

To succumb to the temptation, however, of treating every jot and tittle as a pillar of the faith, as has been our tendency, threatens to turn the whole into a house of cards, one that is too dangerous to touch lest it collapse. And if the joy of discovery thus disappears, genuine spiritual life is at risk, a concern pointedly expressed by Ellen White:

When no new questions are started by investigation of the Scriptures, when no difference of opinion arises which will set men to searching the Bible for themselves to make sure that they have the truth, there will be many now, as in ancient times, who will hold to tradition and worship they know not what.[2]

---

[1] *The Editorial Eye*, December 1993.
[2] White, *Testimonies* 5:707 (1889).

We must recognize, however, that simple people are not the only ones who struggle with the specter of losing their faith. And if we do not learn how to provide a safe home for inquiring believers, we will lose more and more of the young people who are graduating from our colleges and universities. We must develop a more dynamic model for the interpretation of Scripture, one that provides both structure and flexibility. And we must make it possible to worship.

Can it happen? Yes, if we will listen to our friends the sociologists. Indeed, I believe they can help us understand not only how to build and maintain such a model, but also how to enable sophisticated people to believe in Sabbath and Advent and in a personal God who is active and present in our world.

Peter Berger and other sociologists have written extensively on the "social construction of reality," the formation and grounding of our world view and social relations by human activity. They argue that humans cannot maintain belief in much of anything without "social support." And what we call reasonable is often nothing more than the consensus of those around us. As C. S. Lewis put it, "The society of unbelievers makes Faith harder even when they are people whose opinions on any other subject are known to be worthless."[1]

In his *Sacred Canopy*, Berger includes a striking comment about the challenges facing the so-called neo-orthodox in their attempt to recover a transcendent deity in our modern world: "Put crudely, if one is to believe what neo-orthodoxy wants one to believe, in the contemporary situation, then one must be rather careful to huddle together closely and continuously with one's fellow believers."[2] Shades of a verse from Hebrews that many of us once memorized: "Not neglecting to meet together, as is the habit of some, but encouraging one another, and all the more as you see the Day approaching."[3] Hebrews is no sociological text, but it preserves a keen sociological insight.

Adventist scholars, however much they wish to be faithful to their roots, still have to live in a world tinged with scorn. In his famous "demythologizing" essay (1941), Rudolph Bultmann declared that it was "impossible to use electric light and the wireless and to avail ourselves of modern medical and surgical discoveries, and at the same time to believe in the New Testament world of spirits and miracles." The return of Jesus then becomes untenable "for the

---

[1] C. S. Lewis, "Religion: Reality or Substitute?" *Christian Reflections*, ed. Walter Hooper (Grand Rapids: Eerdmans 1967) 42.
[2] Peter Berger, *The Sacred Canopy* (Garden City, NY: Anchor-Doubleday 1969) 164.
[3] Heb. 10:25.

simple reason that the parousia of Christ never took place as the New Testament expected. History did not come to an end, and, as every schoolboy knows, it will continue to run its course."[1]

One does not have to look far to find more recent voices that speak with similar scorn. In his best-selling *Rescuing the Bible from Fundamentalism*, Episcopalian bishop and ex-fundamentalist, John Shelby Spong, rejects the miraculous out of hand. Speaking of the virgin birth, he declares:

> Stars do not wander, angels do not sing, virgins do not give birth, magi do not travel to a distant land to present gifts to a baby, and shepherds do not go in search of a newborn savior. I know of no reputable biblical scholar in the world today who takes these birth narratives literally.[2]

But mysteries never end, nor do wild swings of the pendulum. Some forty years after Bultmann declared that electricity and modern medical discoveries had extracted miracles from his world, one of his students, Eta Linnemann, put them back in again—at least back into her world. In Kansas City, in November, 1991, I listened to her tell the story of her conversion to evangelical Christianity and to a belief in a personal God. With a great hunger in her heart and facing a personal crisis, she accepted Jesus as Lord. I was particularly struck by a comment that illustrated Berger's theory of the social construction of reality. She was telling about the amazed questions from her former students when they learned about her new life. "And do you believe he is coming again?" they asked. "Not yet," she responded. Then she told how it took several more weeks of fellowship with believing Christians before she, too, could believe in the Second Coming.

Unfortunately, when she returned to faith she went from a thorough-going rationalism to the opposite extreme. Note the intensity with which she rejected her previous world:

> I regard everything that I taught and wrote before I entrusted my life to Jesus as refuse . . . . Whatever of these writings I had in my possession I threw into the trash with my own hands in 1978. I ask you sincerely to do the same thing with any of them you may have on your own bookshelf.[3]

I believe Adventists have a remarkable opportunity to approach Scripture in a way that can eliminate such wild swings of the pendulum. The One eternal principle of love, Jesus' Two great commands, the Ten commandments, Sabbath and Advent. Those are the landmarks that stand out in Scripture. Our church needs to hear

---

[1]Rudolf Bultmann, "New Testament and Mythology," *Kerygma and Myth*, ed. Hans Werner Bartsch, trans. Reginald H. Fuller (New York: Harper 1961) 5.

[2]John Shelby Spong, *Rescuing the Bible from Fundamentalism: A Bishop Rethinks the Meaning of Scripture* (San Francisco: Harper 1992) 215.

[3]Eta Linnemann, *Historical Criticism of the Bible: Methodology or Ideology?* (Grand Rapids: Baker 1990) 20.

its academics say so with clarity. It should expect us to be thoroughly analytical, honest with all that we find in the sacred text. But it should also expect us to treat the text as sacred, the book that leads us in wholehearted and fervent worship. If those who need structure and those who need flexibility can worship together, confessing a common commitment to the commandments of God and the faith of Jesus, recognizing our differing needs, but realizing that the diversity in Scripture is sufficient to meet them all, then we can be one in Christ, a light to the world, a city on a hill that cannot be hid.

# 14

# *Hope*

## John Brunt

I once heard Dale Parnell, a professor at Oregon State University, tell a story about traveling with his pre-school son. I suppose all of us who have traveled with our children have similar stories. Not long after they started out, his son began asking those all too familiar questions: "Are we almost there? When will we get there? Are we there yet?" Finally, the father became so exasperated that with more vigor than the pre-schooler deserved, he told him to be quiet! His father would tell him when they were almost there. He would tell him when they *were* there. He didn't want to hear another question.

The boy was silent for about two more hours. Finally, he could contain himself no longer, and with all innocence asked, "Daddy, how old will I be when we get there?"

Sometimes it appears that to be an Adventist is to be like a child riding in the back seat of a car on a seemingly interminable trip. Adventism began in disappointment in 1844 and it has struggled with disappointing delays ever since. And now, many decades later, how are we to keep hope alive?

Or perhaps we should ask, why should we keep hope alive? Any look at Adventist hope today must be different after Waco. We have seen that Adventist hope is not only plagued by disappointment and delay; we have seen that it can also go awry in devastation and destruction. We may—correctly—distance ourselves from the Branch Davidians by pointing out how different we are from them and how long ago their forebears broke off from us, but we can't deny the fact that many of those who died in the fires of Waco had been in our own Adventist churches listening to Adventist preaching and studying Adventist Sabbath School lessons within just years or even months before they died in the fires. Even though we recoil and want to cry "unfair" when we hear Diane Sawyer on *Prime Time Live* say that Vernon Howell as a youngster

joined the Seventh-day Adventist Church where he learned to
worship a vengeful God who was coming to destroy, we might
have a hard time convincing anyone who watches some of the programs on 3ABN that it wasn't true.

Can we keep Adventist hope alive so many decades after 1844?
Should we keep Adventist hope alive? And if so, how do we do it?

My thesis is that we should keep Adventist hope alive, not
merely because it is an important part of our Adventist heritage, but
because it is an integral part of the gospel of Jesus Christ as presented in the New Testament. However, there are elements in Adventist eschatology that have been present from the beginning which
tend to obscure this vital connection between our hope and the
good news of grace. We will succeed in keeping Adventist hope
alive to the extent that our hope is gospel-oriented and grows out
of our faith in Jesus Christ. It may not be easy for us to do so, but
the New Testament points us to a hope that endures because it is
grounded in the promise of Jesus Christ.

## HISTORICAL SKETCH

Before we move to the New Testament to see the shape of this
enduring hope, however, a brief historical sketch is in order to help
us understand where we have come from and how our past has influenced our hope.

For our founding fathers and mothers, Adventist eschatology
had a strong polemical edge to it. Our pioneers should hardly be
faulted for this. They faced a world where most of Christianity believed that every day in every way the world was getting better and
better. It was moving toward a millennium of peace on earth that
would be brought about through human effort. God led our pioneers to recognize that hope for the future rested in God's grace
and on God's action, not on human action alone. Our first statement of beliefs in 1872 reflects this polemical edge when it speaks
of both the Second Coming and the millennium. Article 8 reads:

> We believe that the doctrine of the world's conversion and temporal
> millennium is a fable of these last days, calculated to lull men into a state
> of carnal security, and cause them to be overtaken by the great day of
> the Lord as a thief in the night; that the Second Coming of Christ is to
> precede not follow the millennium; for until the Lord appears, the papal
> power, with all its abominations, is to continue, the wheat and the tares
> grow together, and evil men and seducers wax worse and worse, as the
> Word of God declares.[1]

---

[1]Seventh-day Adventist statement of belief, 1872, Art. VIII, qtd. Appendix I,
"Seventh-day Adventist Statements of Belief," *Adventism in America,* 2d ed., ed.
Gary Land (Berrien Springs, MI: Andrews UP 1998) 192-3.

Coupled with this polemicism was an element of William Miller's Adventist theology that became an important part of early Adventism. Remember that William Miller had been a Deist. He had believed in a Deistic God, the clock-maker who set up the world and let it go on its own. Then he was converted to belief in a personal God who brought salvation in Jesus Christ and who promised that Jesus would return in the future. However, even though Miller converted from Deism, there was still a kind of Deism left in his bones when he viewed the Second Coming of Christ. For Miller, God had initiated a great prophetic countdown. In Scripture, God gave the sure word of prophecy that enabled humans to calculate this great countdown.

The course of the world's history proceeded precisely according to this plan. Giant gears of prophetic inevitability ground toward the final promise, and this predictable countdown provided motivation for repentance in the face of coming judgment. In a lecture he published in 1836, seven years before he believed the countdown would end, he wrote:

> Not one jot or tittle of the word of God shall fail. If he has spoken, it will come, however inconsistent it may look to us. Be admonished, then, and see to it that you are prepared. Compare *the vision* with the history of the kingdom, and where can you find a failure? Not one. Then, surely, here is evidence strong that the remainder will be accomplished in its time, and that time but seven years. Think, sinner, how good God is to give you notice, and prove it a thousand fold.[1]

For Miller this "sure word of prophecy" was the basis for the Advent hope. With certainty, Miller pointed to what he regarded as Scriptural premonitions of, *e.g.*, the French Revolution and the history of Turkey. Even the Song of Solomon was a prophetic book to Miller.[2]

In 1845, William Miller wrote a letter to Advent believers encouraging them to keep their faith. It was reprinted in the *Review* of August 19, 1851. In it, Miller included this telling sentence as he spoke of the surety of his conviction that Jesus would come again. "This to us is a source of great joy and it shows conclusively where our faith is founded and our hope predicated. It is upon the sure word of prophecy and no other evidence that we rely."

Both this image of the great prophetic countdown and the polemical tone of Advent hope are problematic today, however. First of all, we no longer live in an age characterized by naïve optimism that an earthly millennium is just around the corner. We no longer need to break down false millennial optimism with predictions of

---

[1] William Miller, *Evidence from Scripture and History of the Second Coming of Christ, about the Year 1843; Exhibited in a Course of Lectures* (Boston: Mussey 1840) 58.
[2] Miller 264.

doom and gloom. Instead we live in an age of despair and meaninglessness that doesn't need to hear about doom and gloom. It needs hope. More on that later.

Second, the great prophetic countdown model of hope, which was important as a means of awakening our pioneers to the promise of Christ's coming, nevertheless obscures certain important elements of New Testament hope, and it is New Testament hope, grounded in the gospel, that has the power to endure. Therefore let us notice several aspects of this gospel-oriented hope and examine its enduring qualities. As we do this we will see how certain aspects of Miller's model of the great prophetic countdown are problematic today. This is not to detract from Miller's positive contribution in calling attention to the importance of the second coming of Christ in an age of false optimism, or of his contribution to understanding the 2,300-day prophecy of Daniel. The world needed to hear what our pioneers said. But today it needs to hear the message in a different key, more carefully nuanced by the gospel. With this in mind we turn to five aspects of gospel-oriented hope as revealed in the New Testament.

## Person, Not Events

Hope that endures is a hope founded on the person of Jesus Christ, not on impersonal prophetic events. Notice how Paul, in Romans 5:1-2, bases our hope for the future on God's grace revealed in Jesus Christ. "Therefore, since we are justified by faith, we have peace with God through out Lord Jesus Christ, through whom we have obtained access to this grace in which we stand; and we boast in our hope of sharing the glory of God."[1]

Notice also how Paul ties future deliverance to the deliverance that we have already experienced in Christ. In 2 Cor. 1:9-10, speaking to his own present experience of ministry with eschatological overtones, Paul says, "Indeed, we felt that we had received the sentence of death so that we would rely not on ourselves but on God who raises the dead. He who rescued us from so deadly a peril will continue to rescue us; on him we have set our hope that he will rescue us again." Our hope for the future is tied inexorably to what God has already done for us in Christ Jesus.

John emphasizes the tie between our present experience with Christ and our hope for the future with his concept of eternal life, which begins now. In John 5:24 Jesus says, "Very truly, I tell you, anyone who hears my word and believes him who sent me has

[1]Rom. 5:1, 2. All biblical quotations in this chapter are taken from the 1989 edition of the *New Revised Standard Version*.

eternal life, and does not come under judgment, but has passed from death to life."

Now certainly this is not new to us, and yet there have been elements within Adventist eschatology that have militated against this basic New Testament conviction. The great prophetic countdown model of hope that has been with us since the time of Miller tends to focus on events, rather than the personal promise of Christ. Adventists have often referred to the study of eschatology as the study of "last day events." But for the New Testament the resurrection of Jesus was already a last day event. Eschatology isn't a matter of deciphering prophecy; rather it has to do with Christ's victory and the credibility that this victory gives to his promise.

Yet remember that when Miller spoke of the foundation of his faith upon which hope was predicated, he spoke of the "sure word of prophecy." Even though he believed in Christ as a personal savior, the foundation of hope, the evidence of hope, was this prophetic outline of events. This impersonal foundation of prophetic events as the basis of our hope obscures the New Testament emphasis that *Jesus* is our only basis for hope.

It has also led us to believe that from this great prophetic countdown we can ascertain in Scripture tomorrow's headlines today, and that, in turn, has led to a long tradition of prophetic speculation. But the fact is—whether we're thinking of Uriah Smith confidently predicting the vital role that Turkey would play in earth's history; the two women in the church where I was born rebuking my parents for bringing a child into the world when Armageddon (World War II) was already upon us; other Adventists during World War II predicting that Israel would not become an independent state; Adventists during the Vietnam War proclaiming that the end was at hand because Laos, Cambodia, and Vietnam were the kings of the East and Armageddon was upon us; Adventists during the 1970s gasoline shortage claiming that the National Sunday Law had begun; or Adventists today showing how the fall of Communism fits in with the very final events—we have never been any better than anyone else at predicting what tomorrow's headlines will be. We don't know better than anyone else how the current crisis the Middle East will turn out. History will continue to surprise us as it does everyone else until Christ comes.

But that is alright, for according to the New Testament, hope that endures is not based on impersonal events and our ability to predict them in advance. Our hope is based on the salvation that has come to us through Jesus Christ. It is Christ who has promised to return and because of the amazing grace revealed in Jesus' life, death, and resurrection, we can have hope that this promise will not let us down. If Adventism is to keep its hope alive, it must be a hope built on the foundation of God's grace.

## ASSURANCE, NOT ANXIETY

A second feature of gospel-oriented hope is assurance. We have already seen that Paul speaks of boasting in hope. There is a joyful confidence to New Testament hope. In 2 Cor. 3:12 Paul says, "since we have such a hope, we are very bold." And the author of Hebrews, in chapter 3, verse 6, says that we are God's house if we hold fast our confidence and pride in our hope.

This is not a boastful, arrogant hope in ourselves, but a hope that rests in assurance because it has grasped the reality of God's grace.

Those of us who have grown up in Adventism need only to remember our childhood to know that Adventist hope has not always been filled with assurance. Too often, anxiety and fear have held sway.

A few years ago, when I was teaching an eschatology class, I decided to kick off the first day of class with an exercise that would break the ice. I asked students if they had ever had dreams about the Second Coming. I thought we'd spend about half the period on this. I was unprepared for what followed. We filled the period and more. Most of the fifty students had had dreams about the Second Coming, and as they shared these dreams, the experience was both moving and haunting. One young man told of dreaming that the day came when his whole family saw the cloud the size of a man's hand in the sky. They rejoiced together that Jesus was coming. And as Jesus came down on the cloud, his sister, his mother, and his father started rising into the air to meet Him. He and his brother, on the other hand, stayed on the ground. They started jumping as hard as they could, jumping frantically, but gravity and guilt held them down even though their parents and sister floated up to meet Jesus in the air.

Another student told how he dreamed that he was at a railroad station waiting to get on a train. The conductor began calling the names of those who were to get on the train, and he recognized that the conductor was Jesus. Jesus called the names one by one, and one by one the people got on the train, until there were only a few left. Finally, every name had been called but his. And the conductor said, "All aboard." He went to the conductor and pleaded that he was to be on the train, too. But the conductor said, "Your name isn't here," and shut the door. The train started off from the station without him, and as it left the station, he saw the train lift into the sky and go up into the air, while he stood on the platform crying. He woke up, his pillow was wet with tears. He really was crying.

I asked the class if anyone had ever had a positive dream about the Second Coming. In that class of fifty students, there was not a single one. Can we be terribly surprised if a new generation of Adventists simply pushes eschatology into the background rather than subject their children to the same nightmares that they had as kids? Adventist hope will endure only if eschatology is consistent with salvation. Otherwise, the gospel becomes a good news-bad news joke. We are saved by grace, (or at least forgiven), but unless we get on the stick and get ready, we probably won't make it when Christ comes again. One can speculate that one of the reasons that—as the Valuegenesis study suggests—young people in Adventism have had such a difficult time grasping the reality of salvation by faith, is, at least in part, the contrary message they have heard in so much of our eschatological teaching. Hope that endures will be a hope founded on God's grace from beginning to end, so that grace is just as real in our eschatology as it is at the Cross. Hope that endures is hope with assurance.

## Trust, Not Calculation

It has been the tendency of Christians from the very beginning to wish to calculate the time of Jesus's return. In Acts 1:6, Luke tells us that the disciples were concerned about the time Jesus would restore the kingdom when he met with them after the resurrection and just before the ascension. But Jesus tells them that it is not for them to know the time or seasons God has established. Instead, Jesus pointed them to their mission. They would received the Holy Spirit and be witnesses to the ends of the earth.

The great prophetic time-clock approach to eschatology has never fully been able to break from its initial predilection for time-setting, and so, over and over again, we see offshoot groups who attempt to set dates. But even in the mainstream, there is too much general speculation about time that creates false expectations—the cry-wolf phenomenon—that detracts from the important issues of eschatology.

And there is another problem with this concentration on time. It exacerbates the sense of delay. Christians, of course, sensed a delay even in New Testament times, as we will see in a bit. But the sense of delay becomes greater as we speculate and create false expectations. It has been very hard for us to accept Jesus' very plain words—"It is not for you to know." It may not be for us to know, but we have spent a lot of time trying to figure it out anyway.

This speculation sets people up for disappointment, so that we go on feeling the aftershocks of the Great Disappointment. Now, one might argue that the New Testament already does that by emphasizing that Christ is coming soon. But there is a difference. The basis for New Testament imminence is the conviction that the resurrection of Jesus has already initiated the "last days" (see, *e.g.*, Heb. 1:2). As long as we stand on that foundation, hope can endure even if it seems like a long time for us. But when the foundation for imminence is a never-ending series of dubious speculations about the future that seem to keep pulling the rug from under our feet, hope inevitably wanes.

There is also another danger in all this. Once we create the sense of delay that grows from these false expectations and failed hopes, we are then forced to try and figure out the reason for the delay. And I've noticed something very interesting about this over the years. Those who give a reason for the delay always seem to suggest that it is because of what other people aren't doing. I remember sitting in a worker's meeting once and being told three different times in one day why I was guilty of causing the delay, and the three were contradictory. But if it is not our task to know the times and seasons or calculate the day, neither if is ours to worry about delay. Our focus is on the mission that Christ has given us. If we have assurance, then we can trust Christ and not be preoccupied with time, either the time of the coming, or the reason for the delay.

## Responsibility, Not Passivity

This leads to the important question of what we do while we wait for the Second Coming. New Testament hope is hope with a vision and a responsibility and a mission, not a passive sitting and waiting for Jesus' return. From the beginning, New Testament writers sought to warn their readers of what would appear to be a delay. Certainly, at the time of Matthew, Christians were wondering why the return had taken so long. In the parable of the talents in Matt. 25, the master goes away for a long time. Already it apparently seemed like a long time to Matthew's readers, but Matthew points to Christian responsibility in the interim. Burying the talent in the ground and waiting passively for Jesus' return is the wrong thing to do. Hope that endures, grounded in the gospel, is responsible hope. It is a hope that not only looks for a kingdom of justice and peace and love, but works in the present for justice and peace and love. It is a hope that seeks to multiply the values of the kingdom while the master is away.

As Jesus goes on to show in the final parable of Matt. 25, it is hope that feeds the hungry and clothes the naked and gives drink to the thirsty. Hope that endures is hope with a living, working vision of the kingdom of God that motivates us in the present and gives us assurance for the future.

We have not always understood this as we should. Take, for example, the issue of slavery in early Adventism. An unsigned editorial, presumably by Uriah Smith, published in the *Review* in 1856, argued:

> We say we bid all reforms, Godspeed! but some are laboring for reforms which they will never see accomplished. As much as anyone, from our very soul we detest and abhor that foul blot on our country—slavery! And our sympathies are with those whose hearts burn with the love of freedom, and who would desire to see the bondman loosed from his chains. But he who expects to see the land freed entirely from this curse, or even to see slavery contentedly confine itself within certain limits, we can but regard as laboring under a false hope; for the horned beast (Revelation 13:11), a symbol of our country, is that he shall speak as a dragon![1]

In the same year an R. F. Cottrell, while arguing against voting, wrote:

> "But you can vote against slavery," says one. Very well; supposing I do, what will be the effect? In the last great persecution, which is just before us, the decrees of the image will be against the "bond" as well as the free. Bondmen will exist then until the last—till God interposes to deliver His saints, whether bond or free. My vote then cannot free the slaves; and all apparent progress toward emancipation will only exasperate their master, and cause an aggravation of those evils that it was intended to cure. I cannot therefore, vote against slavery, neither can I vote for it.[2]

Fortunately not all early Adventists took this view. Ellen White spoke and worked against slavery.[3] Hope that endures is a responsible hope. Hope that is genuine never uses the future Kingdom as an excuse for not working toward the values of the Kingdom in the present. If God cares enough about the world to promise a day free from prejudice and suffering, war and oppression, how can we care so little that we fail to do what we can to end prejudice, suffering, war and oppression now.

## INCLUSIVE, NOT EXCLUSIVE

Finally, a gospel-oriented hope that endures is a hope with a view to the world. Those who hold this hope never claim it as their private possession, because they know that Jesus is the savior of the world. Matt. 1:21 and Rom. 15:12 speak of Jesus as the hope of the Gentiles. Christ is even the hope of the whole creation, which groans, waiting to be redeemed, as Paul shows us in Rom. 8:20, 21. In an intriguing passage in 1 Tim. 4:10, we find that Jesus is the savior of all human beings, especially those who believe. This is not

---

[1] "True Reforms and Reformers," *Review and Herald*, June 26, 1856: 68.
[2] R. F. Cottrell, "How Shall I Vote?," *Review and Herald*, Oct. 30, 1856: 205.
[3] See, for example, Ellen White, *Testimonies to the Church*, 9 vols (Mountain View, CA: Pacific 1948) 1: 264.

universalism, but neither is it a narrow sectarianism. Hope has a broad view. It includes a mission and concern for all people. It includes the recognition that God is working in the whole world with all people, not only with us. It took some time for our pioneers to recognize that. They believed the door was shut. But God led them eventually to open the door and reach out in one of the most impressive mission advances in Christianity. But groups easily regress to a private hope that sustains them as they build walls around themselves and wait for the apocalypse. New Testament hope, on the other hand, reaches out in mission and ethical responsibility to the world. Hope that endures is hope that includes all the world in the loving arms of God's gracious embrace.

## CONCLUSION

In a world where there is so much despair and discouragement, Adventists have something to offer: a confident, assured hope grounded in the grace of God which has been revealed in our savior, Jesus Christ. In *The Hobbit*, Christian scholar and fantasist J. R. R. Tolkien tells of a group of dwarves who had been displaced from their land by a mean dragon. These dwarfs sang of the day when a savior would come, their fortunes would be restored, and gold would flow in the rivers. But Tolkien adds, "This pleasant legend did not much affect their daily business."

For Adventists, it is different. Hope transforms daily business into a sense of mission and responsibility for the world. Without this hope, there is no solution to the problem of evil and death. As my friend Glen Greenwalt is fond of saying, "Even on a good day, children die." A God who cares cannot allow that to go on forever. But we have hope that there is a gracious and kind God whose promise can be trusted. That is a hope that the world needs, and that we can proclaim without being ashamed.

Some years ago, at a theological convention, I rode twenty-five floors down an elevator with two New Testament theologians, Robert Jewett and J. Christian Becker. They were arguing about the role of apocalyptic hope in Christian faith, especially Paul's presentation of faith. Becker was arguing, correctly, I believe, that apocalyptic hope is integral to the gospel. Jewett wasn't so sure. It was a fascinating discussion, and when we reached the ground floor and they separated, it was Becker who shot off the parting salvo, saying, "Just remember, without apocalyptic, the whole world is going to hell." And he was right.

And yet, we must remember that misplaced apocalyptic hope can create its own kind of hell right here on this earth, as Waco has demonstrated. It is important that we preserve hope, but it must be the right kind of hope in order to endure—and in order to deserve to endure. We will know that we have the right kind of hope when we can sing with conviction and vigor, "Our hope is built on nothing less than Jesus' blood and righteousness."

## 15

# Adventist Christianity on the Way to the Future

## Fritz Guy

The preceding chapters of this book have looked at particular
aspects of Adventist Christianity,[1] but in this concluding chapter I will try to paint a more general picture of Adventist Christianity on the way to the future.[2] It will be quickly apparent that the
picture I paint is what I perceive through my own eyes. These eyes
are far from perfect, but they are the only eyes I have, and I am
simply going to report what I see.

It may well seem to some—either more "conservative" or more
"liberal" than I—that what I am doing is more normative than de-

[1] As I explained in *Thinking Theologically* (Berrien Spring, MI: Andrews UP
1999), "Instead of the more customary term 'Adventism,' I regularly use 'Adventist Christianity' for two reasons. In the first place, I want to emphasize the
intrinsic relationship of Adventist faith and life to those of the larger Christian
community. . . . In the second place, I want to emphasize the spiritual and theological dynamic, rather than the organizational and institutional baggage of being
Adventist that seems often to be carried by the term 'Adventism'" (10). But
when I refer to Adventist Christianity I mean the Adventist community in North
America. Whatever insight or understanding I may have comes from life and
work almost entirely on this continent, and mostly in southern California (with a
few years each in Maryland and Michigan).

[2] The phrase "on the way" points to the fact of being in process—in transit
and transition. As an approximation of the Latin *in via*, it connotes both movement and incompleteness. The movement is inevitable and intentional—inevitable because the future (and the change it brings) cannot be forestalled; and
intentional because one need not let the future (and change) simply happen (one
can anticipate it, go out to meet it, and help to shape it). The incompleteness is
entailed by the fact that the process continues: it has not yet attained its goal.

The word "future" means, of course, what is coming, what is ahead, what
has not yet arrived; and it also means direction and destination. The idea of the
Adventist future has at least three dimensions: not only Adventist Christianity's
own future, arising from its past and present, but also its relation to the future of
the world and (even more important) to the future of God.

scriptive, and that my prediction is really a disguised prescription. And usually I am more comfortable prescribing rather than predicting. But my intention here is to describe the Adventist future as I think it will actually turn out to be—recognizing, of course, that my vision is faulty even when I look at the present, and that my view of the future may be seriously flawed or distorted or both. But that view is what it is.

The general picture I see is simple, clear, and (I hope) interesting: *The Adventist future will be more "liberalized"*[1] *(that is, more open, inclusive, and culturally aware) and more "pluralistic" (that is, more self-consciously diverse) than is the Adventist present.* I will endeavor to explain this picture by means of four straightforward theses, of which the first is the most important and will receive the most attention.

*Thesis 1: The Adventist future will be shaped in part by a number of "liberalizing" theological factors in the Adventist past and present.*

On the spectrum of contemporary Christianity, Adventist Christianity is obviously on the conservative side. Most of us are comfortable here, with a theology and lifestyle that remain largely traditional, and with sociopolitical views that tend toward the right rather than the left.[2] Nevertheless, in the Adventist heritage are some surprisingly "non-conservative" (even "anti-conservative") "liberalizing" ingredients that deserve attention. Some of these ingredients are primarily theological and some are primarily historical; all are part of the present reality of Adventist Christianity, and all will help to shape its future.

• The first—the earliest and most fundamental—of the theological ingredients is a profound commitment to Scripture. This commitment is reflected in our official affirmation of the Bible as "the infallible revelation of . . . [God's] will"— that is, "the standard of character" and "the test of experience," as well as "the authoritative

---

[1]There is no reason why the connotation of words like "liberal" and "liberalizing" should be determined by persons who are hostile to their authentic content. It may have been the political campaigning of Ronald Reagan that made "the L-word" an epithet; in any case, its use as a negative value-judgment (rather than an objective description) is now common in American political and religious rhetoric. In any event, the word may refer to a particular intellectual position (as in the phrase "nineteenth-century liberalism") or to a general attitude of intellectual openness (as in "liberal-mindedness"). It is in the latter sense that the word is throughout in this discussion. But it is used descriptively, not as a positive or negative value-judgment.

[2]Yet Adventist Christianity is not in general "fundamentalist," and in some ways it is not properly classified as "evangelical," since that once-general term has been commandeered as a partisan self-designation by, for example, the groups that constitute the National Association of Evangelicals. See Roger L. Dudley and Edwin I. Hernandez, "Do Adventist Voters Lean Left or Right?" *Spectrum* 23.3 (Oct. 1993): 5-13.

revealer of doctrines, and the trustworthy record of God's acts in history."[1] The remarkable fact is that reading the Bible—really *reading* it—thoughtfully and intelligently, *document by document* (the way it was written and was originally intended to be read), letting each document speak in its own distinctive voice[2]—leads a person from biblical literalism[3] to biblical literacy.

Curiously, many people who have the most to say about the authority of the Bible seem not to have actually *read* very much of it. For the more we truly read it (instead of merely making claims about it and quoting it to prove that our own theology is correct[4]) the more evident it becomes that biblical literalism is mistaken.[5] The biblical documents were obviously written by a variety of persons with different vocations, temperaments, social environments, and cultural contexts. And they were written for a multiplicity of purposes—to recount ancient stories, to worship and instruct, to comfort and inspire, to evangelize.

And as we read (and listen),[6] it becomes increasingly clear that it is not a sentence or paragraph here or there but the Bible *as a whole* that is "the infallible revelation of . . . [God's] will."[7] The various

---

[1]"Fundamental Beliefs of Seventh-day Adventists," par. 1.

[2]See Charles M. Wood, "The Canon of Christian Understanding" and "Christian Understanding as a Critical Task," *The Formation of Christian Understanding: An Essay in Theological Hermeneutics* (Philadelphia: Westminster 1981) 82-120.

[3]To be precise, one should speak of degrees of literalism; I do not personally know anyone who holds to an absolute literalism, nor do I know anyone who does not let scientific knowledge influence her or his understanding of Scripture. Without any explicit Biblical evidence, readers of Scripture believe, for example, that the earth is spherical, rotates on its axis, and revolves around the sun, and that the sun came into existence at least as soon as the earth. Here I use the term "Biblical literalism" to point to a *relatively* literalistic reading of Scripture, recognizing a minimum of metaphorical and symbolic language.

[4]A danger of theological polemics is the almost irresistible temptation to use Scripture as the servant of one's theology rather than as its master and judge.

[5]See the objections to Alden Thompson, *Inspiration: Hard Questions, Honest Answers* (Hagerstown, MD: Review 1991) raised by various contributors to Frank Holbrook and Leo R. Van Dolson, eds., *Issues in Revelation and Inspiration,* Adventist Theological Society Occasional Papers 1 (Berrien Springs, MI: Adventist Theological Society 1992) 31-199. A curiosity of current Adventist theological discussion is that those who most emphasize the humanity of Christ often have an almost docetic view of Scripture.

[6]See Ellen G. White, *Thoughts from the Mount of Blessing* (Mountain View, CA: Pacific 1896) 1: "Let us in imagination go back to that scene, and, as we sit with the disciple on the mountainside, enter into the thoughts and feelings that filled their hearts. Understanding what the words of Jesus meant to those who heard them, we may discern in them a new vividness and beauty, and may also gather for ourselves their deeper lessons."

[7]See Dalton D. Baldwin, "Openness for Renewal Without Destructive Pluralism: The Dilemma of Doctrinal Dissent," *Christ in the Classroom: Approaches to the Integration of Faith and Learning* 3 (Washington: Department of Education,

authors and documents, with their different purposes and perspectives, are like spotlights of various colors shining on a magnificent sculpture: it is in the totality of illumination that we see most clearly what we are looking at. To turn on a single spotlight may highlight certain features, but for the best comprehension of the sculpture, we need all the light we can get. A preoccupation with "proof texts" and "problem texts"—emphasizing the former and explaining (or explaining away) the latter—is the result of a misunderstanding of the nature and function of the biblical revelation.[1]

• Perhaps the most surprising of all the "liberalizing" ingredients in Adventist Christianity is the gospel. The gospel leads to genuine spiritual liberation as we get clear about the relation of God's love and our behavior.

The truth that God is love is, of course, the heart and center of the gospel, the "good news" of Christianity; and to be "Adventist" is simply to have a particular eschatological perspective on this truth. It is often (and appropriately) noted that in Ellen White's "Conflict of the Ages" series of books, the first three words and the last three words are the simple statement that "God is love"; the whole story of salvation is surrounded by this affirmation of the real nature of God.[2]

And precisely because God *is* love, life now and in the future comes to each of us as a *gift,* not as a reward for being "good enough" or doing "well enough" or thinking "correctly enough." A gift is not something we earn or deserve, and the person who gives it would be insulted if we tried to pay for it. When we receive a gift the only proper response is to accept it with appreciation and thanks.

But (and this is the great paradox of the gospel) this message that God *really is love* is difficult for us to believe and easy to forget. We Adventists have been talking about "Christ our righteousness" at least since 1888,[3] but too many of us are still "closet legalists,"[4]

---

General Conference of Seventh-day Adventists 1989) 65-6: "It is the underlying harmony of the Bible as a whole that is infallible."

[1]A wider recognition of the "canonical" nature of Biblical authority would eliminate much if not all of the opposition to the ordination of women to professional ministry.

[2]*The Story of Patriarchs and Prophets* (Mountain View, CA: Pacific 1913) 33; *The Great Controversy between Christ and Satan* (Mountain View, CA: Pacific 1911) 678.

[3]See Arthur G. Daniells, *Christ Our Righteousness* (Washington: Ministerial Association of Seventh-day Adventists 1926); Norval F. Pease, *By Faith Alone* (Mountain View, CA: Pacific 1962) 107-76; LeRoy Edwin Froom, *Movement of Destiny,* rev. ed. (Washington: Review 1978) *passim*; Robert J. Wieland, *The 1888 Message: An Introduction* (Nashville: Southern 1980).

[4]This phenomenon may be called "the Adventist disease."

and the rest of us are recovering legalists. Somewhere deep inside the Adventist psyche is a suspicion that we will miss salvation if we aren't good *enough*.[1] Even if we know that everlasting life is a gift, we think we have to show by our good behavior that we appreciate it (and thus in some sense retroactively deserve it); and we suspect that if we don't, God will take it back.

We say that human beings are saved by God's grace; but we also say that grace enables us to overcome sin. This is of course true: "God can do more about sin than forgive it." But we often add (by implication if not explicitly) that we had better be overcoming sin, because if we aren't, we are not actually saved and our ultimate destiny is in doubt. Thus overcoming sin becomes a requirement instead of a gift, grace is turned into a demand, and our attention is focused on how well we are doing—how completely we are gaining the "victory over sin." This makes us spiritually anxious and insecure, because we are not at all sure that we are doing *well enough* (or, more correctly, we are quite sure that we are *not* doing well enough). We start wondering and worrying (and arguing) about *how well we have to do* in order to be acceptable to God.[2] Even worse, we start worrying about how well *others* are doing.

But the truth is that we are *already* accepted. The good news is that doing well enough or being good enough or thinking correctly enough is not the crucial issue. There are many reasons for right behavior, good theology, and healthy spirituality; but being accepted by God is not one of those reasons. The gospel is the good news that in Christ salvation has been given to *all humanity,* and that all are saved except those who reject the gift.[3] God respects human freedom; life with God is not forced on anyone. But—and this is

---

[1] See Roger L. Dudley with V. Bailey Gillespie, *Valuegenesis: Faith in the Balance* (Riverside, CA: La Sierra UP 1992) 272: "We have seen that though our youth have heard the words of the Gospel of righteousness by grace through faith, the Adventist emphasis on behavioral standards has led the majority to believe that they must somehow do something to merit salvation. It is very difficult for an Adventist adolescent to emotionally accept the fact that his or her salvation rests entirely on the merits of Jesus Christ and the he or she cannot contribute to it in any way."

[2] On perfectionism, see Hans K. La Rondelle, *Perfection and Perfectionism: A Dogmatic-Ethical Study of Biblical Perfection and Phenomenal Perfectionism* (Berrien Springs, MI: Andrews UP 1971); Herbert E. Douglass, Hans K. La Rondelle, C. Mervyn Maxwell, and Edward Heppenstall, *Perfection: The Impossible Possibility* (Nashville: Anvil-Southern 1975).

[3] In computer jargon, salvation is the "default setting" (analogous to "startup preferences" for type size and style, margins, etc.) for the destiny of every human being, and will be actualized unless it is altered by one's own choice. The familiar and crucial qualifying words of Jn. 3:16, "whoever believes," are best understood as referring to one's acceptance of the reality of God's love for oneself and thus, in the words of our present metaphor, not changing the setting.

the crucial point—the gift has already been *given*. One does not have to *qualify* for it; one has only to *accept* it. For, to put Paul's words into current American language: "Just as one person doing it wrong got all humanity into trouble with God, so one person doing it right put all humanity right with God."[1] God is "the Savior of all humanity."[2] *This* is the good news.

If (and only if) we are clear about the gospel, we can talk fervently (and non-legalistically) about the profound importance of living in the light of the *torah,* the teaching of God.[3] We can be enthusiastic about the spiritual maturity and moral improvement that come through love, justice, and hope.[4] The fact that God's ideal for us is "higher than the highest human thought can reach"[5] can be seen as an invitation, not a demand.

• A third "liberalizing" ingredient in authentic Adventist Christianity is the idea of "present truth,"[6] the spirit of theological discovery. This idea points to the fact that, as Jack Provonsha has written, "each generation must in some ways be a first generation all over again."[7] Each generation is called to build on the foundation of the past, but it is called to *build,* not just *preserve.*[8]

---

[1]Rom. 6:18; translation based on Eugene Peterson's *The Message.* The *NRSV* translation reads, "Just as one man's trespass led to condemnation for all, so one man's act of righteousness leads to justification and life for all." For a brief discussion of the universalistic thrust of the New Testament, see my essay, "The Universality of God's Love," *The Grace of God, The Will of Man: A Case for Arminianism,* ed. Clark H. Pinnock (Grand Rapids: Zondervan 1989), esp. 42-6.

[2]1 Tim. 4:10.

[3]One of the most unfortunate phenomena in the history of religious language has been the translation of the Hebrew word *torah* by the Greek *nomos,* the Latin *lex,* and the English *law.* The positive connotation of teaching or instruction that is prominent in the Hebrew word is eclipsed in the others by the dominant idea of legal compulsion.

[4]The principles are often illustrated rather than specified in the Bible, which is for the most part better understood as a "casebook" than as a "code book." See Thompson, *Inspiration* 98-109.

[5]Ellen G. White, *Education* (Mountain View, CA: Pacific 1903) 18.

[6]*Present Truth* was the name of the first Seventh-day Adventist periodical; it was taken from the King James Version of 2 Pet. 1:12 and explained by James White in an introductory note on the front page of the inaugural issue (1.1, July 1849): "In Peter's time there was present truth, or truth applicable to that present time. The Church . . . [has] ever had a present truth. The present truth now, is that which shows present duty . . . ." Thirty-five years later, Ellen White echoed her husband's words: "There was a present truth in the days of Luther,—a truth at that time of special importance; there is a present truth for the church today" (*Controversy* 118; cp. 143).

[7]Jack W. Provonsha, *A Remnant in Crisis* (Hagerstown: Review 1993) 13.

[8]Ellen White wrote several times about the progressive nature of the truth. See, for example, *Testimonies for the Church,* 9 vols. (Mountain View, CA: Pacific 1949) 5: 706-9 (originally published 1889): "Whenever the people of God are growing in grace, they will be constantly obtaining a clearer understanding of His

The most important lesson to be learned from the experience of 1844 is the fact that after Tuesday, October 22, a day of great disappointment,[1] came Wednesday, October 23, a day of new beginning.[2]

Word. They will discern new light and beauty in its sacred truths. This has been true in the history of the church in all ages, and thus it will continue to the end. But as real spiritual life declines, it has ever been the tendency to cease to advance in the knowledge of the truth. [People] rest satisfied with the light already received from God's Word, and discourage any further investigation of the Scriptures. They become conservative, and seek to avoid discussion. . . ."

"Search the Scriptures," *Advent Review and Sabbath Herald*, July 26, 1892: 465; rptd. *Counsels to Writers and Editors* (Nashville: Southern 1946) 37: "We have many lessons to learn, and many, many to unlearn. God and heaven alone are infallible. Those who think that they will never have to give up a cherished view, never have occasion to change an opinion, will be disappointed."

"Christ Our Hope," *Advent Review and Sabbath Herald*, Dec. 20, 1892: 785; rptd. *Counsels to Writers and Editors* 33: "There is no excuse for anyone in taking the position that there is no more truth to be revealed, and that all our expositions of Scripture are without an error. The fact that certain doctrines have been held as truth for many years by our people is not a proof that our ideas are infallible. Age will not make error into truth, and truth can afford to be fair. No true doctrine will lose anything by close investigation."

[1]See Arthur W. Spalding, *Origin and History of Seventh-day Adventists*, 4 vols. (Washington: Review 1961) 1: 98; C. Mervyn Maxwell, *Tell It to the World: The Story of Seventh-day Adventists*, rev. ed. (Mountain View, CA: Pacific 1977) 48-49; George R. Knight, *Millennial Fever and the End of the World* (Boise, ID: Pacific 1993) 217-24.

The most memorable account is the poignant recollection of Hiram Edson contained in an undated manuscript fragment located in the Heritage Room of the James White Library at Andrews University and published in *The Disappointed: Millerism and Millenarianism in the Nineteenth Century,* ed. Ronald L. Numbers and Jonathan M. Butler (Bloomington: Indians UP 1987) 215:

> . . . Our expectations were raised high, and thus we looked for our coming Lord until the clock tolled 12 at midnight. The day had then passed and our disappointment became a certainty. Our fondest hopes and expectations were blasted, and such a spirit of weeping came over us as I never experienced before. It seemed that the loss of all earthly friends could have been no comparison. We wept, and wept, till the day dawn.
>
> I mused in my own heart, saying, My advent experience has been the richest and brightest of all my christian experience. If this had proved a failure, what was the rest of my christian experience worth? Has the Bible proved a failure? Is there no God—no heaven—no golden home city—no paradise? Is all this but a cunningly devised fable? Is there no reality to our fondest hopes and expectation of these things? And thus we had something to grieve and weep over, if all our fond hopes were lost. As I said, we wept till the day dawn.

[2]Spalding 1: 98-113; Maxwell 51-4; Knight 304-19. Again Edson's memoir provides a vivid account: "Heaven seemed opened to my view, and I saw distinctly, and clearly, that instead of our High Priest coming out of the Most Holy [Place] of the heavenly sanctuary to come to this earth on the tenth day of the seventh month, at the end of the 2300 days, that he for the first time entered on

Cherishing the heritage that gave them their religious identity and vision, the progressive Adventists of 1844 were responsive to new facts, new circumstances, and new needs. This was an Adventist Christianity deeply concerned with "present truth," an Adventist Christianity truly "on the way to the future." The spirit of theological discovery enabled the progressive Adventists to admit that they had been wrong about some things[1] (but not everything) and to move past their disappointment toward the better understandings they knew would come. And theological discoveries did come: the continuing ministry of Christ on behalf of humanity, the seventh day as holy time, the prophetic role of Ellen Harmon, conditional immortality (which eliminated the horrendous notion of a soul suffering in an ever-burning hell),[2] the religious significance of physical health, tithing as the beginning of financial stewardship, and the expansion of the Adventist horizon as the church undertook a literally global mission.[3]

This remarkable series of theological discoveries was complemented[4] by a willingness to abandon invalid or inadequate views—

that day the second apartment of that sanctuary; and that he had a work to perform in the Most Holy before coming to this earth. That he came to the marriage at that time; in other words, to the Ancient of days, to receive a kingdom, dominion, and glory; and we must wait for his return from the wedding; and my mind was directed to the tenth ch. of Rev where I could see the vision had spoken and did not lie; the seventh angel had began [sic] to sound; we had eaten the littl [sic] book; it has been sweet in our mouth, and it had now become bitter in our belly, embittering our whole being. That we must prophesy again, etc., and that when the seventh angel began to sound, the temple of God was opened in heaven, and there was seen in his temple the ark of his testament, etc." (Numbers and Butler 216)

Maxwell 51-2 raises the question of the precise nature of Edson's experience: "Did Hiram Edson, as some suggest, have a prophetic vision in the cornfield? He may have. He does not, however, state that he actually saw Jesus enter the most holy place. Instead, in his best-known account, he says that he saw 'that' Jesus entered it on October 22. In a different account he says nothing about 'seeing' anything, but recalls instead that he heard a voice speaking to him. Possibly he himself did not know exactly how his valuable insights came to him."

[1]See, for example, Joseph Marsh in *Voice of Truth*, Nov. 7, 1844, 166, qtd. Knight 230-1: "We cheerfully admit that we have been mistaken in the *nature* of the event we expected would occur on the tenth of the seventh month. . . ."

[2]See Ellen G. White, *Life Sketches of Ellen G. White* (Mountain View, CA: Pacific 1915) 48-50

[3]See P. Gerard Damsteegt, *Foundations of the Seventh-day Adventist Message and Mission* (Grand Rapids: Eerdmans 1977).

[4]Theological change is evident also in the various ways the doctrine of the sanctuary in heaven has functioned in the history of Adventist Christianity: first as a way of understanding the disappointment of 1844, then as a reinforcement of the continuing importance of the Fourth Commandment, later as a symbol of "victorious living," and more recently as a mark of Adventist identity and orthodoxy, and as a call to moral seriousness. See Roy Adams, *The Sanctuary Doctrine:*

the "shut door,"[1] for example, obedience to the law as the crucial issues in salvation,[2] and opposition to the historic Christian notion of God as Trinity.[3]

• A fourth, unexpectedly "liberalizing" element in Adventist Christianity is the Advent hope: the brightness of an ultimate future with God makes it impossible to be pessimistic about the proximate future. The Advent hope means knowing that the future will bring the completion—not the frustration—of everything that is good in human existence. Whatever one is looking forward to—professional success and satisfaction; children or grandchildren; financial security—the personal presence of Jesus will be even better. It will bring the continuation of the best aspects of humanness—the love of family and friends, the awareness that our lives matter to God, the experience of beauty, and the joy of discovery and understanding. It will also bring transformation into everlasting life in a world where neither human existence nor the natural environment is distorted by the consequences of sin.

So it doesn't make sense for an Adventist to be a pessimist. This doesn't mean that no Adventists *are* pessimists; it means that the pessimism is a temperamental contradiction of one's belief. Because the future is God's future as well as humanity's future, it offers "new possibilities of grace, new challenges for action, new opportunities for joy";[4] and because the final outcome is sure, one need not be overly anxious about what will happen in the meantime. Talk about the "time of trouble," is a reminder that the future will not be all fun and games; but our primary focus of attention should be the ultimate future.

Even the announcement of eschatological judgment[5] is "good news," because it means that God is more real, and therefore more powerful, than all the insanity, perversity, and brutality of our world. The days of misunderstanding, injustice, and violence are numbered; they will not go on forever. This is good news for every person and for the whole world. Everyone knows what it is to be misunderstood and misjudged—to go the second, third, or fourth

---

Three Approaches in the Seventh-day Adventist Church, Andrews U Dissertation Series 1 (Berrien Springs: Andrews UP 1981); and Jon Dybdahl, "The Sanctuary as a Call to Moral Seriousness," Spectrum, 14.1 (Aug. 1983): 47-51.

[1]See Damsteegt 149-64; Knight 313-4.

[2]See the references in note 13 above.

[3]See [LeRoy E. Froom, W. E. Read, and Roy Allen Anderson] Seventh-day Adventists Answer Questions on Doctrine: An Explanation of Certain Major Aspects of Seventh-day Adventist Belief (Washington: Review 1957), 35-37, 645-6. See also LeRoy Edwin Froom, Movement of Destiny (Washington: Review 1971) 322-23.

[4]La Sierra University Church, "A Sabbath Liturgy for Spring," Riverside, 1994.

[5]Rev. 14:6.

mile and be criticized because one didn't run fast enough and carry a back pack. The news media continually bring reports of horrendous tribal warfare by terrorism and atrocity, resulting from hatreds that are deep and old. The fact of final judgment means that, however much misunderstanding and prejudice, domination, and exploitation there is in our world and even in one's own life—however bad things may seem, and however bad they may actually *be*—in the long run God's intention for human existence will be realized.

• A fifth "progressive" and "liberalizing" theological element in authentic Adventist Christianity is its recognition of "spiritual gifts," particularly the idea of a contemporary prophetic witness, which includes by its very nature the possibility of new theological understandings and ecclesial enterprises. It is precisely the vocation of a prophet to articulate insights that go beyond what is already known, believed, and experienced; a prophet is by definition a "theological discoverer."

This has been the actual Adventist experience with the ministry of Ellen White, whose encouragement (and sometimes insistence) helped to initiate major Adventist efforts in publishing, health care, world missions, and education. Theologically, she encouraged and exemplified openness to the possibility of new and more adequate understandings: "The truth," she said, "is an advancing truth, and we must walk in the increasing light."[1]

• A sixth "liberalizing" theological factor is the Sabbath: the experience of time for being fully human relativizes all hierarchical relationships and all efforts to produce, achieve, and accomplish. For Sabbath time is uniquely graced time; it is time that comes, like human existence itself, as a gift. It is a time when no person is defined as master or servant, rich or poor, time when every person experiences the reality and dignity of being a daughter or son of God. It is time that unmasks all human pretensions to power and authority over others, time that discloses humanness in authentic relationship to God, to God's world, and to God's whole human family. It is the liberating (and thus "liberalizing") time of *Shabbat shalom*.

• A seventh "liberalizing" factor in Adventist Christianity is its moral seriousness, which has this kind of impact in at least two different ways. On the one hand, the Adventist understanding of the multidimensional unity of human personhood as the convergence and integration of moral, physical, spiritual, and social dimensions of human existence leads to ethical concerns about racial and gen-

[1] *Counsels to Writers and Editors* 33 (reprinting an article appearing in the March 25, 1890, issue of the *Review and Herald*).

der justice, stewardship of global resources and the natural environment, and the expansion of personal freedom as far as possible. On the other hand, the Adventist sense of stewardship leads to financial discipline and personal frugality, and hence to upward mobility with "liberalizing" tendencies to which I will allude below.

These "liberalizing" theological factors provide the conceptual foundation for a number of historical factors which are much more obvious but would not be so powerful (if, indeed, they would exist at all) without their theological support.

*Thesis 2: The Adventist future will also be shaped in part by a number of "liberalizing" socio-historical factors in the Adventist past and present .*

Clearly the most important historical factor in the "liberalizing" of Adventist Christianity is education, a logical outgrowth of the Adventist idea of "present truth." Knowledge and critical thinking about human experience and the natural world lead to questions about religious doctrine, about lifestyle, and about church policies and practices.

Ever since Socrates was condemned for corrupting the youth of Athens, education has been subversive of established ways of thinking and therefore of established authority.[1] This explains why educational enterprises are usually regarded with considerable ambivalence by organized religion, government, and the general population. Educational institutions are prized for the prestige they bring to their sponsors; and they are at the same time accused of undermining traditional beliefs, practices, and values. Yet we Adventists have been "true believers" in education. In all ethnic groups, Adventists in North America are significantly better educated than the general population.[2]

Paradoxically, to the extent Adventist education is successful in teaching students "to be thinkers, not mere reflectors of other . . . [people's] thought,"[3] it enables them to do their own thinking about religion. When the church prepares its college and university graduates to be "morally courageous" as a countercultural force in

---

[1]See Neil Postman and Charles Weingartner, *Teaching as a Subversive Activity* (New York: Delacorte 1969).

[2]See Monte Sahlin, "Who Are North American Adventists?" *Spectrum,* 21.2 (Mar. 1991): 18: "The percentage of Adventists with less than a high school diploma is half that of the general population in the United States and Canada. Two out of five Adventist males and a third of the females have college degrees. The majority have spent some time in postsecondary schools. . . . The percentage of highly educated church members is significant in all ethnic groups, In fact, the percentage of males with college degrees among black and Hispanic Adventists may be slightly greater than among white Adventists."

[3]White, *Education* 17. See also William G. Johnsson, "Seven Factors Fragmenting the Church," *Adventist Review,* May 5, 1994: 13.

society,[1] it cannot prevent them from becoming a countercultural force in Adventist Christianity too. Furthermore, expanding knowledge and developing skills facilitate upward socioeconomic mobility, often accompanied by an increasing interest in the contemporary world and a corresponding decline in otherworldly concerns and commitments.

• A second historical factor is the Adventist interest and investment in health and healing. This has several consequences. For example, understanding the medical sciences (such as biochemistry and neurophysiology) leads to scientific thinking about the earth sciences (including geology and paleontology). One cannot enthusiastically endorse the medical sciences because they are useful and then simply discount the earth sciences because they are troublesome. Nor can one properly use *a priori* theological arguments to come to conclusions about empirical reality—whether we are considering the nature of biblical inspiration[2] or the age of the earth. If one is going to think scientifically, empirical questions must be answered with objective evidence. And facts are facts. In spite of all we know about the fallibility of science and the foibles of scientists, and about paradigms and paradigm shifts in the history of science,[3] facts and their logical implications[4] must still be taken into account. A failure to do so, however highly motivated by pastoral or ecclesial concerns, undermines our credibility. There is no substitute for honesty with the evidence. "Truth," as Ellen White put it, "can afford to be fair."[5]

The Adventist interest in health has also produced some other "liberalizing" effects. For example,[6] the level of remuneration of

[1]See Robert Folkenberg, "The Challenge for La Sierra University," *University Vitæ Extra* (Feb. 3, 1994) 3. The term "countercultural force" occurred in the public presentation but does not appear in the published version.

[2]For an Adventist endorsement of a deductive approach to an understanding of the nature of Scripture, see John T. Baldwin, "Inspiration, the Natural Sciences, and a Window of Opportunity," *Journal of the Adventist Theological Society* 5.1 (Spring 1994): 134.

[3]Beginning with the influential work of Thomas S. Kuhn, *The Structure of Scientific Revolutions* (Chicago: U of Chicago P 1962). For an example of the ensuing discussion, see Imre Lakatos and Alan Musgrave, eds., *Criticism and the Growth of Knowledge* (Cambridge: CUP 1970).

[4]Science involves more than the reporting of data (facts); it also entails the coherent interpretation of data (theory). So the claim, "We don't dispute the facts; we just reject the theory," is not scientifically credible unless it is accompanied by a more adequate theory.

[5]*Counsels to Writers and Editors* 35 (reprinting a Dec. 20, 1892, article in the *Review and Herald*).

[6]Another example is the prominence of health care in Adventist life and mission, which has encouraged thinking about sin, salvation, and the Christian life using metaphors of disease and healing (or wholeness)—metaphors that soften the legal language of "transgression" and "justification," imply a gradual development

health-care personnel (especially physicians) in the United States facilitates swift upward mobility that is accompanied not only by the
increasing interest in the contemporary world we noted earlier in
connection with education, but also by increasing political influence in the church
  • A third "liberalizing" historical factor is Adventist Christianity's sense of world mission, symbolized by the apocalyptic angel flying across the sky carrying a message for every nation, every ethnic
group, every language, and every culture.[1]
  Communicating the Advent message leads inevitably to interaction with contemporary life and thought. For to communicate successfully requires an understanding of the intended audience, including its language. It is obvious that if we are going to speak to
the Chinese culture, we must learn to speak a Chinese language. It
is perhaps less obvious, but certainly just as true, that if we are going to communicate to a modern, secular, and scientific culture, we
must learn to speak modern, secular, and scientific languages. But
learning a new language entails an investment of time and effort to
understand not only words and sentence structure and grammar,
but also ways of thinking and valuing and being. This means truly
*listening* and *hearing,* and the inevitable result will be new ideas and
insights. For there can be no real communication without genuine
conversation, and genuine conversation changes all its participants.
It goes like this: if I expect you to listen to me, I must truly listen to
you;[2] if I truly listen to you, I will learn from you; and if I learn
from you, I will be a little more like you by the end of the conversation.
  Thus an encounter with cultural diversity, whether ethnic or
intellectual, leads to a recognition of different ways of thinking,
feeling, and acting. The result is not necessarily a thorough-going
cultural relativism, in which all beliefs, attitudes, and values are regarded as equally valid and appropriate. The result is, rather, an
awareness that no one culture or subculture is a perfect expression
of humanness, and that every culture, including one's own, should
be open to the possibility of learning from the others.

---

rather than absolute contrast between life "in the world" and "life in Christ," and
relativize the notion of "perfection." Besides the motto of Loma Linda University, "To make man whole," there is the linguistic connection of the word "salvation" to the Latin *salvus,* which means both "safe" and "healthy."
  [1]Rev. 14:6.
  [2]This is a version of what Dalton D. Baldwin has named "The Golden Rule
of Evangelism." For a more formal description of the "ideal speech situation," see
Jürgen Habermas, *The Theory of Communicative Action,* 2 vols., trans. Thomas
McCarthy (Boston: Beacon 1984-7) 1: 17; and William C. Placher, *Unapologetic
Theology: A Christian Voice in a Pluralistic Conversation* (Louisville: Westmin-
ster/Knox 1989) 76-7, 105-22.

• A fourth "liberalizing" historical factor is the presence and social impact of Adventist institutions, which bring stability, prosperity, and community recognition. These factors in turn lead to a
sense of respectability that contrasts sharply with Adventist Christianity's original self-understanding as a marginalized "remnant." The
persecuted minority becomes a *prophetic* minority.[1] The idea of
"remnant" remains, but its existential meaning is transformed.

Also, as they facilitate interaction with a larger social, cultural,
and intellectual world, Adventist institutions become places of cultural and intellectual openness. They provide contexts for thinking
critically and constructively about what it means to be Adventist as
an academic or as a health-care professional, and for thinking about
the fundamental nature, meaning, and mission of Adventist Christianity.

• Finally (for this discussion), a fifth "liberalizing" historical factor is the Adventist enthusiasm for printing and publishing, which
leads to a proliferation of Adventist voices.

Beginning with the Millerite Adventist *Signs of the Times* in
1840, the Seventh-day Adventist *Present Truth* in 1849, the *Second
Advent Review and Sabbath Herald* in 1850, and *The Youth's Instructor*
in 1952, Adventist Christianity has given birth to a host of periodicals of various sorts (and varying quality). Today's list runs the gam-
ut from general and official publications like the *Adventist Review*
and the union conference papers to specialized magazines like *Ministry* and the *Journal of Adventist Education* and to unofficial publications like *Spectrum, Our Firm Foundation,* and *Adventist Today,* all
promoting particular viewpoints. While the intention and effect of
some periodicals has been anything but progressive, the very fact of
their existence and diversity is in principle a "liberalizing" force.

The same can be said for books. Some have served to preserve
traditional views: we think of *Daniel and Revelation,* by Uriah
Smith;[2] along with *Bible Readings for the Home;*[3] and, more recently,
*Seventh-day Adventists Believe.*[4] Some have encouraged new ideas
along with the old: *Questions on Doctrine,*[5] for example, and the *Sev-

[1]See Jack Provonsha, "The Church as Prophetic Minority," *Pilgrimage of
Hope,* ed. Roy Branson (Takoma Park, MD: Association of Adventist Forums
1986) 98-107.
[2]Uriah Smith, *Daniel and the Revelation: The Response of History to the Voice of
Prophecy* (Nashville: Southern 1897).
[3]*Bible Readings for the Home* (Washington: Review 1915; rev. ed. 1949).
[4][P. Gerard Damsteegt et al.,] *Seventh-day Adventists Believe: A Biblical Exposition of 27 Fundamental Doctrines* (Washington: Ministerial Association, General
Conference of Seventh-day Adventists 1988).
[5]See above for complete reference.

*enth-day Adventist Bible Commentary.*[1] Some have been more deliberately innovated: *Festival of the Sabbath*[2] and *Pilgrimage of Hope,*[3] edited by Roy Branson; *The Openness of God,* by Richard Rice;[4] and
*Inspiration,* by Alden Thompson.[5] Some have offered alternative
views of doctrines and events: *Prophetess of Health,* by Ronald
Numbers;[6] *The Adventist Crisis of Spiritual Identity,* by Desmond and
Gillian Ford;[7] *Betrayal,* by Merikay McLeod;[8] and *The Word Was
Made Flesh,* by Ralph Larson.[9] Whatever their content or intent,
these books reflect a diversity that is both a cause and a consequence of the "liberalizing" of Adventist Christianity.

After thinking about these "liberalizing" factors in Adventist
Christianity, I would offer two observations. The first is the remarkably pervasive influence of Ellen White. While her work is often regarded as a symbol and bulwark of conservatism, I see it also
as a major factor in the "liberalizing" of Adventist Christianity. Not
only did she encourage a thoughtful openness to "new light"; she
was also prominently involved in the initiation, development, and
survival of many of the other "liberalizing" ingredients. She consistently advocated personal Bible reading; she emphasized God's
love and endorsed the doctrine of righteousness by faith; she vigorously supported a long list of education, health care, world mission, and publishing activities; she was a champion of certain kinds
of social responsibility. So, although it will be disputed on both the
left and the right, I want to say that much of the credit (or blame)
for the "liberalizing" of Adventist Christianity properly belongs to
Ellen White.

My second observation is that the continued "liberalizing" of
Adventist Christianity is inevitable. For some people this is good
news; for others it is very bad news. But however the prospect is
evaluated, I think the forces involved are too obvious to be honest-

---

[1] *Seventh-day Adventist Bible Commentary,* ed. Francis D. Nichol *et al.,* 7 vols.
(Washington: Review 1957).

[2] Roy Branson, ed., *Festival of the Sabbath* (Takoma Park, MD: Association of
Adventist Forums 1985).

[3] See above for complete reference.

[4] Richard Rice, *The Openness of God: The Relationship of Divine Foreknowledge
and Human Free Will* (Washington: Review 1980); rptd. *God's Foreknowledge and
Man's Free Will* (Minneapolis: Bethany 1985).

[5] Thompson, *Inspiration.*

[6] Ronald L. Numbers, *Prophetess of Health: A Study of Ellen G. White,* 3d ed.
(Grand Rapids: Eerdmans 2008).

[7] Desmond and Gillian Ford, *The Adventist Crisis of Spiritual Identity* (Newcastle, CA: Ford 1982).

[8] Merikay McLeod, *Betrayal: The Shattering Sex Discrimination Case of Silver* vs.
*Pacific Press Publishing Association* (Loma Linda, CA: Mars Hill 1985).

[9] Ralph Larson, *The Word Was Made Flesh: One Hundred Years of Seventh-day
Adventist Christology, 1852-1952* (Cherry Valley, CA: Cherrystone 1986).

ly denied and too strong to be effectively resisted. This is why I say that the Adventist future will be more "liberalized" rather than that it will be more "liberal." The passive participle points to the fact that the process of "liberalization" is something that is *happening to Adventist Christianity* rather than something that is *chosen by Adventists* (even "liberal" Adventists, whoever they might be).

But this is not the whole picture.

*Thesis 3: The Adventist future will also be shaped by other, "anti-liberalizing" ingredients.*

The intellectual and social development of a religious community is never rapid, easy, or smooth; and there is no reason to suppose that Adventist Christianity on the way to the future will be a special case. These "anti-liberalizing" ingredients are of slightly different kinds. There are "conservative" ingredients that tend to make the Adventist future a *continuation of the present;* and there are "reactive" ingredients that tend to make the Adventist future a *return to the past.*

• I see two main "conservative" ingredients. In the first place, religion is, as Paul Tillich used to say, a matter of "ultimate concern"[1]—and we do not take lightly to religious change. Indeed, we expect religion to be a rock of stability amid the shifting sands of historical, social, and cultural flow. It is a locus of permanence amid the "change and decay" we see all around and, even worse, feel within ourselves.[2] So the theological and moral seriousness that is one of the great strengths of Adventist Christianity also encourages resistance to change. Adventist Christianity is both a theological perspective and a way of life, and change of any sort can be viewed as "lowering the standards" of belief or behavior.

In the second place, institutional structures lead inevitably to hierarchical thinking and bureaucratic practices, both of which reinforce the intellectual and procedural inertia of large organizations. The larger and more complex the organization, the more difficult and costly is any change of thinking. And Adventist Christianity surely qualifies as both large and complex. It is notoriously difficult for us to discontinue any program, policy, department, or institution, even if the reason for its existence has disappeared. And it is just as difficult for us to change our thinking about our beliefs and

---

[1]See Paul Tillich, *Dynamics of Faith* (New York: Harper 1957) 1-4.
[2]See Henry F. Lyte, "Abide with Me," *Seventh-day Adventist Hymnal* (Washington: Review 1985) no. 50:

Swift to its close ebbs out life's little day;
Earth's joys grow dim, its glories pass away;
Change and decay in all around I see;
O Thou who changest not, abide with me.

our mission. And, paradoxically, the more we feel change occurring within the church, the more we feel a need to maintain unity by resisting change. Although there may be wide and deep dissatisfaction with the reality of the present, there is equally wide and deep disagreement about any specific proposal for change.

So there is a strong tendency to try to make the Adventist future an extension of the present. But the present is hardly an ideal model for the future. Adventist Christianity in North America is becoming a sabbatarian version of the kind of mainline Protestantism that is increasingly respectable, increasingly gray, and increasingly bland—culturally comfortable, experientially unimportant, and theologically stagnant; this development is accompanied by decreasing church attendance, decreasing financial support, and decreasing school enrollment. Nobody—not the people, not the pastors, not the church administrators—really wants the future to be a continuation of the present.

• It is not at all surprising, therefore, that there is also a tendency try to make the future a return to the past. This tendency is encouraged by some "reactive" ingredients. For one thing, a long Adventist history of biblical literalism has encouraged simplistic thinking and attitudes. These in turn provide fertile soil for the self-appointed critics who claim to be the only authentic Adventists left amidst widespread apostasy.

For another thing, our typical evangelistic and missionary fundamentalism—that is, our tendency to preach a simple, unambiguous message with complete certainty from a position of religious superiority—has understandably attracted to Adventist Christianity people with a fundamentalist mentality. There is a steady influx of "true believers"—people who not only have a simple faith but for whom simplicity *is* faith.

And for a third thing, our effectiveness in world mission has led to a demographic shift toward continents with traditions of conservative authoritarianism which contrast rather sharply with the tradition of liberal democracy in North America.

But the past turns out to be an even worse model for the future than is the present. Adventist Christianity simply cannot become a nineteenth-century island, or even a twentieth-century island, surrounded by the twenty-first century.

Loren Seibold, a pastor in Palo Alto, and his wife, Carmen, have given me an vivid extended metaphor:

> It's like the old fools you see occasionally—people who are trying to act as if they were younger than they are, as if they were 18, wild and free—people who are fixated on high school as the best time of their lives. Extended adolescence doesn't work.
>
> There are many who've tried to tell us that we can keep the same enthusiasm for the same stuff we had in 1844, but it just ain't gonna

happen. No one can make 1844 mean to us what it meant to James
White."
     Let's mature gracefully, and not try to act like we're still young,
fresh, and energetic. There are marvelous values that can be developed
in aging.

(Remember that the subject here is not our aging as *individual persons,* of which we are all acutely aware, but our aging, changing,
and maturing as a *religious movement,* a *community, which* we often ignore.)

> We become less passionate, but more constant. We fasten on a few ideas
> of importance, having learned ways to let other ideas gracefully fall by
> the wayside. . . . We are more accepting than we used to be, distin-
> guishing people from nutty ideas.
>      Let's embrace the joys of growing older, rather than pining after the
> spiritual passion, the flaming hormones, of our youth, which gave us so
> much energy and caused us to do so many foolish things."[1]

Even if it were possible (which it isn't), it would hardly be desirable to return to an Adventist Christianity committed to biblical
literalism and maintained by tightly defined boundaries of theological purity and behavioral propriety—a "remnant on the run";[2] a
fundamentalism combining fear and certainty, generating an almost
fanatic loyalty, but afflicted with theological sterility; a community
of faith that cares primarily about its own holiness and matters little
to anyone else.
     An attempt to return to the past is not a recovery of faith but a
failure of nerve.[3] For genuine faith is a commitment to the whole
truth—to the truth we do not yet know as well as to the truth we
think we know. It is not so much a "hanging on" as it is a moving
forward, "an unreserved opening of the mind to truth, whatever it
may turn out to be."[4]
     Trying to go back to the past, furthermore, is actually an abdi-
cation of the church's mission to the world, which is necessarily the
world of the present. This abdication is reflected in the fact that
many of the reactionary "independent ministries" have no mission
to the world at all, but are completely parasitic on the Adventist
community.
     Every new generation lives in a new world, with new questions
to address, new challenges to meet, new problems to solve. The
gospel of God's love is everlasting; but our understanding of it—

[1]Loren Seibold, eletter, Feb. 24, 1994.
[2]The phrase was suggested by Alden Thompson.
[3]See Arthur Peacocke, *Theology for a Scientific Age: Being and Becoming—
Natural, Divine, and Human* (Minneapolis: Fortress 1993) x: "The current resusci-
tation of very conservative positions . . . is a sign not so much of a recovery of
faith as of a loss of nerve before the onslaught of new perceptions of the world."
[4]Alan Watts, *The Wisdom of Insecurity* (New York: Vintage-Random 1951)
24.

our theology—is a snapshot of it from a particular perspective at a particular point in time.[1] As Ellen White once said, "The truth is an advancing truth, and we must walk in the increasing light."[2] There is always more to learn, but we can't see the sky if we've covered the windows with blue paint.[3]

So the task of Adventist Christianity on the way to the future is not to try to relive the original Adventist experience or respond to the original Adventist questions with exactly the same answers—any more than it is my duty to go back to Minnesota and live in the place where my grandfather lived and where my father and I were born.

The Adventist future will be shaped by some combination of progressive, conservative, and reactive ingredients, because none of these ingredients in going to capitulate, be converted, or go away. None of them will let itself be swallowed by the others; nor will any one of them become dominant. This situation will yield one of two consequences: pluralism or fragmentation.

*Thesis 4: For better or for worse, Adventist pluralism is already here.*

Since 1980, the word "pluralism" has become something of an obscenity among some church administrators in North America, but whatever one chooses to call the phenomenon—"pluralism" or "diversity" or "pluriformity"—it is a reality. The picture of a universally homogeneous Adventist Christianity—with every believer around the world studying the same Sabbath School lesson, singing the same hymns, having the same lifestyle, and understanding Advent beliefs in the same way—is an illusion.

The evidence of real pluralism is abundant and inescapable. Hundreds of Adventist congregations are identifiable according to ethnicity, language, form of worship, lifestyle, or theological emphasis; some of these are identified officially, some unofficially. Regional and national differences increase the diversity: Adventist Christianity in Argentina is different from Adventist Christianity in

---

[1]See Heinz Zahrnt, *The Question of God: Protestant Theology in the Twentieth Century* (New York: Harcourt 1969) 359: "For only the gospel is eternal, and theology is temporal; it must always translate the eternal gospel anew for the changing times. . . . We must always begin to build once again, and we must always dare once again to do the unheard of thing, which consists of men, sinful, finite, imperfect and mortal men, daring to speak in human words about God. Here too it is God's grace alone which can make good what in every case man does badly. God must also forgive us our theology, our theology perhaps most of all."

[2]Ellen G. White, "Open the Heart to Light," *Advent Review and Sabbath Herald*, Mar. 25, 1890: 177; rptd. *Counsels to Writers and Editors* 33.

[3]See Watts 25: "You can only know God through an open mind just as you can only see the sky through a clear window. You will not see the sky if you have covered the glass with blue paint."

Austria or in Alabama—and it should be. This diversity is not a weakness but a richness. Parachurch organizations institutionalize the diversity: The Adventist Women's Institute, Hope International, SDA Kinship, and the Adventist Theological Society—all illustrate the variety of interests and viewpoints. In Adventist higher education, Southern Adventist, Southwestern Adventist, and Walla Walla Universities are different in more than geography.

Pluralism tends to perpetuate itself by creating space for isolated elements that are immune to dialog and criticism—intellectual and ideological ghettoes for both left-wing liberalism and right wing reaction. These kinds of differences have already made uniformity impossible, and they also make pluralism necessary if Adventist Christianity is going to avoid organizational fragmentation. Attempts to impose uniformity on diversity[1] are never more than temporarily successful; sooner or later they result in some kind of separation. On the other hand, while pluralism makes spiritual unity more difficult to maintain, it does not necessarily subvert it; the subversion of unity comes from attitudes of pride and arrogance, desires to dominate and control, and practices of exclusion

The huge unanswered (and unanswerable) question is the precise future shape of Adventist Christianity, which will be determined by the "mix" of progressive, conservative, and reactive elements. This "mix" will in turn be determined not only by various individuals and groups within the church, but also by social and cultural influences. An economic downturn, for example, encourages caution and conservatism; prosperity encourages venturesomeness and liberalization. In a broader historical context, Western culture is still flowing in the direction of liberalization and pluralization—thanks in part to the communication media. Yet cultural change itself makes us long for religious certainty, and thus attracts us to the immediate security of fundamentalism.

*"When you visit the altars of the past," somebody once said, "bring back the fire, not the ashes."*[2]

"Bringing back the fire" has been the intention of all the chapters making up this book as they have reviewed the past and antici-

---

[1]For an example of such an attempt, see Alan Cowell's report, via the *New York Times* News Service, in the Riverside *Press-Enterprise*, May 31, 1994: "Pope John Paul II told the world's Catholics yesterday to abandon any thought of women being ordained as priests, saying that the issues was not open to debate and that his views must be 'definitively held by all the church's faithful.' Although the pope's words fell just short of a formal statement of infallible doctrine, the particularly severe and authoritative tone of his letter to bishops suggested that he was seeking to remove the idea from the Catholic agenda for decades to come."

[2]Original source unknown.

pated the future. It is always easier, of course, to bring back the ashes. It is also much safer; playing with any kind of fire is hazardous. But in the long run it is better to take the riskier option—choosing the fire rather than the ashes, recognizing that great disappointment is transcended by greater hope.

The "liberalizing" ingredients I see in Adventist Christianity are not merely accidental or incidental; they are some (but obviously not all) of its defining characteristics. They are part of what Adventist Christianity is. They are ingredients of the spirit, the *fire*, of authentic Adventist Christianity. They are also the impetus for moving beyond the present, into an Adventist future that is theologically progressive, spiritually healthy, and organizationally inclusive. They therefore encourage the possibility of envisioning the future as God's future and going out to meet it—with confidence and vigor, freedom and creativity, gratitude and hope.[1]

[1] An earlier version of this chapter appeared as "A More 'Liberalized' Adventist Future," *Spectrum* 24 (Dec. 1994): 18-32; cp. "Adventism on the Way to the Future," *Pacific Union Recorder*, Oct. 17. 1994: 4-5.

# Contributors

ALDEN THOMPSON (PhD, University of Edinburgh) is Professor of Biblical Studies at Walla Walla University. He is the author of books including *Responsibility for Evil in the Theodicy of IV Ezra, Samuel: From the Danger of Chaos to the Danger of Power, Inspiration: Hard Questions, Honest Answers,* and *Who's Afraid of the Old Testament God?*

ARTHUR N. PATRICK (DMin, Christian Theological Seminary; MLitt, University of New England; PhD, University of Newcastle) was the author of *Christianity and Culture in Colonial Australia: Selected Catholic, Anglican, Wesleyan and Adventist Perspectives, 1891-1900.* He served as Chaplain of the Sydney Adventist Hospital in Sydney, Australia, as Visiting Associate Professor of Church History and Pastoral Ministry at La Sierra University, and as editor of *Adventist Heritage.*

CHARLES SCRIVEN (PhD, Graduate Theological Union) recently retired as President of Kettering College of Medical Arts. He is the author of *The Transformation of Culture: Christian Social Ethics after H. Richard Niebuhr, Jubilee of the World, The Promise of Peace,* and *The Demons Have Had It: A Theological ABC,* and the editor of *Into the Arena.*

CHARLES TEEL, JR. (ThM, Harvard University; PhD, Boston University) is Professor of Religion and Society at La Sierra University. He is the editor of *Remnant and Republic: Adventist Themes for Personal and Social Ethics* and the author of articles on issues related to Adventist mission and ethics.

DALTON D. BALDWIN (ThM, Princeton Theological Seminary; PhD, Claremont Graduate School) served as Professor of Religion at Loma Linda University. His byline appeared in journals including *Process Studies* and *Spectrum.*

FRITZ GUY (PhD, University of Chicago; DD *hc*, La Sierra University) is Research Professor of Philosophical Theology at La Sierra University, of which he served as president from 1990 to 1993. A founding member of the *Spectrum* editorial board, he is the author of *Thinking Theologically* and of numerous scholarly and popular articles, the co-author (with Brian S. Bull) of *God, Sky and Land: Genesis 1 as the Ancient Hebrews Heard It,* and the co-editor of *Meeting the Secular Mind: Some Adventist Perspectives, Understanding Genesis: Contemporary Adventist Perspectives,* and *Christianity and Homosexuality: Some Seventh-day Adventist Perspectives.*

GARY CHARTIER (JD, UCLA; PhD, LLD, University of Cambridge) is Distinguished Professor of Law and Business Ethics and Associate Dean of the Tom and Vi Zapara School of Business at La Sierra University. He is the author, editor, or co-editor of ten books, including *The Analogy of Love* and *Vulnerability and Community*; his byline has appeared over forty times in scholarly journals.

JACQUES DOUKHAN (DHL, University of Strasbourg; ThD, Andrews University) is Professor of Hebrew Bible at Andrews University. He is the author of *Hebrew for Theologians: A Textbook for the Study of Biblical Hebrew in Relation to Hebrew Thinking, Israel and the Church: Two Voices for the Same God, Secrets of Revelation: The Apocalypse through Hebrew Eyes, Daniel: The Vision of the End, Secrets of Daniel: Wisdom and Dreams of a Jewish Prince in Exile, Drinking at the Sources,* and *On the Way to Emmaus: Five Messianic Prophecies Explained.* He serves as general editor of the *SDA International Bible Commentary.*

JOHN C. BRUNT (PhD, Emory University) has served as Vice President for Academic Administration at what is now Walla Walla University and as senior pastor of the Azure Hills Seventh-day Adventist Church in Grand Terrace, California. He is the author of books including *Romans: Mercy for All, Now and Not Yet, A Day for Healing: The Meaning of Jesus' Sabbath Miracles,* and *Decisions: How to Use Biblical Guidelines When Making Decisions* and the co-editor of *Introducing the Bible.*

NIELS-ERIK A. ANDREASEN (PhD, Vanderbilt University) is President of Andrews University. A distinguished scholar of Old Testament theology, with a particular emphasis on the Sabbath, he is the author of *The Old Testament Sabbath: A Tradition-Historical Investigation, Rest and Redemption: A Study of the Biblical Sabbath,* and *The Christian Use of Time.*

PAUL J. LANDA (PhD, Vanderbilt University) was Professor of the History of Christianity at La Sierra University. He was the author of *The Reformed Theology of Gérard Roussel* and *Strategic Planning for Churches.*

RANDAL R. WISBEY (DMin, Wesley Theological Seminary) is President of La Sierra University. He previously served as President of Washington Adventist University and of what is now Burman University, and as Associate Professor of Youth Ministry at the SDA Theological Seminary at Andrews University. He has contributed chapters to six books, authored numerous articles, and edited the quarterly youth ministry journal *Giraffe News.*

RICHARD RICE (PhD, University of Chicago) is Professor of Religion at Loma Linda University. He is the author of books including *Suffering and the Search for Meaning: Contemporary Responses to the Problem of Pain, Reason and the Contours of Faith The Reign of God: An Introduction to Christian Theology in Seventh-day Adventist Perspective, God's Foreknowledge and Man's Free Will*, and *Believing, Behaving, Belonging*. He is also a co-author of *The Openness of God: A Biblical Challenge to the Traditional Understanding of God*.

ROY ADAMS (PhD, Andrews University) served as associate editor of the Adventist Review. He is the author of eight books, including *The Sanctuary Doctrine: Three Approaches in the Seventh-day Adventist Church, The Sanctuary: Understanding the Heart of Adventist Theology, The Nature of Christ: Help for a Church Divided over Perfection*, and *Looking for a City: Briefings for Pilgrims on Their Journey Home*.

ROY BRANSON (PhD, Harvard University) was Professor of Religion and Associate Dean of the School of Religion at Loma Linda University. He was the editor of *Pilgrimage of Hope* and *Festival of the Sabbath*. A co-founder of the Association of Adventist Forums, he was for many years editor of the Association's widely respected journal, *Spectrum*.

SAKAE KUBO (PhD, University of Chicago) served in the New Testament department in the Theological Seminary at Andrews University, as dean of the School of Theology at what is now Walla Walla University, as president of Newbold College, and as dean of Atlantic Union College. He retired in 1989. He is the author of books including *Theology and Ethics of Sex, God Meets Man: A Theology of the Sabbath and the Second Advent, A Beginner's Greek New Testament Grammar, A Reader's Greek-English Lexicon of the New Testament*, and *The God of Relationships*.

# Index

Printed in Great Britain
by Amazon